The Myth of Manliness
in Irish National
Culture, 1880–1922

The Myth of Manliness in Irish National Culture, 1880–1922

JOSEPH VALENTE

UNIVERSITY OF
ILLINOIS PRESS
Urbana, Chicago,
and Springfield

Library of Congress Cataloging-in-Publication Data
Valente, Joseph.
The myth of manliness in Irish national culture,
1880–1922 / by Joseph Valente.
p.   cm.
Includes bibliographical references and index.
ISBN 978-0-252-03571-5 (cloth : alk. paper)
1. Masculinity in literature.
2. Irish literature—History and criticism.
3. Masculinity—Ireland—Psychological aspects.
4. Men—Ireland—Psychology.
I. Title.
PN56.M316V35   2010
820.9'3521—dc22   2010007695

For my dad,

William D. Valente,

1924–2008

A Man of the Highest Principles

Contents

Acknowledgments

My greatest continuing debt is to my wife, Joanne, for her ideas, her encouragement, and her editorial assistance. In all endeavors, we are a team.

I am profoundly grateful to the readers of the manuscript, Joe Cleary, Marjorie Howes, and Vicki Mahaffey, for their comments, corrections, and encouragement. I cannot imagine a stronger trio of Irish studies scholars to engage my work.

Special thanks to my friend Jed Esty, whose advice, tireless questioning, and generosity of time and spirit immeasurably improved this study.

I am indebted to my friends at the University of Illinois, in particular Trish Loughran, Siobhan Somerville, Carol Neely, Matt Hart, and Lauren Goodlad, for everything from research suggestions to critical insights to much needed resistance.

Great thanks, as always, to John Paul Riquelme for his many contributions to my intellectual life.

My work has also benefited from intellectual exchange with Margot Norris, Jean-Michel Rabaté, Cheryl Herr, Derek Attridge, John Bishop, Patrick McCarthy, Marilyn Reizbaum, Brandon Kershner, Damien Keane, Michael Sayeau, Sean Kennedy, Ed Madden, Patrick Mullen, Eibher Walshe, Celeste Langan, Sheldon Brivic, Tim Dean, Elisabeth Ladenson, Zack Lesser, Bill Maxwell, Janet Lyon, and Amanda Anderson.

My gratitude, once more, to the late Ted Irving, my first and most important mentor.

Gratitude as well to the wonderful teachers I have had the good fortune to experience: Geoff Harpham, Stuart Curran, Barbara Herrnstein Smith, Arkady Plotnitsky, Carlos Fuentes, Marjorie Levinson, and Francis McGrath.

A debt of gratitude to Willis Regier for all his help at the University of Illinois Press.

Thanks to Alvan Bregman for his assistance with the permissions.

A final note of appreciation to my sometime coauthor, Margot Backus. Working with her has expanded my critical perspective.

I cannot calculate my debt to my parents, Bill and Elizabeth, for all they have done, nor to my son, Matty, for all that he is. It's what the word *love* is for.

Abbreviations

Preface

    This book aims to supply the first contextually precise account of the male gender anxieties and ambivalences haunting the culture of Irish nationalism in the period between the Act of Union and the founding of the Irish Free State. To this end, my focus will fix not on the prevailing category of masculinity, the psychoanalytic contours of which render it anachronistic to the case at hand, but on the Victorian construct of manliness or manhood, the moral and political logic of which proved crucial to both the translation of British rule into British hegemony and the expression of Irish rebellion as Irish *psychomachia*. The construct remains very much alive today, underpinning the neo-imperialist marriage of ruthless aggression and the sanctities of duty, honor, and sacrifice. Mapping its earlier colonial and postcolonial formations can help us to understand its continuing geopolitical appeal and danger.

The Double Bind
of Irish Manhood

Historical Backgrounds
and Conceptual Horizons

To trace the architecture of manliness in Victorian Britain, as distinct from the currently dominant psychoanalytic and feminist conceptions of masculinity, it is easiest to start with two cruxes that have preoccupied the critics and genealogists of manliness and might be said to involve the vertical and horizontal axes of its historical definition. First, what is the relation of manliness to its ground in masculine gender identity? Is the former merely an honorific variant on the latter, or do the two categories differ in some significant respects? Second, what is the scope of manliness, its relationship to the several patterns of character and conduct that invoke its name? Is there an essential species of manliness or many representative types or codes?

Mapping Manliness

Having noted the affiliation of ideas of manliness with Carlyle's ethos of energetic labor, Kingsley's muscular Christianity, the philoathleticism of Victorian public school culture and the quasi-imperialist adventurism of Baden-Powell's Boy Scouts, many scholars have assumed the interchangeability of manliness with a masculinity staked on such conventional phallic attributes as virility, aggression, power, physical courage, resolution, and so on.[1] Still others observe that the preeminent spokesmen in this arena, Thomas Arnold, first dean of Rugby, and his student Thomas Hughes, author of *Tom Brown's Schooldays,* celebrated manliness not as an identity form but as an ethical norm, a mandate designed to transcend the uses and pleasures of physical hardihood in pursuit of the higher virtues of patience, obedience, forbearance, modesty, and respect for others.[2] With these traditionally feminine attainments as its ultimate goal, the argument runs, the imperative of manliness contained an androgynous streak.

Claudia Nelson goes so far as to contend that women were better disposed to achieve manliness and hence were the bearers of its true import.[3]

The important thing to remember in this debate, however, is that manliness was not a fundamentally *ontological* category, as one side assumes, nor a fundamentally *ethical* category, as the other side avers, but a fundamentally *ideological* category. In this regard, we should construe manliness as an instrument of patriarchy tailored to the demands of a gradually democratizing era in the British Isles for a greater degree of moral suasion in the regulation of gender norms. An instrument, then, not of masculine *rule* but of masculine *hegemony*. The honorific title of manliness was at once an assertion of male authority and an apologia for such authority as morally legitimate and conducive to the welfare of the whole community. As such a hegemonic lever, manliness had to remain ontologically affixed to the masculine gender position; otherwise, it could not serve to secure and advance an exclusively male dominion. At the same time, manliness had to be seen to operate at a superior ethical distance from the masculine gender position; otherwise, it could not serve to vindicate male dominion. Manliness, in other words, transcended the masculinity in which it continued to inhere. Stephan Collini is thus right to say that "there is some daylight between the terms manliness and masculinity."[4] But it should be understood that this daylight is *internal* to the concept of manliness: it fills the space between the *is* and the *ought* of its own definition, solidifying the hegemony of actual men under the color of the ideal.

The relationship binding the late Victorian conception of masculinity to its ideal form, manliness or manhood, can best be described as an impacted dialectic, or *discordia concours*. Manliness paradoxically represented both the consummation of the masculine condition, its perfection if you will, and a sublation of the masculine condition into a loftier form. What is surprising, however, is that the "surplus value" comprehended in manhood seems to have derived, at least in the first instance, from its proximity or connection to the lower orders of being. In increasingly polarized opposition to the feminine norm of "passionlessness," "submissiveness and yielding to others,"[5] masculinity came to be defined in terms of the possession and regulated deployment of robust "animal spirits," the source of conventionally "masculine" fortitude, tenacity, assertiveness, and stamina. The ethos of manliness or manhood involved turning those traits inward and thus converting these cruder "animal" virtues into the higher-order spiritual attainments of integrity, self-possession, and self-control. Thus, the doyen of muscular Christianity, Charles Kingsley, celebrated the inherence of plentiful animal spirits to biological maleness and their importance to the production of genuine manliness. "Manly *thumos* [animal passion]," he pronounced, "is the root of all virtue." His compeer in the movement, novelist Thomas Hughes, declared "the foundation of manliness" to be "its lowest or rudest quality . . . not exclusively a human quality at all, but one which we share with the other animals." And James Fitzjames Stephens added to the chorus in the *Edinburgh Review,* affirming "the great importance and value of animal spirits in all the pursuits and accomplishments that are connected with them." Men were, in Kingsley's phrase, "made of coarser stuff," which gave them tougher moral fiber.[6] The "mere animal" in man facilitated his glory as "the Spirit-Animal."[7] On the terms of this *discordia concours,* not only does masculinity stand to garner surplus spiritual nobility from its intimacy with the animal domain, but men's primordial bestiality constitutes the very *cause* of the self-disciplining spirituality that subsumes, legitimates, and dignifies it. The ideal of manhood, in sum, consisted in the simultaneous necessity for and achievement of a vigilant, rational self-control—in *strong passions strongly checked.*

In a study of muscular Christianity, David Rosen writes, "One cannot enter [the lists of manhood] simply by behaving in a manly fashion. . . . [N]o particular behavior but something in men makes them manly."[8] We are now in a position to see why this was the case. Appearances notwithstanding, manliness was less a matter of content than of form; it comprised not a set of sublime properties but a logic of sublimation, a dialectical organization of contents that was located "in men," yes, but *as* men's proper beyond, a fully immanent mode of self-overcoming.

So while manliness must not be conflated with psychoanalytic conceptions of the masculine subject-position, it might be helpful to those familiar with Lacanian theory to consider how manliness partakes of the social value and function attributed to the phallus. Each depends for its continued existence on the same fundamental imposture and *meconnaissance,* the pretense to a substantially unified, self-sufficient, and self-possessed state of being, dialectically achieved. It is not, then, that each "rests upon the denial of castration,"[9] for through their different instantiations, both take stock of the Lack or limit incurred by the subject as the price of its humanity. It is rather that phallic identification and manly identification alike rest on the simultaneously empowering and embattling illusion that this Lack or limit can be transcended without a trace, overcome without any residual weakness or insecurity, contained without remainder. But because any definition of such plenitude automatically reinstates the limit that it proposes to elide, both the phallus and manliness must be reified over and beyond the evidentiary marks of power, virtue, and distinction they bestow. Lacan has famously declared that the phallus "can play its role only when veiled . . . as itself a sign of the latency with which any signifiable is struck," and David Rosen makes substantially the same argument about manliness in disconnecting its social reality from its social insignia. The phallus and manliness alike constitute a sort of x-factor, what we have already designated a "surplus value," something "in [man] more than [man]," as Slavoj Zizek would say, which can be understood only in structural terms.[10]

Having identified manliness as a specific logic of ethico-political being, rather than a bill of particulars, we have already gone a long way to resolving the second crux of Victorian manliness: is it one or many? Most professional historians—Vance, Newsome, Mangan—incline toward the multiplicity thesis, adducing differences between the chivalric model of a Carlyle, the moral version of a Thomas Arnold, the muscular type of a Kingsley or Hughes, the sturdy "game" form associated with headmasters like H. H. Almond and Edmund Ware, and the imperialist species of a Baden-Powell.[11] There has been an equally persistent tendency among literary and cultural critics to treat manliness as a unified construct, often taking one of the dominant varieties as truest to the spirit of the whole array.[12] The important thing to remember in this debate is that the profound ideological power of manliness over the long Victorian age hinged upon its conjunction of internal consistency and outward flexibility, the result, precisely, of its being a deep structure irreducible to the contents that it organizes. So while manliness proves impossible to itemize, it is not impossible to delineate, provided one finds the appropriate level of abstraction.

In each stripe of manliness isolated, the same underlying *discordia concours* of the elemental and the rarefied obtains, and it is precisely this iron logic that gave the construct its astonishingly protracted currency.[13] Whether it be the seminal fluids in Carlyle, rude "liveliness" in Arnold, *thumos* in Kingsley, physical courage in Hughes, or "beastliness" in Baden-Powell, every paradigm of the manly begins with a primal male-identified element of animal vitality that helps to fuel the exercise of sublimating discipline that it so badly requires.[14] And every paradigm of manliness looks to the same consummation, the marshaling of that vitality to moral and spiritual purpose. To be sure, the prominence, persistence, and sublimation of this vital element altered from version to version and so, correspondingly, did the optimal emphasis on animality and spirituality in the manly specimen. Most notably, something of a break is thought to have occurred between the moralized forms of midcentury and the rugged forms geared to a more belligerently imperialist fin de siècle, and it is on this caesura, more than anything else, that the robust "multiplicity thesis" of manliness reposes.[15] But if the balance tipped "from serious earnestness to robust virility . . . integrity to harshness" as the century wore on, there did remain a balance, a ratio of interdependency between these values, which unfolded in the familiar dialectical logic of sublimation. With whatever inflections and recalibrations, Kitson Clarke's view that manliness "converted barbarian virtue into Christian good" invariably held.[16]

Indeed, even the generally acknowledged transition from the moralized manhood of the early Victorian period to the more athletic and aggressive manhood of the later century tends to ratify, rather than qualify, their underlying continuity. Those who emphasized the *Christian* in Christian manliness—such as Rugby's Thomas Arnold or the Religious Tract Society, publisher of the devout *Boy's Own Paper*—nonetheless regarded animal vigor as both the source and the ongoing support of the strenuous spiritual enterprise they propagated. Thomas Hughes's famous pronouncement, "a man's body is given him to be trained and brought into subjection," bespeaks this sense of the physical precondition of all spiritual rigor.[17] On the other side, even the most social Darwinist of devotees to physical culture and the game ethic saw its ultimate objective in spiritual uplift and moral, even chivalric, service: in "fostering courage and endurance" (Loretto headmaster H. H. Almond), in uniting "health of body, health of intellect and health of heart . . . in one form" (Uppingham headmaster Edward Thring), in inculcating "cooperation, unselfishness, and sound character" (Marlborough headmaster G. E. Cotton), in teaching a "noble negation of self" ("games bard" Sir Henry Newbolt), and in instilling "a spirit of companionship and control [of] temper" (Thomas Hughes).[18] Arguing against the equation of athleticism and mere animalism, Marlborough apologist "Trebla" ascribed to team sports like football "a moral training" in "courage, patriotism, hero worship, self-denial" and in "sexual self-control."[19] As this much abbreviated list of endorsements makes clear, the later athletic mode of manliness was understood to express, discharge, and sublimate the most primal of urges—sexuality, survival, self-assertion—as ennobling, other-directed affects of loyalty, solicitude, and devotion to the larger group or team. Even a critic of compulsory team sports conceded that they lent themselves to "moral virtues, pluck, and merging one's interests in the whole," which are of course the same benefits trumpeted in Hughes's landmark philoathletic novel *Tom Brown's Schooldays*.[20]

The homosocial impetus of the games ethic exemplified the cultural logic whereby the rampant lower energies animating the male of the species proved at once the prime object and preferred instrument of moral discipline. At the same time, and for this very reason, it translated smoothly into the dominant articulations of the fin de siècle military-imperialist types of manliness, which were typically thought to draw upon, test, and promote the same virtues on a wider stage. (Not coincidentally, it was during this period that Wellington's apocryphal remark, that the Battle of Waterloo was won on the playing fields of Eton, achieved currency.)[21] The result was what Geoffrey Best calls "the cult of the Christian warrior," in which rectitude and ruthlessness, ferocity in battle and evangelical zeal, the worldly glory of England and the divine glory of God, all counterpose without canceling one another—a *discordia concours* in arms.[22]

The durability of the logic of manliness amid changes in the constellation of manly norms ultimately renders the historical swerve from the ideal of rugged morality to that of moralized ruggedness as difficult to pinpoint as it is now common to assume (or to turn matters around, the difficulty of pinpointing this historical swerve bears out the durability of an undergirding logic). No such assumption, it should be pointed out, reigned among the Victorians themselves, whose sensitivity to the constant ratio of manliness was no less acute for being unconscious. Thus, the "games" bard himself, Sir Henry Newbolt, author of "Play Up," had begun his career writing poems about Camelot and saw the sports mania as an extension of the earlier chivalric ethos of manly service. He was seconded in this respect by John Perceval, who moved from Rugby to become the first headmaster of Clifton, giving that school a strongly marked identity as a site of what one might call "games chivalry." Baden-Powell, in turn, contrived to fuse, and confuse, the moral ethos of chivalry with the bodily ascesis of frontier imperialism in his Boy Scouts training program, even publishing a book on scouting titled *The Young Knights of the Empire*.[23] As for muscular Christians like Kingsley and Hughes, they represented (and continue to represent) the preeminent voices of Victorian manliness precisely because their respective articulations of bodily gusto, competitive aggression, and tribal solidarity with Christian forbearance, self-sacrifice, and earnestness held the defining counterstresses in all but perfect suspension (which is not to say they resolved them).

This chiasmatic logic defined manliness not just as an ideal of being-in-the-world per se but as an ideal specific to the masculine gender position and potential. Hence, there were substantive political, which is to say patriarchal, grounds for its perdurablity. The late Victorian and Edwardian logic of manhood mirrored in reverse the dichotomous stereotype of femininity that was enshrined during the same period.

Woman had, of course, long been defined on a *disjunctive* basis, as either virgin or whore, spiritual ideal or bodily abject, maternal nurturer or dangerous virago, the fetishized sum or the fearful subversion of all cultural values. But during the late nineteenth century, this bipolar profile took a specific biosexological inflection: normative (middle- and upper-class) British women were understood to be emotionally centered yet comparatively delicate or muted in their desires, and therefore passive and reserved in their sexuality, the vessels of an idealized "passionlessness."[24] Active or aggressive female desire counted as not only immoral but abnormal, a mark of psychic disturbance or pathology, but one that seemed to betoken, like hysteria or neurasthenia, the intrinsic weakness of women's rational faculty and the instability of their affective constitution.

By contrast, the Carlylean hero, the muscular gentleman, and the Regency blood were all understood to be rationally capable in some proportion to the strength of their passions; they were seen to be invested with great and effective moral energy *owing* to the active, aggressive, sometimes wayward force of their animal stirrings. Just as manliness defined the normative male as predisposed to spiritual nobility on account of his closer commerce with the bestial element, so it defined him on a highly *conjunctive* or *integrated* basis despite, or rather because of, his internal antagonisms. Male appetite was seen to be animated by the same power as male self-discipline. Hence, the proper or manly man could attain to a fully self-referring tension among his own component drives, with his more urgent and brutish energies not only contesting but actually feeding the effort required to restrain and redirect them.[25] In consequence, the manly ideal could pretend to a self-containment and sufficiency that the feminine ideal could not compass by definition. Indeed, the manly ideal did not really engage the womanly ideal in that traditional complementary opposition of genders, in which male and female properties look to complete one another, but rather did so in a metonymic if incommensurable relation of whole to part, in which the manly comprehends and commands a morally regenerative tension that the feminine *properly* lacks. It was to the precarious feat of maintaining this dynamic equipoise of forces, rather than the value of the forces themselves, that the enormous social and symbolic authority of manliness ultimately pertained.

The converse was no less true. It was only insofar as the *discordia concours* of manliness was maintained and the unbalanced exhibition of any one of its aspects avoided that the claim to its social and symbolic authority could be credited. Precisely because manliness was so much more than the sum of its parts, the disaggregation of those parts not only vitiated what Kingsley called "the divineness of the whole manhood," but also signified a descent into some other(ed) less cohesive form of life, be it man's internal other (the animal) or external other (the woman).[26] The visible unleashing of *thumos,* for example, could evince a certain disjunction of manhood's component energies and so a breakdown in its distinguishing faculty of rational self-possession. At the extreme, such a manifestation of aggression could signal a lapse into emotional excess, even frenzy, which bore the unmistakable imprint of the bestial. On the other side, a completely successful suppression of animal *thumos,* to the point of its extinction, would entail a complementary imbalance in the component energies of manhood, issuing in a feminized passivity or submissiveness.

At the same time, it is a measure of the hegemonic power of the manly ideal that its vulnerability to such wholesale default, including a default on its masculine basis, actually enhanced its ideological utility. Whereas the condition of femininity and the womanly ideal were thought to be organically linked, at least in theory, as a function of women's "natural" piety and passivity, manliness could be represented as being exclusively grounded in masculinity and yet a nonetheless notable accomplishment, something *intrinsic yet decidedly not automatic* in men. Thus, Samuel Smiles, the inventor of "self-help," designated the manly element to be an effect coterminous with the volition producing it: "Energy of will [is] the very central character of man—in a word, it is the man himself." Charles Kingsley's famous dictum, "The prerogative of man is to be bold against himself," still more succinctly captures both the structure and the effect of manhood's double inscription: its simultaneously descriptive and prescriptive import, which enables a mutually empowering play between naturalized self-interest ("man's prerogative") and praiseworthy self-denial ("bold against himself").[27] Under the rubric of manliness, in other words, male privilege *itself* comes by nature and yet through industry, fulfilling the contradictory terms of all bourgeois orders of merit.

It is this double articulation of manliness—as irreducibly animal/spirit, born/made—that permits the gendered terrain of manliness, which we have been mapping, to open up on the geopolitical terrain of manliness, to which we now turn.

Manliness; or, The Logic of English Hegemony

Of course, it goes without saying that manliness in Victorian Britain was ardently believed to be peculiar to *Englishness,* a joint benison of an Anglo-Saxon and an Anglican-Protestant heritage. Values that English spokesmen ascribed to their Teutonic origins (pluck, realism, stoic calm) and to their Protestant traditions (individuality, independence, rationality) were regularly taken to underpin or derive from the signature manliness of the race. Politically, Anglo-Saxon manliness was advanced as both explanation and warrant for the liberties England enjoyed and for the dominion they exercised abroad. In *The Races of Man* anatomist Robert Knox pronounced the Saxon "nature's democrat—the respecter of law when the law is made by *himself.*" And it was in this manly English power for self-rule that Anglo-Saxonist historians and ethnologists discovered, in the legal sense of the term, an English right to rule others, based on their inferred capacity to do so disinterestedly: "There is no disputing strength," J. A. Froude wrote, "nor happily is there need to dispute, for the strength which gives a right to freedom, implies the presence of those qualities which ensure that it will be rightly used."[28] This sort of naked identification of manly might and English right was by no means uncommon. Apologists for the different manifestations of manliness—moral, sporting, chivalric, sturdy—typically held their respective character regimes to enhance the virtues native to the English people and necessary to their exercise of power, both military and civilizing, throughout the world. Building on this argument, the boy magazines of the late nineteenth century promoted the inveterate pluck of the British "lad" as not only enabling but also justifying colonial ventures, that is, as indicating the special English suitability "for taking up the white man's burden."[29]

But while such noisy ideological manipulation has held the attention of most contemporary critics of empire, the properly hegemonic labor of manliness was performed in the silent logic of its articulation, beginning with the systematic play of its de- and prescriptive aspects, its dual function as symbolic capital and symbolic mandate. As symbolic capital, the *descriptive* category of manhood designated and enriched or bypassed and impoverished individual or corporate subjects on politically contingent grounds, thereby introducing into the texture of gender identity apparently extrinsic factors like class or racial origin. Thus, true manhood could and did take shape as the ontological essence of a very limited and specialized type of subject, the metropolitan gentleman, whose defining virtues could be indexed, but never *proven or achieved,* through exemplary displays of conventionally virile qualities. In this vein, manhood presupposed a subject fully empowered to dispose of himself and recognized as such, a subject possessed of the traditionally male-identified endowments of autonomy and self-command. For this normative subject, the metropolitan gentleman, the enactment of lawful self-discipline was received in the larger social arena as a supreme expression of masculine aggression, strength, and fortitude. It bespoke a social cachet and authority too assured to be flaunted, a possession of the phallus in appropriately veiled terms. As Thomas Hughes put it in *The Manliness of Christ,* "Self-restraint is the highest form of self-assertion."[30] Working under these cultural assumptions, every act of obedience stood to be recuperated as self-government, every act of obeisance as self-control, every act of compromise as fidelity to a higher principle or more reasonable judgment. Consequently, the state of manliness could and did effectively pose as the essential predicate for possessing in full the rights and privileges of democratic citizenship. Further, as the condition of personal independence, manliness could and did emerge as a leading trope of national self-determination. Whereas in the political code of the time the retiring ideal woman bore the dubious prerogative of protection, hence of being a protectorate, individual and collective manliness equaled fitness for freedom.

In figuring such a socially approved "fitness for freedom," manliness represented not just an exclusive mode of symbolic capital but also a universal symbolic mandate. Its *prescriptive* summons to a certain mode of self-fashioning, the attendant rewards it offered for success, these embraced all aspirants to liberal, democratic rights and responsibilities, thereby extending the dynamics of gender hierarchy into wide-ranging contests over class enfranchisement and colonial rule. Indeed, the authority of this honorific category was so comprehensive in this regard that it passed directly into the political lexicon of the time; advocating the claims of any group to greater political stature became synonymous with summoning, expressing, or defending their manhood.

But a crucial part of the political efficacy of manliness was that while it presented itself as a broadly available prospect, it remained a stubbornly restricted prerogative. Precisely because it could not, as Rosen argues, be demonstrated by conduct or demeanor alone, the ethical *prescriptions* it enjoined (rationality, self-possession, fortitude) could be recognizably fulfilled only by subjects answering to the statutory *description* it encoded (metropolitan, bourgeois, male). And because manliness presupposed such an *already* enfranchised subject, its role as compulsory ideal presented the subdominant subject or group with a nearly insoluble double bind, which intruded on the internal logic of the construct itself. Whereas the dialectical play in manhood's relation to masculinity manifested itself as *bildung* for the elite metropolitan—the training and development of inborn possibilities—the same play manifested itself as *spaltung* for the racial or colonial subaltern, a performative contradiction in which the assertion or enactment of one forfeited or belied the other. For these racial and colonial subalterns, the exercise of self-restraint and self-discipline, within the terms of the existing sociopolitical regime, could not be easily distinguished from passivity, docility, acquiescence, or weakness, all of which signaled the absence or loss of the stalwart masculinity necessary to justify any bid for liberation. Instead of an achieved expression of masculine value, a subaltern's conformity to the ethos of manliness would likely be read as a testament to his colonial emasculation. He could hardly lay viable claim to self-mastery in lawfully abiding the mastery of an alien power. On the other side, the forms available to the subaltern subject or group for the direct assertion of masculinity per se, whether as violent force or aggressive virility, tended to violate the self-disciplinary canons of bourgeois manliness, its call to energetic self-restraint. Such transgression of a compulsory ideal synonymous with the fitness for freedom gave hostages to the apologists for imperial rule, evincing the subaltern's incapacity for self-government.[31] In either case, through lawful acquiescence or lawless, even violent opposition, the subaltern can only seek what George Mosse calls the "quiet grandeur" of the manly estate by proving himself fundamentally unworthy thereof.[32]

Tellingly, the respective positions of the metropolitan gentleman and the colonial subaltern vis-à-vis the honorific estate of manliness replicated the respective positions of male and female within the patriarchal sex/gender system. In other words, there obtains a structural unmanning of the subdominant subject that is a prior condition of the more familiar imperialist discourses of feminization. For the caste of metropolitan gentleman, the de- and prescriptive functions align themselves *conjunctively,* so that their possession of its dignified moral status and the accompanying symbolic capital might paradoxically seem *natural* yet *earned.* Thus, the cultural stipulation of metropolitan bourgeois manliness served to invest the attributes, attitudes, and exploits of the pertinent subject-class with an aura of manly attainment, so that these attitudes, attributes, and exploits could, in turn, vindicate the initial cultural stipulation. For subdominant castes of subject, conversely, the de- and prescriptive functions of manhood were arranged *disjunctively* (the burden of the feminine, as we have seen), so that the acquisition of its dignified moral status and accompanying symbolic

capital might paradoxically be *compulsory* yet *impossible.* The cultural stipulation of subaltern unmanliness or premanliness invested the attributes, attitudes,
and exploits of the pertinent subject-class with a sense of inveterate deficiency
that both demands and defies remedy. In this way, manhood functioned as the
ideological engine of "flexible positional superiority," wherein the hegemonic
group legitimated their power and privilege by manipulating either side of a
given, politically charged binarism to their advantage.[33]

The particular suitability of manhood for this task rests in turn upon its *discordia concours* of animality and spirituality, which enabled subaltern claims
on manhood to be undermined by referring any positive evidence of manly
bearing or accomplishment to whatever notional equilibrium of these contrary
elements seemed best defined to refute it. Subaltern groups could be classified
as embodying a hypertrophy of some component part of manhood, its internal
other or external other, the enactment of which counted as unnatural in much
the same way as feminine displays of aggressive desire. "The divineness of the
whole manhood," conversely, remained the preserve of metropolitan gentlemen.
Thus, in the class register, bestialized representations were directed against the
Chartists, whose agitation for proletarian enfranchisement convinced an arbiter
of manliness like Kingsley that the "workers of England" were not yet "fit to be
free."[34] In the colonial register, the racially diverse subaltern peoples of the East
were regularly subjected to feminizing modes of representation.[35]

As "metrocolonials," at once members and wards of the British metropole, as
white "natives," at once racially similar and subjacent to the British imperialist,
the Irish occupied, even constituted, a decisive negative border to the Imaginary
self-portrait of English manhood.[36] We should not be surprised, therefore, that
when it came to the Irish, this double bind took its most visible and powerful
form. It materialized and was implemented on either side by the feminizing
discourse of Celticism and the bestializing discourse of simianization, which
cooperated in representing the "mere" Irish as racially deficient in manhood and
so unready for emancipation. Literary and cultural critics, myself included, have
addressed Irish feminization and simianization from a variety of perspectives.[37]
What the accounts to date have failed to delineate, however, is the dialectical
interplay of these racial figurations over time, the unconscious syntax that gave
the Irish stereotype its "stereo," self-ratifying effects. The ideological formation
orchestrating these contrapuntal tropes and lending them their hegemonic
power of containment and exclusion was the compulsory norm of manliness.

Typing Irishmen

Ideological coherence is typically the residue of historical convergence. Such
was certainly the case with the representation of Irish manhood. As a home

colony, Ireland had long been susceptible of familial metaphors that functioned to naturalize British political sovereignty over its neighbor: for example, the "Sister Isle" and later, with the controversial Act of Union, the wife in a "metropolitan marriage." But the early anthropological and ethnographic discourses, otherwise known as the racial sciences, helped to shift the epicenter of Irish femininity from the national to the racial dimension. The Irish were depicted as genetically feminine and so, on the reigning patriarchal logic, congenitally attuned to obeying the will of a masculine race like the Anglo-Saxon, provided it was robustly asserted. By inscribing the presumed inferiority of the Irish in biological terms, this shift of register lent their political subordination an air of inner necessity, historical inevitability, and, above all, *permanence.*

More important, this maneuver participated in a larger shift in the specific value of gender as the ideological currency of *metro-colonization,* a change occasioned by the development of liberal principles and institutions next door in the metropole proper. The discourse of modernity in Britain was staked on the contradictory coherence of economic and political liberalism, the former openly demanding imperialistic occupation as a method for expanding markets, acquiring resources, and accessing cheap labor, the latter implicitly deploring such conquests as a vitiation of the democratic ideal. The strain between these collateral variants grew decisive with respect to the Irish question, owing to the geographical proximity of the two islands, the resulting mobility of resources and information, and the seven hundred years' engagement of the English and Irish cultural traditions. As historian Richard Lebow writes, "The discrepancy between the values of British society and the means employed to preserve colonial domination over Ireland grew steadily more apparent. . . . While Britain was becoming more democratic [through the Reform Acts, the Married Woman's Property Act, and so on], British rule in Ireland continued to rely on force and coercion and became more undemocratic in relation to the emerging value structure of British society."[38] Under these circumstances, the stereotypical feminization of the metro- or semicolonial other began to operate as a vehicle of imperialist apologia—which is to say it operated under the pressure of a felt inconsistency.

The gender system acted as a uniquely serviceable frame for discriminating the English from the Irish in a hierarchical manner, in order to rationalize British authoritarianism while at the same time acknowledging the cultural intimacy of colonized and colonizer. That is to say, the feminization of the Irish aimed precisely to place them both in a complementary relation to the British, in which each polis would "naturally" ally itself with the other (like woman and man in the heterosexual Imaginary), and in a synechdochic relation to the British, in which Irish judgments and interests were always "partial" (fractional and emotionally biased) when seen from a putatively balanced and comprehensive British perspective.[39]

In suggesting that the metrocolonial staus quo reflected or responded to certain defining needs and proclivities of the Irish character, the imperialist gender allegory further implied that British rule was not only for the best, in a general sense, but was also about doing the best for its metrocolonial wards—hence that it was a fundamentally humane enterprise. In failing to recognize or respect as much, conversely, Irish resistance to said rule could be accounted perverse or unnatural; it could even, for that reason, be seen to bespeak subhuman(e) tendencies, of which anthropoid species had for some time been the approved emblem. Beginning in the 1840s, with the Repeal Campaign, the simianization of the Irish intensified with each access of ungrateful protest against the political fact or the socioeconomic means of colonial governance—the Young Ireland démarche, the rise of Fenianism, the success of the Land League, the militarization of Sinn Fein, and the like—and then abated as each movement waned. This rhythmic fluctuation afforded one of the period's most reliable typological constants.

Nevertheless, the same anthropological and ethnological discourses that altered the grounds of Irish feminization worked a similarly decisive change in the focus of Irish simianization. In the late 1840s, the Irish ape still possessed a mano a mano quality, so to speak. Cartoonist John Leech and others limned individual figures, such as John Mitchel, as "the Irish Monkey," and the Irish in general were frequently imaged as brutes and primitives, the catchphrase "wild Irish" epitomizing their putatively uncivilized being-in-the-world. (The English even coined an Irish sobriquet for their *own* urban barbarians, "hooligans," which remains current in the soccer culture of today.) But the specific connection between perceived racial savagery and the anthropoid kingdom had not yet crystallized. It was only once the Victorian preoccupation with evolutionary models of human ancestry (galvanized by the 1859 publication of Darwin's *Origin of Species*) informed the new racial sciences that the Irish monkey finally metamorphosed into the Irish *as* monkey.

The introduction of this ethnological weapon consolidated the role of racial-colonial supremacism as a modern secular theodicy, justifying the abrogation of liberal political ideals (democratic participation, freedom of persons) in the service of liberal political economy (generalized commodity exchange, freedom of markets). With the figuration of the subaltern as subspecies, it became evident that the ironic corollary of the extension of political rights to more and more persons was the selective extenuation of the status of personhood itself. Whereas feminization implied that the political rights of the Irish were vested in their British masters, much as a wife's suffrage was understood to be vested in her "lord and master," the burden of simianization was to throw into question whether the Irish properly owned any political rights in the first place. The former represented colonial rule as companionable protection, the latter as exigent control.

With the typological stars thus aligned, the logic of manliness conjured forth an English-identified ideal of autonomous, self-regulating plenitude, of which these Irish-identified profiles were the complementary but unsynthesizable fragments, the symmetrical yet antagonistic modes of otherness. As such an ideal whole, manliness functioned not just as a standard against which these alternating figures of Irish inferiority were judged but also, and more important, as the hinge that held them together, interchangeably, as the dual effects of a characteristically Irish failure to meet the magnanimous summons to normative, liberal, which is to say British, subjectivity. What I have called the ideal's hegemonic power of containment and exclusion is all the more evident when one considers that the failure in question was inherent not in the Irish character, as colonial propaganda insisted, but in the very structure of manliness itself, specifically in its constitutive confusion of *ethnos* and *ethos,* de- and prescriptive criteria. Indeed, it is precisely this confusion that enabled the gendered superiority of the English and the gendered abjection of the Irish to be consolidated in and through one another. Ideologically, England's ethnic advantages in claiming manliness cast the Irish inability to do so as an ethical demerit; conversely, Irish ethnic impediments to attaining manly status underwrote English success as an ethical achievement.

Even with this double-edged ideological efficacy in mind, it is striking and remarkable, though not altogether surprising, that almost all of the leading theoreticians of English manliness were also among the major exponents of Irish feminization *and* bestialization. Thomas Carlyle, early prophet of the chivalric style of manliness, denounced the Irish as a "brawling unreasonable" people and Ireland as a "human swinery" and a "black howling Babel of superstitious savages."[40] On the other side of the ledger, he also created the emblematic figure of the "Irish widow" to allegorize the cross-contagion of bodily and moral infirmity.[41] Thomas Arnold, leading spokesman for Christian manliness, found the Irish to be "barbarians," a "savage people," and spoke of going over and "civilizing them."[42] In a perfect instance of Oedipal rivalry and identification, his son Matthew proposed to erase the invidious Saxon-Celt divide on which he had been raised only to lend it a subtler and more obdurate form. Arguing explicitly from the idea of manhood as self-disciplined excess, Arnold defines the Celtic personality as "sentimental, not unlike the much lionized Greek, but without the latter's sense of measure." "Do not let us wish," writes Arnold, "that the Celt had less sensibility but that he had been more master of it." From this lack of self-mastery, Arnold infers that "the sensibility of the Celtic nature . . . its nervous exaltation, have something feminine in them, and the Celt is peculiarly disposed to feel the spell of feminine idiosyncrasy; he has an affinity to it; he is not far from its secret."[43] The eminent historian and male supremacist J. A. Froude (whom we saw equate British might with British right) believed the

Irish suffered an "incompleteness of character," which made them "the spend-thrift sisters of the arian race." He further held that the "unbridled passion" of the Celts made them patently unfit for self-rule: "Passionate in everything . . . [t]hey are without the manliness which will give strength and stability to the sentimental [read: feminine] part of their disposition." Completing the circuit, Froude also declared the Irish "more like squalid apes than human beings."[44]

In a literary vein, Alfred Lord Tennyson, whose major work, *In Memoriam,* did so much to focus the Victorian debate on the nature of manhood, deplored in that very poem "the blind hysteria of the Celt," a characterization that patholo-gized the racial femininity it invoked.[45] The animalistic stereotype materializes in the sequel to *Tom Brown's Schooldays, Tom Brown at Oxford.* Thomas Arnold's apostle, novelist Thomas Hughes, epitomizes failed manliness in a drunken, violent, buffoonish Irishman named Donovan, who manages to corral Brown himself in his folly, threatening the moral progress of perhaps the most beloved protagonist in "manly" literature.[46] The allegorical tendency of the scene is to question whether the Irish are sufficiently evolved to occupy or benefit from the elite character factories of England, and whether given the rootedness of manliness itself in "animal spirits," the presence of the "wild Irish" cannot but prove a contagion.

Finally, the man who personified "muscular Christianity," Charles Kingsley, authored perhaps the most notorious of the simianizing blood-libels upon the Irish: "I am haunted by the human chimpanzees I saw along that hundred miles of horrible country. I don't believe they are our fault. I believe there are not only many more of them than of old, but that they are happier, better, more com-fortably fed and lodged under our rule than they ever were. But to see white chimpanzees is dreadful; if they were black, one would not feel it so much, but their skins . . . are as white as ours."[47] What haunts Kingsley, as his discomfort at Irish whiteness denotes, is the sense of English ("our") proximity to these "human chimpanzees." An ardent imperialist, Kingsley attributed Britain's ex-tensive colonial superiority to the manly possession of primordial *thumos* by the Anglo-Saxon race, and the bestial impression left by the Irish could not but seem the mirror image, the same yet reversed, of this great conquering passion. Kingsley's anxious dismissal of English responsibility for the horrific condition of Ireland belies a suspicion of some kinship between imperial (animal) aggres-sion and colonial (bestial) abjection not unlike that which he posits between the Irish and the anthropoid. That is to say, because Kingsley holds "animal passion" to be "the root of all virtue," his Irish "missing link" does not fully insulate English manliness from the simianizing implications of Darwinism. Kingsley only finds reassurance in his faith in the supremacy of English industry and providence, which have left these still unimaginably wretched Irish better off in every way "than they ever were." Irish unmanliness thus serves as alibi for the primal aggressor of imperial manhood, showing it to be sanctified and beneficial by comparison.

Perhaps because this bilateral allegory of Celtic unmanliness was simultaneously a vehicle of English self-congratulation and reassurance, it circulated widely and in various forms among the mass cultural media of Victorian Britain and Ireland, including:

1. Popular novels and melodramas, such as Boucicault's *Shaughraun,* which figures the Irish alternately as a prospective bride for the English colonizer (Claire) and a barbarous if charming lout (Conn), frequently compared to animal life (goats, pigs)
2. Newspaper articles, humor, and opinion magazines, like *Punch,* where a notorious satire discerned the lineaments of Irishness in London Zoo's first ape:

   > A gulf, certainly, does appear to yawn between the Gorilla and the Negro. The woods and wilds of Africa do not exhibit an example of any intermediate animal. But . . . [a] creature manifestly between the Gorilla and the Negro . . . comes from Ireland. . . . [I]t belongs in fact to a tribe of Irish savages: the lowest species of Irish Yahoo. . . . The Irish Yahoo generally confines itself within the limits of its own colony. . . . Sometimes, however, it sallies forth in states of excitement, and attacks civilized human beings that have provoked its fury.[48]

   The *Punch* satire disavows (displays/dissimulates) the Victorian anxiety at the newly discovered descent of man from ape by displacing the proximity of the two species onto the Irish other: the function of the so-called missing link here, as everywhere, is not only to mediate but, in mediating, to absorb unto itself humanity's genealogical kinship with the lower orders and thus to divest "true" humanity of that humbling derivation. In this case, the Irishman's role as missing link is intimately bound up with his debased masculinity. In his susceptibility to furious "states of excitement," he bodies forth the universal male complement of "animal spirits," which the metropolitan gentleman effectively discharges through a socially ratified habit of self-regulation.

3. A rich tradition of political illustrations portraying the Irish either in feminine or simian guise, most prominently the work of Sir John Tenniel. Two of his pieces in particular—"The Fenian-Pest" (figure 1), and "Two Forces" (figure 2)—encapsulate the sort of gendered vise set out for nationally, let alone nationalistically, minded Irishman.

As L. P. Curtis remarks, "The Fenian-Pest" follows the narrative outline of beauty and the beast and features a stern, sturdy Britannia protecting a hyperfeminized Hibernia from the simian blandishments of a Fenian insurgent.[49] Like another Tenniel cartoon, "The Mad Doctor," this one dichotomizes the Irish people-nation into charming and compliant loyalists, who accept their

THE FENIAN-PEST.

Hibernia. "O MY DEAR SISTER, WHAT ARE WE TO DO WITH THESE TROUBLESOME PEOPLE?"
Britannia. "TRY ISOLATION FIRST, MY DEAR, AND THEN——"

Figure 1. "The Fenian-Pest," *Punch,* March 3, 1866. Courtesy of the Rare Book & Manuscript Library, University of Illinois at Urbana-Champaign.

feminine place under Britain's dominion, and odious, savage nationalists, whose insistence on masculine aggression has made monkeys of them. Whereas the Irish figures image the external alterity of manhood as *sexual* difference and the internal alterity of manhood as *species* difference, the bearing of Britannia, at once phallic and androgynous, graceful yet military, marks her as the fully integrated "Spirit-Animal," the preferred estate of manliness.

Composed much later, during the Land League crisis, "Two Forces" takes the allegorical implications of the beauty-and-the-beast motif even further in the same direction.[50] Like "The Fenian-Pest," this cartoon predicates its political message—that the Irish must embrace British rule to save themselves from themselves—upon a gendered anatomy of the Irish as fissured between the antagonistic components of manly character. But here the apish Fenian is less conspiratorial and more bellicose, and the cartoon identifies him simply as "anarchy," a label that effectively dissociates the violence he threatens from any rational agenda. Whereas in "The Fenian-Pest," Hibernia appears distressed and deferential toward Britannia, here she appears clingy and helpless, her body buried against Britannia's strong upright form, her face hidden, all sense of her personality extinguished. Britannia herself strikes a more imposing and mannish figure than previously. Planted in the middle ground of the picture,

Figure 2. "Two Forces,"
Punch, October 29, 1881.
Courtesy of the Rare Book
& Manuscript Library,
University of Illinois at
Urbana-Champaign.

her phallic sword, "the law," creates a prophylactic barrier between the inimical sides of the Irish spirit, while marking Britannia herself as the figure of their impossible synthesis or conjunction. Identifying the very possibility of good democratic order with a racially saturated manhood, the sword redoubles the 1860s opposition of a simianized Fenian and a feminized Loyalism into an opposition between the law-giving British nation and the law-starved Irish people. The "Two Forces" splitting Ireland translate immediately into the "Two Forces" contesting the United Kingdom. Or to put it another way: whereas the Irish explained their internal fissures as the effect of colonial oppression or even the precise aim of Britain's divide-and-conquer strategy, the British, like Tenniel, justified colonial rule on the basis of Ireland's unmanly internal divisions.

The *Edinburgh Review* articulated the specifically political lesson to be distilled from all such verbal and visual *figura:* "The Irish are deficient in the unquiet energy [feminine] . . . deficient too in the faculty of self-government [bestial] without which free institutions can neither flourish nor be permanently maintained."[51]

Manliness and the Metrocolonial Double Bind

This ideological ensemble of high and pop cultural discourses unfolded the logic of manliness in a manner calculated to exacerbate the distinctive conflicts and anxieties of a "metrocolonial" people. On one side, the Irish were enlisted as foot soldiers of empire, and so bound to the ethos of manliness; on the other, they were reduced to inmates of empire, and thus stigmatized as manhood's other. As a consequence of this hierarchical self-division, many politically articulate Irishmen wound up internalizing the broad Eurocentric ideology of gendered racial stereotyping, in which Anglo-Saxon supremacism, the discourse of their dispossession, quickened and flourished. The contradictory semicolonial in-scription of the Irish often passed into a contradictory semi-imperial attitude on the part of the Irish, who were effectively interpellated to endorse certain invidi-ous assumptions fundamental to the colonial authority, moral and otherwise, that disenfranchised them. They were, in other words, caught in a dynamic of identification and rivalry with the English over the terms of ethnic (self-)defi-nition, which were vital in turn to the struggle for national self-determination. And, for reasons already adduced, the estate of manhood was both the most valuable and the most elusive stake in this ideological competition.

The saliency of the manly ideal to this deeply emulous Irish self-conception only intensified as the century wore on. An increasing number of Anglo-Irish boys attended British public schools—the factories of manliness—forming a particularly strong contingent, for example, at Cheltenham.[52] At the same time, a growing number of Irish Catholic boys, often from nationalist families, attended native academies modeled, in their fetishism of the manly, upon their British counterparts, a circumstance ironized in Joyce's depiction of Stephen Dedalus at Clongowes Wood.[53] Even Pearse's übernationalist St. Enda's Academy closely followed this pattern. Such institutional cross-pollination heightened the Irish sense of identification and rivalry with their colonial rulers, for they found them-selves excluded, as an ethnic group, from the fruits of the disciplined mode of self-fashioning in which more and more of their number were inculcated and practiced as individual subjects (of the Crown).[54]

The historical evidence of this competitive identification and the collective *psychomachia* it wrought can be discerned in each phase of Irish nationalist resistance leading up to the Anglo-Irish war. No sooner did the metropolitan ethnologies of the Celt take hold in the 1840s than the nationalist vanguard of the time, Young Ireland, began to exhort its adherents to a collective enactment of British-style manliness. Leaders urged resolution, endurance, self-discipline, and respectability, while warning against a "womanly" indulgence in loquacious tirades, protests, and lamentations. As Sean Ryder has proposed, the immemorial Irish practice of allegorizing the land, nation, and people as a beautiful maiden or goddess grew increasingly problematic under the masculinist sway of the new racial sciences: "The femininity which at one moment is used to define Ireland as a nation which . . . has been treated unjustly, becomes at another moment an embarrassment to a nationalism which internalizes . . . those values which privilege masculine traits such as activity, vigour, strength and courage."[55] But if we are to understand how this sort of iconographical discomfiture might actually compel nationalist leaders to rethink entrenched modes of popular self-conception and presentation, we must look to the pervasive ideological power of the manly ideal. It is this ideal that articulates masculinity not as a final form, a goal in itself, but as the basic condition, the raw material of individual and collective self-government—which is to say the *primary* desideratum of any colonized people.

In 1843, the Young Ireland leader Charles Gavan Duffy took the bait of manliness in an especially public way. He admonished the readers of his movement's paper, *The Nation,* that "brave men . . . endure when it is not wise to act—they act when it is no longer needful to endure. But the women's weapon of complaint and recrimination they seem to use never. . . . [T]hese are the men to build a nation."[56] Duffy's position, however, contained a potentially crippling performative contradiction that cut against his professed cause in two paradoxically related ways. The "women's weapon" he deplores as contemptible, unworthy of the muscular business of nation building, was one of the sole resorts for a disempowered people to win redress of grievances. No less important, it remained a critical first step in organizing the efforts of decolonization that must precede the prize of national independence. By conceding, in effect, the justice of colonial subjugation insofar as the Irish persist in displaying the feminine traits ascribed them, Duffy expresses a masculinized identification with the aggressor that can serve only, in practical terms, to stymie nationalist advocacy in its very emergence.

In that self-betrayal and self-suppression, moreover, and here is the paradox, Duffy's posture helped to foster just the collective gender status he would denigrate and avoid. The hegemonic design of Victorian manliness solicited the Irish subaltern to an emulation of its prescriptive conventions, while simultaneously precluding, on descriptive or statutory grounds, his appropriation of the estate itself and its collateral social privileges and political entitlement. In this manner, it bid fair to transfer the worrisome social regulation of the dispossessed, refractory Irish subalterns to the subalterns themselves, in the form of *self-regulation,* offering the empty promise that the fitness for freedom indicated by such rectitude would somehow conduce and ultimately lead to the reality of freedom itself. In the circumstances of colonial subordination, however, the self-restraining conduct recommended as manly was indistinguishable from an easily feminized pattern of forbearance. Thus, in accepting this ideological simulacrum of a political objective, the early Young Ireland anticipated the inaugural posture of subsequent moral force movements, including Home Rule and Sinn Fein. Each found itself confronted with the first side or phase of what I am calling the double bind of Irish manhood.

THE METROCOLONIAL DOUBLE BIND, PART 1

If the metrocolonial subject, individual or collective, elected to enact the manly ethos and to demonstrate thereby his capacity for self-control and respectable self-government, he had to restrain and regulate his conduct in conformity with the received canons of gender and social practice. But by pursuing this regimen, he would perforce testify to his potential (gentle)manliness at the price of abiding the order of his oppression and so lending at least tacit support to its legitimacy and the correlative legitimacy of his own exclusion from the rights and liberties of manhood. For the Irish subaltern, observing the manly norms of self-repression amounted to acquiescing in the feminine stereotype of passivity, pliancy, and submissiveness to others that British opinion regularly invoked as proof of the essentially Celtic desire to be ruled.[57]

However manly on its own terms, such conduct tended to strengthen British confidence that the Irish lacked the staying power to sustain political resistance of any sort or to earn its wages. Referring to Ireland's professed right of self-determination, Major Saunderson declared, "No race is free until it's strong enough and brave enough to be free. England is free because she fought to be free."[58]

The problem is nicely illustrated in Thomas Davis's 1845 essay, "Memorials of Wexford."[59] Davis begins a paean to Wexford masculinity by praising its inhabitants' restraint of aggressive passion in almost programmatic conformity with the conventions of Victorian manliness. He pronounces his subjects "as good a mass of men as ever sustained a state by honest franchise, by peace, virtue, and intelligent industry." In Wexford, Davis pointedly remarks, "outrages are unknown," and he proceeds to attribute an exhaustive catalog of manly qualities to the peasants there: their "honest dealings" and patient endurance of high rents; their self-respecting "gaze that heeds no lordling's frown" yet does not prevent this "Catholic people" from remaining on "excellent terms with their Protestant landlords"; their upright manner and address—"The Wexford men have neither the base bend nor the baser craft of slaves"—that translates into honorable participation in the electoral mechanisms of their own national subjacency; their social respectability, manifest in a "snug homestead, kept clean," and a similarly scrupulous attention to "every religious duty"; and their "industriousness and skill," which produces uncommon prosperity. On the strength of these factors, and the disciplined rationality they betoken, Davis organizes the first movement of his essay around the proposition that "no county is fitter for freedom than Wexford," the phrase "fit for freedom" being, of course, a stock formula of Victorian manliness.

But given the mayhem committed by the famed "boys of Wexford" in '98, their present habit of law-abiding, disciplined, and prosperous respectability lent credence to the Anglo-Saxonist commonplace that the unmanly character of the Irish responded better to authoritarian rule than to independence. Nor could a strong nationalist like Davis find the stereotype of native Irish deference sufficiently challenged by the self-control with which Wexford men tolerated their subordination.

Accordingly, Davis begins the second, contrapuntal, movement of the piece by taking stock of the underlying political inefficacy of Wexford's manly modus vivendi: "Wexford is not all that it might be. . . . [T]here is something to blame and something to lament, here a vice sustained, and there a misfortune laxly borne." He finds himself welcoming in Wexford's recent nationalist demands (which seem not unlike Duffy's reviled "complaints") some glimmer of the "rude vitality" exhibited so spectacularly by the fabled "boys of '98." A highly mythologized rendition of their military exploits occupies the remainder of the essay. While Davis labors to preserve a sense of continuity between the "honest dealings" and self-respecting demeanor of Wexford present and the bloody doings and ferocious outlawry of Wexford past ("Theirs was no treacherous assassination—theirs no stupid riot—theirs no pale mutiny"), he clearly departs from the celebration of high Victorian manhood in favor of the compensatory agenda of colonial hypermasculinity: a competitive identification with the conqueror on the basis of fighting strength and ferocity alone.[60] Moreover, in contrast with his heartfelt yet slightly skeptical manner of complimenting contemporary Wexford, he reconstructs the martial experience of the '98 with a fulsome poetic verve, suggesting something of a conversion experience on his part. As a result, when he returns to the present in his coda, the threadbare generalities he uses to exhort his audience—"press your organization, work at your education, and increase your political power"—serve both to announce the strategic limits of Wexford's current embrace of manliness and to encipher a call to more virile opposition.

The rhetorical trajectory of Davis's essay, from dignified self-regulation to militant aggression, models the political itinerary of each of the moral force movements, as they drifted into league with the physical force wing of the struggle. The progress of Young Ireland itself is a case in point, turning as it did from a pre-Famine alliance with the diligently law-abiding O'Connell to the post-Famine Rising of 1848, which ushered in the Fenian era of violent separatism. Once again, the Home Rule campaign switched from its genteel parliamentary advocacy under Butt's leadership to the New Departure cov-

enant, which tacitly incorporated a new highly volatile strain of agrarian terrorism. It was Butt's commitment to a respectably self-restrained deportment
in the movement's diplomatic and parliamentary dealings—his commitment
to political manliness as he understood it—that restricted the Home Rulers to
a feminized strategy of unrelieved supplication and ultimately led to his ouster.
Even Sinn Fein sketched a similar path, proceeding from a rigorously nonviolent
philosophy under Arthur Griffith to an adventitious yet decisive identification
with the martyred Volunteers of 1916. To some degree, these trajectories, like that
of Davis's essay, sketched unconsciously defensive responses to the hegemonic
operation of the ideal of manliness, specifically to the conflicting pressures it
exerted and anxieties it aroused in the metrocolonial subaltern. Since for a nationalist Irishman the ruling passion to be strongly checked was precisely the
passion for political manhood itself, that is, ethnonational self-determination,
the ends that interpellated them to the manly estate were perennially defeated by
the prescribed means of achieving it. Here we arrive at a more deep-structural
feminization than image and typology enacted. For the Irish, the manly norm
of aggressive self-restraint was *in itself* the acknowledged "feminine" norm of
submission to others—gender being finally determined in these circumstances
not by the content of one's racial performance but by one's relation to the masculinized locus of concentrated social power.

That an unconscious defensiveness shaped the life cycle of these major moral
force movements may be deduced in part from the rhetorical practices of Fenianism, with which each of them ultimately dovetailed. Leaders of the Irish Revolutionary Brotherhood (IRB) and its political and cultural confederates sought to
nominally attach the militaristic, hypermasculine ethos they promulgated to the
ideal of manliness from which it *substantially* diverged. "In a number of ways,"
Toby Joyce writes, "the Irish Fenians of the 1860's were typical mid-century
Victorians," and they were accordingly responsive to the ideological worth of a
manly repute, the social value of which appealed to their (middle-) class interests
and aspirations.[61] One finds men such as James Stephens, O'Donovan Rossa,
Michael Cusack, Joseph Roche, and Michael Doheny selectively deploying the
vocabulary of manhood so as to reduce the ideal they brandished to its martial
component alone. The sainted dynamitard O'Donovan Rossa, for example, used
the term *manhood* interchangeably with *group discipline*. Joseph Roche wrote
of "manly bearing and tone" as the equivalent of soldierly demeanor. American
"head centre" Michael Doheny equated manhood "in the highest acceptation
of the term" with "the use of arms."[62]

James Stephens's article "Liberty or Destruction" captures this physical force
synecdoche of Victorian manhood perfectly: "We witness the periodical slaughter of our people; we see the grass growing on our hearths; we watch the stalwart
manhood and virtuous womanhood of our race flying to distant lands—and

seeing all this we must be men. . . . You are our vanguard. Be prepared to meet the foe in ordered phalanx, and your measured tramps shall hush the voice of denunciation. . . . United Ireland leaping to her feet, shall, with one sweep of her unfettered arm, hurl the invader into the sea."[63] This passage seems to recommend the Victorian ideal of manhood but in fact reverses its defining logic and so defaults on its very essence. Instead of marshaling aggressive force to the ends of self-discipline and mastery (invoked in the phrase "stalwart manhood"), this hypermasculine rhetoric mobilizes forms of discipline ("ordered phalanx," "measured tramps") as a means to enhance a release of an aggressive force that was not only uncontrolled ("shall, with one sweep of her *unfettered* arm, *hurl* the invader into the sea") but in its repeatedly instanced futility, profoundly undisciplined as well. Far from being casual, this reversal indicates how the *realpolitical* objectives of Fenianism virtually compelled the movement to simplify, distort, violate, and ultimately reject the normative manliness to which it remained ideologically attached. Whereas the efforts of moral force nationalism to appropriate the symbolic capital of manliness tended to vitiate their agenda of practical resistance (the first side of the double bind), the Fenians' attempt to appropriate the manly code to their practical agenda tended to vitiate their claim on its symbolic capital—triggering the second side of the double bind.

THE METROCOLONIAL DOUBLE BIND, PART 2

If the metrocolonial subject, individual or collective, elected to assert his masculinity in defiance of the self-regulatory norm or the political regime that it served—if he sought, for example, the violent overthrow of his subordination— his course of action would indicate an inability to keep his passions in check, an absence of the self-control that was the hallmark of normative manliness and hence the fitness for freedom. By this path, too, the Irish could only testify to the legitimacy of their marginalization. That which *went* uncontrolled in this sort of lawless aggression was an excess of "animal spirits," bespeaking a racial and cultural subhumanity.

The high point in the simianization of such presumed barbarism came in the 1880s, powered on one side by the Land League outrages and on the other by new pseudoanthropological conceits, such as John Beddoes's "Index of Nigrescence," that floated in the wake of Darwin's discoveries.[64] As a result of these developments, the Irish ape was produced in greater numbers than before, by more diverse hands, and with a more decidedly racial edge. During the same period, the efforts of a nascent revivalist nationalism to controvert Calibanesque stereotypes of Irish brutality, with proclamations of the innate idealism and incomparable spirituality of the Celtic race, were appropriated from the start to an Arnoldian framework of Celtic femininity, whose central tenets it recalled and reinforced. Just as the resistance of Irish *political* nationalism to racial feminization tended to ratify the concomitant imperialist discourse of racial simianization, so the resistance of Irish *cultural* nationalism to simianization tended to ratify the concomitant imperialist discourse of feminization.[65]

With this closure of the ideological circuit, finally, the slippage I posited at the outset between late Victorian manhood and masculinity reveals its hegemonic import in yet another version of the gendered double bind. On one side, the British elite could deny the Irish their collective manhood for *failing to meet* the fundamental standard of virile masculinity, that is, for being insufficiently courageous, powerful, and unyielding in their resistance to colonial rule; on the other side, the British elite could deny the Irish their collective manhood for *exceeding* the fundamental standard of virile masculinity, that is, for being excessively violent and refractory in their resistance to colonial rule.

Coda

Just as the imperialist operation of the manly ideal lay not in the properties mandated but in the logic of their arrangement, so the means of frustrating the imperialist instrumentality of the manly ideal lay not in the degree of the Irish acceptance or rejection thereof but rather in the particular manner of its internalization and reappropriation, a receptivity to the pressure of its immediate social currency that winds up unwittingly altering the larger economy of its potential.

Parnellism comprised just this sort of unconsciously innovative ideological reassemblage in the pursuit of a comparatively orthodox political agenda. Nor is this distance between method and yield accidental. Insofar as any open avowal or pretense of manliness would necessarily vitiate the self-repressive, self-sublimating modus operandi of the ideal, manliness represents one of those estates—like humility or dignity—that cannot be attained by direct approach but must come as a by-product. The manliness of Parnell was distilled, and could only have been distilled, from such distinct registers of praxis that no sovereign will could possibly have directed its cultivation or controlled its reception. It is precisely this structural condition that enabled the manliness he embodied for Ireland to exert its full impact, which presupposed a certain absence of awareness or understanding on the part of both his allies and his adversaries. Readers of Slavoj Zizek will recognize in this paradox his delineation of "ideology" per se: not a generalized misrecognition of the reality of particular social relations but rather social relations that depend for their consistency, hence their particular reality, on a generalized misrecognition.[66]

1

The Manliness of Parnell

Irish political and cultural historians have long pondered the reasons behind the tenacious hold that Charles Stewart Parnell exerted on the imagination of his compatriots. But while they have succeeded in amassing voluminous and fairly consistent evidence as to the sources and dimensions of his public appeal, they have failed, by and large, to satisfy themselves with a comprehensive explanation of what Labouchere calls "the Irish fetishism of Parnell."[1] In trying to qualify the achievement of a figure similarly revered and martyred, mystified and then deified within his own oppressed community, Spike Lee's film *Malcolm X* celebrates the eponymous hero for giving Afro-Americans their "manhood," and I believe an analogous claim can be made for the impression Parnell left upon both the Anglo- and the Gaelo-Irish community of his time, not to mention the English themselves. Every aspect of his political life, from his widespread popularity to the internecine nationalist conflict occasioned by his demise, can be better assessed if one considers the importance of his gender performance, broadly conceived, on two levels: the way in which his personal style of address coordinated with his political agenda to project an air of manliness that had a special currency under the regime of domestic colonialism and the way in which the air of manliness he projected became the locus of collective transference and identification, allowing Parnell to defy colonial emasculation in the name of the Irish people.

This is one of those occasions, I would submit, when a cultural studies methodology can legitimately supplement the discourse of history, by taking up inadequately explicated events or phenomena on conceptual lines not ordinarily applied to them. Thus, at the conclusion of his massive biography of Parnell, F. S. L. Lyons proclaims that Parnell "gave back to the Irish people their self-respect,"[2] but he does not have an optic available to clarify the meaning of his own intuition, and so he reverts, here and elsewhere, to a vaguely moralizing disappointment with the politically immature and self-mystifying disciples who so venerated Parnell in the first place.[3] An analytic lever like gender performance, however, can help to contextualize the rather amorphous notion of colonial respect, to illuminate the ideological constraints placed on its achievement, and to concatenate the elements of Parnell's career that engaged or challenged those constraints.

Having invoked cultural studies, however, I want to dissociate my use of the term *performance* from the claims of volitional agency that it often carries, along with its relatives *performative* and *performativity,* in much of that discourse. Indeed, as the ensuing discussion shows, the ideal of manliness itself was less a substantive or performative than a structural category, a mode of organizing the basic elements of character, private and public, individual and collective. As a result, the manliness embodied individually by Parnell for the ethnos at large could not finally reside in the enactment of specific forms of policy or self-presentation but only in the logic of their arrangement. The manliness of Charles Stewart Parnell in particular was articulated across several dimensions of his political profile and practice (personal, rhetorical, tactical, strategic), and it was on the basis of this concerted development—the way each register answered the others at a figurative remove—that its idealized aura radiated from Parnell to the people-nation, from exemplary Irishman to Irish Man.

In this regard, it is worth remarking that the contemporaneous memoirs and the subsequent biographies of Parnell regularly discover in him the cardinal properties associated with late Victorian manhood, yet none of them sees fit to foreground the gender coding of these attitudes or to constellate them on an explicitly gendered basis. Small as it may seem, this persistent oversight constitutes one of those crucial blind spots upon which ideological reproduction depends. For this elision of gender performance (outside of a casual reference or two) shelters a crucial element of the Parnell "enigma," and hence of his charisma, even in those narratives bent on dissecting or debunking his mystique, and, in so doing, it plays a key role in the generally acknowledged failure of all of these documents to penetrate the "Irish fetishism" of their "Chief."

A Man for Ireland

Accounts of Parnell's achievement tend to break down along a public-private axis, the same axis that came to figure so prominently in the scandalous denouement of his career. Contemporaneous accounts tend to trace Parnell's seignorial éclat primarily to his interior resources, deeply personal qualities of spirit, bearing, and temperament, and only secondarily to the policies he fashioned or the tactical maneuverings he actuated. As one might imagine, however, this "extraordinary man" thesis runs toward hagiography rather than history and does less to explain Parnell's cult of personality than to affirm and legitimate it. Furthermore, melding old-fashioned heroic romance with the assumptions of liberal individualism, this thesis all but precludes a sociopolitical analysis of Parnell's appeal. On this view, even his most broadly public impact, the mass identification of the Irish people with his movement, boils down to a sentimental embrace aroused by his personal charm. His fellow politician T. P. O'Connor opines, "I can't think anyone outside Ireland can understand what a charm Mr. Parnell has for the Irish heart; that wonderful personality of his, his proud bearing, his handsome strong face, the distinction of looks . . . all these are irresistible to the artistic Irish."[4] More recent accounts downplay the personal romance of Parnell and analyze his success primarily in terms of comparatively objective sociopolitical conditions, needs, and objectives, to which his personality is seen as a cultivated response. What this perspective misses, however, is precisely that which mesmerizes (and stupefies) the earlier one: the visceral nature of the Parnell effect upon people, from the immediate impression he left on allies, to the influence he exerted within the rarefied political culture of Westminster, to the loyalty he inspired in the Irish masses, but a tiny fraction of whom had ever laid eyes upon him. In reducing the so-called Parnell myth to the terms of modern political rationality, this perspective does less to explain Parnell's cult of personality than to discount or instrumentalize it.

Let us take a classic example. Conor Cruise O'Brien's landmark text *Parnell and His Party* locates the efficacy of Parnellism in its studied ambiguity, even duplicity, through which it contrived to win the sustained adherence of multiple, conflicting, and sometimes antagonistic constituencies: revolutionaries and constitutionalists, Home Rulers and separatists, advanced Irish nationalists and their far more conservative English sympathizers. According to O'Brien, the "romantic," charismatic persona of Parnell functions strictly as a piece of necessary political camouflage, a mask under which the shrewd political maneuvering of a "realistic" politician could proceed. To be specific, Parnell's "mysterious awe-inspiring" figure gave him an aura of romantic Irish radicalism, which allowed him to pursue his more modest political objectives without splitting his own coalition and while retaining a "vague penumbra" of revolutionary blackmail in his dealings with the English. "The ambiguity of the system must be crystallized in terms of personality. . . . [T]he prestige of achievement, the magnetism of great ability previously established, these drew to the personality of the leader the enthusiasm generated by the revolutionary policies which he was felt to symbolize. Then he was able to carry out, with the aid of his party, and of non-revolutionary elements in the country, his constitutional policy."[5] Useful as this analysis is, O'Brien conveniently forgets that the uncanny magnetism of Parnell attracted the ethnic and nationalistic identification of the "non-revolutionary elements" of Irish society, not to mention the fraternal admiration of the British public (under the "Union of Hearts"), no less effectively than it pleased the revolutionary hard-liners. To put this objection another way, the masterful enigma of Parnell's public persona attracted a multiple and mass political investment and so can hardly be reduced to a mere symbolic stalking horse for "revolutionary policies," which drew only marginal and declining support during this period. Moreover, none of these constituencies seized upon Parnell as the image of the romantic revolutionary, for which Robert Emmet, the Manchester Martyrs, and the "bold Fenian boys" had already established such a vivid and recognizably different profile.[6] Rather, these various competing groups lionized Parnell, or approved of him, or simply tolerated him, for possessing some phantasmatic trait that the revolutionary tradition did *not* contain. Indeed, it was positively crucial, as one would expect O'Brien to recognize, that this trait resist alignment with any one strain or school of Irish nationalism, or any particular agenda whatever, if Parnell was to perform his definitive role of sustaining and even personifying a fractious coalitional solidarity. In this sense, Parnell's magnetic image had to be something more than an instrumental element of the system; it had, in fact, to exceed politics, in its narrowly rational form, if it was to produce the politically mobilizing effects that it did.

Summarizing these two species of historical account, we might say that each marks the insufficiency of the other with its own. The "system" speaks to the politically intelligible aspect of Parnell's élan that exceeds personal charm, presence, or charisma; personality names the affective element of Parnell's aura that exceeds rational instrumentalization. As a preeminent normative discourse interweaving individual ethical predispositions with collective ethnic essences, manliness represents a privileged meeting place for the complementary lacunae in Parnell studies.[7] This is particularly the case insofar as Parnell was a public figure, the site of mass identification, whose signature issue, the Irish question, had come to speak to the gendered character of the entire ethnos. Under these peculiarly overdetermined circumstances, the discursive grid of manliness served to interlink Parnell's individual presence, with its aura of romance, and his public policy, with its reputation for clear-eyed realism, to such a degree that each formed the necessary and sufficient condition for the manly valence of the other. Parnell's demeanor sexualized his politics, rendering it the object of personal investment by his supporters, while the associated virility of his policies helped to infuse his demeanor with allegorical significance, making it a manly signifier of the Irish nation. That is to say, Parnell's appeal turns out to reside neither in the romantic elements of an heroic personality nor in the realpolitik of stratagem and policy but in the manner of their articulation, or rather their double articulation: the way in which the personal and policy dimensions of Parnell's career are coordinated, at the level of their ideological form, by the discursive grid of manliness, which gives them their specific political weight, and the way in which this coordination itself works to countervail the imperialist bias of the manly ideal, so that Parnell might give it a specifically Irish embodiment.

To understand how deeply the various levels of Parnell's praxis—personal, rhetorical, tactical, strategic—are imbricated in one another, one might first ponder that the most private dimensions of the Parnell mystique were thoroughly geopoliticized by the persistent tendency, among supporters and detractors alike, to read Parnell's physique and his general mien in the most complex ethnonational terms imaginable: as the Anglo-Protestant, quasi-aristocratic vehicle of Gaelo-Catholic colonial resistance. Thus, the Anglo elite discovered in him the qualities they prized in themselves, and they did so to affirm rather than to qualify their gendered abjection of the native Irish. The Tory Ulsterman St. John Ervine proclaimed, "Parnell was of Anglo-Saxon blood, the blood of authority and leadership, while his followers were Celts, in whose veins flowed the blood of obedience and submission."[8] Lord Cowper agreed: "His very passion was English, his coolness was English, his reserve was English." Sir Henry Thompson queried, "Was Parnell an Irishman?" musing, "I would have taken him, and did take him, for a quiet, modest, dignified English gentleman."[9] While by Anglo-Protestant lights he was on the wrong side, he was nonetheless "of the right stock and the right stuff."[10]

Parnell, however, was in fact a Celt on his distaff side, a descendant of the famous Scottish American admiral Charles Stewart. More important, since adolescence he had not only identified as unequivocally Irish but also suspected himself liable to English mistreatment on these grounds. He told his brother John, "The Englishman despises us because we are Irish, but we must stand up to them." And again, "That fellow despises us because we are Irish, but the Irish can make themselves felt everywhere if they are self-reliant and stick to each other."[11] He held to this idea over the course of his career, reformulating it in various ways. The resulting sense of intense mutual solidarity between Parnell and his "people" allowed for a kind of reverse discourse in which the Irish masses felt themselves virilized by the gendered esteem that Parnell won from their common adversaries. That is to say, they took the exception the English made for Parnell as a concession to the Irish nation as a whole.[12]

While this high opinion of Parnell was rarely couched in direct references to manhood or manliness, the qualities regularly attributed to him by the English and Anglo-Irish comprised many of the conventional indices of that ideal. One British politician pronounced Parnell's "calm self-control and air of complete detachment" to be "remarkable things." Sir Charles Dilke praised his "aloofness . . . iron will . . . inexorable tenacity, sound judgment and the faculty of controlling himself and others."[13] A well-known correspondent for the *Daily*

News, J. MacDonald, called him "the sternest of the stern . . . whose great gifts are an iron will and resolution."[14] Henry Harrison remarked, "His courage and self-possession never failed. His steadfastness . . . endured unshaken," while Sir William Butler pronounced him "a strong-souled man."[15] The Unionist *Irish Times* spoke of his "iciness of attitude" and "provoking self-possession under the gravest circumstances." The arch conservative *Pall Mall Gazette* declared, "Under a slim and almost effeminate exterior, he has an iron will, calm, cool and bloodless, he is a man who nothing can move," and then goes on to contrast him with more stereotypically Irish politicians: "O'Connor Power grows savage . . . and O'Connell hisses . . . with ill-disguised resentment. . . . Parnell remains invariably imperturbable."[16] We can at this point grasp the crucial importance of Parnell's socioethnic background to his leadership of the Irish cause. The all-important British audience could perceive him—in contrast with the Great Liberator, the Gaelic Daniel O'Connell—as answering the statutory descriptive criteria of manliness and so were prepared to credit and even extol his fulfillment of the ethical criteria.

In keeping with this assessment, even those British political caricatures antagonistic to Parnell did not cast him in feminine or simian guise. There was, for example, a famous series of political cartoons known as Irish Frankenstein, in which post-Darwin, advanced Irish nationalists were simianized to the point of monstrosity or limned as monsters with simian properties. In the most famous of these, by John Tenniel (figure 3),[17] Parnell is inculpated in the Phoenix Park murders, but as a professional, even gentlemanly, agent provocateur of the monstrous assassin figure. Instead of the Irish Frankenstein, whose lineaments in this rendition are markedly subhuman, Parnell represents the Irish *Dr.* Frankenstein (note the caption: "'The baneful and blood-stained monster! . . . Had I not breathed into it my own spirit?' . . . C. S. P-rn-ll, M.P."). Another cartoon, J. G. Thompson's "Irish Monkey Grinder," in which a well-attired Parnell trains a simianized Fenian to dance to his tune, suggests that this line of portraiture was more than casual. Even after Parnell's fall, London and Dublin cartoonists spared him the facial distortions suffered by certain of his nationalist colleagues.[18]

Whatever accolades Parnell extracted from the English were registered in a freer manner and more fulsome key in Irish public opinion. Parliamentary colleague T. P. O'Connor notes Parnell's "personal dignity and imperturbability," his "cold courage," "massive strength," "unfailing nerve," "impenetrable reserve," and, above all, "perfect self-possession."[19] Michael Davitt found him, at his peak, "the very picture of manly strength," and Standish O'Grady remarked "the rigidity of his back," the "sternness of his front," and his general athleticism. Parnell's lieutenant, William O'Brien, draws the connection between his physical deportment and his psychic resources, an "icy coolness" and "deliberate

THE IRISH FRANKENSTEIN.

Figure 3. "The Irish Franken-
stein," *Punch,* May 20, 1882.
Courtesy of the Rare Book
& Manuscript Library, Uni-
versity of Illinois at Urbana-
Champaign.

reserve."[20] Here again the contrast with the great Daniel O'Connell is striking. Even at his most hypermasculine—in his physical prime, accepting challenges to duel—O'Connell was always a figure of drama; Parnell at his most harried was a figure of stoic calm.

Parnell's bodily and psychic dispositions thus answered one another, or were seen to answer one another, in a way that enabled him to be not just an instance but an icon of manly virtue. His lieutenant and successor, John Redmond, claimed that Parnell not only exhibited but also "taught Irishmen self-respect and self-reliance," a judgment seconded by Parnell himself: "I have always endeavoured to teach my countrymen . . . the lesson of self-reliance."[21] Since Parnell's contact with his own people was so minimal, these last comments suggest how personal demeanor can pass into communal or national iconography by way of its stipulated value. Parnell's characteristic posture of autonomy and dignity came to occupy the very center of his mythos because it could be held up as a model for the Irish people—a *role* model whose assumed effectiveness would make it an *allegorical* model as well. Parnell's great disciple become nemesis, Tim Healy, spoke eloquently to this psychosocial effect: "We seized upon the idea of the man, his superb silences, his historic name, his determination, his self-control, his aloofness—we seized that as the canvas of a great national hero."[22]

The topical "canvas" of the day was the political cartoon, and those favorable to Parnell encapsulated this allegorical arc from personal conduct to national character. His caricatures in the *Weekly Freeman* and *United Ireland* (figures 4–6) exhibit an extraordinarily erect carriage. Even when he is leaning back, as in "The Labourer Is Worthy of His Hire" (figure 4) and "A Fair Field in Bonnie Scotland" (figure 7), or forward, as in "A Game Two Can Play At" (figure 5), the depiction still manages to convey a sense of his ramrod bearing, which is immediately linked with some struggle or achievement on behalf of the Irish people. In "The Labourer," for example, the Land League's successes effected with the "ax" of "Parliamentary Agitation" clear the dense thickets of a superannuated feudalism. In "The Master" (figure 6), the upright posture of Parnell, in gentleman's dress, contrasts with the stooped obeisance of "flunkies" Salisbury and Gladstone, in livery, to suggest that a superior dignity now attaches to the "Irish interests" that Parnell carries, precisely by reason of his insistence on attending to them independently. Parnell is "Master" here inasmuch as he retains his *self*-mastery, refusing prerogatives that might breed dependency, and in this sense, the cartoon suggests, the quality that Parnell models for the nation is indeed one of manliness.

Through this figural exercise, oft-repeated in different media, Parnell's air of self-reliance became the proleptic mark of Irish national independence. As one separatist put it, "In him there was not only success, there was national self-respect embodied." James Loughlin's comment, "Parnell was adored less as a man than as a national icon," is at best half-right.[23] Parnell was a national icon to be adored precisely inasmuch as he was perceived as a man, or *the man,* in an honorific sense. He embodied an analogy between personal self-government, the defining virtue of achieved manliness, and collective self-government, the aim of Irish nationalism, an analogy that functioned to enthrone Parnell as the exemplary figure, in every sense, of the movement he headed. He seemed to possess something akin to a Home Rule of the soul.

Cataloging these gendered apprehensions of Parnell, one begins to sense that they do not register the impression left by an individual so much as they reflect and participate in the construction of an epitome or abstract, even, or especially those reports that rely upon the illusion of a personal encounter. In such portrayals, Parnell not only is characterized by generalized epithets like "self-command" or "calm in crisis" but is seen as personifying and projecting in his everyday demeanor *an explosive yet controlled tension* that was essential to the late Victorian vision of manliness, though once again the category is never deployed. The *ascesis* of strong passions strongly checked is reported to

Figure 4. "The Labourer Is Worthy of His Hire," *Weekly Freeman*, April 14, 1883. Courtesy of the Rare Book & Manuscript Library, University of Illinois at Urbana-Champaign.

Figure 5. "A Game Two Can Play At," *Weekly Freeman*, January 7, 1885. Courtesy of the Rare Book & Manuscript Library, University of Illinois at Urbana-Champaign.

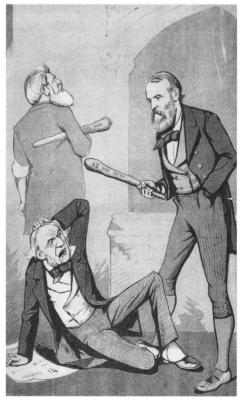

Figure 6. "The Master," *Weekly Freeman,* January 16, 1886. Courtesy of the Rare Book & Manuscript Library, University of Illinois at Urbana-Champaign.

Figure 7. "A Fair Field in Bonnie Scotland," *United Ireland,* August 18, 1888. Courtesy of the Rare Book & Manuscript Library, University of Illinois at Urbana-Champaign.

have become all but visible in his lineaments, rather like the classical figure of Laocoon, who had become a paragon of manliness in the Victorian age.[24]

The Irish member of Parliament (MP) T. P. O'Connor offers the most comprehensive summary of this take on Parnell: "First, as to Parnell's appearance, as he was, so he looked. The iron resolution, the impenetrable reserve . . . the frigid fanaticism was written in his lithe figure and still more in the strange, striking unique countenance." What is strange and striking here is precisely the odd, almost novelistic legibility of a symbolic property never to be named. Elsewhere O'Connor remarks that "behind the cold and impassive exterior of Parnell there was a volcanic energy and also a ruthless determination."[25] O'Connor was not alone in apprehending such "volcanic abysses" in Parnell's temperament.[26] Assessing one of the Chief's parliamentary interventions, one politician recalled a "frigid voice, but with a certain suppressed intensity beneath the almost negligent manner." Even at his most familiar, one of Parnell's Fenian contacts observed, "He was always encased in steel."[27] W. B. Yeats, following the same line, seized upon "Parnell's ability to keep his person in subjection" in order "to show an impassive, rock-like face," which was apparently never confused with a merely passive feminized address. Indeed, Yeats's favorite anecdote on Parnell's character has the man confronting parliamentary charges of "abetting assassination" with a seemingly insouciant calm while all the time tearing his hands bloody with his own fingernails in order to restrain his violent emotions. According to John Kelly, it was precisely in his willfully self-cloistered affect that Parnell inspired a whole generation of Irish literati including Yeats, Robinson, Gregory, Martyn, and Joyce, who could be counted on to reproduce and refurbish his legend.[28] Several of these, Catherine Tynan, Lionel Johnston, William O'Brien, and Standish O'Grady, developed a series of formulaic fire and ice metaphors to convey "the coexistence in Parnell of extraordinarily passionate feelings and a rigid self-control." O'Grady's was the most famous—"the ice clear, ice cold intellect working as if in the midst of fire"—and was adopted in several venues, most luridly by Parnell's party newspaper, *United Ireland,* to describe his final end: "He flamed out in the last struggle, like an unsuspected volcano breaking in red devastation through its accumulated ice."[29]

This slippage between spontaneous impression and intertextual embellishment is bound to intensify our leeriness at locating the manly image of Parnell in his bodily presence, as well as our curiosity about the psychosocial basis upon which this implicitly gendered idea of Parnell emerged. The mythologizing accounts themselves cannot be expected to offer us any direct assistance. They do, however, express substantially uniform agreement—in a further sign of their formulaic quality—on the cardinal sign of the "volcanic abysses" they detect: the silence of the man. Parnell's constitutional reticence is construed over and over again as crucial to the power he exerted and the distinctive impression he made. Thus, as indicated above, T. P. O'Connor yokes Parnell's "iron resolution" to his "impenetrable reserve," suggesting a familiar gendered logic wherein inexpressiveness equates with inviolability. J. L. Garvin invokes the same implicit logic in locating Parnell's command in the "power of silence."[30] So does the Irish historian Paul Bew, in linking Parnell's "legendary frigidity of demeanor, impenetrable reserve, and strange sphinx-like silences" with "the hint of steel" in his character. One quite famous cartoon, of course, actually depicted Parnell as "the Irish Sphinx."[31] In truth, though, the stillness of the sketch medium itself, in the sense of both silence and stasis, greatly enhanced the contribution of many political illustrations to the manly image of Parnell. The freezing of his passion at the moment of expression in "Hide and Seek" (figure 8) or "Loaded with Infamy" (figure 9) projects a kind of visual correlative, à la Laocoon, to the logic of sublimation.

For Parnell's English antagonists, and even some of his Irish allies, his majestic silences proved remarkable for their divergence from gendered national type. Certainly, the last great Irish leader, Daniel O'Connell, earned a reputation as a great talker as well as speaker, and his volubility helped to foster the assumption that on this score an Irishman would lead his fellows by playing to rather than against type. Parnell's taciturn ways thus appeared all the more impressive for being unexpected. He was dubbed by one English contemporary a "locked mouth master of loose lipped men" and by another "the very strong still man . . . in a most loquacious land."[32] "What struck you most about Parnell," one Fenian remarked, was "his silence. All Irish agitators talked. He didn't." Such generalizations helped to prepare the previously cited arguments of Cowper and Dilke that Parnell's noble reserve and aloofness expressed his English makeup. Indeed, these attributes convinced observers on both sides of St. George's Channel that, Irish or no, Parnell had "not a bit of the Celt in him," that "he was a regular Englishman," his maternal lineage notwithstanding. This was a view shared in certain Fenian quarters as well: "He was the man to fight the English, he was so like themselves, cool, callous, inexorable."[33] If silence were next to Englishness and Englishness to manliness, Parnell was, in sometimes incompatible ways, next to all three.

To Parnell's friends and supporters, conversely, his imperturbable reticence not only defied prevailing ethnonational ideologies but also acted to reverse them, frustrating his English adversaries and reducing them to "impotent fury."[34] Of a confrontation with Gladstone himself, William O'Brien wrote, "For the first time in the collision of the weak and passionate race with the strong and stolid one, it was the Englishman who lost his head and the Irishman who went on his way with a calmness too self-restrained to be even contemptuous." J. D. Reigh's cartoon "The Bumptious Pygmy and the Contemptuous Giant"

Figure 8. "Hide and Seek," *Weekly Freeman*, August 4, 1888. Courtesy of the Rare Book & Manuscript Library, University of Illinois at Urbana-Champaign.

Figure 9. "Loaded with Infamy," *United Ireland*, August 11, 1888. Courtesy of the Rare Book & Manuscript Library, University of Illinois at Urbana-Champaign.

(figure 10) does a *Gulliver's Travels* spoof on this very scenario, in which Parnell's magisterial silence, aplomb, and self-possession puts to rout the frantic excess of a Lilliputian British leader. Yeats, characteristically, elaborated upon this reversal to the point of dialectical synthesis: "The Englishman is reserved because of his want of sensibility—Parnell is reserved in spite of it."[35]

Where Nationalist and Unionist accounts do concur is in treating Parnell's bodily deportment and social mien as both a moral signifier, the index of a "self-possession that never failed," and an element of ethnonational gender allegory, a display of manliness attaching not just to the individual but to the people, Anglo or Irish, who could claim him. However dubious in their own right, the racial judgments on both sides provide compelling testimony to the efficacy of Parnell's political performance, which was, as James Loughlin has it, "designed to contrast with the perception of Irish-Celtic characteristics, especially verbosity, emotionalism, and gesticulation"—the very traits, I would observe, that were used to impugn the manly character of the Irish.[36]

Figure 10. "The Bumptious Pygmy and the Contemptuous Giant," *United Ireland,* May 11, 1889. Courtesy of the Rare Book & Manuscript Library, University of Illinois at Urbana-Champaign.

The ironic thing about the allegorical value assigned Parnell's silence is that his reticence was, at least in part, the effect of an individual limitation. As Joyce develops in *Finnegans Wake,* Parnell had a speech impediment, a stammer or stutter; so what Conor Cruise O'Brien has called the "weight of silence behind his words" answered in some degree to his difficulty in forming them.[37] Indeed, contemporaries and historians alike have expressed surprise at Parnell's meteoric rise as a public figure given his lackluster skills as a public speaker.[38] If one considers how far his romantic aura of manliness hung upon his taciturn demeanor, however, one can see his stammer as representing just the sort of felix culpa that it comes to represent in *Finnegans Wake.* The less likely Parnell was to hit the rhetorical high notes, so to speak, the more assured the manly timber of his political voice—especially since neglect of oratorical flourish helped to distance him further from the stereotype of the volubly hyperemotional Celt. O'Grady captures the paradoxical surplus value of Parnell's verbal limitations in noting that "his words had something of the hardness and solidity of fact."[39] Having no penchant for rhetorical flight, Parnell was credited with unwonted gravity.

Even when Parnell's legendary ineloquence passed into striking inconsiderateness, the gender cachet of his political performance proved sufficiently impressive, glamorous, and vital to the interests of his constituents to redeem it in full. Consider his acceptance of the Parnell National Tribute, an outpouring of trust and affection from his followers amounting to forty thousand pounds sterling. Upon receipt of the award at a testimonial banquet, Parnell managed just "two cold sentences," expressing not his feelings of gratitude but his reluctance "to express his feelings."[40] While his reticence on this occasion could be seen as graceless in the extreme, and was certainly seen as singular, it was not taken, on the whole, as insulting. Lord Spencer marveled, "Here is this handsome sum of money collected for him. He does not make reference to it and gives offense to nobody. . . . [I]t showed the immense power of the man."[41] More than his immense power, however, the incident testified to his *specific* iconic value. His unforthcoming response was easily read as another sign of personal and by extension national self-mastery won through rigorous control over deep passion.

In a sense, the testimonial itself represented something of a threat to Parnell's image of manly self-possession, which his flinty acceptance aimed to recuperate. The National Tribute responded not only to Parnell's service but also to his insolvency, to the wreckage of his fortunes in the cause. As such, it was testament *both* to his secure and lofty reputation *and* to his financial vulnerability and decline, to weakness no less than power. It showed him to be a prince and a pauper in one. In declining to display the virtue of gratitude, Parnell declined to acknowledge the condition that made such gratitude a necessity, and in so doing, he stubbornly clung to the iconic mantle of manliness that had earned him the tribute in the first place. Thus, with an unerring sense of gender expectations, Parnell held up the unspoken compact he had with the Irish people: to embody their claim to collective manhood, in this case by refusing to concede his dependency upon their collective support.

While Parnell's oratorical skills were so poor he had to make a virtue of his deficiencies, he was not entirely without resources as a rhetorician. On occasion he did exhibit a talent for putting the weight of well-chosen words behind his silence. His few truly memorable turns of phrase—the entire canon of his bon mots—served to recommend and project a national posture of self-restrained aggression, to frame irredentist sentiments that imparted an aura of manliness to the Irish people-nation at large. Replying to a preemptive warning from Gladstone, Parnell issued the manifesto of the Irish National League in which he grandly announced, "Ireland has been knocking at the English door for long enough with kid gloves. I tell the English people to beware and be wise in time. Ireland will soon throw off the kid gloves and she will knock with a mailed hand."[42] The English public evidently responded to the mailed hand as a direct and rather chilling threat. But the key to Parnell's metaphor is that while he is showing the mailed hand beneath the kid glove, he, and Ireland, is *still knocking*. If the mailed hand betokens armed force beneath the kid glove of political supplication, the continued act of knocking—rather than breaking in, smiting, and so on—restrains the threatened aggression within a polite social gesture. The mailed knock enacts the manners that control the implied force or violence of its concussion. As such, it is the very image of aggressive passion, aggressively curbed, a subtle emblem of achieved manhood.

Addressing a Land League meeting at Westport in 1879, Parnell asked the crowd what the tenant farmer must do when faced with eviction, and he answered his own question with the words, "You must show the landlords that you intend to hold a firm grip on your homesteads and land. You must not allow yourselves to be dispossessed as you were dispossessed in 1847."[43] With the redoubling of "hold" and "firm grip," Parnell's figure of speech unmistakably invokes the exercise of "muscle" against the threat of eviction, but a muscle that in its very retentiveness seems restrained and forbearing rather than barbarous and destructive, the expression of a controlling passion that is itself held in control ("not allow yourselves"). He is clearly playing with the idea of physical-force militancy, perhaps acknowledging its necessity, but at the same time, he is dissociating his people from anything like belligerence or unleashed violence. The phrase "to hold a firm grip" grew into the motto of this land-agitation movement, and it did so, I submit, because it hit a visceral sweet spot centered in the morality of manliness.[44]

In an equally well-known speech at Ennis in 1880, Parnell asked those assembled another question: "Now what are you to do to a tenant who bids for a farm from which his neighbor has been evicted?" to which the crowd replied,

"Shoot him, shoot him." Again answering his own question, Parnell declared, "I wish to point out to you a very much better way. . . . You must show him . . . by leaving him severely alone, by putting him into a moral Coventry . . . your detestation of the crime he has committed."[45] Once again, Parnell chose a figure of aggression ("severely alone"), one that is not only more spiritual than physical but also constraining rather than invasive—to put in "moral Coventry"—a figure that mimes the moral dynamics of muscular manhood. What is more, having been rehearsed in Peoria, Illinois, earlier that year, Parnell's sudden interrogation of the crowd may be seen as a set piece contributing to the same general effect.[46] In asking his inflamed audience what is to be done with such a scoundrel, Parnell solicits the extremist response he receives, precisely so that he might counter its violent sentiments with a counsel of self-restraint. He thereby enacts the dynamic of manly sublimation in his relationship with his own supporters. They are called upon to supply a show of unbridled (mob) passion so that he might furnish the spectacle of impeccable (national) self-control.[47]

The visual rhetoric of the cartoonists supportive of the Irish Party tended to replicate Parnell's verbal rhetoric: that is, they cast his agenda as an actively contained or displaced form of political aggression and Parnell himself as the manly leader of a manly movement. To this end, a pictorial grammar evolved in which his championing of Home Rule could be seen to implicate a certain play of violence, real and symbolic, while the violence itself could not be directly seen at all. Sometimes, as in "Hide and Seek" and "Loaded with Infamy," a stern Parnell appears ready and able to exert an overmastering physical force that is rendered unnecessary by the cowering of his enemies before the fact. Other caricatures frame allegorical scenarios of parliamentary combat after the fact. In "A Game Two Can Play At" (see figure 5), for example, Gladstone seems to have been floored by a blow to the head, and a coolly respectable, well-heeled, even genteel Parnell stands by with the offending instrument, the club of parliamentary obstruction. He does so not to brandish the weapon but to call the stunned prime minister's attention to the "42 Irish votes" that it signifies: the source, that is, of Parnell's *proper, lawful authority.* Finally, some cartoons, like "The Rally" (figure 11), invoke the marshaling of concerted militaristic force around the figure of Parnell, not to be unleashed upon any object or hostile agency but as the very condition of political solidarity, much as *thumos* represented the ground of moral organization in the Victorian imaginary.

Moving from the rhetorical to the tactical register of Parnellism, we find that manliness constitutes more than a value center in each; it serves as a conceptual instrument for conjoining them, for articulating nationalist word and nationalist deed in a *politically normative assault on the political norms of British rule in Ireland.* With his famous speech at Ennis, Parnell effectively instituted the practice of boycotting, which has been a staple of nonviolent protest ever

Figure 11. "The Rally," *United Ireland,* December 20, 1890. Courtesy of the Rare Book & Manuscript Library, University of Illinois at Urbana-Champaign.

since. Boycotting had certain specifically legal and political attractions for the Irish Land League: it was an unprosecutable method of militancy that accordingly fostered the broadest popular participation. But these were indissociable from its cultural and ideological appeal: its enactment on a collective scale of the approved dynamics of manliness, which translated as a living claim on this honored estate by the Irish people. A negative political gesture, boycotting operated within and yet athwart the liberal individualistic spirit of British law. It managed to be aggressive without being at all violent and so respectable in its very assault on the respectable status quo of colonial landlordism. Moreover, it was stringent in its restraint, registering the depth and intensity of public feeling through a mass, self-enforced withdrawal of affect. And such an organized display of resolve could not, properly undertaken, partake of anything turbulent or unruly, but required the strictest discipline. The racial feminization and simianization of the Irish were thus confuted on the very terms on which they were launched.

The other political tactic most closely identified with Parnell bears an uncannily similar structure. Indeed, one might well say that as boycotting was to the land agitation, parliamentary obstruction was to Home Rule. As is well known, Parnell presided over a policy of taking advantage of every opportunity to jam the operations of Great Britain's legislative body. Like boycotting, the practice worked simultaneously within and against the law in order to give controlled yet effective vent to Irish grievances and the passions they aroused. Like boycotting too, the practice was at once too pugnacious to be feminized and too ingenious and peaceable to be simianized.[48] Here again, moreover, the practice impressed even the foes of Home Rule because it demonstrated enormous collective discipline, in direct contradiction to the reigning stereotypes of the Irish as emotionally incontinent: consumed by "nervous exaltation" on the one hand and addicted to "brawling" on the other. For obstruction to succeed, as it did, it was necessary for the Irish Party members to act and vote in perfect solidarity, a lockstep regimen made manifest in the airtight Pledge with which they all bound themselves to the leadership of Parnell, who, for his part, became the universally acknowledged enforcer and embodiment of this discipline. Beyond evincing the oft-disputed Irish capacity for self-government, a political correlative of the manly ideal, the party's obstruction of Parliament threatened to make Britain and its empire ungovernable, and, as a result, this filibustering tactic produced some of the same hystericizing effects upon the English members as Parnell's own intractable silences.[49]

With respect to both of these signature agendas, boycotting and obstruction, the symbolic weight of Irish manhood borne by Parnell cast him as the focus of a highly fraught dynamic of transferential identification. To both his nationalist allies and his imperialist adversaries, Parnell stood as the main and perhaps only restraint keeping an endemically quarrelsome and disorderly people in line.[50] He was generally seen, that is to say, as the immovably strong check on the otherwise irresistibly strong passions characteristic of the Irish race. As his performance at Ennis evinced, Parnell looked to cultivate this reputation and did so again, quite famously, on the eve of his arrest for orchestrating the No Rent campaign. Asked who would replace him during his time in Kilmainham, Parnell stared over the rim of his champagne glass, an accoutrement of his gentlemanly status, and replied, "Ah, if I am arrested, Captain Moonlight will take my place," referring to the mythical avatar of Land League Fenianism.[51] He thereby positioned himself as the main, if not only, sublimating tether on runaway Irish political passion. In this role, he paradoxically represented Irish manhood while tacitly ratifying the unmanly stereotype of his followers, by being what they were not and disdaining what they supposedly displayed. Still more paradoxically, in performing this role efficaciously, he contrived to imbue those he represented, in their own eyes and those of their English audience, with the same qualities of manliness that they presumptively lacked. Most paradoxically of all, these structural moments, Parnell as image and Parnell as counterimage of Irishness, could not be disentangled from one another but existed in a kind of abrasive symbiosis, testifying to the persistence of the stereotype in the very struggle to dismantle it.

Parnell himself seems to have factored this symbiosis, finally, into his *strategic* calculations. The convergence of the moral force Home Rule movement with the Fenian movement (the New Departure) occurred precisely with the ouster of Isaac Butt by Parnell as the head of the Irish Nationalist Party. But unlike the other cited instances of such dovetailing (Young Ireland, Sinn Fein), this one resulted not in the appropriation of nonviolent to "advanced" nationalism but rather the opposite, the uneasy containment of physical by moral force. In 1878, the man from Avondale secured the agreement of the Fenians in both Ireland and the United States to suspend for a time military operations in deference to constitutional maneuvering, while he nevertheless maintained an ongoing public dalliance with the physical force option, refusing to foreclose on martial insurgency altogether. As Parnellite biographer Barry O'Brien writes, "Parnell had . . . the strongest sympathies with Fenianism, but he was resolved not to be managed by the Fenians. His policy was to keep Parliamentarianism well in front and to mass the revolutionists behind it. The Fenians were to be his reserves."[52] The Fenians would prove not only active reserves but also active *as* reserves. The hard-liners put insurrectionary violence at the disposal of the Home Rulers, not to use or deploy but *to check, and to make a continual show of checking.* Law-abiding forms of concession or temporizing, which under Butt's decorous leadership would resonate as pliant or quiescent, vindicating the feminine profile of the Irish as secretly desirous of strong rule, could under the new dispensation or "departure" be seen as effective steps to bring the more truculent Irish elements under discipline. The bestialized stereotypes of the Irish people at large were thus undercut while "a bold spirit of resistance" was maintained.

Parnell's symbolic status vis-à-vis his Fenian partners, however, like his status vis-à-vis his parliamentary followers, bore deeply ambivalent gender implications, admitting diametrically opposed constructions. Barry O'Brien's view, that he became something like the acceptable face of Fenianism, accords Parnell a representative function strangely constituted in his perceived distance or difference from the object represented—not unlike, it will be noted, his figuration of Irish masculinity.[53] As noted above, antinationalist voices in England and Ireland alike stressed such racialized differences in order to refute Parnell's representative function and its affirmative value. For those supportive of Parnellism, however, the moral appropriation of the physical-force constituencies amounted to not just a brilliant political stroke, adding both sinew and flexibility to the constitutional agenda, but a great cultural coup as well, the unification of the fractious and volatile Irish people nation on a disciplined and purposeful basis. That is to say, Parnellites tended to view the assimilation of Fenianism as a kind of structural analogue to the *discordia concours* of manliness itself, with physical-force radicalism expressing the collective *thumos* or animal passion upon which Parnell himself acted as a doggedly rational control. This collective *discordia concours* was in turn congruent with and doubtless tributary to the manly contours of Parnell's personal legend. His struggle to channel violent revolutionary energies to vigorous devolutionary ends undoubtedly contributed to his personal image as a Laocoon figure. Contemporaries may have read those "volcanic abysses" into Parnell and extrapolated his "ruthless determination" to command them as at least in part a projective translation of his known efforts both to tap and to tame the explosive potential of Fenian radicalism. Because the normative script of manly sublimation gave a certain symbolic value and mode of intelligibility to the whole of his praxis, shaping its reception at every phase, the shadowy "Fenian reserves" of the parliamentary movement could become unconsciously identified with the "impenetrable reserve" of his own manner.

Parnell and the Ladies (Land League)

As we shall observe on several occasions in this study, the manly ideal continues to fortify the domestic patriarchal economy, even as it leavens the larger geopolitical sphere of operations. Perhaps no clearer evidence of this dual function can be found than in Parnell's own evolving assessment, tacit instrumentalization, and strategic termination of the Ladies Land League, which was spearheaded by his formidable sister Anna.

It is a truth universally acknowledged that Parnell disapproved from the outset of the institution of a female-run contingent to the Land League in Ireland, despite the success of an American Ladies Land League in the United States, founded by his other sister Fanny. While the purported reason for his resistance differs slightly from one account to another, they converge in buttressing the suspicion that Parnell viewed the prospective organization as a threat to the manly image of his movement and his leadership. Irish feminist Francis Sheehy Skeffington held the opposition of Parnell and his associates to be "imbued with the old 'protective' idea of man's relation to woman."[54] In his view, the Parnellites saw themselves as defaulting upon the chivalric responsibility attendant to male authority—a crucial, sentimentally charged component of the manly ethos—should they countenance women incurring the danger of political militancy. According to historians such as Robert Kee and F. S. L. Lyons, the Chief was more precisely worried about the "ridicule" that he and the Land League might attract for placing women in positions of likely physical and legal peril.[55] On this account, the perception that he and his movement shrank from the rigors of chivalric duty disquieted him more urgently than the fact of the dereliction itself. If the latter concern seems the more extraneous of the two, indexing a pragmatic reckoning with social mores and political risks rather than the reflexive prompting of an ego ideal, it nonetheless grapples with a deeper and more comprehensive slough of unmanning. The kind of derision that Parnell apprehended would not only call attention to a nationalist break with the normative canons of manliness but also call into question the ontological condition of collective Irish masculinity necessary to meet such a standard. Such ridicule would, in short, conjure from a contingent lapse in manliness the revenant of ethnonational emasculation.

Ultimately, Parnell allowed the Ladies Land League to fill the organizational void created by the incarceration of the male leadership of the Land League, himself included, for disrupting the 1881 Land Act. He presumably surmised that being locked in Kilmainham, neither he nor his lieutenants would be diminished in the popular imagination by any jeopardy the women encountered in their absence. As it turned out, however, the actual conduct of the Ladies Land League—its efficiency, its vehemence, its unforeseen radicalism—might well have served to undermine the manly cachet of the Irish party and its constituency groups in ways that Parnell had never anticipated. (No less a revolutionary éminence grise than John O' Leary, for example, proclaimed "the women . . . more serious and more honest than the men.")[56] Yet just the opposite proved to be the case, in part through the gender-savvy machinations of Parnell himself.

In the first place, the extremism of the Ladies Land League, and of Anna Parnell in particular, contributed materially to the detention of her brother. That is to say, the Ladies Land League helped to make good on Parnell's famous warning that "if I am arrested, Captain Moonlight will take my place." Indeed, E. H. O'Donnell famously characterized the women Leaguers as "Captain Moonlight in petticoats" and, mixing in a *sansculotte* reference, denominated Anna herself "the grand mademoiselle."[57] A number of commentators, contemporary and historical, concurred in the judgment that the Ladies Land League was a good deal more "savage" than its male-dominated predecessor had been.[58] In his *Memoirs,* the nationalist member T. P. O'Connor declares that "the woman revolutionary is always more violent than the man" and that Anna Parnell was "the most violent of the women zealots." Along the same lines, F. S. L. Lyons discerns "a tincture of revolutionary fanaticism about Anna Parnell." And according to R. F. Foster, Anna Parnell's "counsels" grew more extreme over time, mounting to "passionate appeals to the Irish tenants to choose open war instead of appeasement" (that is, reliance on the newly instituted Land Courts).[59] Ultimately, the Ladies Land League even went from *exhorting* to *extorting* violent action from its peasant clients: if no outrages were committed in a given district, the Ladies Land League would refuse all requests for funding because, in their words, "no trace of manly opposition can be detected in your county."[60] This identification, one might say confusion, of "manly opposition" with hypermasculine belligerence served to benefit Parnell personally by convincing the ruling British elites that his permanent removal from hands-on authority would only bring permanent anarchy to Ireland. Thus, Lord Cowper conceded, "the central executive of the

Land League did exercise some controlling influence over the wilder spirits in the country districts. But no controlling influence was exercised now [under the Ladies Land League]."[61]

Parnell himself repeatedly echoed these sentiments, both from his prison quarters and upon his release.[62] He apparently pressed Tim Healy to write articles critical of the Ladies League; he confided to his brother John Howard that it had become "an uncontrollable and mischievous agency";[63] he confirmed his sister's reputation for "recklessness" among parliamentary allies like T. P. O'Connor;[64] to his paramour Kitty O'Shea, he claimed to have admonished his sister for "the folly of criminality for which the Ladies League, now, solely exists";[65] most notoriously, once freed from jail, he complained to Michael Davitt of "the state of the country," the "anarchy" the Ladies League had wrought, "as if he were a British minister bringing a Coercion Bill," and then promised to starve the League financially for squandering the moneys he had already allotted it.[66] All of this ranting led many of his contemporaries and most historians to conclude that he was "infuriated" with his sister and her cohorts.[67] But such a reading entirely misses the strategic impetus of the position Parnell assumed. There was a secondary measure of profit for him in the Ladies League activities, an ideological surplus value accruing to his own iconic manly profile, but he could only realize this profit by condemning the group's radicalism emphatically.

As we have noted, Parnell was effective in deploying violent extremism and extremists as a shadowy, untapped reserve in the service of his "vigorously disciplined gradualism."[68] If, in his own words, "the physical force tradition is an imperishable force . . . which gives me vitality and power," the "tradition" was vitalizing and above all "imperishable" only insofar as Parnell remained poised to actuate the physical-force option without ever actually doing so.[69] In her public suborning of outrage, Anna Parnell openly rejected the classic Parnellite tactics of *using* without *committing* violence, causing her brother to doubt her judgment even as he admired her indomitable tenacity. So whereas at Ennis Parnell had baited the crowd to call for murder in order that he might set them upon a more temperate course, thereby establishing himself as the governor of mob passion, Anna set out the same rhetorical lure for a crowd at Drumcolliher, only to approve their answering cries for blood, thereby demonstrating that she was, as Cowper said, "no controlling influence" whatsoever.[70] In this departure from Parnell's policy, however, Anna and the League broadly served his purpose, handing him the opportunity of displaying his singularly manful capacity for keeping revolutionary mayhem at bay as well as at hand. That is to say, in refusing to hold physical force in reserve, the Ladies Land League came to form a historically actualized specimen of Parnell's own "advanced" reserve, to embody the explosive political passion that he always managed to contain, discipline, sublimate. Whereas the Fenians put insurrectionary force at his disposal not to deploy but to check and to make a continual show of check-ing, the Ladies League, rather less willingly, put the institutional advocacy of such force at Parnell's disposal not to inflame but to silence and, through his repeated condemnations, to make a conspicuous show of silencing. Parnell was thus enabled once again to impress restraint upon his nationalist constituency *in the name of that constituency* and so to personify the virtue of self-command for the collective at large. What Anna Parnell bitterly, and not unreasonably, called "hiding behind the women's petticoats" simultaneously proved to be a sovereign enactment of manliness.[71]

In this respect, the entire incident can be understood to demonstrate the rel-evance of Giorgio Agamben's recently prominent theory of sovereignty to the gender politics of decolonization. Agamben sees the sovereignty of nation-states as operating through a logic of exception, whereby certain conditions, popula-tions, identities, or activities are included in the juridical-symbolic order, but only in the mode of exclusion, as counterexamples to the normative legitimat-ing values and attributes of the nation-state itself.[72] The same logic is at work in the consolidation of what we might call ideological sovereignty as well, that is, the effective self-determination of comparatively hegemonic groups within the cultural-symbolic order. Thus, the British included the Irish within the metropolitan polity of the United Kingdom but only in the mode of exclusion: by setting the Irish up, for example, as counterinstances, feminine and bestial by turns, of the manliness that represented the signature self-identifying virtue of the English "race." In dissolving the Ladies Land League for cause, Parnell moved not just to vindicate Irish manhood vis-à-vis the British, to refute the logic of exception undergirding "home" colonialism, but also to reclaim the gendered authority of Irish men vis-à-vis Irish women. To this end, his policy decision counterposed the self-contained power and tempered aggression of the original male-dominated Land League to the putative excesses—financial, affective, and criminal—of the women's version.[73] In so doing, he immediately resurrected the logic of sovereign exception within the Irish nation itself. That is, he expounded a manliness that encompassed, by definition, all of the Irish people qua ethnonational subjects, but included women only in the mode of exclusion, as the negative example that legitimated by contrast the authentic purchase Irish men enjoyed on this gender(ed) ideal. As the Ladies Land League debacle reveals, women were not just necessary to yet expelled from the norma-tive space of manliness, they were necessary precisely in their expulsion. We will see this dynamic of gendered exceptionality (inclusion-exclusion, immanence-exile) reassert itself in the literature of the Revival as the motif of the "double" woman, one of whom apotheosizes an Ireland "fit to be free" and another who must be extruded to realize that apotheosis.

If one examines Parnell's evolving response to the Ladies Land League, from its inception to its demise, the classic disjunctive or bipolarizing logic of the feminine stereotype emerges rather starkly. At the outset, the women appeared too delicate for the dangerous task at hand, in need of a protection the imprisoned men could not extend. By the end, the women appeared too violent and reckless for their difficult mission, in need of the restraint that Parnell was eager to exert. Over the course of the journey, Parnell's opposition to the Ladies League, his insistence on reining in their headstrong courses, attracted the support of the most conservative element of the Catholic hierarchy, such as Archbishop McCabe, who decried the "immodesty" of women engaging in political activism, let alone insurgency.[74] The irony of this patriarchal alliance spoke for itself a scant decade later when the same Catholic hierarchy vigorously defended the ideal of self-controlled manliness by urging that Parnell be deposed as party Chief for engaging in his own, still graver, "immodesty."

The Fall of Parnell

The same cultural script helped to shape the reception of his notorious sexual scandal and, with it, the repercussions of his downfall. In an irony unfailingly noted in the histories of modern Ireland, the fall of Parnell unfolded in the immediate aftermath of his greatest succès d'estime, the exposure of Richard Piggot as the forger of letters supposedly incriminating Parnell in the planning of Fenian outrages. Less fully remarked has been the symbolic propinquity of these events, centered on the racialized question of manliness. Beyond leveling a charge of political criminality at Parnell, the Times Commission bid to reverse the increasing identification of Irish nationalism with the acknowledged dignity and integrity of Parnell himself by impugning that integrity and dignity on the grounds of his association with the simianized exponents of revolutionary violence.

Parnell's advocates in the press seem to have grasped the gendered stakes of the inquiry. Over the long investigation, a series of cartoons in *United Ireland* and the *Weekly Freeman* allegorized Parnell's successes in the legal struggle as victories in man-to-man combat of various sorts: brawling ("Hide and Seek" [figure 8] and "Another Knockdown" [figure 12]), dueling ("A Fair Field in Bonnie Scotland" [figure 7]), cudgeling ("Throwing It Up" [figure 13]), swordplay ("Loaded with Infamy" [figure 9]), and total war ("Victory" [figure 14]). In each sketch, once again, there is but the anticipation or inference of violence rather than its immediate execution, a strategy consistent with what is, after all, the point of celebration: Parnell's exculpation of any direct involvement in political violence. At the same time, since such triumphs amounted to a restoration of Parnell's (and thus the Irish) title to manliness, some sort of virile assertive representation thereof—the kind associated with violent conquest—predictably recommended itself. One cartoon, "Hawkeye Turns on His Torturers" (figure 15), finds something of a solution to this tenor-vehicle paradox. It shows Parnell catching and then brandishing a tomahawk thrown at him by racially othered,

Figure 12. "Another Knockdown!" *Weekly Freeman,* May 11, 1889. Courtesy of the Rare Book & Manuscript Library, University of Illinois at Urbana-Champaign.

Figure 13. "Throwing It Up," *Weekly Freeman,* February 8, 1890. Courtesy of the Rare Book & Manuscript Library, University of Illinois at Urbana-Champaign.

Figure 14. "Victory!!!" *Weekly Freeman,* March 9, 1889. Courtesy of the Rare Book & Manuscript Library, University of Illinois at Urbana-Champaign.

Figure 15. "Hawkeye Turns on His Torturers," *United Ireland,* September 27, 1888. Courtesy of the Rare Book & Manuscript Library, University of Illinois at Urbana-Champaign.

primitivized members of the *Times* inquiry. The image sends a plain signal that Parnell's virile aggression reflects in a more controlled, dignified, racially evolved manner the violence barbarically visited upon him, a conclusion that consorted well with his ultimate vindication.

The arraignment of Parnell backfired spectacularly on its own terms, conferring upon him the very mantle, in both Britain and Ireland, that it had sought to despoil. But it did pave the way for the troubles to come, by playing upon the structural instability of the manly ideal, by indicating that the passionate depths of his being, the putative object of his vaunted self-control, might instead be the concealed source of abandon and excess, the repository of an uncontrolled *thumos*. What is more, in clearing Parnell of political skullduggery, further enshrining him as the very epitome of noble Irish manhood, the Commission hearings salted in advance the collective trauma of the public emasculation to come.

In the context delineated here, immediate and extended, the adulterous liaison of Parnell and Catherine O'Shea could only have tarnished his reputation for manliness, evincing a signal failure to control the private, affective side of himself and his life. But the damage was decisively aggravated by Parnell's recklessness in allowing the circumstances of his affair to spill into the political arena where his resolute image had been forged. In purchasing the connivance of Catherine's husband with a parliamentary seat, despite Captain O'Shea's refusal to take the all-important party pledge, Parnell committed a shockingly venal breach of the celebrated discipline that he had himself imposed. Further, in using his paramour, his English paramour, as an intermediary in negotiations with Gladstone, Parnell created the impression that he was all too susceptible to her political views and machinations. He seemed to have permitted unrestrained amorous sentiment to lead him into the "feminine" realm of personal intrigue that had long been viewed as an insidious threat to the masculine political order of rational, clear-cut opposition: us versus them, imperialist versus nationalist, English versus Irish, and so forth. The autocratic leader had turned out a uxorious lover, and, in the process, an apparently manipulable statesman. Emblematizing Parnell's predicament, even the nationalist press began referring to Kitty as "O'Shea who must be obeyed," an epithet less derisive of the woman herself than of Parnell for being captive to and henpecked by her.[75] Having evaded the bestialized side of the Irish double-bind during the Piggot nightmare, he awoke to find himself roundly feminized by the O'Shea divorce case.

Irishmen on both sides of the ensuing leadership crisis apprehended and attempted to exploit its gender implications. For the Parnellites, dismissing their man in conformity with the express wish of Gladstone and the liberals amounted to forsaking the manly stance of autonomy and self-command that had fused in the popular mind the image of Parnell and the cause of Home Rule. As a new Fenian recruit to parliamentarianism put it, reflexively adopting the lexicon of manliness, "What do you think every self-respecting man in the world will think of you when you have done this thing? Why, that you are cowards, that you have no self-reliance, that you do not deserve freedom."[76] Parnell himself played the gender card in a similar yet still more explicit fashion. Instead of directly refuting the moral indictments leveled at him by the Catholic hierarchy and the British government, he elected to contest the aura of manly respectability in which his accusers typically wrapped themselves, reducing their demonstrated attitudes to a womanish fastidiousness and self-display, at once feminine and feminizing. During the Kilkenny elections, Parnell asked the Irish people not "to give into all the old women and humbugs in England who are taking their opportunity of airing their virtue all over the country."[77] He also ridiculed the new party head, Justin McCarthy, as "a nice old gentleman for a tea party."[78]

Given the nature of Parnell's recent embarrassments, of course, this particular gender offensive carried its own dangers of reversal. The single nastiest moment in the bitter fracas in Committee Room 15—what Lyons calls "the final impossible word"—vividly illustrates as much. Noting the absence of strong leadership in Parnell's absence, John Redmond declared Gladstone the likely new "master of the Party," to which Tim Healy retorted, "And who is to be mistress of the party?"[79] Beyond baldly insulting Kitty O'Shea, Healy's words succinctly revile Parnell himself for betraying the party into female hands and reducing it to a feminized state. More than that, his aspersions pithily interlink Parnell's sexual immorality, his political deception, and his uxorious enthrallment as symptoms of his unmanly character. Healy expanded on this gender tropology elsewhere, denouncing Parnell for "prostituting a seat in Parliament to the interests of his own private intrigue," an offense that, given Parnell's position, symbolic and otherwise, appears indistinguishable from the corruption of the manly spirit of the Irish political enterprise.[80]

Although Healy's sexualized censures resonated in Irish political culture for their insolence and indecency, they set the tone for the dismantling not just of Parnell's political fortunes but of his public image as well, his conversion from paragon to antitype of (Irish) manliness. If not the source, Healy's aspersions on Parnell's mistress and his later accusation of embezzlement were certainly a subtext for a series of cartoons in the *Weekly Nationalist Press* that were devastating in their ridicule of a morally effeminate, not to say degenerate, political has-been. For example, Fitzpatrick's "He Managed to Catch the Train This Time" (figure 16) and "A Startling Contrast" (figure 17) both cast Parnell as a dandy or fancy man carrying off the embezzled Paris Funds in his pursuit of the affair with or marriage to Kitty O'Shea. In either illustration, he dresses gaudily (a yellow plaid belted topcoat in one, a checked vest, spats, and ribbons in the other), signifying his commitment to self-indulgence; he shows either cavalier indifference or condescending aversion to the burdens of public responsibility, and in "A Startling Contrast," he waxes positively sybaritic in his single-minded concern with his own welfare: "As for myself, I may truly say that I am now enjoying a

Figure 16. "He Managed to Catch the Train This Time," *Weekly National Press,* July 4, 1891. Courtesy of the Rare Book & Manuscript Library, University of Illinois at Urbana-Champaign.

Figure 17. "A Startling Contrast," *Weekly National Press,* July 18, 1891. Courtesy of the Rare Book & Manuscript Library, University of Illinois at Urbana-Champaign.

greater happiness than I have ever experienced . . . in my previous life."[81] Now at this moment in Victorian culture, with Oscar Wilde riding high in London theatrical society, the dandy counted not just as the antithesis, but as a travesty of the manly ideal, a figure who deployed considerable powers for discipline and self-management to desublimating ends, of which his carefully aestheticized self-presentation was taken to be a sign. In painting Parnell in dandyish hues, these illustrations play upon his past reputation for iron self-government, and, rather than debunking it altogether, they suggest Parnell himself has come to pervert his own virtues. Indeed, the eponymous "Startling Contrast" exists not only between Parnell's new estate and that of the peasant family he carelessly abandons, as the caption indicates, but also, implicitly, between the old heroic Parnell who labored manfully on behalf of those same peasants and the new effeminate Parnell brought to moral "ruin" by a "shameless hussy."

Given that heroic reputation, however, and Parnell's long-standing identification with the Irish people-nation, this sort of campaign against his manliness could well be deplored as corrosive to the image of Irish manliness generally. Certainly, that was the position adopted by the *Weekly Freeman* in its illustration "To the Rescue" (figure 18). In this cartoon, Healy, McCarthy, and other anti-

Figure 18. "To the Rescue!" *Weekly Freeman,* April 4, 1891. Courtesy of the Rare Book & Manuscript Library, University of Illinois at Urbana-Champaign.

Parnellites swoop down as taloned harpies—the feminine emasculating monsters of Greek mythology—in search of political "place," the venal correlative of Parnell's Paris Funds. They engage the figure of Parnell, dressed as a classical warrior, who remains superbly defensive and self-restrained in his aggression, acting merely as a formidable shield for the real victim of their dastardly attack, the "spirit of nationality," personified by the goddess Erin bound.

In the end, it was less the attacks mounted on either side that damaged the (self-) image of Irish manliness than the spectacle of vicious debate they combined to generate. The larger pattern of petulant and intemperate recrimination on both sides of the power struggle ensured that the destruction of Parnell's manly stature would redound upon his party and his people, much as the stature itself had. Nothing could have ratified the stereotype of the fractious, undisciplined Irish more graphically than the political donnybrook surrounding Parnell's fall. The point is acidly confirmed by Sir William Harcourt's snide report on the colloquy in Committee Room 15: "The Irishmen were upstairs fighting like Kilkenny cats [an image that nicely conflates the feminine and the animal], coming out at intervals to have drinks all round."[82] As the acrimonious infighting continued past Parnell's professional and bodily demise, Harcourt's vision of Irish Party fractiousness found echoes in *United Ireland,* where Reigh's caricatures began to lampoon its leaders as unruly schoolboys, not yet graduated to manhood in anything but their comically inappropriate facial hair, or similarly hirsute toddlers, biddable by "Nurse" Gladstone (see figures 19–22).

If, as I have endeavored to show, the mystery of Parnell's charisma needs to be explained in terms of the self-repressive image of manliness that he helped to stamp upon the nation, this strangely traumatic reaction to his collapse in the years following, even among Irishmen instrumental in the final result, is perhaps best explained by the destruction of the image thus stamped, a return of the repressed wherein Parnell and his political colleagues forfeited that form of national as well as personal self-respect with which they were identified. Years after his death, it was precisely the forceful self-possession of Parnell's person and his policies that lingered in the often wistful recollection of his countrymen. Political illustrations commemorating his passing, such as Reigh's "Our Leader Still" (figure 23) and "On Guard" (figure 24) looked to resurrect this collective sense of manliness in military tableaux of a classical and purely ceremonial sort, in which the conventional trappings of physical aggression are marshaled in an iconographical code emphasizing austere orderliness. They stand in sharp and explicitly gendered contrast to the caricatures of the Irish leaders who would take his "monumental" place (see also "The Redmondite Design for the Parnell Monument" [figure 25]).

More telling, perhaps, was the political resurrection of Parnellism in the new century by the early Sinn Fein party whose leaders, most notably Arthur Griffith,

Figure 19. "Justin McCarthy's Boys at School," *United Ireland,* March 24, 1894. Courtesy of the Rare Book & Manuscript Library, University of Illinois at Urbana-Champaign.

Figure 20. "The New 'National' School," *United Ireland,* June 27, 1891. Courtesy of the Rare Book & Manuscript Library, University of Illinois at Urbana-Champaign.

Figure 21. "The Most Dangerous Enemies to Irish Freedom," *United Ireland*, December 12, 1891. Courtesy of the Rare Book & Manuscript Library, University of Illinois at Urbana-Champaign.

Figure 22. "Featheration," *United Ireland*, September 19, 1891. Courtesy of the Rare Book & Manuscript Library, University of Illinois at Urbana-Champaign.

Figure 23. "Our Leader Still!" *United Ireland,* October 15, 1893. Courtesy of the Rare Book & Manuscript Library, University of Illinois at Urbana-Champaign.

saw themselves as the heirs to the Chief's "self-respecting, self-relying" legacy,[83] now fitted to the task of resisting, in limited, problematic, but politically effective ways, the regime of domestic colonialism. More telling too was the resurrection of Parnell that transpired during the era devoted to such endeavors, the Irish Renaissance or Revival. More than fixing in the Irish historical memory that "fetishism of Parnell" that came to be called his "myth," the multiple registers of Revivalism—political, cultural, and literary—drew upon the established legend of the Chief, his iconic name and narrative, in fashioning new answers to the conundrum posed by the manly ideal. It is to these events we now turn.

Figure 24. "On Guard!" *United Ireland,*
January 9, 1892. Courtesy of the Rare
Book & Manuscript Library, University of
Illinois at Urbana-Champaign.

Figure 25. "The Redmondite Design for the
Parnell Monument," *United Ireland,*
October 14, 1899. Courtesy of the Rare
Book & Manuscript Library, University of
Illinois at Urbana-Champaign.

2

Afterlives of Parnell:
Political, Cultural, Literary

In his Nobel Prize lecture, "The Irish Dramatic Movement," W. B. Yeats famously located the origins of the Irish Revival in the fall of Parnell and the collapse of the constitutional politics for which he stood:

> The modern literature of Ireland, and indeed all that stir of thought which prepared for the Anglo-Irish War, began when Parnell fell from power in 1891. A disillusioned and embittered Ireland turned from Parliamentary politics; an event was conceived; and the race began, as I think, to be troubled by that event's long gestation. Dr. Hyde founded the Gaelic League, which was for many years to substitute for political argument a Gaelic grammar, and for political meetings village gatherings. . . . Meanwhile I had begun a literary movement in English. . . . The nationalism we had called up—the nationalism every generation had called up in moments of discouragement—was romantic and poetical.[1]

With respect to Parnellism in particular, however, Yeats's sense of causation requires a correction from both ends of the temporal spectrum. As Roy Foster has argued, "The cultural revival in fact had begun several years before [Parnell's death] as a function of constitutional nationalism's success not its failure"; that is, it had begun in the expectation of Parnell's success in delivering the domestic autonomy necessary to build the nation along aboriginal lines.[2] It is no less true that even after the movements of Hyde and Yeats were well established, the figure of Parnell remained a source of inspiration strangely consonant with rather than exotically distant from the "romantic nationalism" that had supplanted his agenda.

Parnellism and the Gaelic Athletic Association

At the beginning there was the Gaelic Athletic Association (GAA), the prototype for the revival as a whole and its first full-fledged constituency group. It was founded at or near the apogee of Parnell's political influence and under his joint sponsorship (with Maurice Davin and Archbishop Croke), and the split following his disgrace dealt it a nearly fatal blow. Now the GAA took as its explicit decolonizing goal the resuscitation of ancient Gaelic physical culture to the wholesale exclusion of imported competitions, such as football, cricket, and rugby. So while Parnell's reputation for a certain athleticism—along with his political standing—rendered him a fit patron for the new organization, his related widely known affection for the "shoneen" game of cricket would seem to have disqualified him. That it did no such thing indicates something more was at stake in the formation and operation of the GAA than the games themselves and their ethnic provenance. The orthodox way of explaining this additional yet essential element that wed the early fate of Irish athletics to Parnell has been to see the GAA as a glorified front and recruiting organization for the "hillside men" who pitched their lot in with his from the time of the "New Departure" through to the final by-election. But however closely bound the GAA was to the Fenian cause—whether it actually formed a private army, supplied convenient occasions for swearing in new members, or, more indirectly, helped to train an army of national defense by improving the Irish physique—its simultaneous affiliation with Parnell did not arise solely from the realpolitik of violent separatism any more than it did from the ideology of cultural nativism.[3] To the contrary, it spoke to that unadmitted point of Irish identification with the metropole upon which separatism and nativism alike reposed: the important standard of manliness that Parnell epitomized for his nation and so could warrant in other symbolic representatives, like the GAA.

The sports culture of nationalist Ireland not only shared but echoed the gendered rhetoric of the British public school, experienced firsthand by landed gentry like Parnell himself and at an imitative remove by the scions of a growingly affluent Catholic middle class.[4] As on the neighboring isle, the promotion of an athletic agenda in Ireland involved panegyrics upon the ancestral virtue and vitality of the native race, cast in the unmistakable vocabulary of Victorian manliness:

> The Irish Celt is distinguished among the races, for height and strength, manly vigour and womanly grace. . . . [D]espite wars and domestic disabilities, the stamina of the race has survived almost in its pristine perfection.
>
> A matchless athlete, sober, pure in mind, speech and deed, self-possessed, self-reliant, self-respecting, loving his religion and his country . . . earnest in thought and effective in action.[5]

Commenting on these passages, W. F. Mandle wryly notes that "Tom Brown could not have aspired to a more glorious apotheosis." Indeed, while the pedigree given this "matchless athlete" typically harks back to the lore of Celtic myths or the luster of classical Greece, its more direct, decisive genealogy proceeded by way of such Anglocratic staples of manliness as the public school novel, memorial, and apologia. Thus, the Gaelic Athletic Association manual of 1887 includes excerpts from Charles Kickham's *Knocknagrow,* a hurling narrative of homosocial exploit and adhesion exhaustively indebted to the "games" set pieces of *Tom Brown's School Days.* It is not too much to say, with Mandle, that "writers and publicists who extolled the traditional manly vigor of the Celt; who emphasized the morality [of the] Catholic; who set up hurling as a game that was more than a game were unconscious imitators of the English writers who were doing the same . . . for a Saxon tradition . . . a Protestant faith and for cricket."[6] The key term in this observation, however, is *unconscious,* which in a broadly social context always implies structural or discursive constraint. The Irish philo-athleticists did not set about to emulate the English. But in seeking to constitute themselves in opposition to prevailing imperialist stereotypes, they assimilated the English agenda of manliness to native practices, rituals, and signifiers that would in turn dissimulate its origins.

Even as Irish sports propagandists preened themselves on the sterling aboriginal qualities of the Irish people, they called for a programmatic regeneration and enhancement of the race based on the sort of post-Darwinian, quasi-eugenic principles that arch imperialists like Froude, Dilke, MacIntosh, and Beddoes invoked to downgrade the Celt and justify his permanent subjugation. During the weeks the GAA came into existence, Parnell's party newspaper, *United Ireland,* pressed the nationalist brief for athletic revival on (d)evolutionary grounds.

> Voluntary neglect of such [National] pastimes is a sure sign of National decay and approaching dissolution, the strength and energy of a race all largely dependent on the national pastimes for the development of a spirit of courage and endurance. War-like races ever fond of games requiring skill, strength, and staying power. But when a race is declining in martial spirit . . . the national games are neglected at first and then forgotten. And as the corrupting and degrading influences manifest themselves . . . we find the national pastime and racial characteristics first fade and disappear.[7]

More than a decade later, on the pages of *Sinn Fein,* the "Celt" predicated nothing less than the "survival" of the ethnos upon the cultivation of its indigenous pastimes: "What a woeful tale might we not have to tell if the heart of the race, sinking under the weight of adversity, failed to feed the veins with invigorating blood, and to stir . . . the muscles of manhood? What a charnel heritage would we not have received of debility and degeneracy?" An article titled "Irish Athleticism," published the following year, offered more forward-looking and more explicitly evolutionary reinforcement: "And they [the GAA] are doing manful work in the rebuilding of the Nation. . . . For what, after all, is the meaning of the Irish revival if it is not a movement based on the conviction that it is as Irishmen we will . . . reach that higher stage of human development to which all races aspire?"[8]

What is most important about this evolutionary defense, from our perspective, is also what seals its structural identification with a characteristically British philo-athleticism. In keying the broad advance of the race to the fate of its physical culture in particular, the argument tacitly posits the impacted dialectic of manliness as the normative course of collective *bildung*. On this account, bodily energies in specific must be cultivated and trained because they, like their conceptual siblings, "animal spirits," form the indispensable condition and effective instrument of moral, intellectual, and spiritual discipline as well and thus of ethnocultural progress generally. Thus, we find the Celt insisting that "to create an Ireland . . . mentally alert and politically untrammeled which would be but a shadow and reproach to the muscular traditions of our race, could only be equaled in irony by the development of a hoard of muscular beings devoid of racial and national dignity. Mind and courage may shape the destiny and mold the policies of a people, but it is the manhood alone . . . which can safeguard its frontiers and enforce its sovereign will."[9] For this reason he can "conceive of no element . . . so important . . . in our national upraising as our physical strength intimately allied with an intelligent consciousness of that strength. For the mine, for the workshop, for the farm, in the counsel, country house and college, the higher the physical tone, the better, the greater, and the happier the labour." His rhetorical ascent here from menial to cognitive labor, from the underground toils of the mine to the ivory towers of the college, affirms not only the "mutual relations for good between mind and muscle" but the continuing precedence of the latter in ensuring success at each upward realm.[10] His formulation plays out in pragmatic or occupational terms the fundamental paradox of manliness, whereby the lower somatic forces give rise to the higher mental and moral forms through their self-surpassing reflexivity, their capacity for "intelligent," which is to say disciplined, "consciousness of themselves." Given the isomorphism between the *social* dynamics of athletic training and development and the personal dynamics of manly self-fashioning, it stands to reason that athletes themselves, both as individuals and as team members, would have emerged in this discourse as paragons of manhood, the repositories of all of its signature properties. Columnist "Amerigen" illustrated as much in locating the essence of Irish athletics in moral training rather than in competitive prowess and in defining proper Irish athletes as "men of discipline, of self control and self respect, men of sober habits, and having what may be called . . . greater esprit de corps, men who cherish and zealously guard the good name and prestige of the club."[11] As we saw with Parnell and the Ladies Land League, the positive political valence attached to this sort of exemplary gender construction inevitably carries over from the unified-field allegory of nationhood ("We Irish are like that") to the internally differentiated Symbolic of civil society ("Some of us are more like that"). To embody the authoritative ideal of manliness in the name of the Irish people is also to accumulate a certain authority over those people and to distribute that authority, in whole or in part, among discrete representatives of that people: a movement, the men of that movement, or even, as in the case of the GAA, a certain type of man or performance of manhood at the expense of others.

The cultural authority enjoyed by Irish athleticism naturally helped to consolidate the social authority of the middle and upper orders, which had greatest ideological and institutional access to the games ethic of manliness. Precisely because the GAA was organized along primarily nationalist rather than caste lines, however, it played a crucial role in disseminating the manly ideal more broadly, drawing in working- as well as middle-class subjects. Marilyn Silverman has noted that the GAA "socialized some labourers to the idea of a Gaelic nation," and I would argue that the appeal of mainstream middle-class nationalism proved ultimately inseparable from the more visceral yet more universalizable appeal of middle-class gender norms.[12] For their part, the working class was already a supremely embodied order in the popular Imaginary, possessors of a rude bodily vigor that promised athletic prowess and required athletic discipline. In this respect, the sports movement stood in the same relation to the working-class body as the manly faculty of sublimation stood toward the virile animal spirits that were both its fuel and its object of mastery. Thus, in enlisting the laborers in its physical program of manly development, the GAA rehearsed the symbolic logic underpinning that program as a logic of class difference. This praxis is one neither of benign inclusion nor of invidious distinction, but the kind of soft hegemony typically evinced in missionary work.[13]

Nothing in the internal class or ethnogender politics of the GAA stood at variance with its reputation or critical role as a front organization for the Irish Republican Brotherhood. Quite the opposite. A GAA identified with and credentialed by the classic manly constellation of bodily sinew restrained for the common good or purpose (a working definition of esprit de corps) served the interests and enhanced the image of the Fenians in two opposed yet interconnected ways that reflected the colonial double bind in reverse order. On the one hand, having built up their physical power, stamina, and endurance, whetted their aggression and agonistic zeal, all in the context of a cohesive group dynamic, the GAA members gave the appearance, perhaps illusory, of being fully prepared to form a fierce and efficient military force. As the "Celt" put it, "I do not regard the GAA as a purely match playing organization, but rather a training ground for the Irish physique—the successor of the Fianna, a voluntary national militia."[14] On the other hand, the disciplinary aspect of the GAA, its channeling of such agonistic ferocity into intramural rule-governed play, its cultivation of the self-control necessary to contain aggression within the bounds of healthy competition—this allowed the body to function simultaneously as the public face of the new (or New Departure) Fenianism, at once an instrument and a totem of its provisional turn from extreme to respectable nationalism. Instead of representing merely the preliminary expression of revolutionary violence, the GAA could, or could also, be seen as its final sublimation. In this regard, the relationship of the hillside men and the GAA follows from and analogizes to the relationship of Fenianism and Parnell himself. Even as Parnell was maintaining the hillside men as a physical force "reserve," in part to stage his own political manliness by keeping them in check, the Fenians were developing the GAA as a front organization, in part to stage their political manliness by apparently allowing "physical force" to be restrained and redirected in athletic exertion.

The GAA men's famous demonstration at Parnell's funeral (of all the apt venues) provided an elegantly condensed, street-theatrical allegory of their ambivalent yet ambidextrous engagement with physical force nationalism. Quoting from Association historian Marcus de Burca, the funeral was "one of the biggest political demonstrations ever seen in Dublin. Occupying a prominent place in the cortege were the men of the GAA—said by some to number as many as 2000—who walked each carrying a hurley draped in black and held in reverse to resemble a rifle, through the city to Glasnevin cemetery." Contemporary accounts amplify this description to telling effect: "Stout burly fellows all, each ruffled with a camàn dressed in black . . . they marched six abreast with splendid military precision. . . . The Gales raised their camàns aloft and a wail rose from the people."[15]

What gives this ritual enactment its startling iconic power, the signifier that concentrates its different layers and conflicting valences in a single gesture of political passion, is the black draping that adorns the camàns. As a species of crepe, it expresses grief and reverence for Parnell, and as a mode of concealment it links these sentiments to the GAA's purposefully undecidable status as a type of the "Fianna" or "a voluntary national militia." It is the coverings that enable the reversed camàns to simulate rifles, converting the stout, burly fellows from athletes into warriors, lending their choreography the effect of "military precision."[16] Thanks to the coverings, in other words, the hurlies could be identified as guns, the GAA itself could be identified as a redoubt of colonial resistance, not to say a school for sedition, and its obsequies for Parnell could be identified with his own increasingly vocal attachment to the Fenian tradition during his terminal election campaigns. The ceremonial trappings, or wrappings, mark the cortege as a symbolically curtained or protected space wherein the elements of constitutional, cultural, and insurgent nationalism could formally align themselves at the most belligerent, hypermasculine end of their shared potential.

But the drapings not only figured the camàns as firearms, they served to ritually muzzle the rifles they evoked. In allegorical terms, the covers both acted as an emblematic shield for an especially ballistic expression of revolutionary desire and simultaneously signified a desire to place a shield, a "safety," on the revolutionary ballistics themselves. The hurley shrouds function, one might say, much like the veil in its specifically Derridian usage, something that makes and marks sense in the same motion. But in this case the veil screens what has been announced in and by the very act of screening. Moreover, it does so to quite specific political affect. If by turning the plowshares into swords, so to speak, the covers betoken the solidarity of the GAA with physical-force militancy, then by sheathing those swords, the covers betoken the temporizing affect that the GAA, like Parnell before them, proposed to have upon physical force militancy. Thus, the ceremonial cloaks *also* work to align constitutional, cultural, and insurgent nationalism under the sign of "restraint."

In the event itself, of course, and in its impact on the assembled, these conflicting lines of implication had no existence, no legible consistency, apart from one another. They formed not a simple mixture of senses but a volatile, symbolic compound. As the bearers of same, the hurley shrouds heralded both a collective (physical) forcefulness that had not yet passed into feral savagery and a collective forbearance that had not yet lapsed into feminine passivity. Condensing aggression and self-repression, in the manner of a *discordia concours,* the public gesture of draping the camàns furnished the funeral with the defining emblem of Irish manliness and diffused a sense of this political aspiration through each ritual performance. The culmination of the dynamics was also the culmination of the ceremony, the final spectacle of grief and grievance combined. The athletes "raised" their camàns (weapons) "aloft" in the single most belligerent, hypermasculine gesture in the entire affair (one that calls to mind the later use of firearms at IRA funerals), and the people "wailed" like banshees, undertaking on a mass basis the traditionally feminine task of keening the dead. In striking a fine equipoise between menace and sentimentality and between the component parts or others of manliness that these attitudes earmarked, the ritual action redoubles the symbolic labor performed by the covered camàns themselves in order to effect a truly fitting tribute to the man who gave the Irish back their manhood.

It is no less appropriate, however, that this moment of aggrandized ethnonational purchase on the manly ideal should have occurred at Parnell's funeral. First, as we saw in the previous chapter, the demise of the "Chief" brought down the curtain on a provisionally successful engagement of Irish political leadership with the gendered double bind of colonialism. But it did so in such a traumatic

way as to trigger the need to grapple with that legacy amid a new set of negotiations with the prevailing gender ideal. Second, while the funeral commemo-
rates symbolically the ultimate human experience of materiality ("Remember
man that thou art dust"), it is in itself a symbolically overdetermined space
comparatively free of the material constraints that inform sociopolitical interchange. Such comparative liberty, which increases as one approaches a purely
ceremonial state, most easily accommodates what Jameson calls the merely
formal resolution of real social contradictions, including those, like colonial
manliness, that manifest primarily in discursive terms.[17] One of the challenges
for any nationalist aesthetic, such as that which characterized or evolved from
the Irish Revival, was to commit to formal resolutions, their common ground
with ritual, only insofar as they could be translated back into social practice.

Parnell and Muscular Sinn Fein

Two decades after the founding of the GAA, patriotic groups like Cumann Na
nGaedhal and the Dungannon Clubs joined forces under the organizational
umbrella of Sinn Fein, which sought both to support the manifold forms of
cultural nationalism that had sprung up in the interim and to mobilize them
to more definitively political ends. In keeping with this broadly nativist affinity, Sinn Fein and its leader, Arthur Griffith, took as their signature policy the
removal of Irish members from Parliament at Westminster. Just as the Gaelic
league established institutions for promoting the indigenous language, and the
educational movement, spearheaded by Gaelicists like Standish O'Grady and
Patrick Pearse, endeavored to establish authentically Irish institutions of learning, so Sinn Fein advocated the resurrection of fully separatist Irish political
institutions. A still closer analogy might be drawn with the Gaelic Athletic Association, to which, as we saw in the previous section, the Sinn Fein newspa-
pers (*United Ireland* and *Sinn Fein*) gave full-throated support. For the GAA,
the return to aboriginal Irish sport required a wholesale rejection of the games
imported from elsewhere in Britain, a posture notoriously formalized in the
so-called Ban, which was to last into the 1970s. Grounded in the belief that
"the first principle of nationhood is self-government," the Sinn Fein project of
"inculcating self-reliance among the people" took a similarly rejectionist cast,
substituting the refusal of one form of participation for another.[18]

But if, asks Richard Davis, "abstentionism . . . was regarded by many as the
crux of the Sinn Fein programme," how is it that Parnell, "who spent his whole
political life as a member of the House of Commons, is nevertheless regarded
as a Sinn Fein hero?" How is it, in other words, that Parnell's political legacy,
which Davis himself traces to that early form of parliamentary engagement
known as obstructionism, should endure in and receive credit from the pro-

ponents of parliamentary disengagement and withdrawal? Why would Sinn Fein bother to insist that they and not the parliamentary party "were the true inheritors of Parnell's mantle"?[19] Well, there did exist a membrane of strategic affiliation: Parliamentary withdrawal did after all constitute a species of boycott, the practice Parnell had popularized with his speech at Ennis. Moreover, Parnell himself had dallied with a parliamentary boycott as well, worrying Gladstone by his consideration of a "Hungarian policy" that Griffith would later trademark. But ultimately Parnell's importance for Sinn Fein did not reside in any specific political agenda or calculus to be pursued, so much as a symbolic value to be recovered, an ideal of contained aggression and aggressive self-containment—Ourselves Alone—inextricably bound up with Victorian gender norms. At bottom, then, Sinn Fein's hero worship of Parnell remained a matter of ideology, and specifically gendered ideology, rather than policy.

The nativist rhetoric of Sinn Fein imported heavily, and without ironic self-awareness, from the imperialist vocabulary of British manliness, and did so even more explicitly and consistently than the rhetoric of its compatriots in the GAA. As we have already begun to see, Sinn Fein regularly couched its defining agenda of nonviolent separatism as conducive if not equivalent to an ethos of collective self-reliance, a virtue summoned in turn to warrant a claim to national self-determination. One column from the Sinn Fein weekly was particularly telling in this regard. Preparatory to rallying Sinn Fein "adherence" to support Irish athletics, the "Celt" characterizes its policy as "involving one principle—self-reliance; and one medium of practice—national activity."[20] This synopsis unfolds under the title "MUSCULAR SINN FEIN," a reference to the robust physical culture that the Celt is promoting, but also an unmistakable if unwitting allusion to muscular Christianity, the movement in England most exhaustively identified with the cult of manly self-fashioning.

The aptness of the allusion, however accidental, runs deep. Not only does the "one principle" in forming Sinn Fein policy represent the cardinal virtue of an idealized Victorian masculinity, but the cardinal virtue that Sinn Fein adherents attached to "national activity," its "one medium of practice," was a masculinized strength or show of resistance. Griffith's own "Hungarian policy" was originally endorsed by Cumann Na nGaedhal, the immediate ancestor of Sinn Fein, as "a manly substitute for parliamentarianism." And the Sinn Fein constitution, framed three years later, "determined to make use of any powers we have, or may have at any time in the future, to work for Ireland's advancement and the creation of a prosperous, virile, and independent nation." For the "Celt," writing shortly thereafter, virile is as virile does: "In the arena of human conflict, policy without physique is the shadow without the substance, the voice without the vitality of manhood. . . . There is always a time when policies alone are useless and power alone is permanently effective." For the columnist of *The Peasant*, even the efficacy of Sinn Fein's activities made a poor consideration next to the forcefulness they displayed. He offers glowing commentary on what he can only describe as a futile if not pointless demonstration of Sinn Fein against parliamentary style Home Rule. In the process, both the title and the body of his column reveal the phrase "virile agitation" to be an all but official designation of preferred Sinn Fein tactics (rather like the phrase *passive resistance* for the post-Gandhi civil rights movement), one that carries a healthy measure of gendered identification with the conqueror's methods.[21] It is not surprising in this light that Griffith managed to combine a policy of absolute separatism with hopes for a partnership with England in the administration of empire: the will to manly self-containment on the national scale meets the masculinized will to mastery on the international scale.

Countering the Parliamentary Party's invocation of a "lost leader," from whom they claim direct descent, Sinn Fein enshrined Parnell as a token of the political virility that they themselves had rediscovered. They were thus able to tap into what remained vital about Parnell even after his demise, what that "new stir" Yeats spoke of built upon rather than replaced: not the mechanism of his policies, upon which the mainstream Home Rulers staked their allegiance, but his impersonation of national indomitability, which could easily be seen as underpinning diverse, even conflicting, political tactics at different times and in disparate historical circumstances. By affecting a gendered bond with a memory of Parnell, by canonizing him in the same masculinized terms they used to characterize their own agenda, the Sinn Feiners were able to install the dead Chief as a forerunner of their movement, despite the evident discrepancies in their respective programs, in order to simultaneously burnish and borrow his mythic prestige as a form of secessionist prophecy, without needing to supply a bill of shared positions. Like Sinn Fein itself, Parnell was seen to have "cast defiance" in "the face of the world's greatest power" through his stratagem of obstruction, while "the slavish reliance" of his successor, John Redmond, on other likewise "parliamentary methods" was castigated not only for its fecklessness but also for being "contrary to the teachings of Parnell." Beyond exempting obstruction from "the normal strictures against parliamentarianism," Sinn Fein chose to regard this démarche as "a form of physical force . . . of war by other means," conducted as if by a "foreign power."[22] In this way Parnell's perceived virility and aggression ("form of war") came to stand in for the separatists' objective ("foreign power") that he never actually pursued. If Parnell-like obstruction represented a "form of physical force," however, it was a highly sublimated one indeed, a species of assault so disciplined as to be in itself a proof against violence. As we saw in the last chapter, it was the rule-governed, self-contained quality of Parnell's strategy that lent it the cachet of a manliness derived from a finally British scale of cultural value. That Sinn Fein elected to recuperate Parnellism on these Anglified gender grounds only goes to show that a separatist ideology is no guarantee of ideological separatism.

More generally, in lionizing Parnell for practices at distinct variance from its own, Sinn Fein showed that when Irish manhood was at stake, it came not just to harness symbolic politics but to embrace them as well. A *United Irishman* editorial on the proper memorializing of Parnell confirms as much under color of denial. Denouncing the "Parnell Commemoration Association," a frequent target of Sinn Fein and a synechdoche for the parliamentary party, Arthur Griffith decries the tawdry symbolism with which Parnell's grave at Glasnevin had been festooned: "But the . . . procession mongers have placed a plaster of paris bust in the centre of the plot. This atrocious thing . . . the brow of this sham thing is frayed and a large piece of paint has been chipped off the nose. . . . [A] cheap photograph of Parnell is placed in a cheap frame, covered with cheap glass and exhibited on a cheap iron." Far from demanding custodial repair or improvement of Parnell's grave site, Griffith advocates a minimalist approach that aims to square with the essence of Parnell's achievement, rather than the inevitable pomp attending his memory: "There is no statue of Parnell over his grave. He needs none. The man who put spirit into the slaves of the landlords and taught them they were men, can afford to leave his immortality more to history than to sculpture."[23] The spirit of true "men," suggests Griffith, requires no ornamental emblem, for it is authenticity itself, and having forged the rightful character of a nation, Parnell lives on in the very tissues of its memory, unbeholden to the vulgarities of symbolic expression. Griffith's position on this point, however, fails to acknowledge the enormous allegorical freight secreted in his usage of the word *men,* a signifying nexus wherein notions of ethical normativity, political fitness, and rights of enfranchisement affix themselves to what we might call the trappings of gender, that is, socially ranked styles of performance and self-presentation. Yeats's rhetoric of a "turn" from parliamentary politics notwithstanding, it was in fact this masculinist ideology that underpinned the historical bridge from the liberal nationalism of Parnell to the cultural nationalism of the Irish Revival, a bridge that owed much to the early stirrings of Sinn Fein.

Tricks of Memory: Lady Gregory and the Revival of Parnell

Parnell's skill at aligning the tensions among the various wings of nationalist resistance with the *discordia concours* of his own manly profile served, among other things, to authorize divergent interpretations of his political methods and commitments in the literature representing him. At the same time, because Parnell's strategy in this regard was precisely to articulate diverse modes of resistance inextricably, the differences among the posthumous literary interpretations amounted in large measure to differences of emphasis. The more radical

Parnell found in the revivalist iconography of a Gregory or a Pearse always stopped short of being a full-blooded insurrectionist; the Parnell emblematizing the inherent dignity of a more conservative, gentrified nationalism, à la the later Yeats, never entirely loses his revolutionary éclat. In the end, this constitutive gendered duality of the Parnell legend becomes an object of reflection itself, a basis for James Joyce's critique of imperialist and nationalist manliness alike.

It is at once ironic and apposite that one of the more recognizable portraits of Parnell as an "advanced" nationalist should have sprung from the aristocratic Imaginary of Augusta Gregory. Ironic, because she inveighed against Parnellism during the life of its architect for mounting such a doggedly aggressive assault on the conditions of landed entitlement. Apposite, because for a much longer time she had cherished the romantic image of a still more implacable, hypermasculine foe of Ascendancy rule, the "treason-felon" or revolutionary, who paid with life or liberty for a violent pursuit of Irish self-determination. Indeed, it was this latter passion that fueled in turn her famous redactions of Gaelic legends like the myth of Sovereignty and the Cuchulain Cycle, literary achievements that made her perhaps the chief architect of revivalist manhood. In these split if not conflicting investments, we can discern the peculiar psychic agon of the metrocolonial mandarin, caught between an identification with her Anglo-Irish caste and with a birth nation whose fortunes were increasingly defined in terms of a Gaelo-Catholic irredentism. Understandably, the figure of Charles Stewart Parnell, a great Ascendancy landowner and the leader of a largely native Catholic-Irish devolutionary movement, represented an especially fraught object of this psychomachia.

Stationed in Egypt as a member of her elderly husband's diplomatic entourage, Lady Gregory joined her lover, Wilfred Blunt, in cultivating public support for the Felaheen nationalist movement. To this end, she sought to humanize its leader in British eyes by publishing a sentimental portrait of his family and domestic situation in *The Times*.[24] Having taken this step, which was daring for a woman so tightly ensconced in the imperialist establishment, Gregory nevertheless discountenanced Blunt's sympathy for the similarly irredentist Home Rule campaign and privately reproached his subsequent involvement in related Land League agitation. Blunt's feeling that her seeming inconsistency on this score stemmed from class ideology, what he called her "property-owning blindness," was only reinforced by her counterclaim that Parnellism constituted a "vulgar and virulent" program, unworthy of "the Irish people, the poor, who are courteous and full of tact [which is to say deferential] even in their discontent." To put the matter in Victorian gendered terms, Gregory scored Parnellism for being masculine without being manly, for being assertive without submitting to the tether of chivalric decorum. When Blunt described for her the brutality and pathos of the evictions he had witnessed, Gregory, "who had never been to an eviction," was inclined to discount the severity of the measures taken, confiding to her diary the report of a "bedridden old man found to have his boots on and was shamming."[25]

Following her disagreement with Blunt, Gregory grew steadily gloomier over the future security and life prospects of her only child, Robert. Near experience told her that the Anglo-Irish seigniory to which he was heir had entered a period of continuing erosion by the crosscurrents of agrarian outrage (her brother, Algernon, a land agent, required a bodyguard of garrisoned soldiers), the Land War (the fiercest agitation targeted the estate of Lord Clanricarde, Gregory's neighbor and fellow diplomat), rent strikes and land courts, where the tenants at Coole would soon win a 25 percent rent reduction (giving her financial trouble), and parliamentary concessions to the restive Irish Party, such as the Land Bill of 1881 and the Ashbourne Act of 1885 (the first land-purchase bill). Amid this endlessly protracted crisis for her class, she welcomed the outright defeat of the first Home Rule Bill (1886), the centerpiece of Parnell's career as Irish leader.[26]

A few years later, after Parnell had died, Gregory continued to make her case for unionism in a piece that might have seemed, from Blunt's perspective, a negative counterpart to "Arabi and His Household." Anonymously published just prior to the second Home Rule Bill (1893), with the intention of helping to defeat it, the dystopian fantasy, "The Phantom's Pilgrimage; or, Home Ruin," sees Gladstone returned to the Ireland of the future to behold the appalling socio-economic consequences of the Home Rule policy that he and his collaborative adversary, the Irish Party, had implemented: renewed famine among the tenants, landlords ruined, brigandry rampant, the entire institutional fabric in shreds. An expression of her inherited Ascendancy outlook, the patrician Unionism of the piece embarrassed the later cultural nationalist Gregory into an unbroken silence on its existence, let alone its authorship.[27] Not that her developing cultural nationalism translated automatically or comprehensively into political nationalism anyway. By the testimony of her own revisionist autobiography, "Even my growing friendship with W. B. Yeats [circa 1897] did not bring me into that national struggle in which he had a hand."[28] To the contrary, she spent the next five or so years of revivalist collaboration trying to draw him out of that national struggle. Thus, a year after she claims "my feeling against Home Rule had been gradually changing," she could still primly inform Yeats that it was the duty of the upper orders to teach the people how to "starve with courage," if it came to that, rather than encouraging them in lawless means of survival—a posture that would continue to reject the tenor of much Parnell-like Land League activity even under more dire circumstances than actually obtained in late Victorian Ireland. By the end of the century, Gregory's Ascendancy background and experience had taught her to "dislike and distrust England," to love Ireland, but to reject nonetheless the policy that would spell their partial separation.[29]

As James Pethica observes, however, in "The Phantom's Pilgrimage; or, Home Ruin," Gregory's most public, proactive denunciation of Parnell-like Home Rule, she makes a deliberate exception for the figure of Parnell himself, striking a somewhat discordant note in an otherwise orthodox Unionist symphony.[30] Instead of casting Parnell as a traitor to his Ascendancy tribe and heritage, an indictment in keeping with Gregory's own caste-based distaste for the National League, she anticipates her much later revivalist drama, *The Deliverer,* in depicting Parnell as the victim of treachery, a figure sacrificed to the venal ambitions of his disciples. His betrayal and martyrdom in turn served to enhance and ennoble his afterimage on the lens of Gregory's imagined history, overriding any residual pique she had at his class errancy. In this regard, it is worth noting that while Gregory apparently saved no memorabilia whatever from Parnell's storied political reign, she did keep among her private papers an account of his funeral, one of his last photographs, and a copy of Catherine Tynan's "Lament" for the fallen leader.[31]

Out of kilter, perhaps, with Gregory's political leanings at the time, her commemoration of Parnell in "Home Ruin" did consist after a fashion with her abiding passion for the memory of Ireland's martyred hillside men, from the great leaders of the '98 to the executed foot soldiers of Manchester fame. As a young girl, Augusta Persse devoted her entire allowance to purchasing Ireland's Songs of Rebellion at her local stationer's shop.[32] As a middle-aged widow, she married her fascination with the romantic Irish rebel to her developing interest in folklore to produce her first properly revivalist piece of writing, "The Felons of Our Land," which gathers the verse, chronicles the historical occasions, catalogs the authors, and recalls the heroes that constituted the popular eulogistic strain of Irish nationalist literature. So lovingly does Gregory retail the sacrificial idealism putatively animating the rebel tradition that she found herself admonished by her peers for the seditious overtones of her study, and her response, recorded in her diary, was to pledge "not to go so far toward political nationality in anything I write again," in part "to keep out of politics and work only for literature" and in part to maintain imperialistic solidarity with her only son.[33] Just as Parnell emerges unexpectedly unscathed by Gregory's strictures on Home Rule in "The Phantom's Pilgrimage," so he holds an unexpectedly honored place in the martyrology of "The Felons," with Yeats's "Mourn—and then Onward" serving as the exemplary paean ("F," 631).

There is a marked paradox, then, at the heart of Gregory's fin de siècle attitude toward Parnell: she strictly dissociates the symbolic value of the politician from her dour estimate of the campaign to which he gave his political life and from which he took his iconic identity. This paradox, in turn, answers to a second, more encompassing, paradox characteristic of Gregory's metrocolonial ideology: her disdain for the masculine virulence of Parnell's Home Rule campaign, which she felt to menace the future well-being of her family and class, was matched or exceeded in intensity by her affection for the more violent, hypermasculine lineage of physical force martyrdom, and for the fallen Parnell insofar as he could be annexed to it. Reading for a relatively coherent political belief system, existing scholarship has filtered out the apparent contradictions and equivocations in Gregory's attitude by recourse to an opposed pair of interpretive schema. On one side, Gregory has been framed as fundamentally a unionist, whose literary investment in the Irish felon was not an avowal but a strategic deferral of nationalistic affiliation. Biographical critics such as Mary Lou Kohlfeldt and Elizabeth Longford draw support for this argument, not just from Gregory's repudiation of Parnellism and her later enthusiastic support for Horace Plunkett's unionist alternative—the socioeconomic policies popularly known as "Killing Home Rule with Kindness"—but also from her enduring "formula" for the Anglo-Irish literary revivalism that she came to personify. "But I felt less and less interest in politics as other interests came in. I had soon laid down a formula for myself: 'Not working for Home Rule but preparing for it,' and this by adding dignity to the country through our work. But it is hard to keep quite clear."[34] On the other side, Gregory's attachment to the cult of fallen patriots has been adduced to demonstrate that she was a sound nationalist all along, without professing or even knowing as much. For Pethica, her incongruous commemoration of Parnell in "The Phantom's Pilgrimage" signals an original "deviance from [the] political orthodoxy" she seemingly affirmed, while Lucy McDiarmid, going a step further, sees Gregory as having espoused a "soft Fenianism" from girlhood to the grave.[35] Both sides state the cogency of Gregory's ideological position on the substantial elision of one of her primary competing adherences. In the process, both sides wind up unwittingly conflating the structural coordinates whereby they propose (as Gregory herself did) to map that position, the endeavors of "politics" and "literature," or political and cultural nationalism, respectively. Either Lady Gregory should not be viewed as a full-blooded cultural nationalist because her revivalism did not intend, will, or pursue the political autonomy of the Irish nation, but to the contrary unfolded under muted unionist colors, or Lady Gregory should be understood as a political, because a full-blooded cultural, nationalist—her celebration of revolutionary balladry evidencing her protoseparatist inclinations. Either way, the attempts to streamline Gregory's complex articulation of the political and the cultural have only borne out her wry comment upon her own famous "formula" for doing so: "But it is hard to keep quite clear."

One way of going beyond the interpretive impasse created by Gregory's affiliative ambivalences is to return to their admittedly eccentric site of maximum concentration, her treatment of Parnell, understood not as a mere effect of this colonial psychomachia but as a symptom thereof, in the properly psychoanalytic sense of the term. What might this mean? In Slavoj Zizek's parlance, the symptom makes manifest the "Logic of Exception," whereby an item excluded from or marginal to a normative field of operations proves for this very reason representative of that field's inner reality.[36] Observable as a contingent if powerful disturbance in a given subjective or symbolic economy, the symptom simultaneously epitomizes, in its very distortion, the hidden, always divided structure of the whole. Now in "The Phantom's Pilgrimage" and again in *The Deliverer,* Gregory's favorable evocation of Parnell ill consists with both of her primary, deeply polarized political cathexes: her rejection of Parnellism in favor of a benignant unionism and her promotion of violently nationalist treason-felony in spite of her unionism. She enshrines Parnell in this manner, however, precisely because he exemplifies a still more foundational affinity of hers, the idea of martyrdom, which likewise informs, whether in fear or admiration, those same warring political attachments. So while Parnell remains at most an incidental figure in her extensive literary and polemical oeuvre, he stands forth as its first universal "exception," crystallizing the antagonism between the radical and conservative hemispheres of her political sensibility, at the very place where they can be seen to join.

More important, as the "extruded" middle of Gregory's political self-division—the chief exception to and link between her unionistic allegiances and Fenian sympathies—her take on Parnell helps to make legible the torturous ideological agenda refracting them both and the underlying principle around which that agenda struggles to cohere. Her agenda comprises one of the Irish Revival's most intriguing dialectical negotiations between cultural and political nationalism, one that illuminates the effective asymmetry of the two species. A truly reciprocal interaction or mutual interpenetration of political and cultural nationalism does *not,* as one might expect, serve the interests of both species equally, nor does it serve to equalize their influence. On one side, such interaction or interpenetration means that neither agenda can simply enlist and exploit the other, precluding the instrumentalist, means-ends logic that is the hallmark of a properly political nationalism. On the other, such mutuality or reciprocity means that the two must cooperate through a layer of symbolic mediation, which, being the hallmark of the cultural form, inevitably conduces to its hegemony. The telos of this dialectic, in Gregory's case, is a robust yet restrictive cultural nationalism or, more precisely, a cultural nationalism augmented, made robust, by the political nationalism it incorporates and restricts. Her revivalism was virile in that, violating her own guiding precept, it was about "working for independence" as well as merely preparing for it. But it was circumscribed in that the work it performed and, more important, the work it defined political nationalism as performing remained strictly preparatory in nature. The crucial lever in this nicely calibrated revivalist machinery was the concept of "dignity."

Drawn from Gregory's "Ascendancy code," John Kelly observes, "dignity became her watchword and its promotion the goal of her Irish plans." She measured the worth of nationalist endeavor, whatever its form, by whether it advanced the tone of Irish dignity, as opposed to furthering the Irish cause. It is for this reason that in later years Gregory could use the quoted phrase "adding dignity to the country" to profess the politically disinterested nature of "our [revivalist] work."[37] In point of fact, however, essays like "The Felons of Our Land" and plays like *The Deliverer, The Rising of the Moon,* and *Cathleen Ni Houlihan* could be (mis)read as radical or activist incitements in large part because they succeeded in accomplishing something more politically concrete than merely strengthening the moral fiber or raising the consciousness of Ireland in preparation for Home Rule. Most of Gregory's "High" revivalist efforts serve not to augment but to vindicate Irish dignity, and to vindicate Irish dignity as a warrant for Irish liberty. Dignity became a profoundly radicalized desideratum in the imperialist discourse of the time (including Gregory's own "Ascendancy code"), an intangible attribute or quality awarded to the "dearer" and denied the "cheaper" races as a means of legitimating colonial dominion and disenfranchisement, super- and subordination, respectively. When Lord Salisbury oppugned the first Home Rule Bill with a comparison of Irishmen to Hottentots in their unfitness for the sort of "representative self-government" responsibly enjoyed by people of "teutonic" extraction, he was making an argument to the unequal dignity of the races, implicitly relying for evidence upon the long parade of helpless women, dim ineffectual paddies, brawling drunkards, irresponsible buckleppers, and dangerous, chattering simians that passed for Irishmen in the British cultural Imaginary.[38] In this ideological atmosphere, asserting the collective dignity of a colonized people like the Irish could not but hold them up as subjects of right: human, political, even liberal-democratic.

This same practice is not, in itself, however, to lay claim to the *exercise* of said rights. To stand on one's dignity, as Gregory fashions her work to do, is precisely also to refuse to make a "movement" or cause of that dignity. In this sense, it is a deeply and yet incompletely political measure. Thus, in her manifesto on the Irish national theater, Gregory could recommend countering the "misrepresentations" of Irish "buffoonery" as a task "outside of all the political questions that divide us," even though such buffoonery, in the shape of the stage Irishman, had long tended to naturalize Irish subjacency.[39] Whatever its politicizing potential, such an assertion of Irish dignity could always stand clear of even fundamental partisan issues insofar as dignity itself connotes a certain self-containment or self-effacement bound up with respect for propriety, authority, and order, as the clichéd pairing of "long-suffering" with "quiet dignity" attests. Moreover, the vindication of that dignity, if it is to be effective with the same projected audience, *must itself be dignified,* be respectful of the terms in which dignity operates and "tells," be modest in its address, even in its challenge to an aggrieving world. Gregory's concessionary phrase "outside of all the political questions that divide us" shows her mindfulness of this need. Indeed, asserting or vindicating Irish dignity need not even be construed as incompatible with Gregory's chilling tenet that the peasants were better taught to "starve with courage" than steal to survive. In sum, Gregory's cherished social virtues and revivalist principles tended to demonstrate an Irish "fitness for freedom," without in any way demonstrating *for* Irish freedom, that is, without implying the necessity of overturning British rule or garrison privilege. Such virtues and principles could be readily tailored to unionist as well as nationalist sentiment.

The ideological connection between dignity and fitness for freedom helped to power the discourse of manliness, enabling what was inculcated as a personal ethos to function as an instrument of geopolitical as well as gender hegemony. Conversely, the discourse of manliness riveted the connection itself. As an arrangement or calculus of concrete gendered signifiers, it literally gave flesh to the otherwise diffuse notions of collective dignity and fitness, facilitating the personification at both the individual and the group level. It is therefore hardly surprising that Gregory should have recourse to the narrative figurations and symbolic trappings of manliness in her attempts to vindicate Irish dignity as a warrant for Irish liberty, particularly since the structural preemption of Irish manliness through simultaneous feminization and bestialization had long been the dominant British cultural strategy for denying that warrant. Thus, her representations of Parnell and the Fenians take their dignity from the reflective light of the manly ideal. With the Fenians in particular, Gregory availed herself of the discourse of chivalry, which, like the broader norm of manliness, had its nineteenth-century epicenter in the land of the colonizer.[40] An intrinsically elite ethos of hyperbolic self-denial, sacrifice, and service, latter-day chivalry not only squared nicely with Gregory's aristocratic disposition, it did so precisely in the moralized terms she preferred. If the ideal of manliness served to confer dignity upon the entitled subject in fin de siècle Britain, chivalric forms served to supplement the dignity of manliness itself.

At the same time, Gregory clearly felt that the reflexive dignity of her own work—the aptitude of her writing to be the very warrant it would adduce—finally hinged upon the relationship she struck between the cultural and political nationalisms coincided in her project. On this score as well, Gregory draws upon the construct of manliness, not as a set of outward, gender-specific signs but as an internal logic. The peculiar dialectical architecture of manliness, which we have been tracing in this study, enables her to articulate politics and culture together, in partnership, precisely by sublating (canceling and preserving) the former in the latter. Given the premium Gregory placed on containing the partisan political charge of Irish cultural self-validation, manliness can be understood not just as the representational mechanism but as the deep structural correlative of Gregory's idea of collective dignity.

Lady Gregory's portraits of the Irish "Chief" and the Irish felon as manly paragons of struggle and sacrifice share certain crucial features, one involving the methodology and the other the substance of her reflections. On the question of method, the commendations of both Chief and felon are decisively mediated throughout "Phantom's Pilgrimage" and "Felons of Our Land." In neither text does Lady Gregory laud her subject directly; rather, she takes the measure, critically or affirmatively, of a broader Irish response to the figures and their legacy. In this way, she is able to burnish the dignity of their profiles in the mirror of others' regard, without granting her endorsement to their respective political aspirations or means of achieving them. More generally, she is able to enhance, without insisting upon, the claims to nationhood for which the men remembered variously stood. On the question of substance, the dignity that Gregory adduces in her subjects is invariably bound up with the thwarting of their anticolonial purposes, with the unavailing nature of their struggle and sacrifice. (Since on the face of things, the deeds of her stalwarts might seem more than a little politically self-interested, at least in the collective sense, they can only pretend to the purity of chivalric self-conquest insofar as they fail in their objective.) With this gambit, of course, Gregory follows a well-worn Celticist tradition, extending from Arnold to the early Yeats, of ennobling, aestheticizing, and spiritualizing Irish political reversals. In thus apotheosizing the exploits of her subjects on grounds antithetical to their own agonistic code, she further heightens the distance or degree of mediation between her cultural and their political spheres of operation. But she does so in the mode of the opposite, as a closing together or mutual embrace. Through this synergy of distinctive rhetorical method and particular substantive focus, her portraits of Irish patriotism constitute acts of nationalist auto-appropriation, cannibalizing political failures as cultural achievements in the name of Irish glory.

What Pethica deems "hints of a lingering admiration of the dead . . . Parnell" in "The Phantom's Pilgrimage" reside exclusively in the narrative staging of Gregory's contempt for the treachery of Parnell's acolytes. Vilifying O'Brien with calls of "Traitor," "Judas," and "Who slew his master," an angry mob sends up a "New Testament antiphon" to Gregory's private comparison of O'Brien to the faithless servant Zimri, who "slew his master," Elah, and the entire house of Baasha in 1 Kings 16:9.[41] Her use of master-slave tropes in both cases indicates that her moral outrage focuses specifically upon the affront to social hierarchy, the impertinent overthrow of fellow landed gentry by a pack of upstarts. *The effect is to mold the ouster of Parnell as Irish Party head into a hieroglyph for the ouster of the Ascendancy by the same nationalist forces.* In its negatively triangulated mode of expression, Gregory's "lingering admiration of "the dead . . . Parnell," far from an exercise in "unorthodoxy," proves startlingly consonant with her unionist adherences at that juncture, and turns out to be prototypical of her later penchant for conjuring with a radicalism that she does not finally espouse. In this instance, by dislocating Parnell's romantic cachet from the material aspirations of Parnellism, Gregory's caste rhetoric cunningly sets the two in political opposition to one another.

More than that, however, because Gregory's ambivalence toward Parnell was metonymic of an extensive chain of internal ideologically charged conflicts (over her relation to her peers and "the people," her role in any national cause, her own hyphenated Irishness), his image came to function as an exploratory vehicle for her correspondingly personal yet broad-based solution: to stipulate a general yet always provisional discontinuity between her symbolic interventions and the activist incitements or programs they might be thought to entail. On the occasion of Parnell's death, Gregory felt such revulsion for his newly minted foes that she urged Sir William to stand for Parliament as a Parnellite, notwithstanding their shared distrust of Home Rule.[42] That gesture, however fleeting, clearly illustrates how Gregory's powerful sociosymbolic investments could translate into fits of unwonted political attachment. But it also throws into sharp relief how Gregory's later more considered response, "The Phantom's Pilgrimage," admits no such conversion whatever. Her decision to set a mass castigation of the wrong done Parnell against a panorama of the wrong done Ireland by Parnell and his policies introduces the sharpest of caesuras between the mythopoetic concerns of her developing cultural nationalism and the prudential considerations—economic, juridical, institutional, and the like—endemic to political nationalism and antinationalism alike. In "The Phantom's Pilgrimage," the privileging of Parnell the symbolic presence at the expense of Parnell the statesman serves to announce the self-privileging of cultural artisanry over political advocacy in her own work. Gregory's highly oblique reflection on the Chief's passing frames him as an oblique anticipation of her own future.

Not even the representational immediacy of the stage-play format could deter Gregory from resuming her mediated method of portraying Parnell in *The Deliverer* (1911). Here, the strategy works to all but erase the policy dimension of Parnell's career in favor of its cultural import. A biblical allegory, the play trades on the Chief's reputation as the Irish Moses, which Parnell sought to consolidate in a speech delivered shortly after his ouster: "If I am to leave you tonight I should like—and it is not an unfair thing for me to ask—that I should come within sight of the promised land."[43] Gregory's theater audience encounters Parnell much earlier in the biblical narrative, as a royal heir, born to wealth and privilege. Over the course of the action, he turns against the ruling house, takes up the cause of the "Israelite" slaves whose blood he is rumored to share, suffers betrayal and death at their hands, and then reappears to their desperate imaginations as an imperishable spirit. Embellished with Irish allusions, both mythic and topical, and retrofitted with Kiltartan dialect, the biblical framework of the drama is sufficiently familiar and specific to render the figure of Parnell unmistakable, but sufficiently remote and generic to render the character of Parnell obscure and the politics of Parnellism irrelevant. Revealingly, in fact, the King's Nurseling rarely occupies the stage and has considerably less than 5 percent of the spoken lines. In the entire play, he commits just one, albeit significant, deed, the slaying of an Egyptian overseer, the allegorical effect of which is to align Parnell with the physical-force element of his National League front. As we shall see, this dramatic identification of Parnell with the "treason-felon" of Gregory's beloved rebel verse not only enhances the masculine profile of the Nurseling in the play itself but also proves crucial to the larger significance that Parnell comes to hold in Gregory's increasingly gendered nationalism. For all that, however, the unclear motive for the killing (does he act in defense of the Israelites or his own standing as a full-blooded Egyptian?), combined with its being almost a reflex action, balks any attempt to connect it with contemporary Irish political events, known tactics of the National League or Irish Party, or specific incidents in Parnell's life. The briefly mooted plans for a slave "exodus" whereby the Nurseling's leadership is established likewise sustain biblical parallels in preference to specific points of correlation with Irish anticolonial activity. It is, instead, the dissemination of the various facets and phases of the Parnell legend throughout the slave nation that constitutes both the bulk of the dramatic byplay and the epicenter of its historical allegory. Instead of Lady Gregory's Parnell play, as Yeats had it, *The Deliverer* is her "Parnell" play, a drama about *the discourse, the stories, the quotes enveloping Parnell rather than the man himself.*

The action opens with the Israelites complaining of their miserable life conditions, which they bitterly contrast with the opulence of the Pharaoh's household, personified by the impeccably attired King's Nurseling, "a holy circus for grandeur" (*TD,* 260). In the ensuing parley, the female helots in particular recirculate in allegorical mode the received opinion, canvassed in the previous chapter, as to the aristocratic bearing and physique that gave Parnell an heir of personal manliness: "He is so well-shaped," "No one can become a suit better," "His head held up so lofty and so high" (*TD,* 260–61). When the King's Nurseling subsequently slays the sadistic steward, it is the narrative chorus of the male helots that transubstantiates his inadvertent homicide into proof of the sort of virile nerve and hardihood that Parnell's many hagiographers placed at the core of his political leadership:

> Dan: "That was a good blow and no mistake."
> Ard: "He has killed him with one blow of the hurl."
> Malachi: "You stood up well to him. It took you to tackle him. You behaved well in doing that. But I'm in dread it will bring you under trouble." (*TD*, 265)

At this moment, the King's Nurseling accedes to the status of Chief Israelite, not as a matter of lineal fact necessarily, nor even through the totemic power of his deed, but on the formative word of the slaves themselves ("You are a good man's son" [*TD*, 265]). Their voice is decisive in identifying his assault on Egyptian power with his presumed blood membership in the Israelite community, much as the Irish people-nation determine that the Anglo-Irish landlord of Avondale belonged to them on account of his struggle against British rule and garrison exploitation.

The judgment of the Hebrew bondsmen inaugurates the second, Messianic, division of the play, which hints at an antitypical parody of the opening verse of John's panoptic gospel: "In the beginning was the Word, and the Word was with God, and the Word was God" (John 1:1). Having vowed to elevate his "crushed, miserable race" (*TD*, 266), the King's Nurseling promptly disappears to devise the escape plans, and it is in his prolonged absence that he ascends to the station of Messiah, that is, deliverer and sacrificial lamb in one, all by the power of the spoken word alone. Years earlier, in the comedy *Spreading the News,* Lady Gregory skillfully sets in motion a dizzyingly rapid, polyphonic acceleration of gossip and inference, rumor and foregone conclusion, that breaks the "reality barrier," so to speak, and produces the social datum, a supposed murder, to which it mistakenly refers. Here, in a tragicomic variation on that scenario, the bondsmen, anticipating their exodus, pour forth rapidly and with escalating momentum ever more fulsome expressions of belief and identification, hope and hero worship, loyalty and expectation, until they have an engendered semidivine reality to which they refer, the Nurseling-as-Savior. And then, just as zanily, their conversation reverses itself, layering suspicion upon censure, disaffiliation upon self-loathing, servility upon resentment, until the Israelites themselves are split, and their new idol, returning suddenly, is broken at their hands, the victim of a herd killing that parallels his own killing of the overseer. The strophic measure of dialogue deifies the King's Nurseling for imagined strengths and virtues redolent of the tactical and strategic components of Parnell's steely command, in particular his canniness in using agrarian Fenianism as a "reserve" army ("that one has a good head for plans"; "Every enemy has

any complaint against Pharaoh will be on our side. . . . [H]e is a great for plans";
"He is the best we ever met!"; "A real blood he is!"; "The sea and the hills would
go bail for him!" (*TD,* 267–69). The antistrophic measure of dialogue in turn
demonizes the King's Nurseling for imagined or rumored faults drawn from the
annals of the Parnell scandal, in particular an unmanly duplicity, vanity, and
intemperateness, stemming from an irreligiosity already decried by the clerics
of their sect. "It is what the priest was saying, the lad is proud and he is giddy";
"He is in no way religious. . . . I am told he's a real regular Pagan"; "I am a very
bad lover of deceit and treachery" (*TD,* 271–72). But ultimately the allegorical content of these rhetorical counterblasts signifies less than the symmetry
that Gregory has fashioned between them. To put it another way, the carefully
maintained symmetry between these opposed views holds the ultimate key to
their significance.

The conventional allegorical reading of *The Deliverer,* that it not only depicts
but openly deplores the repudiation of a great leader and the loss of the signal
liberatory opportunity he represented, presupposes the play's implicit endorsement of Parnell and his Home Rule agenda. It is therefore important to observe
that the pendular equipoise that Gregory strikes between the initial enraptured
canonization of the King's Nurseling and the later embittered condemnation of
him—both emanating from the same precincts—comes to rest squarely upon a
void. That is to say, there is no warrant within the limits of the dramatic action
itself for either of these judgments, and hence, given the abortive outcome, there
is no warrant for determining the Nurseling's definitive relation—ironic, parodic,
ambivalent, straightforward—to the allegorical framework. Indeed, the play
refers the question of whether the Nurseling was really a Moses figure destined
to lead the Israelites out of bondage to the verdicts of the slaves themselves. All
of this is to say that Gregory suspends the stories and opinions about the Nurseling in dichotomous balance, pro and con, for and aft, while at the same time
so foregrounding these stories and opinions that, in aggregate, they eclipse the
figure they claim to elucidate. On the one hand, Gregory refuses to take sides
in a bygone controversy. On the other, she broadcasts how the constructions
of Parnell on either side of that controversy have always, for better or worse,
outstripped the historical reality. This effect is precisely what she had in mind
when she wrote in *Our Irish Theater* that *The Deliverer* is the story of Parnell's
betrayal "as the people tell it."[44] The play must not be understood, accordingly,
as condemning, or even pivoting upon the people's betrayal of a great man and
his efforts. It is rather about an oppressed people's betrayal of their own self-
generated ideal and the role of oppression itself in the dynamic. Its treatment of
Parnell, like that in "The Phantom's Pilgrimage," is really about his *image,* and
it is no accident that Gregory entitles her drama on nationalist memorial, in
which Parnell's name figures prominently, simply *The Image.* Like that play, *The*

Deliverer is not really a vehicle of political nationalism at all; rather, it attempts a certain cultural anatomy of political nationalism. Indeed, on the surface, the strictly political implications of this cultural anatomy might be seen as more unionist than nationalist. The inconstancy of the Hebrew slaves in abandoning the political ideal they created speaks allegorically to similar irresponsibility in the Irish masses who in Gregory's view have long played an equal and collabora- tive part with British misrule in the depleted state of the country.

Where this anatomy bleeds into Gregory's specifically cultural nationalism, however, is in generating the doleful insight that such political immaturity on the part of the Irish people is determined by the very colonial subjacency that it helps to perpetuate. On this basis Gregory was able to discover in the arti- facts of native Irish culture, and to adduce in her aesthetic and ethnographic endeavors, certain evidence of her countrymen's inherent "fitness for freedom" that remained at loggerheads with their circumstantial disabilities. Consider Gregory's testimonial for the ballad "A Sorrowful Lament for Ireland" in her revivalist classic *Poets and Dreamers:* "I like it for its own beauty, and because its writer does not, as so many Irish writers have done, attribute the many griefs of Ireland only to 'the horsemen of the Gall' but also to the faults and shortcom- ings to which the people of a country broken up by conquest are perhaps more liable than the people of a country that has kept its own settled rule."[45] In this assessment, we can grasp just how Lady Gregory's revivalism can be said to work for independence, but in a preparatory, self-braking mode. Putting a nationalist spin on Arnoldian Celticism, she holds the popular cultural archive of the Irish, exemplified by the "Lament," to evince the worthiness of self-determination, the "dignity," that Irish civil society sadly belied.

The possibility of imaginative redemption in *The Deliverer* comes with the last scene, the resurrection of the Nurseling in the mind of a still-enslaved people:

> Malachi: It is sorrow you will sleep with from this out. You will not
>   find the like of him from the rising to the setting sun.
> Dan's Wife: Look! He is living yet! He is passing!
> *King's Nurseling passes slowly at the foot of steps . . . His clothes are torn*
>   *and blood-stained, and he walks with difficulty.*
> Dan: It is but his ghost. He is vanished from us.
> Dan's Wife: I wish I didn't turn against him. I am thinking he might be
>   an angel.
> Dan: (*to* Malachi) Will he ever come back to us? (*TD,* 277)

Owing to Gregory's deftly unconventional adaptation of the tragicomic genre, moving from tragedy to comedy instead of vice versa, this scene functions not just as a crisis but as an alembic, suddenly transmuting the allegorical purport of the drama in a manner utterly consistent with its overall structure. In his compelling, uncertain existence, the King's Nurseling is, on Gregory's reading of history, the authentic Parnell, a figure of collective phantasmatic desire, at once insubstantial and more than substantial, a mere ghost and a true god. His ephemerality in afterlife answers to his having been generated in the first place out of the breath of the people, as an effect, necessarily comic, of their overheated discourse. But having survived the collective internecine self-betrayal of that discourse, the image of the Nurseling/Parnell is raised to the stature of a saving remnant. Whereas the biblical avatar of Parnell is in his stage life too insubstantial an agency, too thin a character, to fulfill the tragic role to which the action calls him, his afterimage acquires the gravity of defeat, of opportunity lost, and with it the power to confer that tragic stature upon the people themselves, who must abide the defeat and suffer the loss. In a sudden access of prophetic insight, the inherited tragic stature of the bondsman stands revealed: "Malachi: I won't tell you what I don't know. Wandering, wandering I see, through a score and through two score years . . . and no man will see the body is put in the grave. A strange thing to get the goal, the lad of the goal being dead" (*TD,* 277). The vision (hallucination/epiphany) of the Nurseling thus restores to the people the dignity they forfeited in forsaking their ideal in the first place, a restoration project that the play itself, constructed to showcase this final exaltation of the leader, serves to perform with regard to Parnell.

Unlike "The Phantom's Pilgrimage," *The Deliverer* beatifies both Parnell and Parnellism at the moment of their joint demise. At its worst, the gesture might be understood as mawkishly bewailing in death a movement for which Gregory had no use in its prime, perhaps for the purpose of accruing greater nationalist credibility in the eyes of an increasingly dominant and militant native middle-class audience. At best, the gesture might be understood as taking the semiautonomy of the political and cultural spheres to mean that even an entirely wrongheaded partisan campaign could harbor a spiritual or mythopoetic value as profound as it is unintended. But the articulation, in the final scene, of the renewed collective dignity of the subaltern group with their continued endurance of self-aggravated adversity and futility points to something deeper than unconscious opportunism, on the one hand, or the subtle reconciliation of political ambivalence, on the other. It suggests that the superficial unionism noted earlier in the play is but the outward sign of a structural fault line in the nationalism that Gregory came to espouse. Briefly put, in identifying her cardinal virtue of dignity with the individual and collective ability to bear with loss and withstand defeat, Gregory would seem to have devised a spiritual-cultural warrant for nationhood that is not just misaligned or incommensurable with the goal of political independence but even hostile to and preemptive of it. The preparatory work taken by Gregory's revivalism—the emancipatory justification it endeavors to supply—would seem to hold valid only insofar as the Irish continue to be denied independence and to be spiritually and culturally justified and sanctified by that denial.

Her sentimental portrait of the Irish revolutionary tradition "The Felons of Our Land" (1900) at once confirms and complicates this suspicion, particularly in light of the often overlooked properties that it shares with both her earlier and her later renditions of Parnell(-ism). After "Felons" appeared, Gregory declared that she would "never go that far . . . in anything I write again," and the main effect of her words has been to produce the critical misimpression that she went much further in the piece than she actually did. One salient internal limit that has gone ignored is precisely Gregory's signature strategy of rhetorical mediation, which creates a firewall whereby she can emotionally invest in a cause without actively promoting it. Lucy McDiarmid, for example, has denominated Gregory "the unofficial publicist of the Fenian tradition" on the basis of "Felons," which she likens to a Fenian "monument," in that it "systematizes and consolidates elements of Fenian culture." But whereas the monument in question, the Cork Memorial, enshrines the occasions (1798, 1803, 1848, and 1867) and the "righteous men" of a century-long revolutionary tradition, systematizing and consolidating their names and their memory, Gregory's essay remembers in reverential terms the occasions and the expressive bent of a century-long verse tradition, and verse tradition only, systematizing the ballads and lyrics, protagonists, and patriotic sentiments that compose it. While disclosing a profound attachment to a figure of the "treason-felon," she does not extol or even examine him directly; she certainly does not monumentalize him as she does the verse ("There is a redeeming intensity and continuity of purpose through even such doggerel verses as these; they are not without Dignity" ["F," 631]). She enlists herself as the unofficial publicist not of the Fenians themselves but of *their* unofficial publicists, the makers of their poetic monuments, and in this distinction between propaganda and folklore lies a world of difference. McDiarmid argues that "Felons" is in the business of "transferring terms of praise from political actions to poetry" such as "intensity," "continuity of purpose," and "dignity."[46] But in fact these "terms of praise" play rather conventionally in both the political and the poetic registers, and Gregory's decision to confine them to the latter is further evidence of her desire to concentrate value, and the reader's mind, on the cultural medium rather than its revolutionary object.

The opening sentence of the essay deliberately establishes an aesthetic rather than political focus: "For a century past, to go back no further, the song-writers of England have been singing of victory; the song-writers of Ireland only of defeat" ("F," 622). The first sentence of the following paragraph widens the frame of reference to include the people-nation at large, but remains firmly within a cultural arena, marking the essay as a work of political ethnography rather than political engagement: "It is not of conquerors or of victories our poets have writ-

ten and our people have sung . . . but of defeat and of prison and of death" ("F,"
622–23). Throughout the remainder of the article, Gregory adheres scrupulously
to the ethnographic protocols of participatory observation, positioning and
identifying herself as an amanuensis of demotic nationalism, an echo chamber
for its voice: "A Felon has come to me," "a chief ornament of many a cottage,"
"I have known the hillsides to blaze," "at little Catholic bookshops," "the ballads are written to keep in honour," "They have their stories so often told," "In
Ireland a peasant has always before his eyes" ("F," 622–34). Even when Gregory
delivers her own summary judgment on the phenomenon of rebel poetry, she
speaks from the position of its makers and consumers: "In Ireland [the poet] is in
touch with a people whose thoughts have long been dwelling on an idea; whose
heroes have been the failures, the men 'who went out to battle and who always
fell,' who went out to a battle that was already lost" ("F," 634). It is this cultural
bond forged through the expression of shared suffering that concerns Gregory,
rather than the specifically political solidarity forged in shared resistance.

Lady Gregory came from a family bent on converting the native Irish to
Protestantism, and although she forsook that project in her youth, its animating
impulse, missionary zeal, does indeed hang over her collation of revolutionary
verse in "Felons," accounting perhaps for its reception as a Fenian document.
Gregory's strategy of mediated commentary serves to frame the many ballads
quoted or reproduced in the essay as items of value worthy of cultural allegiance
in and for themselves, rather than as they were intended, as means for winning
allegiance to the armed struggle against the colonizer.

Certain of Gregory's best-known plays for the Irish National Theatre dramatized just this power of politically charged verbal artifacts to magnetize attention and mobilize passion to de-politicized ends. At the end of *The Gaol
Gate,* Mary Cahel celebrates her son's martyrdom not for any positive gain it
might yield his fellow moonlighters in the campaign they served, nor even for
the freedom it secured his comrades, but rather for the honor it wins him, the
infamy it correspondingly spares him, and, in particular, for the lofty place he
will assume in ballads, popular histories, and local anecdotes, which Mary is
already giving a Christological turn: "I will call the people and the singers at
the fair to make a great praise for Denis. . . . I will never be tired with praising
. . . til we'll shout it through the roads, Denis Cahel died for his neighbor." In
The Rising of the Moon, one year later, a notorious rebel leader wins a policeman's leave to escape not by persuading him to sedition, though he tries, but
by singing him the ballad of the title and thereby playing on his nostalgic attachment to the communal associations of tune and lyric. In neither play do
the characters conceive a new appreciation of advanced nationalism, owing to
their engagement with revolutionary song and story. Quite the contrary. As the
last line of *The Gaol Gate* denotes, Mary Cahel envisages an ethnoreligious, not

a political, line of testimonials for her son, while the policeman in *The Rising of the Moon* wonders, "Am I as great a fool as I think I am?" after the strains of the ballad and the man who sung it have vanished.[47] The playwright, it would seem, construes that the power of this popular discourse to instill or heighten feelings of group solidarity exists in inverse ratio to its weak, strictly political instrumentality.

But it is on just this point that the substance of Gregory's argument in "The Felons" most perfectly answers its rhetorical method. As the cited passages above indicate, the aspect of popular rebel verse that Gregory dwells upon longest and venerates most is its passionate embrace of "defeat, prison, and death," which is to say its sanctification of Irish revolutionary praxis at its most instrumentally challenged. But make no mistake—this verse does not to Gregory's mind mourn the ineffectuality of Fenian-style insurrectionism, from the '98 to the present, so much as it discovers redemptive virtue in the dogged Fenian commitment to an apparently unwinnable cause: the heroic selflessness required, the chivalric idealism exhibited, the collective nobility modeled. Even as popular metropolitan periodicals like *Punch* and *Tomahawk* singled out the Fenian for simianization, glossing physical force itself as a metonym of Irish beastiality, this colonial counterdiscourse, on Gregory's reading, singles out the "treason-felon" as an emblem of a uniquely Irish spirituality, an ethnically specific capacity for devotion to an idea.

On the one hand, Gregory projects onto this literary tradition a rather more politicized version of the aim that she pursues in such plays as *The Deliverer* and *The Gaol Gate:* to identify Irish dignity as resurgent in the failed attempt at national liberation, for which that dignity and hence that failure stand as a recursive moral warrant. Perhaps that is why this is the one topic upon which she feels free to infringe ethnographic protocol and inject her own value judgment directly: "The song-writer, the poet, would find a better mission were he to tell of the meaning of failure, of the gain that may lie in the wake of a lost battle" ("F," 622). On the other hand, she draws from this tradition the means of extending the reach of cultural nationalism even further than her own plays do. In the "better mission" of sanctifying defeat, the verse tradition not only kindles its own desires, loyalties, and sense of community at some remove from the physical force resistance it celebrates; it also recenters the very import of that resistance in a more aesthetic and moral register. That is to say, the poetic lineage constructed in "Felons of Our Land" subtly alters the relation of cultural to political nationalism in terms favorable to Gregory's own robust definition of the former. Instead of cultural discourse doing the preparatory work for independence, articulating or dramatizing the moral claims that political action will look to sustain by less savory tactics of aggression (Parnellism) or force of arms (Fenianism), doomed insurgency is seen to do the still more preparatory work of providing the poets and songwriters the occasion to lodge that claim in the first place: a fatal, foreseeably unrequited, and so spiritually pure nationalist sacrifice. Here cultural nationalism appropriates not just the ambient energies but the very agenda of its political counterpart to its own differently proportioned objectives. It internalizes and sublimates the futility of repeated trauma into the dignity of tragic ritual. On this score, Gregory's reading anticipates Patrick Pearse's well-known elaboration of blood sacrifice in something like reverse order. She aestheticizes Fenianism as a cultural defense *against* its politics; he will aestheticize Fenianism as a cultural defense *of* its politics.

We have now arrived at a place where what I have called the "exceptionality" of Parnell in Lady Gregory's early ideological imagination can be fully elucidated. Gregory first came to the figure of the "treason-felon" by way of a demotic poetry that she, given her Anglo-Irish background, was especially liable to read in Celticist terms, that is, as consecrating the spiritual wages of agonistic futility. As a result, she understood Fenianism as a movement whose potentially terrifying violence was paradoxically always already under a certain control, was in fact but the initial phase of a cycle of collective sublimation that dignified the native while leaving Ascendancy interests relatively secure. This sort of "cultural Fenianism" managed, accordingly, to square the vicious circle of Gregory's competing nationalist and unionist sympathies.

The same could not, of course, be said of Parnellism, which Gregory first encountered as a living force rather than a literary phenomenon. Parnell's Irish Party organized the National League with the sole aim of achieving material success, in the form of both political devolution and, still more baleful for Gregory's class interests, land transfer and appropriation. It was less the official means of Parnell-like agitation—boycotting, obstruction, rent strikes—than their *utter disregard for the consolations of defeat* that prompted Gregory to see Home Rulers as more "vulgar and virulent" than their harder-line compatriots. Here, then, we have the origins of one side of her paradoxical attitude toward Parnell and his movement. On the other side, with the demise of Parnell, both political and physical, his legend not only grew in stature but became more palpably literary and, in the process, took on the tragic dimensions of an honorable though unavailing, or honorable *because* unavailing, martyrdom. Parnell himself shifted from the historical arena of realpolitik, however mythologized, to the aesthetic arena of ritual tragedy, attached, in Gregory's eyes, to the distinctively Irish cult of sanctified ruin. It was on these grounds that she came to include Parnell in the honor roll of poetically feted rebels in "Felons" and then to identify him, in an allegorical abuse of history, with revolutionary violence in *The Deliverer*. This (mis)appropriation of Parnell to the Fenian party is of crucial importance for our understanding of Gregory's developing ideological position, for it indicates that the dynamic of sublimation, whereby she sought to compose her diverse overlapping conflicts (unionism/nationalism, cultural/political nationalism, Parnell/Parnellism), proceeded in two directions simultaneously, or, to put it another way, constituted a true *discordia concours.*

The image of "Ireland militant, bound, dependent, male," writes Lucy McDiarmid, "is the source and grounding of Gregory's imagination," because it appeals to her maternal solicitude and because it empowers her specifically as a woman writer.[48] Without disputing this canny appraisal, our analysis suggests that the Prometheus-as–political prisoner trope inspired Gregory because it encapsulated the peculiar tensions informing her complex ideal of Irish patriotism. If the Irish people were to obtain the dignity consistent with Gregory's "Ascendancy code" and, collaterally, her Ascendancy interests, then the hypermasculine belligerence and savagery of "militant Ireland" needed to be constrained by the practical discipline of defeat in battle and the moral discipline of a literary tradition valorizing that defeat as the crucible of a higher good. Gregory's "treasonfelon," that is to say, must always exemplify the political version of a chivalric *ascesis,* a submission to the purifying frustration of desire or will on behalf of a "mere" ideal. They must be not only "male," in the most ferocious sense of that term, they must also, and for that very reason, be "bound." Conversely, however, if the poetic cult of defeat that Gregory favors in "Felons" is not to be a passive, supine failure of energetic nationalism but a spiritually uplifting nationalism of energetic failure, then the cult requires a savage "physical force" to discipline in the first place. By the same token, insofar as Gregory's "Ascendancy code" of dignity presupposed the operation of disciplinary constraint, it not only envisaged some unruly passion to be constrained but also pegged the moral splendor of the dignity achieved to the strength of the passion effectively and graciously regulated. Gregory's "treason-felons," accordingly, must be "bound" within the disciplinary hoops we have described, while remaining decidedly and forcefully "male." On this symbolic logic, we can see why the decision to enroll Parnell in the canon of patriot-martyrs inclined, if it did not compel Gregory to affiliate him with the Fenian party.

The symbolic logic in question is that of manliness. This is only to be expected. The Ascendancy code of dignity that Gregory so prized was largely fashioned within and imported from British public school culture, where manliness served as the ethical grounds for both male and metropolitan hegemony. Moreover, the double bind that the manly ideal imposed upon the (Irish) subaltern, for the purpose of making morally legitimate resistance impossible, maps uncannily onto Gregory's metrocolonial psychomachia—the clash of her landed and national allegiances—which she seems to resolve by morally legitimating Irish resistance as practically speaking impossible. That agenda, the strategic heart of "Felons" and *The Deliverer,* amounts to an ideological deployment of the manly logic of sublimation in both the form of patriotic resistance Gregory comes to approve and the discursive mechanism whereby she expresses her approval. That is to say, the same common, now familiar dynamic of strong passions, strongly checked, characterizes not only Gregory's idealized Irish martyr, whose revolutionary force is tempered by the sanctified futility of his quest, but also, and more important, the dialectic of political and cultural nationalism that propagates this sainted figure. On Gregory's account, Irish cultural nationalism, whether in the form of popular balladry or her own revivalist drama, subjects in advance the violent passions of political and especially revolutionary nationalism to the possibility of a sublimating restraint, by locating its essence and its telos in the spiritual discipline of repeated striving and defeat, the ritual glorification of which in turn constitutes a crucial ingredient of the cultural nationalist program. At the same time, this doubly articulated cultural discipline is itself grounded in the supposition of violent political passion (patriotism, tribal solidarity, love of country or freedom, and so on) that, overriding all prudential considerations, sustains an enthusiasm for the *ascesis* of "the battle already lost." Harnessed to Gregory's "better mission," this enthusiasm in turn infuses the literature in question with the patriotic fervor and the political charge that it both carries and contains.

Thus, at the textual level, the *discordia concours* of manliness can be seen to provide the ideological currency necessary for the conversion of treason-felon into martyr-incorruptible. At the systemic level, given its historical saliency and specific relevance to Gregory's project, manliness can be seen to provide the very template of her revivalist dialectic: just as animal spirits fuel and empower the manly moral exertion that curbs and controls their hyperaggressive force, so a "virulent" Irish political nationalism energizes a literary culture that tames its savage potential in hallowed images and narratives of its chivalric self-immolation. Finally, at the theoretical level, the impacted dialectic of manliness, its transcendence of the male-identified properties that continue to ground it, provides a model of the vanishing symbolic mediation whereby cultural nationalism tends to subsume, precisely in joining forces with, political nationalism.

As befits this female architect of revivalist manhood, the *discordia concours* defining her patriotic ideal and her ideological method comes together most powerfully in a drama, *Cathleen Ni Houlihan,* which draws upon the ancient Gaelic myth of a woman defining male sovereignty.

3

The Mother of All Sovereignty

More than just contributing some dialogue to Yeats's blockbuster *Cathleen Ni Houlihan,* more than collaborating in its construction, Augusta Gregory did the lion's share of its composition and deserves at the very least to be acknowledged as coauthor. Such is the gathering critical consensus on the true creative source of this Revivalist landmark. With the words "all mine alone," scrawled on the first draft, Gregory herself laid claim to everything in the play up to and including the entrance of the Poor Old Woman. If her proprietary note is true, and Yeats all but conceded as much, then it is nearly impossible, as Nicholas Grene remarks, to attribute the dramatic intercourse between the Old Woman and the Gillane family to anyone other than Gregory.[1] Yeats probably wrote some of Cathleen's declamatory set pieces, but the defining elements of the play—its dialogue, action, and political impetus—now seem to belong primarily to Lady Gregory.

Our own reading of Gregory to this point adds substantive evidence to this largely circumstantial brief. It indicates that *Cathleen* is strikingly consistent with Gregory's other treatments of revolutionary martyrdom. In the political register, *Cathleen* helped to resuscitate and popularize the Fenian cult of blood sacrifice, which had taken hold after the 1803 rising of Robert Emmet, and it set the terms for the more considered self-martyrdom of Easter week 1916. In the cultural register, Gregory helped to revivify and popularize the ancient Gaelic myth of Sovereignty. Her recovery project not only instituted a signature Revivalist genre, the Sovereignty play (for example, Gonne's *Dawn*, Robinson's *Patriots,* and especially Pearse's *Singer*), but also lent blood sacrifice the dignity of a precolonial origin at once native and noble, aboriginal and aristocratic.[2]

Paradoxically, however, the crucial element mediating these cultural and political registers was that pervasive colonial import, the manly ideal, which acted to transform a myth of succession into a dramatic spectacle of self-sacrifice. As we shall see, moreover, the ideal in this case takes a peculiarly chivalric cast or complexion that encodes a largely unrecognized (and unconscious) filiation of the Irish Literary Revival to its unabashedly imperialist counterpart in late Victorian England, the "Medieval Revival."[3]

The Sovereignty Myth

According to the Gaelic myth of Sovereignty, any candidate for kingship accedes to the crown by way of a mating ritual in which the Sovereign Hag (Erin, the Poor Old Woman, the Shan Van Vocht, the Cailleach Beare, Cathleen) attempts to seduce or accost him and, then, upon sexual consummation, undergoes a metamorphosis into a beautiful young woman. The Hag is not just synonymous, as Liz Cullingford has argued, with the land of Ireland; the Sovereignty myth, that is, is not just a fertility myth. The Hag, rather, signifies the property of legitimate national authority, and she specifically identifies herself as such in the most famous version of the myth, the elevation of Niall of the Nine Hostages: "and who art thou, he pursued / royal rule am I, she answered."[4] This symbolic value takes hold in the contour of the narrative itself. The Hag's sexual aggressiveness is tantamount in the political domain to a right of nomination, and hence to a substantive measure of autonomy and agency, while the potential king is limited to the more passive rite of acceptance or refusal, of authorizing her choice or failing to do so.

There has been considerable debate over whether the priority the Hag enjoys, or the proactivity she displays, in this ritual "correlates with the relatively favorable legal status of pre-conquest women."[5] Without determining that vexed issue, we can say that this piece of the mythic Imaginary does suggest the patriarchal rule that somehow exists without an originary division into dominant and recessive gender polarities. It is perhaps significant that the shift from Irish Brehon law (which the conquerors viewed as the epitome of native backwardness) to British common law had as one of its more conspicuous effects a deterioration in the status of espoused women from joint stockholders in the marital estate to the virtual chattel of their husbands. The imperialistic appropriation and oppression of Ireland, famously structured along gender lines, brought along a modern form of gender oppression, structured along colonizing, appropriative lines.

The Sovereignty mythos, accordingly, offered contemporary literary nationalists an opportunity to contest not just the colonial application but the colonizing structure of the modern bourgeois gender system, and to identify its ills with the British occupation, as they regularly did with any number of other social problems. But in Yeats and Gregory's *Cathleen Ni Houlihan,* and in the Sovereignty dramas that followed it, literary nationalists chose instead to remodel the myth in a manner that served to reinforce the prevailing gender system. In their particular strategy for doing so, one can clearly discern the effect of the internalized double bind of manhood: the desire, on one side, to avert the more obvious threat of feminization and, on the other, the care to sublate (cancel and preserve) any compensatory hypermasculinity in order to avert the stigma of simianization.

The Sovereignty Drama

As Robert Welch astutely observes, the Sovereignty play not only "enacted a scene of translation"—the Old Woman become young girl—but also "accomplished an act of translation, whereby the emblems and figures out of the Irish cultural memory were carried over into the twentieth century and given renewed life and shocking relevance." But like many acts of Revivalist translation, the Sovereignty play came to be distinguished not only by its rehearsal of the source material but also by the decisive revisions it introduced into that material. In the case of the Yeats and Gregory play, the lusty persona of the Cailleach Beare is changed into a desexualized mother/maiden figure. As Cathleen catalogs the heroes who have died in her name, she makes a special, almost inordinate, point of declaring, "With all the lovers who brought me their love, I never set out the bed for any."[6] In Patrick Pearse's *Singer*, Maire is listed simply as "Mother of MacDara," the title character and revolutionary protagonist, and she is explicitly linked to "Mary, mother of us all," her virginal prototype. Maire shares her sovereignty status with her adoptive daughter and MacDara's prospective sweetheart, the preternaturally innocent Sighle. In *Dawn*, Maud Gonne likewise distributes the Sovereignty function between a mother and a daughter who is also a mother, and here, too, no biological father is in evidence or evidently missed.

Correspondingly, in these plays, the heroic self-immolation of blood sacrifice replaces the act of sexual congress as a means of attaining Sovereignty and inducing the Old Woman's transformation. As Cullingford points out, "Although the Old Woman is metamorphosed into a springtime bride, it is the shedding of male blood, not the emission of male semen that accomplishes the miracle."[7] What's more, blood does not function as a metaphor for male semen, as it clearly does in Joseph Plunkett's famous aisling poem, "The Little Black Rose":

> when at last the blood
> O'erleaps the final barrier to find
> Only one source wherein to spend its strength
> And we two lovers
> . . . are made one flesh at length."[8]

On the contrary, in the Sovereignty drama, male blood substitutes for the sexual substance in a preemption of the sexual function. Indeed, both *Cathleen* and *The Singer* lay particular stress upon this exclusionary dynamic by having the commitment to blood sacrifice directly interrupt or preclude a prospective marital commitment. In *Cathleen,* the Shan Van Vocht intrudes upon the wedding preparations of Michael Gillane and Delia Cahel to solicit assistance in recovering her "four beautiful green fields" from " the stranger." Michael's willingness to undergo death as an expression of devotion to Cathleen thus proves an elegant way of excluding any sexual relation whatever.[9] And it is Michael's simultaneous and indissociable decisions to break off his marital engagement and to pursue a fatal engagement with Erin's enemies that catalyzes Erin's final transformation. As for *The Singer,* MacDara commits himself to perish in hopeless battle against the British and, in the very same moment, renounces the desire to kiss Sighle even once as a way of sealing their long-deferred love affair. The prospect of the battle, in turn, rejuvenates MacDara's worn-out mother, the Sovereignty figure, who announces that her son "has quickened the dead years and all the quiet dust" with his blood.[10] The mother's speech thereby links the fertility motif to the captivity motif, the resuscitation of the land to the reappropriation of sovereignty, while implicitly locating her son's fertility-god status in his refusal of sexuality itself.

Now the feminine agency originally attaching to the Sovereignty myth constituted a specifically *sexual* agency, and it was this agency, indissolubly bound as it was to a legitimating right of election, that might have posed a symbolic challenge to the gendered hierarchies governing modern political arrangements, colonialism in particular. Accordingly, the first aspect of the Revivalist revision, the desexualization of the Poor Old Woman, works to transfer primary moral authority for the ritual transformation to the male protagonist.[11] In the modern Sovereignty play, the Hag is less of a kingmaker and more of a supplicant. As Lionel Polkington has noted, even as the Sovereignty play came to portray revolution as a matter of "individual volition," the mythic emblem of collective power, the Hag is made to forfeit the capacity "to act on her own behalf."[12] In this regard, the modern Hag might seem to recall not her Gaelic original so much as its Norman transcription, the much invoked "Roisin Dubh," or its postascendancy heir, the Spéirbhean of aisling verse, both of whom reflect the learned helplessness of colonial enthrallment in the passivity with which they abide the remote prospect of their deliverance. Unlike those figures, however, the modern Hag depends not upon a foreign adventurer, like the Jacobite prince, "coming over" the sea, but upon a native courtier "stepping up" in an act of valorous self-negation that is also an act of manly self-conquest. The overall effect of the genre, accordingly, is to assert Irish masculinity at the cost of a certain Oedipal identification with the conqueror, or, to put it another way, to disavow the stigma of racial feminization at the cost of forgoing a critique of the patri-archal brand of colonialism that produced it.[13]

This effect becomes clearer once we take the second part of the Revivalist revi-sion into consideration. More than a concession to the puritanical Catholicism of the imagined audience, the foregrounded substitution of blood sacrifice for restorative sexual intercourse frames nationalist allegiance as a form of chivalric pledge, an expression of fealty and devotion to an Ireland envisaged as a spotless maiden/mother icon, and hence as a variant on the "courtly lady" of medieval romance: imperious, enchanting, inviolate—not someone to lay down *with,* but to lay down one's life *for.* Cathleen claims the title in reciting an honor roll of aristocratic rebels who "died for love of me" (*C,* 8) and accepted a grave in lieu of the bed she refused them. It is perhaps going too far to view her as la belle dame sans merci, since the knights do "think themselves well paid" in the end, but she clearly boasts a kindred literary and cultural provenance.[14]

By the same token, Cathleen's account tends to cast her elect, structurally speak-ing, as *chevalier servanti,* who fight and die, fight *to* die, on behalf of a wrongly dispossessed "damsel in distress." In elevating Cathleen as a sexually untouchable object of romantic veneration, Yeats and Gregory predicate the metamorphosis of Erin (Woman/Nation) upon the impeccably chivalric performance of her courtier ("he must give me himself, he must give me all" [*C,* 8]) no less than the nationalist zeal it signifies. Here again, the contrast between the Sovereignty drama and the loosely related aisling verse proves instructive. In the aisling, the Spéirbhean and her suitor alike represent a native Irish political agency that has been nullified by colonial occupation, and so they must look to external aid for the consummation of their allegorical romance. In the Sovereignty drama, however, the Shan Van Vocht and her courtiers combine to represent a colonial dilemma in which na-tive political agency may be generated or recovered through a practice of heroic self-nullification, a practice that precludes any romantic consummation, even as it represents a type of "blood wedding."

The doubly articulated nexus of self-denial endemic to the Sovereignty drama gave the genre a correspondingly dual appeal for Patrick Pearse. The diegetic format adumbrated, in a glamorous light, the very sort of martyrological strat-egy that Pearse dreamed of implementing as a myth come true. Thus, by simply following the formula laid down by *Cathleen,* a play he much admired, Pearse was able to compose *The Singer* in late 1915 as a virtual prospectus for the Eas-ter Rising and a herald of the totemic leadership he would provide. But the Sovereignty drama's mediation of the ultimate sacrificial display through an ennobling crisis of heterosexual romance proved a still more propitious feature of the genre for Pearse, on strictly personal grounds. According to Séan Moran, Pearse had written plays of heterosexual passion in his youth, but left off in adolescence so as to avoid the necessity of "facing his own instinctual drives," specifically his suppressed affectional preference for boys, a longing disparaged in Irish society as the essence of unmanliness.[15] Given, however, the persistent and persistently self-closeted character of this pedo-homoeroticism, and given the manifold religious, political, and personal anxieties Pearse must have suffered on that account, it is extraordinarily telling that when he finally came to craft his own Sovereignty drama, he was able to return to the theme of sexual desire and attraction, and even to place them in an unmistakably autobiographical context. Such, I would submit, was the sense of security he derived from the comparatively rigid and therefore impersonalizing conventions of the genre.

Pearse not only communicated his own sexual propensities to his protagonist, MacDara, but also took the arguably riskier step of attaching them to the same sort of pedagogical interchange that had stirred his own libidinal energies as the headmaster of St. Enda's. While in exile from his role as a revolutionary firebrand, MacDara enlists as a tutor and forges such a strong bond with his boy student as to rival the boy's love for his mother and arouse her jealousy. The scenario represents an allegorical translation of a conflict between an Oedipalized homo- and heterosexual object choice. That MacDara has internalized this conflict himself becomes evident in his narration of his year in the wilderness. Describing his struggle to esteem worldly beauty aright, he tells his elder Maoilsheachlainn that when he "stopped to look at the white limbs of some beautiful child," he would wish to "blind" his eyes against the temptation of "an unholy thing," keeping himself "cold and chaste as the top of a high mountain" (*S*, 26–27). But now he has returned home to find himself corrected by the beauty of Sighle, which "must be holy" (*S*, 27). Of course, MacDara's return to Sighle and hence his resolution of the unadmitted sexual conflict is programmed into the very form of the Sovereignty drama, which makes that drama an ideal mechanism of Freudian disavowal. Pearse can encode a confrontation with his own sexual ambivalence, can even allow the resulting homoerotic undercurrents to swirl about his alter ego—for his chosen dramatic format ultimately requires a marriage plot and thus a naturalized expression of cross-sex desire. That is to say, the generic formula of the Sovereignty drama makes a perfect "beard": it dissimulates the sexual ambivalence informing Pearse/MacDara's history while ensuring against any sense of inauthenticity in the dissimulation.

But there remains one further twist of the screw. MacDara returns to Sighle not in pursuit of romantic or sexual fulfillment but in compliance with a generic imperative to romantic and sexual *renunciation*. Against the background of his previously intimated homoerotic stirrings, MacDara's relinquishing of connubial love, highlighted by his declining a last (and only) kiss, cannot but smack of an evasion or refusal of normative heterosexual destiny. Although undertaken in the name of Mother Ireland, a heterosexual and reproductive ideal of the nation, MacDara's particular act of resistance to both elements of this ideal bears an import that outstrips the generic guidelines approving the act itself. That is to say, his chivalric *ascesis* manages to contain (in every sense) elements of a taboo sexual difference, if not dissidence. By the same token, because his evasion of heteronormativity, highlighted by that refused last kiss, unfolds according to the approved chivalric protocols, it presents itself as manly self-sacrifice and the fitness for freedom so denoted, the very things it would otherwise be taken to betray and dishonor. By the end of *The Singer,* MacDara's *sexual* resistance merges all but seamlessly with a socially conservative movement of *national* resistance that would vigorously reprehend it. Or, to put it another way, Pearse uses the Sovereignty formula to square the circle of his unadmitted sexual desires and his proud but incompatible moral and political beliefs. Thus, Pearse's ultimate rendition of blood sacrifice makes for arguably the most erotically charged scene in the play: MacDara envisions himself "hung naked" before the enemy soldiers and ecstatically strips off his clothes to meet them. At this point, his homosexual energies receive not just a species of deniability or "cover" but a kind of sanction from the political agenda they have been regulated to serve.

Even as the reconstruction of the Sovereignty Hag as a paragon of feminine virtue can act to disguise the desublimation of her warriors' illicit homoerotic affections, it corresponds with a rigorous sublimation of the masculine violence to which those warriors have committed themselves. As Mark Girouard observes in *The Return to Camelot,* medieval chivalry evolved as "a warrior code that accepted fighting as a necessary and indeed glorious activity, but set out to soften potential barbarity" by subjecting it to the "high standards" associated with the ethical and romantic ideals of the aristocracy.[16] In thus permitting the discharge of brute animal force within a disciplinary regime of honor and propriety, the chivalric ethos stood as both a prototype and a variant of Victorian manliness, whose shaping logic, strong passions strongly checked, it roundly approximates. Operating in the context of Irish nationalism, the identification of blood sacrifice with chivalric heroism promised to square the double bind of (colonial) manliness. On one side, blood sacrifice could be seen to exemplify the traditional warrior values of courage, valor, resiliency, and duty, and hence to constitute a refusal of racial feminization. On the other, construed as a romantic, quasi-religious mode of bodily self-overcoming and transcendence, blood sacrifice provides a fully martial alternative to and stay against hypermasculine ferocity, belying the charges of racialized bestiality or simianization.[17] Understood in this light, blood sacrifice brings to perfection the convergence of chivalric idealism and the manly norm. Directing aggression inward in the service of Woman/Nation, the practice offers a summary instantiation of the philosophy at work in the famous dictums of Kingsley and Hughes:

A man's prerogative is to be bold against himself.[18]

So far as I know the least of the muscular Christians has heard of the old chivalrous and Christian belief that a man's body is given him to be trained and brought into subjection, and then used for the protection of the weak.[19]

Now for a man to spill his life's blood, not as a contingency but by design, and to do so in the service of not just an old woman or a young maid but a figure who is alternately one or the other, could not that be seen, from a certain angle, as taking the injunction "to be bold against himself" in "the protection of the weak" to an unprecedented extreme? Could it not be seen as attaining to a new perfection of the manly ideal?

Blood sacrifice could indeed bear such an import. But to do so, it had to carry forth a symbolic logic at once irreducible to the instrumentalism of political action yet somehow productive of corollary effects, cultural or spiritual, that could be seen to influence, enhance, or override such action. Fixed within the domain of "ordinary politics," blood sacrifice could only enact a principled defeatism that was no less defeatist for being principled. The construction of a Sovereignty play like *Cathleen Ni Houlihan* evinces as much. Written between the passage of the Local Government Act and Wyndham's Land Act, *Cathleen* self-consciously reflects, and reflects upon, the contemporary socioeconomic conditions of agrarian Ireland.[20] Bridget Gillane's comment that her younger son Patrick will have "no place of his own" indicates that the inheritance rules in Ireland have altered from subdivision to primogeniture (*C,* 5). The expectation Bridget's husband, Peter, nurtures of acquiring another ten acres upon the death of Dempsey speaks to the decline in sharecropping and the rise of peasant proprietorship in the wake of Parnell's leadership. Finally, the conflation of romantic alliance with financial arrangement in the nuptials of Michael and Delia points to the recent consolidation of the "familialist" social regime. But in heeding Cathleen's summons to death and glory at play's end, Michael goes off to enlist in the Rising of '98, which had, of course, long since passed into the annals of Irish failure. That is to say, Michael does more than simply emulate those heroes Cathleen sings of, more than replace them, more than reincarnate them; he marches back in time, past the more recent debacles of 1847 and 1867, and *joins* them. What *Cathleen Ni Houlilan* stages, accordingly, is something other than a repetitive view of history, wherein each rising might be thought to reproduce and build upon the last; it offers something other, too, than a displacement of the logic of historic development by the logic of mythic recurrence, wherein each rising and the splendid sacrifice it entails is of a piece with the others, a continuing testament to the essential principles of Irish nationhood on an "eternal plane."[21] In conjuring so overtly with historical specifics and then just as conspicuously setting them out of joint, Gregory and Yeats stage an audacious rhetorical anachronism: an exhortation of Michael and, by extension, the audience to rally behind a cause *already defunct.* The climactic maneuver is perfectly calibrated to register Gregory's characteristic sentiment that nothing sanctifies Irish physical force like the edifying inevitability of its disappointment. The object of that sanctification is the collective spirit, the expression of which resides in the symbolic-cultural arena. For Gregory and

Yeats, in particular, the politically enabling and the culturally ennobling stood at odds, at least in Ireland.[22]

Their play *Cathleen Ni Houlihan* is often taken to invoke, in proper Revivalist mode, a long-established, characteristically Irish tradition of noble failure, manifest in the lineage of martyrdom already adduced. But if the cult of martyrdom indexed a history of failure for revolutionary nationalism, it nonetheless embraced the idea of an ultimate triumph (both in principle and as a practical goal) for which martyrdom itself was a fractional substitute, a means of asserting indomitability under the yoke of domination. It was, rather, the Revivalists themselves who bestowed upon the bearing of defeat a surplus value for the culture defeated, the Revivalists who turned the already lost cause into a kind of ethnospiritual legacy. If there is a tradition at work here, it is what Eric Hobsbawm designates an *invented tradition,* one of the many improvised inheritances springing up, to various ideological ends, out of the rapid, deeply felt deracinations of late imperialism.[23] In their modern combination, the Myth of Sovereignty and the cult of blood sacrifice constitute another such invented tradition, a virilizing correlative of the first. A play like *Cathleen Ni Houlihan* not only stages in laudatory terms the spiritually uplifting embrace of an inevitable military and operational defeat, it "freeze-frames" the closing action at the moment the heroic gesture to die defending Erin is undertaken, thereby eternalizing the jouissance of spiritual uplift and eternally deferring the disabling political consequences of the defeat itself. The Old Woman's last words, as Michael goes marching off, reinforce this strategy from inside the frame: "They shall be speaking forever / The people shall hear them forever" (*C,* 10).

The same dramatic strategy of freeze-framing also functions to identify the manliness displayed in the doomed revolutionary gesture with the spiritual uplift that it produces. In this way, the play counters with a sublimated vision of masculine vigor and courage the more feminized implications of the Arnoldian sense of Irish destiny that it projects: "They always went forth, but they always fell." It is only Irish manliness, self-conquest in the defense of the downtrodden, that could effect Cathleen's glorious translation, even if that translation indexes not material success to come but the ethnospiritual perfection already wrought in the embrace of the long-lost cause. No less than its reversible form, no less than its doubly inscribed historical milieu, the political meaning of Cathleen's metamorphosis partakes of the logic of an anachronism.

The same embrace occurs, all but literally, in the climactic finale to *The Singer,* and with much the same ideological complexity. The mutually renovative effects of blood sacrifice are set in countervailing juxtaposition to the doubtful material-political consequences of the practice, while the juxtaposition itself—violence as resistance versus violence as *ascesis*—aims to slip or controvert the double bind pathologizing Irish nationalist masculinity. Taken in the context of Pearse's and Gregory's longer careers, however, the two texts may be seen to traverse this double bind in reverse order. Whereas Gregory deployed the sovereignty format to introduce a strenuous if already sublimated masculine assertiveness into her earlier profile of Irish self-immolation, "The Felons of Our Land," Pearse used the format to modulate a sometimes sanguinary, hypermasculine articulation of Irish nationalism in a more resolutely disciplined self-constraining direction.

As Susan Cannon Harris remarks, Pearse enjoys a reputation for "blood thirstiness" on account of certain political speeches and writings in the years leading up to the Easter Rising.[24] The most notorious of these seems to link the property of manhood directly with the capacity and enthusiasm for armed violence:

1. "I hold that before we do any work, any *men's* work, we must first realize ourselves as men. . . . For we suffer things that men do not suffer and we seek to redress grievances by means which men do not employ. We have, for instance, allowed ourselves to be disarmed."

2. "Men who have ceased to be men cannot claim the rights of men, and men who have suffered themselves to be deprived of their manhood have suffered the greatest of all indignities and deserved the most shameful of penalties. . . . In allowing ourselves to be disarmed, in acquiescing in a perpetual disarmament . . . we in effect abnegate our manhood. Unable to exercise men's rights we do not deserve men's privileges. We are, in a strict sense, not fit for freedom."

3. ". . . Bloodshed is a cleansing and a sanctifying thing, and the nation which regards it as the final horror has lost its manhood. There are many things more horrible than bloodshed; and slavery is one of them."[25]

But Pearse's statements are never, as J. J. Lee points out, quite so categorical in their bloodlust as they first appear.[26] Even in Pearse's most truculent promotion of Irish hypermasculinity, there lurks an awareness of and attachment to the moralized Victorian norms of manly self-possession, which blood sacrifice looked to reclaim. The loss of manhood, for Pearse, ultimately centered not on the loss of arms, or even the loss of freedom, but on a willingness to abide "slavery," a heteronomy so profound as to be internalized. If in "suffering [themselves] to be disarmed, in acquiescing in [their] perpetual disarmament," the Irish have "abnegate[d]" their "manhood," that manhood can nonetheless be understood to consist not in the courage of armed conviction per se but in the spirit of self-determination that it signifies. Pearse makes this equation quite explicit in the second declaration: "Unable to exercise men's rights," we are "not fit for freedom." In identifying manhood with a fitness for freedom, Pearse aligns himself with the quasi-official discourse of manliness, at least at the level of slogan. But more than that, he implicitly reduces his beloved force of arms to a material-political means for vindicating the manly estate, rather than a direct expression of the manly estate, which itself continues to inhabit a distinctly symbolic-spiritual dimension.

On this conception—as an underdetermined, and hence always contestable, fitness for freedom—Pearse's "manhood" participated in an allegorical-depth model structurally congruent with the strategy of blood sacrifice that he increasingly espouses. *That is to say, the inner reality of manhood could not be deduced, nor its possession established, from the ordinary external indices of virility, just as the underlying spiritual import of the Sovereignty quest could not be reckoned by the ordinary calculations of military advantage or material-political benefit.* It is no accident that Pearse interfuses these respective allegories, the gender and the national, all but indistinguishably in order to generate the considerable rhetorical power of the finale to *The Singer*. MacDara declares, "I will talk to you more strangely yet. . . . [T]he battle is won whether you go or not. . . . The fifteen were too many. . . . You should have kept all back but one. One man can free a people as one Man redeemed the world. . . . I will go into battle with bare hands. I will stand up before the Gall as Christ hung naked before men on the Tree" (*S*, 43). Here, at this late moment in his literary avocation, after so many proclamations extolling "the sword" and linking the recovery of Irish manhood with a call to arms, Pearse comes to define the manhood animating the highest forms of armed nationalism as, if not separate from the resources of aggression, then at least sublating (canceling, preserving, uplifting) the use of those resources. MacDara's signature (speech) act frames national deliverance not as the *imposition* of masculine will but as the *exposition* of manly character. To actualize this manly force of character, MacDara proposes, one must first strip away the elements of hypermasculine force—from the concerted ranks of the soldiers to the engines of warfare they deploy. One must stand "naked," revealing an inner strength accentuated by outer deprivation. At the same time, of course, MacDara's speech functions in the mode of recruitment, enjoining his fellows to "rise" along the lines of physical force, their hypermasculine démarche now ideologically sheltered by his manly sacrifice.

As the quoted passage makes clear, Pearse ultimately held up the crucified Christ not just as the archetype of blood sacrifice, with all of the liturgical overtones of sacred blood at work, but as an exemplar of the inward manliness the act required. His figural itinerary in this respect strikingly paralleled that of Thomas Hughes, who likewise counterbalanced his own rather combative pattern of manhood in *Tom Brown's Schooldays* with a celebration of the Savior's paradigmatically self-restraining, self-conquering virtue in *The Manliness of Christ*. Indeed, MacDara's climactic performance, wherein moral and gender self-fashionings fuse around the idea of stalwart Christological valor, comes right out of Hughes's argument in *Manliness*.[27] Among other things, the very existence of this direct link speaks to the politically incorrect, not to say inimical, sources of Pearse's sacrificial ethos.

The heavily Roman Catholic iconography pervading Pearse's rhetoric has helped to camouflage the extent of his indebtedness to a peculiarly English Protestantism for his conception of Christ as an emblem or ideal of masculinity. Through much of the Victorian era, middle-class Anglican culture entertained a robust Medieval Revival, extending from works of philosophy (Carlyle's *Past and Present*), fictions (Kingsley's *Alton Locke*), poetry (Tennyson's *Idylls of the King*), conduct books (Digby's *Broad Stone of Honor: Rules for an English Gentleman*), public school artwork and architecture (the stained-glass panels at Clifton), and catalogs of national heroes (the Black Prince, Arthur, St. George).[28] In this movement, the questing knight, whether a Galahad or a Red Cross, emerged as a paragon of manliness precisely by way of an *imitatio Christi* that informed his chivalric deportment in those particulars on which the Victorians had placed a special emphasis, such as sexual chastity.[29] Implicit in this medievalist script was a double chain of mediation, wherein Jesus represented the touchstone of manliness while supporting a warrior ethos distinct from his own in manner and mores, if not in its core principles.

Many of the names listed here will be recognized from my introduction as leading exponents of the sexual ethnology that made a bid to preempt the Irish, structurally, from any claim to manliness. It is therefore all the bolder and yet more compromised of Pearse to appropriate their own gendered construction of Christ to manufacture a manly warrant for the Fenian-style activities that they and their compatriots regularly simianized. As chivalric exemplar, Christ provides Pearse with a figure of the spiritual heroism at work in Irish insurrection, while his crucifixion provides Pearse with an analogue of blood sacrifice that was already accepted as the epitome of manly (self-)conquest, rather than brute savagery or feminized capitulation. With the figure of Christ the chevalier, Pearse "doubled down," as it were, on the *imported ideologeme,* Arthurian chivalry, that was paradoxically instrumental in modernizing the ancient myth of sovereignty as an allegory of *native self-possession.* In so doing, Pearse realized the full propagandistic potential of the Sovereignty drama, and made it, in a sense, the last word in Irish patriotism.

But Pearse's success on that head could not entirely efface the internal rift in the symbolic burden of the genre, a fracture both incidental to and emblematic of its metrocolonial origins: the dramatic content intended to interpolate and mold the ideal Irish rebel draws substantially upon an authoritative norm instituted by his target of rebellion. The resulting problem should be obvious. Because the chivalric style of manliness came to signify national integrity and cultural autonomy under a specifically British imprimatur and within a specifically British frame of reference, its "naturalization" by Irish Revivalists and separatists like Pearse could easily be taken to signify just the opposite state of affairs, that is, the confirmed decenteredness and subjacency of the Celtic fringe. However militantly executed, the appropriation of the colonizer's totemic conceits inevitably clashes with the discourse of authenticity and autonomy that is a staple of cultural nationalisms. The icons of the entitled other cannot be assimilated without threatening the sense of native self-identity under (re)construction.

This profound quandary might be classified as the ill to which Irish identity politics was heir, which is also to say that it was the eternal limit on Irish manliness in its properly symbolic-spiritual dimension. In the following chapter, I will trace in some detail the Revivalists' preoccupation with and negotiation of this symbolic limit. Still more pressing, however, for the Sovereignty drama per se, was the severely limited purchase that sacrificial manliness in the chivalric mode could give the subaltern subject or community in the material-political register—what I earlier called the domain of ordinary politics.

If form follows function, as the anthropological proverb has it, then function follows sociopolitical origin. As the protocol for an aristocratic warrior class, chivalry evolved to lend statutory distinctions of class and gender a seemingly unimpeachable moral justification. Given the Great Chain of Being that constituted the dominant cosmology of the medieval era, chivalric rule amounted to a type of secular theodicy. Predictably, the imperialism nurturing the resurgence of this rule in the nineteenth century was itself a neofeudal regime, whose articulation of higher-bred classes, "dearer races," and superior nations-states ran against the liberal enlightenment currents that helped to drive the project at large. The main proponents of this resurgence, as Girouard observes, were the antidemocratic spokesmen of manliness—like Carlyle, Froude, and Kingsley— "who dreamed of creating strongly paternalistic, hierarchical, and quasi-feudal societies." On the one hand, the chivalric tradition of noblesse oblige allowed the imperial mission to be construed as a moral quest, an exercise in knight-errantry writ large as geopolitical virtue. In Lacanian terms, this tradition operated as an elite metropolitan Imaginary: a self-congratulatory frame of ethical self-conception in which the real economic and political stakes of empire could be misrecognized, its brutal exploitative impetus overlooked. On the other hand, the same chivalric tradition framed the imperial mission as a moral *test* "aimed to produce a ruling class that *deserved* to rule because it possessed the moral qualities necessary to rulers."[30] More important, perhaps, the very revival of this tradition could be invoked to corroborate the claim that such a class had in fact already been produced. In either mode, as prescription or self-description, modern chivalry served the imperialist subject as a discourse of romanticized sublimation, in which the objectives of world conquest and self-conquest mirror in order to embellish one another.

The chivalric code is so adaptable to imperialist purposes because at its heart there always resided a political dialectic of *surplus authority,* loosely analogous to the Marxist economic dialectic of surplus value. From the start, chivalry presupposed agencies with a certain reserve of structural power and prestige to be invested sacrificially in the cause of others, preferably the vulnerable and virtuous, and in opposition to the immediate desires of the self, or at least without any calculation of return. It simultaneously presupposed, though not openly, that such service would only consolidate the power and prestige invested—that it would only augment the preexisting reserve of social capital. Thus, in the prototypical field of courtly romance, the chevalier devotes himself entirely to the regal lady whose pedestaled immobility, distressed or otherwise, underwrites not only the knight's reputation as a champion but also the moral authority of the patriarchy that bestows that dignified role upon him. Translating this scenario into world-historical dimensions, the modern credo of chivalry demanded that the sway the empire wielded over its vanquished and consequently feminized wards be invested in their "improvement," and this now familiar "soul-making mission" in turn served to deepen, diversify, and legitimate the practices of colonial surveillance and mastery. Like the manly ethos with which it came to dovetail, the chivalric order in its various manifestations effected an *aufhebung* of masculine power, a negation and deferral of its self-interested aggression in the interest of moralizing and thereby strengthening its purchase.

Looked at the other way around, chivalry, like manliness, represented an elite discourse in a very specific yet deep-structural sense. It functions as what Jean Baudrillard has designated an alibi of power, a pragmatic formation that permits the established hierarchy to extend itself in the form of its own suspension or withdrawal.[31] Absent a preexisting fund of social capital to draw upon, the chivalric program possesses none of its customary political efficacy. As thematized in the Sovereignty drama, the act of self-martyrdom on behalf of the Woman/Nation crystallizes—while strenuously disavowing—this very impotency.

The doctrine of blood sacrifice in both *Cathleen* and *The Singer* proves to be, quite literally, a dead end for the drama as well as the protagonist, a suicidal gesture without any constructive political impact that can be *plausibly staged.* In his groundbreaking book *Intimate Enemies,* Ashis Nandy has elaborated on how the mind-set of "colonial hyper-masculinity," the overidentification with the aggressor in his aggression, tends to betray the cause it asserts by engaging the struggle for independence on ideological grounds that play to the continuing advantages (military, industrial, technological) of the conqueror.[32] It is part of the colonial double bind, I would submit, that the same might be said of the divergent, if not contrary, mind-set of chivalric manliness enacted in these plays. In subliminally identifying with the imperial power in its morally self-aggrandizing strategies of renunciation and disaccumulation, the *colonial hypergallantry* of a figure like MacDara plays into the continuing *disadvantage* of his colonial position, its paucity of power reserves.

The Sovereignty drama, of course, pretends to a resolution of the very impasse in which it is cornered. The essential feature of its Imaginary structure is to identify metonymically the act of chivalric self-immolation with the salvation of Erin (Woman/Nation). Her physical metamorphosis at play's end thus not only evinces but also literalizes the sort of magical thinking that Freud famously attributed to aesthetic creation. Indeed, drama, with its public embodiment of an Imaginary universe, has perhaps the greatest power to license such thinking, particularly when, as in Revivalist drama, the fantasy explicitly partakes of a shared national agenda. Pearse's extraordinary campaign of pursuing political revolution as dramatic ritual takes this brand of wish fulfillment one step further by reversing its terms, by giving an imaginary mythopoetic aura to concrete mortal bodies. It should be remembered, however, that the measure of success Pearse's strategy ultimately enjoyed arose not from the chivalric valor of the Irish volunteers, who are marched off to prison to the execrations of their fellow citizens, but from the widely reviled offense against chivalry on the part of the modern British "knights" who summarily executed them.[33] It is one of the ironies of the metrocolonial situation that the failed sacrifice of those who could not afford it can be redeemed by a lack of forbearance on the part of those who could.

THE DOUBLE WOMAN

But that is not the last of such ironies. If Irishmen qua *Irish* men wanted the necessary capital to realize the self-aggrandizing potential of chivalric sacrifice, they continued to possess that capital and to reap that recompense qua Irish *men*. That is to say, the requisite entitlement that was lacking for the feminized subjects of empire remained in force for the admittedly embattled male subjects of a colonized patriarchy, who managed to solidify their domestic privilege through the unavailing ritualistic nobility of their resistance to foreign subordination. The same master trope of the Nation as Woman that facilitated a peculiarly chivalric enactment of patriotic service allowed that service to function as a condensed site of masculine hegemony, predicated not just upon a heroic ideal but also upon the disjunctive, bipolar construction of Woman discussed in our opening chapter. The Sovereignty drama in particular helped to make this return to the sexual-political roots of the chivalric order a crucial part of the Irish nationalist aesthetic. In translating the early Gaelic myth of succession into the sexually repressive terms of the Medieval Revival, the genre not only converted the Sovereignty goddess herself into a courtly lady, but in the process introduced into the nationalist discourse what we might call the differential gender equation: a hierarchy of opposed feminine types (Madonna-whore, virgin-virago, sum-subversion of cultural value) that serves both to dissimulate and to justify the hierarchy of men over women. Through this strategy of the double woman, an outcropping of the chivalric code, the Sovereignty drama acted to stabilize normative gender disjunction and authority at the allegorical level.

The Sovereignty dramas of Gregory, Pearse, Gonne, and Lennox Robinson all bifurcate the mythic personification of Irish society into an avowedly iconic woman and a plainly literal woman—a symbolic figure representing what Lacan calls The Woman, who underwrites the (founding) father's law, and a quotidian figure representing the individual women who remain subject to that law—in short, the legitimating and excluded other of a paternal nationalism. Anne McClintock has argued that "women are typically constructed as the symbolic bearers of the nation, but denied any direct relation to national agency."[34] The double-woman motif of the Sovereignty drama takes this strategy a crucial step further, openly placing individual female agency at odds with national agency, whether as an impediment to or a betrayal of it.

In Lacanian terms, Yeats and Gregory stage the feminine binary as comprising a phallic mother (the Poor Old Woman, Cathleen) and the woman as phallus or object of exchange (the bride to be, Delia).[35] Not coincidentally, the dramatic identity of the latter seems almost entirely comprehended in her dowry, her exchange value, which arrives onstage, to fetishistic acclaim, long before she does. This order of appearance serves to emphasize the comparative nullity of Delia vis-à-vis the symbolic plenitude of Cathleen. Indeed, Delia shows up to claim her bridegroom only after Michael has been magnetized by Cathleen's exhortation to be "putting the strangers out of my house" (C, 9), *strangers* being the recognized code word for the British occupiers. At this juncture, Delia's only words to the bewitched Michael, "Why do you look at me like a stranger?" (C, 11), subtly mark her as part of the colonial problem. Not content with having Delia's desires silenced or ventriloquized, the play sees her desire rudely invalidated by the mother figure, whose function is to sanctify what she herself describes as an aristocratic, male-dominated enterprise: "There was a red man of the O'Donnells of the North and a man of the O'Sullivans of the South and there was one Brian that lost his life by Clontarf by the sea" (C, 8). While Delia's desperation to keep her fiancé from enlisting in the blood sacrifice is dramatically necessary, insofar as it points out the value of what is being sacrificed, it must also seem politically selfish and immature in failing to appreciate the overriding value of the sacrifice itself. If the symbolic woman ratifies the virtue of a male warrior elite by inspiring them to chivalric deeds, the literal woman, Delia, evidences the maleness of that chivalric virtue by failing to recognize or appreciate its self-denying standard.

It is therefore of allegorical moment that Delia's only second in this dilemma, Michael Gillane's literal mother, Bridget, is likewise identified with her dowry, which emerges as a dramatic symbol of narrow, familial self-interest. Elizabeth Cullingford has praised the play for putting distance between the phallic mother, whose overwhelming importance to the child always reverberates with the threat of death, and a real, living mother, who always seeks her children's safety.[36] But while Bridget's plea to her husband, "Tell him not to go" (*C*, 11), is dramatically necessary for the same reason as Delia's, it likewise rates private domestic concerns higher than those collective nationalist aspirations and the service ethic that advances them, a stereotypically feminine attitude with which this play expresses little sympathy. On this point, it is worth noting the conduct of the other male subjects in the play. Bridget's husband, Peter, was scripted and originally played as such a venal buffoon that he discomfited an otherwise dazzled audience.[37] Yet as Michael leaves to join the pale-cheeked heroes, his father yields neither to his wife's entreaty nor to his own expressed wish to secure the dowry he painstakingly negotiated, but rather to the greater mastery of patriotic sacrifice invoked by Cathleen. Michael's younger brother Patrick, whose dramatic function throughout is to act as a dispassionate observer, is given the privilege of witnessing and reporting the great mythic transformation that ennobled manhood has wrought: "I saw a young girl, and she had the walk of a queen" (*C*, 11). At the end of the play, Gregory aligns the men, including Peter, with the chivalric ethos, which opens onto the future of the larger community, symbolized by the out-of-doors, the sublime beyond of the stage set into which Michael disappears. She aligns the women, excepting Cathleen, with the contemporary freeholding ideology known as familialism, which closes upon a present of domestic-self absorption, symbolized by the narrow bounds of the cottage interior.

That *Cathleen* should pit an elite patriarchal institution, the chivalric revival, against a populist one, familialism, evinces the impact of class-sectarian difference within the nationalist movement. That the play should resolve the conflict by assigning the one a manly valance and sphere of operation and the other a feminine valance and sphere of operation reflects the importance of gender tropologies in mediating and shoring up other modes of hierarchizing discourses, be they classist, ethnic, sectarian, or imperialist.

On one hand, in its representation of blood sacrifice, *Cathleen* retrofits an ethical doctrine espoused by knights and nobles of pre-Reformation feudalism on to a still older roll call of Gaelic potentates: "a red man [Hugh] of the O'Donnells . . . and a man [Donal] of the O'Sullivans . . . and one Brian [Boru] who lost his life at Clontarf" (*C*, 8). The play thereby affirms an aristocratic Irish lineage antedating the rancorous divisions between the Protestant settler Ascendancy and the Catholic people-nation, a lineage of which Anglo-Protestants like Gregory, Yeats, and their Revivalist forebear, Samuel Ferguson, saw themselves as a saving remnant. The layered historical analogy was that the warrior chieftains were to the Gaelic tribes, and the knights of Christendom were to their vassals and charges, what the gentry is to contemporary Irish society, rightful (natural/upright) leaders. On the other hand, in drawing along strongly masculinist lines its invidious contrast between such high-minded, mandarin rules of conduct and the scrambling practices of the freeholding class, *Cathleen* permits and even solicits its largely Catholic middle-class audience to counteridentify with the elitist, aristocratic traditions on gender grounds alone.

A miracle play in effect as in form, *Cathleen Ni Houlihan* contrived to square the circle between introducing social antagonism and enforcing social hegemony. It affirms moralized class-sectarian hierarchy at the level of its codes of action. But in gendering these codes masculine and feminine, respectively, and then mapping them onto either side of the double woman, the play manages to convert caste self-assertion into patriarchal consensus. As the goddess of a perpetually rejuvenated Sovereignty, the Symbolic Woman stands for the so-called virtual Irish nation, already free and whole, with which the manly courage and selflessness of an elite chivalric brotherhood is linked as its condition of possibility. In selfishly impeding this prospect of revolution and renewal, the literal women stand for the mean, fragmented colonial actuality, with which the feminized self-interest of a rising middle class is linked as its condition of persistence. Evoking factional strains only to override them, *Cathleen* ultimately induces its audience to equate advanced nationalism itself with an ethos predicated upon aristocratic leadership, a textbook specimen of discursive hegemony in action.

This gambit rests upon the canny intuition that the various class and sect constituencies of the nationalist movement and the cultural revival find a less reliable common ground in their respective notions of effective decolonization than in their patriarchal attitudes and commitments, hardened as they were by the psychic scars of imperialist feminization. As an allegorical strategy, the motif of the double woman enables Yeats and Gregory both to tap and to allay the ethno-gender anxieties of their audience: to invoke Irish feminization as a shared problem pegged to the colonial condition, the better to refute it as a racial characteristic or cultural finality. The phallic Mother/Sovereignty figures the indigenous, authentic Ireland of the Revivalist imagination. In recruiting a warrior band, inspiring their efforts, enjoining chivalric sacrifice, and countermanding all merely domestic values, she personifies that Ireland *both* as a site of virile opposition to British rule *and* as the domain of masculine authority over literal Irish women, who for their part signify the fallen, feminized Ireland that English policy sought to foster. In the final magical transformation, the "young girl" not only replaces the Hag as the visible symbol of the state of Ireland, marking her renewed claim to self-determination, she also replaces the literal Irish woman as the proper "mate" for the heroic men, lodging that claim in blood. With this dramatic climax, the manliness that would bring about the new "queen"/Ireland strides forth as the only reigning gender ideal, while the "woman of the house" lingers as an emblem of the colonial predicament to be overcome.

The Sovereignty dramas that followed *Cathleen* responded at various removes to the calls of "encore" that greeted its production. Not surprisingly, each rang a variation on its double-woman structure, wherein the dissimulation of an elitist agenda served only to sharpen the nationalist provocation. The most derivative and least successful of these sequels, Maud Gonne's *Dawn,* tries to adapt the Sovereignty myth without the gender scapegoating.[38] Thus, Gonne distinguishes the phallic Mother, Bride, from her victimized daughter, Brideen, in terms of their respective strength, endurance, personal stature, and indominability: Bride signifies Ireland's unbreakable resolve, always available for regeneration, while Brideen signifies Ireland's broken spirit, ever in need of regeneration. But Gonne does not oppose the Symbolic Woman and the literal woman on any matter of moral, cultural, or political import—she interpolates no invidious division in the feminine archetype—and as a result Brideen is able to return after her death as a Symbolic Woman after all. Given the constraints of the format, however, Gonne's approach spells the absence of any truly viable crisis of decision that would offer the play focus, energy, and suspense—any evaluative complexity, that is, that would secure the play a modicum of depth. The justice of the Irish cause, imagined in the wretchedness of a starving peasantry, and propounded in utterance after plaintive utterance, finally asserts itself in the deus ex machina translation of Mother Ireland that encapsulates the mechanically propagandistic nature of the play as a whole. The flatness of *Dawn* as a dramatic experience does, however, help to elucidate precisely how the double-woman formula, and so the Sovereignty drama itself, draws for its aesthetic and ideological effects upon the masculinist sexual politics that Gonne carefully excised. On the one hand, it is the device of the double woman that enables patriotic identification to be a source of dramatic tension rather than a reflex of pious orthodoxy; on the other, it is the chivalric framework that the double woman entails that enables this conflict to be resolved through acts of peculiarly masculine self-renunciation in which nationalist and patriarchal authority fuse indissociably. Linked by the Irish themselves with unremitting suffering, as in Pearse's punning verse "Mise Éire" (I am Éire/Misery), the value of Irish feminization is turned on its head in this dramatic structure.[39] The same suffering, voluntarily undertaken by a warrior class, instantiates a self-discipline that not only recuperates but also regenders the nation, along the distinctive lines of Victorian manliness.

The misogynistic potential of this generic project bubbles to the surface in the play *Patriots* by Gregory and Yeats's protégé Lennox Robinson, whose nationalist ardor was first kindled by a performance of *Cathleen Ni Houlihan.*[40] Written a year before the Easter Rising, in the belief that the United Irish League, with its markedly familialistic platform, had stifled the spirit of rebellion altogether, the play records the release of James Nugent, leading Fenian, from a life sentence for the murder of an informer. Having redeemed the code of revolutionary honor in this fashion, Nugent finds the cause betrayed again, this time by the self-serving complacency and timidity of his friends and family. At the center of this depressing spectacle is Nugent's wife, Anne, an eminently capable woman who had the temerity to flourish in his absence by pursuing self-interested financial goals rather than his brand of sacrificial militancy. As Nugent's erstwhile revolutionary muse, Anne had once proved the proper object of chivalric manliness cast in the register of anticolonial struggle. She had played the role of the Symbolic Woman, in calling patriots to lay down their lives for the Irish cause, her cause. In the dramatic present, by contrast, she is involved in traducing the cause and trampling upon its chivalric ideals. How? By becoming a quotidian shopkeeper, a literal woman—but not just any literal woman—her extraordinary success as a merchant and landlord marks her out as a type of the New Woman emerging over the past decade or so in the British Isles.

In a really clever dramatic gambit, Robinson pairs a diegetic inversion of the Sovereignty myth with a poetic or metaphoric inversion of the New Woman figure. Anne observes that upon her husband's arrest, when she was a young woman, her hair turned gray overnight—"as grey as it is now," some twenty years later. Toting up the toll James's patriotic zeal has taken upon her—"my health, my strength, my beauty, my money"—Anne complains that "at twenty-six I found myself old and ugly and grey and worn out" (*PA,* 47), a young woman changed instantaneously, even magically, into an old Hag. *Patriots,* then, in a supplement to the mythic provisions of *Cathleen Ni Houlihan,* suggests that the failure to appreciate the sacrifice of the warrior-suitor has the effect of reversing the process of the Cailleach Beare's rejuvenation. What is more, this reversal seems to be itself irreversible. When James tries to woo Anne with his "enthusiasm" and "eloquence" about the prospect of a "free country, a happy people, liberty at last," she explains her inability to renew her lapsed dedication on the grounds that she is "too old" (*PA,* 48).

In fact, Anne's disposition to regard her husband's actions not as chivalric services rendered but rather as unreasonable demands exacted represents her initial default in the role of Symbolic Woman, figure of the nation as a whole, in favor of her life as an individual woman, a regular female subject, preoccupied with personal matters ("my health, my strength, my beauty, my money"). Anne's default as a Mother Ireland is, in turn, glaringly analogous to the fault popularly attributed to the New Woman, who was seen as abandoning her properly feminine investment in the well-being of the family in order to secure the same sort of personal interest, and to do so by taking much the same market-oriented path to self-actualization and economic independence as Anne. With her distinctively metropolitan provenance, the New Woman had by this time emerged as a leading emblem of the disruption of customary, organic forms of life by commercial pursuits and priorities. For Robinson's Hibernian audience, accordingly, such a woman could not but be viewed as a specter of the sneaking domination of Irish culture by British materialism, which was unflaggingly decried by Revivalist spokesmen (Douglas Hyde, D. P. Moran, and others) as the most toxic fruit of British military and political rule. On the terms *Patriots* sets out, in other words, Anne Nugent's rejection of sacrificial nationalism is continuous with her embrace of the commercial standard of value for which the British occupier had long been notorious. She thus combines in her dramatic persona the unreconstructed Hag and the deracinating New Woman as the two sides, symbolically speaking, of the colonial plight.

Even as Anne personifies, in one aspect, the entire Irish community, Robinson identifies her, as a mark of her symbolic collaboration, with its single most dishonorable element, the Gombeen Man, made legendary in Irish melodrama as an underhanded, self-serving foil to the daring, noble-minded Fenian hero. The most prominent social perception of the Gombeen Man was that he extended credit and then secured defaulted landholdings, which allied him hand and glove with the British soldiery during the Land War of the 1880s.[41] The exigencies of business, which is to say the profit motive, compel Anne to do likewise in a manner calculated to appall Robinson's audience. Over the protests of her outraged husband, she evicts Nugent's old comrade in arms, Dan Sullivan, and his family, in an errant betrayal of nationalist solidarity. But, what is more, Mrs. Sullivan is herself Anne's best friend, indicating that Anne lacks even the most basic sense of fellowship.

Whereas the symbolic, courtly woman legitimates the codes of political and martial brotherhood, while remaining at their phantasmatic fringe, Anne shows herself incapable of sponsoring the solidarity necessary to any kind of collective action, and particularly one involving ultimate sacrifice. Indeed, precisely by evicting the Sullivans, she prevented their son, Willy, the one revolutionary soul left in town, from following his master, James Nugent, on a campaign of incitement. Thanks to Anne, Willy dies not *for* the cause but *to* the cause. From this turn of events, Anne's reverse transformation, from young to old woman, may be understood to betoken her part in arresting or precluding the political transformation or the spiritual renewal of her country.

In the Sovereignty drama, the phallic Mother (Ireland), or Shan Van Vocht, is more than a persona of advanced nationalism and nativist Revivalism; she is the nexus, the *point de capiton,* where their substantially divergent agendas may be sutured together. Hence, Anne's rejection of her suitor-husband's consuming revolutionary commitment places her in breach not just of the physical force politics dramatized in the play but of the cultural politics of the dramatization itself. The denigration to which Anne is accordingly subject, both in and by the play, ironically ratifies her experience that the courtly idealization of woman as national icon does indeed lay demands upon ordinary women that are as crushingly heavy as the price of refusing them is exorbitantly high. Here we can see how the burden of the double bind attaching to Irish manliness was, through the specifically chivalric expression of that manliness, transferred to Irish womanhood.

By virtue of Patrick Pearse's primary affiliation with the Catholic people-nation of Irish-Ireland, he tended to disavow not only the British but also the aristocratic origins of the chivalric ideal in whose image he molded his version of blood sacrifice. Unlike a Gregory or a Robinson, Pearse did not take the self-abnegation extolled in the Sovereignty drama and in his own revolutionary creed to represent an elite tradition at odds with middle-class familialism, but rather took it as a grassroots practice consistent with the sexual abstention mandated by that familialism on mixed moral and prudential grounds. Whereas for Yeats, Gregory, and Robinson, blood sacrifice was a vehicle for renovating everyday Irish culture, for Pearse, blood sacrifice was a means of expressing and thus redeeming everyday Irish culture in its innermost reality, of allowing it to become what, by a Nietzschean logic, it already was. This confounding of the virtual and the actual Irish nation came to inform Pearse's construction of the double woman. It prompted him to treat all of his female characters as already maternal, as mothers in the making at least, and to enshrine them on that basis as likely personae of Ireland.

In *The Singer,* Pearse does partition the Cailleach Beare into a Symbolic Woman (Maire) and a literal woman (her adopted daughter, Sighle) and draw certain generally prescribed distinctions between them as to stature, attitude, and dramatic function. Maire, who repeatedly dispenses drink in token of her Sovereignty role, approves the imminent national sacrifice, willingly consigning her sons, MacDara and Colm, to the slaughter and admonishing Sighle not to grudge their lives to the cause—not to act, in other words, like Delia Cahel. Sighle rather perplexedly finds herself to be a romantic temptation that both brothers forgo for the sake of Irish freedom and, in the process, a symbolic nexus mediating their relationship as spiritual leaders and designated victims of the coming insurrection. Once again, we have the phallic Mother, object of homosocial veneration, and the woman as phallus, object of homosocial exchange. But in this case, Sighle clearly follows the lead of her mother, sharing in her activities and striving to emulate her outlook. As a result of this filial piety, the distance between the Symbolic and the literal woman is reframed along the lines of potentiality and actualization, and is shown to vanish over the course of the action.

The mode of that vanishing, however, is itself crucial to the strain of masculinist ideology with which Pearse infuses his nationalist faith. Alone with Maire at the outset of the play, Sighle confides that she has long felt herself an object of romantic affection for both of the young men and has recently found herself the focus of some unspoken rivalry between them, a rivalry that seems to be undermining the psychic well-being of the resident son, Colm, in particular. In asking Maire to forgive her this entanglement, Sighle reveals her obscure yet powerful awareness of posing some sort of danger not just to the boys themselves but to their revolutionary mission, a danger we can now recognize as fully consonant with Sighle's role as the literal woman. Sighle has become the site of the valuation of personal desires and concerns that conflict with the collective goals of decolonization and national liberation. Thus, in the terms of the dramatic allegory, Colm's attraction to Sighle as a marriageable young woman may come to interfere with the blood tribute he is to make in consummation of a higher marriage with her as avatar of Ireland.

For her part, Sighle expresses her reciprocation of the young men's feelings by openly regretting the brothers' imminent death on the battlefield: "I shiver when I think of them all going out to fight. They will go out laughing: I see them with their cheeks flushed and their red lips apart. And then they will lie very still on the hillside,—so still and white, with no red on their cheeks. . . . Colm's hair will be dabbled with blood" (*S* 9).

There is an unmistakable allusion in these words to the parting solicitation of the Old Woman in Cathleen ("They that have red cheeks will have pale cheeks for my sake, and for all that, they will think they are well paid" [*C*, 10]), and it serves to underscore the anti-Sovereignty tenor of Sighle's elegy, its grudging of the young lives who do not seem so obviously "well paid." Maire, the Old Woman's counterpart in *The Singer,* immediately, and for the only time, finds occasion to reprove Sighle, enjoining sentiments more compatible with their iconographic role: "Whist daughter, that is no talk for one that was reared in this house. I am his mother and I do not grudge him" (*S*, 9–10). Sighle's contrite response is noteworthy on two counts. First, she recognizes that her lament was not just politically heterodox but would also count as self-centered, in keeping with the literal-woman syndrome: "Forgive me, you have known more sorrow than I, and I think only of my own sorrow." Second, thanks to the perfectly pitched rhetoric of blood sacrifice in her retraction, populist yet eroticized, her mea culpa slides almost seamlessly into her maiden address as a Sovereignty figure: "I am proud other times to think of so many young men, young men with straight strong limbs, and smooth white flesh, going out in great peril because a voice has called them to right the wrong of the people" (*S*, 10).

As a still potential mother (Ireland), Sighle functions as a figure of disciplinary instruction in the play. To its presumed edification, the audience watches her internalize the gender norms that will shape her as a proper object of nationalist fealty, norms that the literal-woman types in earlier Sovereignty dramas infringed or even flouted. At the same time, as a Symbolic Mother to be, whose potentiality is always absorbed within the reality of her status, Sighle comes by her lofty destiny *automatically,* as an effect of her identity. Like Ireland itself, in Pearse's conception, Sighle faces the task of becoming what in essence she already is. The register of Being takes clear precedence over the register of doing. Indeed, to say that women are all in some sense mothers and sanctified on that basis—and Pearse makes this case quite explicitly in his short story "The Mother"[42]—is to say that women like Sighle are constituted as organic moral agencies, their *bildung* a foregone conclusion. Accordingly, individuated, personally motivated subjectivity, as represented by the literal woman, is here glanced at just long enough to be not so much rejected (rejection implying choice) as *actively precluded.*

This organic mode of *bildung* in turn has its preordained telos in the iconographic immobility of the mature Maire, her enshrinement as a fully, which is also to say merely, Symbolic Woman. Unlike the Old Woman in *Cathleen,* Maire does not incite rebellion; she merely approves it. The right of royal nomination that was the traditional province of the Cailleach Beare has passed here into a more quiescent rite of confirmation, instancing a more definitively phallocentric division of authority. In sectarian terms, the forceful goddess Ireland of pagan lore, favored by Anglo-Protestant Revivalists, gives way to a docile Mother Ireland molded by the Catholic-identified tradition of Mariolatry central to (Pearse's) Irish-Irelandism. Indeed, Pearse goes out of his way to give Maire a role in the insurgency that emblematizes the glorified passivity of her status by invoking the dominant ritual enactment of Marian devotionalism: the vigil. A vigil is an acting out of an intense form of inaction, of pure waiting, abiding, suffering (in its original sense); it is also the occupation of a distinct formative frame or stage, here a sacralized stage, that is constitutively *off*stage, a margin defining the main event. In either respect, once cast as a specifically feminine preserve, the vigil keeping throws into contradictory relief the aggressive masculine dimension of the blood sacrifice that it patiently contemplates. By this contrast, such vigil keeping helps to show that far from lacking active, agonistic elements, blood sacrifice brings such elements under control in an exercise of manliness. Given the religious associations of the vigil and the liturgical valence of redemptive bloodletting, the "manliness of Christ" would seem again to be the ultimate point of gender reference. In a classic instance of chivalric compensation, the male warriors adduce woman's role in keeping "all the great vigils" as proof she is "too good . . . for us" (*S,* 15), thereby fixing her on a pedestal that both exalts and immobilizes her. Where earlier Sovereignty dramas deployed the Symbolic and literal woman's split to recommend doing for the nation instead of oneself, Pearse deploys the same motif to exhort women not to *do* for the nation but rather to *stand* for (and by) the nation, to perfect themselves as a national trope and to restrict themselves to that tropic existence.

Pearse's last drama seeks a new assemblage, in the Deleuzian sense, of the Woman/Nation complex: it endeavors to reverse the becoming-woman of Ireland, its feminization under the so-called metropolitan marriage, with a becoming-nation of woman, the projection of woman as a static ideal of collective life, enabling and ennobling masculinized agency on its behalf. If in this *The Singer* exaggerates rather than epitomizes the patriarchalism at work in the other Sovereignty dramas, its extremity does bring to the fore a trenchant, contextually specific political agenda common to all: even as they speak Irish truth to British power, after their fashion, all Sovereignty dramas also speak male power to female disenfranchisement.

SOVEREIGNTY, SUFFERING, SUFFRAGE

The period over which the Sovereignty drama took its course, 1902–1915, was also the period of most heated contention regarding women's right to vote, whether under the present colonial dispensation, as a guarantee under the Home Rule provisions of 1913, or in the Republic of the future. As chronicled by Rosemary Cullen Owens, Margaret Ward, and Cliona Murphy, the tensions between Irish women's suffrage and Irish nationalism, in both the evolutionist and separatist models, were configured in a rather lopsided fashion.[43] While these tensions increased with the militancy of the former, they originated with and were caused by the masculinist antagonism of the latter. It is, in my view, impossible to imagine that a genre so preoccupied with gender norming under an insurgent nationalist aegis would not be both conceived and received, in its various specimens, as bearing upon that salient controversy.[44] Indeed, I would submit that the Sovereignty drama had greater unconscious effect on the suffrage debate for seeming to ignore the pointed issue and its constitutionalist horizon of pertinence altogether.

Opposition to expanding electoral rights for women was urged on two different fronts, the flagrantly normative and the putatively pragmatic. The flagrantly normative argument typically came from the Irish-Ireland wing of the nationalist movement in ideological solidarity with its confessional affiliate, the Catholic Church. It held that "allowing women the right of suffrage is incompatible with the unity of domestic life" and, further, that women's participation in public affairs would corrode "the passive virtues of humility, patience, meekness, forbearance and self-repression" that constitute the "special province of the female soul."[45] The *Catholic Bulletin* published a contemporary parable titled "Kitty and the Fight for Freedom," in which the misadventures of the innocent protagonist with suffrage viragos only go to prove that "women are made to be cherished and shielded from contact with a rough world" by the "chivalrous nature" of stout men like her fiancé.[46] Although the propaganda value of Pearse's *Singer* seems to lie elsewhere, it not only endorses the separate-spheres argument but also raises it to the level of national allegory, where gender norms function as both patriotic obligations and political identity forms. Whereas in "Kitty" a "chivalrous nature" represents the social property of men, and dependence thereupon the social propriety of women, in *The Singer* chivalric manliness and passive, retiring femininity *also* represent the very meaning of Irishness in its respectively gendered forms. Without even mentioning female suffrage, the play can be felt to exclude it qua political action or intervention.

The putatively pragmatic opposition to women's franchise held the policy to be just in principle but misguided and finally unacceptable under the range of present or immediately foreseeable contingencies affecting Irish national ambitions. The suffragettes were, for instance, admonished not to seek the franchise from Westminster, lest they lend legitimacy to continued colonial rule in Ireland.[47] To this objection, one can say only that the freedom from collaborationist taint enjoyed by the Catholic Relief Act, which granted male franchise, and Catholic Emancipation shows just how "putative" this pragmatism could be. Later, the mainstream Redmondites refused to entertain provisions for female suffrage in the third Home Rule Bill, lest such an amendment, to which they were chilly anyway, queer support for the measure as a whole.[48] In either case, the social dictum levied at politically minded Irish women was to defer or set aside their individual aspiration to the franchise for the purpose of helping to ensure collective, but exclusively male, self-determination, to put aside personal desire for national good, or rather the good as nation.[49]

Sovereignty drama lends still more striking allegorical support for this pragmatic objection to suffragism than it does for the strictly normative objection, or, rather, it gives added bite to the pragmatic objection by raising it to the dignity of a normative judgment. The cardinal feature of the Sovereignty drama's generic structure, the double woman, in fact models with uncanny precision the social dictum imposed, as a Hobson's choice, on women seeking electoral rights. The Symbolic Woman *is* of course Sovereignty, the fantasy figure of collective destiny, while the literal woman is defined by her care for some degree of personal sovereignty, some input into the actual unfolding of her life narrative, whether in marriage, career, family life, and so forth. Paradoxically, whereas the phantasmatic Sovereignty represents the one plenary reality in these plays (the very substance of Irish political identity), the literal woman bears a merely privative reality, only emerging as the substance of a political negation, a drag on the concerted national being that Mother Ireland would mobilize. In this manner, the dramatic format succeeds in framing the entire question with an antisuffragist bias without framing the question *as such* in the first place. That is, the possibility of a woman's personal sovereignty does not appear a worthy desideratum alongside national Sovereignty; nor a necessary constituent of a truly national Sovereignty, as the suffragists themselves insisted; nor even a discreet option in conflict with national Sovereignty, as the mainstream Redmondites maintained. The Sovereignty drama encodes women's personal sovereignty instead as a simple moral failing—weakness, woefulness, selfishness, or some amalgam thereof—to the effect of casting upon the fledgling feminist movement an ideological taint that was all the more insidious for being allegorical and therefore lateral, unsourced, unconfrontable.

More than that, in the dramatic context of blood sacrifice, with young men volunteering to perish for the Woman/Nation, Sovereignty drama set up the female concern with personal sovereignty, of which suffragism was the most clamorous public display, to resonate as a betrayal of the woman's part in the chivalric compact, a refusal to pay in the coin of liberty, autonomy, or agency for the goods of manly protection, devotion, and self-denial.[50] Through this oscillating dichotomy and identification of Woman and women, the courtly relations staged in the genre draw upon existing gender inequities and the power reserves they reflect to exert a certain political instrumentality that extends beyond the proposed objectives. If the chivalric blood sacrifice these plays recommend fails to benefit the Nation as Woman, playing to both the material and the cultural strengths of the colonizer, it likewise fails to benefit the woman as citizen, depriving her of a standing even as it offered her a pedestal. The difference between these two outcomes, of course, is the difference between an unintended consequence and an unconscious motive.

Sovereignty Spoofs

THE SHADOW OF THE GLEN

A strong connection between John Synge's *Shadow of the Glen* and *Cathleen Ni Houlihan* was immediately intuited on all sides of the Revivalist movement. Those elite Anglo-Protestant directors of the Irish Literary Theatre, Gregory and Yeats, elected to debut *Shadow* (October 8, 1903) on a double bill with *Cathleen,* which was then about a year into its triumphant engagement with Irish nationalist sentiment. The arrangement invited a comparative reading, to say the least. The leader of Catholic Sinn Fein, Arthur Griffith, rose promptly to the bait. Amid his famous rant against the supposedly un-Irish, unpatriotic sexual morality of Synge's maiden offering ("Sometimes the woman lives in bitterness—sometimes she dies of a broken heart—but she does not go away with a Tramp"), Griffith discerned in the production and the theater an attempt to offer a "substitute" for the more politically orthodox *Cathleen.*[51] Taking her

cue from Griffith's vitriolic critique, his sometime partner in Irish-Ireland militancy, Maud Gonne, organized a flamboyant walkout on *Shadow* designed to
evoke her likewise flamboyant entrance as the title character in the premier of
Cathleen.[52] Such gestural displays of this intuition, however, have only helped to
render the precise tenor of the connection itself perennially elusive. A century
later, critics still wonder: does *Shadow* simply share a topos or problematic with
Cathleen—be it petit bourgeois familialism (Doggett), the mythic supernatural
(Grene), or gendered nationalism (Hoyt, Quinn)—or does *Shadow* address its
iconic antecedent more directly?[53] Is the relationship of *Shadow* to *Cathleen*
largely analogical, as Ben Levitas suggests, or has Synge crafted a more strictly
dialogical transaction? Can one even trace *Shadow*'s filiation to *Cathleen* in
the lineaments of the play itself, or is it rather the felt effect of contextual pressures surrounding the play's original reception? As Nicholas Grene puts this
unanswered question, "Was [*Shadow*] conceived as an ironic antidote to the
idealizing *Cathleen,* or were Synge's very different intentions wrested toward
politics by the Dublin audiences and the nationalist press?"[54]

Taking a page from the New Formalism, I would conjecture that the difficulty in resolving this matter arises in part from the thematic bias to which our
favored methodology in Irish studies, a fine-grained historicism, is sometimes
prone.[55] *Genre represents the primary language in which literary works speak to
one another.* So to compare these particular dramas on the basis of a content
unmediated by the generic protocols that frame them is to turn something of
a deaf ear to their intertextual dialogue, to attempt to decode it in the absence
of the underlying code. It is also to forfeit the tools for discriminating textual
cohabitation from textual conversation, that is, the sharing of a sociocultural
universe (objects of critique or validation, target audiences, conditions of discursive possibility, and so forth) from the joining of a debate over the defining
proportions and demands of that universe. Accordingly, what might prove useful
in the scholarship on *Shadow* is a detailed discussion of its careful, sometimes
parodic manipulation of Sovereignty flourishes and conventions, for this is the
means whereby the play announces not just its generalized ties to *Cathleen* but
its critical stance toward *Cathleen* and the brand of gendered nationalism that
it sponsors.

Synge drew *The Shadow of the Glen* from a violently misogynistic folk tale
current throughout Ireland, "The Man Who Pretended to Be Dead," the Galway
variant of which he heard from an Aran Islands acquaintance, Pat Dirane.[56]
Certain of the most sweeping alterations Synge made to the story have been
well documented,[57] but certain other underconsidered embellishments are directed mainly at focusing an ironic lens upon the Sovereignty drama in general
and upon *Cathleen* specifically. First of all, instead of greeting Nora with the
title "Ma'am," as in the Dirane, Synge's Tramp calls her "lady of the house," a

formulation sufficiently out of place to attract Griffith's derisive notice in his review.[58] Now given that this "lady" is soon to be evicted from her "house," and given that she calls the Tramp "stranger," it is impossible *not* to hear the voice of Cathleen complaining of "too many strangers in the house" and hoping to get "my beautiful fields back again" and put "the strangers out of my house." The precursor of the evicted Nora, both in her own mind and in the fulminations of her husband, Dan, is one Peggy Cavanaugh, another addition to Dirane's story, who spends her time "begging money at the crossroads, or selling songs to the men" (*SH,* 13), activities that recall the precursor of Cathleen Ni Houlihan in the Yeats and Gregory play, one Winny of the Cross Roads, known for peddling gossip. Synge thus sets up an analogy—Peggy is to Nora as Winny is to Cathleen—that places his heroine in the purely structural position of Sovereignty, a dramatic replication of the construction of women in nationalist ideology.

In a further elaboration of this allusive pattern, before Nora offers her guest tea, as in the folk tale, she pours him whiskey, a token practice of the Sovereignty goddess. Once she fetches Michael Dara and the tea has been served (and here again Synge has added to the original story), Nora gives the two men an account of her existence that resonates distinctly with the self-description Cathleen provides Michael and Peter Gillane. Like Cathleen, she boasts of her intimacy with "a power of men." Like Cathleen she praises them as "fine men" all, and like Cathleen, she represents this commerce as following from her own "imperious demands": "I was a hard child to please and a hard girl to please . . . and it's a hard woman I am to please this day" (*SH,* 11). Yeats and Gregory's Cathleen is, of course, so hard to please that "if anyone would give me help . . . he must give me all" (*C,* 8). Moreover, with all of the men Nora has known, forever "talking to someone" and "looking for someone" (*SH,* 10), it is by no means clear that she has, in Cathleen's words, "set out the bed for any" (*C,* 9). Mary Fitzgerald-Hoyt incisively takes this ambiguity as a dramatic strategy for indicating that "what Nora truly desires is not sex, but rather transcendence."[59] It is no less a strategy, however, for sustaining the heroine in an allegorical relationship with the Shan Van Vocht, whose similarly peripatetic sexuality is, in the Sovereignty drama, likewise displaced onto an ideal of transcendence.

None of this is intended to reduce Nora to a type of the Woman/Nation, or to discount the dramatic realism (as opposed to the documentary reality) at which Synge is aiming. However, I do mean to show that Synge fashioned Nora to *evoke* the symbolic Éire figure, even as she enacted the *literal*-woman role, what the Tramp tags "a woman only" (*SH,* 5). That is to say, *The Shadow of the Glen* does not merely ignore or discard but actively inverts the double-woman motif that *Cathleen Ni Houlihan* instituted as a template of gendered nationalism. Understood in a feminist vein, the proposed effect of this intervention was far from straightforward.

On the one hand, the play not only displaces the Woman/Nation's troubles by the personal distress of Nora Burke, as Antoinette Quinn observes, it quite deliberately restages that displacement as a reversal of the Revivalist ideology for which the Irish Literary Theatre had earned widespread if temporary plaudits. By inverting without dissolving the terms of the double woman, Synge calls critical notice to the *prior* displacement of the concrete "personal distress" of Irish women by the feminine symbolization of national "Troubles" in the Sovereignty drama. To this extent, the dramatic action in *Shadow* might well seem to point, as Quinn claims, to "the liberation of the Irish female from her iconic fate into human vulnerability . . . the characterization of female desire and destiny as personal and individual." On the other hand, by inverting but steadfastly refusing to dissolve the double woman, the play in effect allows that such a culturally generated feminist "liberation" is, under the reigning ideological circumstances in Ireland, all but impossible. Because the iconic Woman/Nation can attain conceptual and political consistency only through a dialectical negation of actual women, as the double-woman motif itself attests, the hegemonic power of this allegory in the Revival prevents the complete detachment, and certainly the complete *literary* detachment, of the representation of individual women from the normative magnetic field of the Symbolic Woman. Synge's inversion, one might say, anticipates in another register one of Jacques Lacan's signature formulations. Lacan proclaimed that "Woman does not exist," being always already constructed in accordance with male fantasies.[60] Synge's construction of Nora Burke suggests that (Irish) women do not exist, being a fantasy effect of patriarchal nationalism that casts its "shadow" over the ordinary women of the "glen." The accessories or markings of the Sovereignty with which Synge contours his "realistic" heroine nudge the audience to recognize the indelibility of that "shadow," particularly for those who would indeed seize upon the heroine as a national type. Where there is the Woman/Nation, there can be no "woman only."

Synge's parodic turn on the Sovereignty drama, then, delineates what we might call the Revivalist double bind of Irish *womanhood*. But that is only half the story. Turned upon the male characters, the same parodic strategy serves to trace this impasse to a doubly articulated Irish paternalism, either wing of which smacks of a recognizably British cultural standard.

Gender criticism of *Shadow* has mainly focused upon its critique of patriarchy in the so-called bourgeois nationalist mode, as embodied in Nora's once and prospective husbands, Dan Burke and Michael Dara. In a manner that unmistakably recalls Peter Gillane "handling" the Cahel dowry, Michael Dara calculates the nest egg he will enjoy with Nora now that Dan Burke is dead; Dan, in turn, spitefully envisions the destitution Nora must suffer now that he has risen. The two men's signature actions, both additions to the original tale, fully accord in identifying male authority with material accumulation, a posture that joins the men, at play's end, in a smug, homosocial "marriage" of respectability. Both are obsessively concerned with controlling the elements of their environment, of which Nora is one, by taking and hoarding possession thereof, which in Nora's case tends toward social confinement and sexual repression. In the context of a Sovereignty spoof, Michael and Dan's ideological kinship points to a key masculinist analogy encoded in the trope of the Woman/Nation: on one side, the domestic assumption of male dominion, understood as a shared commerce in and possession of women; on the other, the public good of self-determination, understood as a shared ethnic possession of a land or country. The domestic assumption gives a naturalizing, familial aura to the public good, while the public good warrants the domestic assumption as the indispensable building block of national formation and reproduction. For Synge, woman *is* Sovereignty in exactly the same way as Woman, for Lacan, *is* the phallus: she is the enabling site of power, the ground of (male) agency; she upholds the framework of patriarchy/nationalism, symbolically ratifying its authority by remaining materially subject to it.

At the same time, the "grudging materialism" that Dan and Michael expound as the currency of their pinched mastery was deeply associated in the Irish mind with the British middle classes, the main exponents of colonial rule.[61] As the object of this avaricious mastery, Nora embodies a different type of Irish *figura:* not the Woman as Nation but the native as feminized—and feminized, as it were, *from within.* The metropolitan marriage, *Shadow* proposes, has been installed in the rural Irish homestead, the privileged space of aboriginal authenticity for the Revival and Irish-Ireland alike.[62]

The power and tenacity of this critique, however, have led many viewers and scholars of the play to adapt a correspondingly romanticized view of the other male couple (the Tramp—Patch Darcy) and the offices they supposedly perform for Nora. These two men have been understood as follows:

a) To signify and facilitate the release of Nora's sexual desires from the puritanical encumbrances of Irish familialism[63]

b) To help Nora "rediscover the delights of Nature" and thus to adopt an openness to experience at odds, symbolically as well as practically, with the stifling conventions of bourgeois sociality[64]

c) To "arouse Nora's imaginative reserves," which have been deadened by the routines of agrarian subsistence[65]

d) To put Nora in touch with a "lost heroic ideal" that stands in stark contrast to the petty venality of her male familiars[66]

Given this collective alignment of social, sexual, political, and poetic liberation, it is little wonder that the sympathetic nature of the wife and the Tramp in relation to one another should be deemed the single greatest alteration that Synge wrought on Dirane's original story.[67]

Such a reading of the Tramp would seem, on the face of things, consistent with Synge's use of the Sovereignty drama and specifically *Cathleen Ni Houlihan* as an intertextual framework. Just as Dan and Michael must be seen as reincarnating the spirit of Peter Gillane, in all of its stinting, paternalistic respectability, the Tramp, along with his idol Darcy, must be seen to reprise the role of Michael Gillane in agreeing to serve and defend an evicted woman in what amounts to an act of symbolic betrothal. Moreover, the Tramp's "courteousness," his "constant references to Nora as 'lady of the house,'" and his final assurance of protection for her ("You'll not be getting your death with myself, lady of the house" [*SH*, 14]) not only sharpen the satire of Dan's "bourgeois orthodoxy," as Paul Murphy observes, they also evince the chivalric attitudes and commitments proper to the Sovereignty hero qua specimen of Irish manliness. The Tramp's ultimate geste, which Murphy aptly describes as a "cavalier rescue of the damsel in distress," *is* the definitive consummation of the Sovereignty drama, which likewise draws upon "the classic fairytale ending where the valiant knight leads the beleaguered princess" to freedom.[68]

But *The Shadow of the Glen* is, after all, a Sovereignty spoof rather than a Sovereignty pastiche, and on the masculine side Synge structures his parodic intervention by cleverly manipulating the critical distance on his prototype as he moves from one set of analogies to another. The correspondence between the established peasantry, Dan/Michael and Peter, unfolds in straightforward fashion, while the correspondence between the revolutionary mavericks is so transvalued as to bring its new principal, the Tramp, into unacknowledged alliance with his bourgeois antagonist. In the Tramp, that is, Synge transposes the sort of gallantry displayed by Michael Gillane from the gender-inflected register of national politics to a national-inflected register of gender politics, where the complicity of the chivalric ethos with the more conventional assertions of masculine dominance grows more legible.[69]

Evidence of this agonistic partnership emerges with the Tramp's very first demurral at Dan's eviction of Nora:

> Tramp [pointing at Michael]: Maybe himself would take her.
> Nora: What would he do with me now?
> Tramp: Give you the half of a dry bed, and a good food in your mouth.
>   (*SH,* 14)

The Tramp's proposed homosocial transfer of a woman between apparent rivals assumes and enacts the homosocial fungibility of Woman, as construct, between apparently opposed strains of patriarchal discourse, the familialist and the romantic or courtly. The manner in which the Tramp commends Nora to Michael's unforthcoming care envisages chivalric conduct to be coextensive with the male superintendence and proprietorship that formed the bedrock of bourgeois familialism. Metaphorically speaking, therefore, the initial escape route that the Tramp sketches for Nora leads nowhere at all, issuing in another, and a closely related, mode of confinement.

The action, or nonaction, of the play literalizes this ideological bind, beginning, ironically, with the figure of Patch Darcy, whose memory joins the Tramp and Nora in an attitude of bereaved reverence. Darcy was mentor to the gallant Tramp, protector of the isolated damsel, and a "good shepherd" by contrast to the hapless Michael Dara. In combination, these attributes define Patch not just as a sainted man but as a saint of chivalric manliness. He stands as the model for the courteous solicitude toward Nora that the Tramp now espouses, just as Christ, to whom the play's biblical imagery explicitly links Patch, was the received archetype of the idealized masculinity that such stalwart gentility evinces. Yet, and this is the key point, Darcy's messianic profile does not carry, indeed it conspicuously lacks, any redemptive function or potential. His attention to Nora, however unflagging and uplifting, has neither ameliorated her situation nor alchemized her destiny. The *poesis* of the drama seems to enthrone Patch in the prospective role of Savior precisely so that the *diegesis* might strip him of that title, revealing a practical void at the heart of the ethos he represents.

In pronouncing himself "the last one heard [Patch's] living voice in the whole world" (*SH,* 6), the Tramp lays claim to something like apostolic succession from old Patch, especially because he only discovered who owned the voice on the "third day," suggesting that Patch's spirit (voice) has been resurrected in him. That Darcy's message proves not divine and ineffable but deranged and inchoate, however, augurs ill for the Tramp's performative identification with him. As Eugene Benson has argued, "The life of the Tramp offers no hope for Nora," and so his offer to guard her in that life, like the earlier tutelage of Patch, amounts to service without benefit.[70] Tellingly, Nora agrees, openly and immediately, with this depreciation of the Tramp's devoirs. With Darcy's end fixed in her mind, she replies to the Tramp's invitation: "What good is a grand morning when I'm destroyed surely, and I going out to get my death walking the roads?" (*SH,* 14). Nora's sentiments illuminate in the Tramp's subsequent cajolery a hidden element of masculine presumption, in every sense of the term, to which the chivalric mode of address is typically liable. The rhetoric in which the Tramp frames his promises of a better day, while extravagantly other-directed in form, not only misses but also seeks to override the woman's desires, to which it seemingly makes its appeal. His speech sets about, and here the affinity to courtly rhetoric is unmistakable, to cast Nora's longing in the image of his idealization of her, an idealization that is in turn conditioned by the Tramp's own meager resources of gratification: "Come along with me now, lady of the house, and it's not my blather you'll be hearing only, but you'll be hearing the herons crying out over the black lakes . . . the grouse and the owls with them . . . and the larks and the big thrushes. . . . [I]t's fine songs you'll be hearing when the sun goes up" (*SH*, 15). Far from promising a genuine liberation, of whatever stripe, the Tramp's offer repeats a familiar masculinist gesture: to ventriloquize the desire of a woman in professed dedication to her fulfillment, to substitute the male "should want" for the female "does want."

Though forced to leave with the Tramp, Nora clearly remains unpersuaded by his "fine bit of talk," which she knows to be mere "blather" (*SH*, 15). For her, the naked exposure to nature, however poeticized, is inseparable from the "debt of nature," the physical decline and demise that her new vagrancy will inevitably hasten. Being an inversion of the double woman of the Sovereignty drama, she experiences its climactic event, the blood sacrifice, in reverse order. Whereas the Shan Van Vocht is given back her youth and delivered from bondage, her homeland restored, through a gallant death incurred at her urging, Nora is consigned to old age, homelessness, and "her death" by accepting, under compulsion, a like form of chivalry, here revealed to be an integral part of the ideological landscape of her disenfranchisement.

Synge thus completes his pincer attack on gendered nationalism. Having invoked Revivalist mythology to expose the stifling of female aspirations under the prudential regime of familialism, he turns around and shows how the noble impracticality celebrated in that mythology harbors a complementary sexual politics. Synge in turn counted upon his audience to discern in these paired modes of patriarchal domination, material constraint, and discursive construction a mirror image of the twin engines of colonial mastery: dispossession and stereotype. It is as the victim, and perhaps only as the victim, of these respective nationalist and imperialist agendas, at once antagonistic and isomorphic, that Nora's identity as Irish Woman/Woman-Ireland achieves some sort of synchrony.

The upshot of Synge's dual critique is a radical utopianism, in the etymological sense. By that I mean that the dramatic action finally leaves the audience "no place" to stand, or no stand to take, that is answerable to the exigencies it sets forth. This phenomenon, characteristic of Synge's dramaturgy, has in the case of *Shadow* been notably misread as an effect of the play's attack on bourgeois nationalism alone, and in the light of this interpretation, *Shadow* appears to represent a more conventional nostalgic utopianism. Seamus Deane, for instance, asserts that "for Synge nationalism was a moment of resistance to the inevitable transformation of traditional life. . . . [I]n Synge, the cause is always lost, the order of things is not regenerated." Taking this gloss on board, Rob Doggett has drawn out its implied gender politics: Synge seeks to establish an "a priori authenticity" and to that end constructs his heroine as a reification of "a romantic primitive Ireland that has been forever lost." In endeavoring to signify a "secret" Ireland "prior to the intrusion of the nationalist patriarchal apparatus," Synge winds up "completing its phallic circuit": "The peasant female symbolizing a coherent nation in the present has been replaced by a peasant woman symbolizing a coherent nation in the past."[71] As our reading demonstrates, however, the Synge of *Shadow* specifically refuses the identification of Woman with Nation, past or present (the revivalist and bourgeois options, respectively). But in taking seriously the patriarchal discourse that joins these alternatives, he simultaneously acknowledges that Irish women, qua dramatic personae, cannot be fully extricated from such iconographical accretions or sedimentations. Rather than failing "in the restoration of the native female to any true position," as Doggett holds, *Shadow* disputes the very possibility of said "restoration" and deploys constructs like chivalric manliness to reveal how "any true position" comes to our collective mise-en-scène already contoured by layers of ideological investment. It is precisely owing to this Nietzschean awareness of the constitutive, and constitutively tendentious, power of figuration—patriarchal, nationalist, and so forth—that Synge disposes more effectively than Doggett thinks of both the native woman's stock enshrinement as vehicle of authenticity and, by extension, the broader equation of authenticity with aboriginality itself. Beyond simply rejecting any organic linkage of the Native/Woman with a condition of precolonial authenticity, Synge cast doubts upon the postcolonial possibility of there being any one "true position" for the Native/Woman, any organic standard of authenticity proper to her.

With this last point we are in a position to return to Deane's more comprehensive formulation and introduce a nuanced amendment. Instead of saying that "in Synge" an idyllic, traditional "order of things" is not *re*generated, we would say that Synge shows that such an order, inferable from the things that are, has never been generated at all. It is not that "a cause is always lost," but that some more desirable possibility has always already been preempted— politically, ideologically, discursively. Unlike a "traditional way of life," whether as "order" or "cause," such utopian potentiality does not admit of dramatic objectification. It can only be suggested through what Adorno has theorized as a process of *negative allegory:* a prospect nowhere signifiable in the contents of the work is evoked as a residuum of the aesthetic form or gestalt.[72] In *Shadow,* the simultaneous negation of competing styles of patriarchal nationalism, which together constitute the entire field of social intercourse, traces a purely formal prospect of ethno-gender liberation strictly coterminous with the dramatic experience itself.

According to Adorno, such negative allegory forms the keystone of modernist innovation, instituting a shift from mimesis to assemblage as the dominant representational strategy.[73] Its operation in *Shadow* (and again in *Playboy*) helps to explain why Synge's plays have entered the modernist canon while those of his Revivalist peers—Colum, Robinson, Milligan, Cousins, Martyn, Moore, and even Gregory—have not. It further helps us understand how it is that Synge's peasant plays bear far closer affinity to the postmodern theater of Beckett than to the Irish National Theatre in which they played. It is, finally, a testament both to the ecumenical sweep of Synge's critique of gendered nationalism and to the protomodernist eccentricity of his work that while Lady Gregory tirelessly promoted his greatest and most controversial plays, she joined Arthur Griffith in disliking and even resenting them.[74]

THE CHARWOMAN'S DAUGHTER

James Stephens's first novel unfolds a tale of individual *bildung* and an allegory of national promise.[75] It combines without fully synthesizing mythic and realistic strategies of representation, so that the effects of its gentle irony on either of these stylistic and generic modes might be the more readily discerned. On one side, the "ways of world-making" practiced by Mrs. Makebelieve and the pattern of growth followed by her daughter, Mary, take shape at the intersection of fairy tale, chivalric romance, and Irish legend, an intersection most conspicuously occupied by the Sovereignty myth in its modern Revivalist adaptation. On the other side, the social and material world occupied by the Makebelieves acts to translate this Sovereignty myth into the register of domestic comedy, in two interrelated senses: first, a conventional romantic comedy, capped by the kind of prospective marriage so hauntingly transfigured in the fatal tryst of the Irish martyr and the Old Woman/Nation, and second, a comedy of domestic politics, in which the national struggle symbolized by the Shan Van Vocht targets not the enemy invader, or Stranger, but the enemy within, the *seoinin,* or "shoneen," whose aping of English ways leaves him "a stranger in his own house." The latter phrase comes from one of the essays Stephens wrote in *Sinn Féin* denouncing that figure and what he stands for: a broader Irish propensity, born of the metro-colonial condition, to internalize the values, tastes, and pretensions of the British colonizers and their Anglo-Irish garrison.[76] In *The Charwoman's Daughter,* this inward turn of cultural resistance tends to assimilate the racial categories of English and Irish to the caste categories of "aristocracy" and "people" or "mass,"[77] and it is this elision that creates a space for Stephens's distinctive contribution to the Revivalist literature of manliness, his representation of a working-class variation on and spoof of this inveterately middle-class thematic.

The disappointingly few full-fledged readings of *The Charwoman's Daughter* have properly isolated motifs and scenarios that point to the Sovereignty drama as the organizing allegorical frame of the novel. The Makebelieves, ensconced in their high turret-like tenement, assume the role of fairy-tale damsels in distress, awaiting deliverance from their unlovely, economically straitened circumstances.[78] But they do not represent just any damsels in distress. Mother and maid—soldered together by the daughter's Christian name, Mary, the name of not only the arch maiden of Christendom but also the most popular Catholic version of Mother Ireland—the pair update the double Sovereignty goddess, Poor Old Woman and beautiful young girl. A slavey by trade, Mrs. Makebelieve repeatedly loses gigs for venting her umbrage that "these folk [her employers] have houses of their own" and she does not, that is, for an embittered sense of dispossession and internal exile that recalls the Shan Van Vocht (*CD*, 28). For Mary's part, she is the focus of the two women's shared dream of a marriage that would transform their lives utterly. But even as the Sovereignty narrative seems to be following approved Revivalist lines, Stephens is busily demystifying its veiled complicity with the standards of the colonizer and its traffic in the (debased) coinage of Seoininism. As Jochen Achilles remarks, the consummation envisioned by Mrs. Makebelieve consists either in "an aristocratic ambience of sublime lifelessness" or in "bourgeois surroundings oozing respectability." This glorious destiny finds its corresponding means of achievement in the advent of some "absurdly heroic . . . absurdly rich nobleman," a "lord" of "knightly aura," for Mary to wed.[79] By thus assembling the women's joint fantasy out of gallantry and fabulous wealth, Stephens shows that the patrician materialism fueling the mother's desire complements and is complemented by the medieval romanticism framing the daughter's fulfillment. In this respect, the chivalric caste of Revivalist discourse could not but cooperate in the Seoininism it officially reprehends, helping to enthrall its audience to a set of "non-Irish" values.[80]

This enthrallment of the Makebelieves' fantasy life to an alien ideal is soon externalized in the family with whom mother and maiden alike remain entangled for most of the novel: the O'Connors, an affluent clan of *seoinins*. Mrs. Makebelieve assumes the position of cleaning woman in the house of Mrs. O'Connor, which, as Achilles points out, features a living room that is "almost an exact replica" of her own "dreams of happiness."[81] Shortly thereafter, Mary, who wanders at large during the workday, takes up with an O'Connor scion designated simply "the policeman." The suit this policeman pays the young girl seems to place him in the pre-scripted role of Prince Charming, the anticipated savior of the Makebelieves' fortunes. It is therefore telling that he is the one character in the novel most consistently and comprehensively identified with imperialist agency. By profession, of course, he enforces the legal and political authority of a foreign power; by election, he promotes the cultural authority of that same power. For example, seeking to impress Mary with his knowledge of Dublin, the policeman dismisses "the local newspaper whose opinion might be biased by patriotism" in favor of "the more stable testimony of reputable English journals," which stand in his mind for "exact truth" (*CD*, 37). In other words, his pronouncements claim authority, here a decidedly paternalistic authority, by deploying prevalent racial stereotypes—sentimental Irish versus objective

English—to their approved ends, the greater glory of the hegemonic group. The policeman thus exemplifies Stephens's "Irish Englishman"; he identifies with the foreign masters in order to put on the raiment of their mastery at "home."

The policeman's complicity with alien rule is amplified, psychically and allegorically, in his dalliance with Mary, where he plays a robust John Bull to her shrinking Éire. Mary herself regards her well-heeled suitor as "the adequate monarch of his world," and he in turn seeks from her the "homage" such a potentate is due (*CD*, 81, 39). He even comes over time to regard himself as a type of "conqueror" for whom Mary is the well-deserved "loot" and site of occupation (*CD*, 101–2). Stephens objectifies the sense of domination attending the couple's vastly different social ranks as a vast disproportion in bodily size. Not only is the policeman, by everyone's account, abnormally big (as per Dublin Metropolitan Police [DMP] requirements), his massive frame enhances his sense of class and gender entitlement. Not only is Mary just a "slip of a girl," the contrast between her physical dimensions and the policeman's leaves her "awe-stricken" and contributes to a conscious loss of "self-possession" on her part (*CD*, 100, 38, 40). At the same time, however, owing to the cultural association of muscular power and the masculine ideal, Mary eroticizes male violence and feels a "terrible attraction" to "being hit by a man," an attraction to which the policeman's imposing frame seems especially designed to cater (*CD*, 18). That is to say, Mary responds to the policeman's forcible bodily presence not only with a sense of vulnerability bordering on fear but also with an excitement bordering on libidinal desire: "Everything desirable in manhood was concentrated in his tremendous body" (*CD,* 20). On the allegorical plane, the same profile that recommends the policeman as the chevalier of Mary's emancipation fantasies simultaneously taps an ingrained sexual and colonial dependency that leaves her vulnerable to abjection at his "great hand" (*CD*, 38).

For the reader, the policeman's double inscription straddles the line between the Imaginary and the Symbolic registers of the novel, between his placement within Mary's inner fantasy frame and his social reality as defender of the established regime. The locale of the pair's initial reencounter, Phoenix Park, encapsulates this duality in the cleavage between the perpetual rejuvenation encoded in its name and the regulatory program enacted on its grounds. The policeman introduces the topic of the eponymous phoenix, whose "singular habits," its eternal rebirth from the flames of its own destruction, raise the bird to an emblem of all manner of renewal: personal regeneration, cultural revival, and Christian resurrection. The policeman's narrative association with the phoenix speaks to his prospective status as Mary Makebelieve's suitor-savior and, by allegorical extension, as Sovereignty's heroic servant. The policeman goes on, however, to indicate that owing to these same "singular habits," the bird likely never had "a real, but only a mythical existence—that is it was a makebelieve bird, a kind of fairy tale" (*CD*, 37). With the appended clause, the policeman contrives to signal his own fantasy role at the level of the name (he is the great Makebelieve hope), while puncturing it at the level of the word (he is *only* a makebelieve hope). Through his offices, literal and figural, the personal signifier of redemptive promise gives way to the common term for mere pretending, for a fiction no one believes.

The public and uncannily germane function of the couple's immediate surroundings gives ironic contextual emphasis to this verbal play of disenchantment. From 1907 on, and so at the time of their meeting, Phoenix Park was the training headquarters both for the Royal Irish Constabulary (RIC), a semi-military police enforcing colonial rule on the Emerald Isle and for British police forces throughout the empire. Such was the influence, at this historical juncture, of the so-called Irish model of colonial policing. Although this model was most valued for its efficiency in rural areas, the Constabulary system proved no less significant in the largest towns, as the command station in Dublin betokened.[82] The RIC remained an Anglo-identified squadron as compared with the Irish-identified DMP, but given the proximity in their urban mission and the actual similarity in their ethnic and sectarian composition,[83] the policeman's membership in the DMP can be seen to bear the same relation to colonial law enforcement as his *seoininism* does to British culture generally. Phoenix Park, as the initial grounds on which the couple first meets, likewise raises expectations of native renewal at the level of symbol only to dash them on the material plane of colonial governance.

It is therefore unsurprising that far from undergoing any sense of personal refreshment at the time of her daughter's first "date," Mrs. Makebelieve, honorary Shan Van Vocht, slides inexplicably into illness on that occasion. Following a narrative line as schematic as it is magical, her decline worsens in tally with her daughter's continued assignations and then reaches a nadir on the same day that Mary distances herself from her mother (and so her heritage) by lying about her occupation: "She said her mother was a dress maker" (*CD*, 51). In an incident that rivets the component strains of bildungsroman and national allegory, Mary's misrepresentation expresses adolescent shame at her parentage that resonates with class and colonial mortification as well.

As a result of her mother's convalescence, and as symbolic retribution for her own disavowal, Mary must serve as maid in the O'Connor household. This amounts to a mini-parody of the Sovereignty myth, wherein Mary is seen to replace the old(er) woman not with "the walk of a queen" but in the crouch of a scrubwoman. Witnessing her in this posture, the policeman comes to apprehend the family secret she had labored to conceal, and the knowledge seems to infect his attitude toward Mary along lines that underscore his own *seoinin* status. Each of the changes Mary is chagrined to observe in the policeman thereafter smacks of a specifically colonial disposition on his part; his subsequent conduct toward her rehearses in miniature features commonly associated with the British domination of Ireland. First, there is Mary's sense that the policeman has her under a type of surveillance: "His advent hinted at a gross espionage, at a mind which was no longer a man's but a detective's, who tracked everybody by instinct" (*CD,* 86). Second, there is her feeling that his bodily address contains an incipient violence of possession: "He did not keep his arms quiet, but tapped his remarks into her blouse and her shoulder. Each time his hands touched her they remained a trifle longer. . . . [T]hey would grip her round and squeeze her clammily while his face spiked her to death with its mustache" (*CD,* 88). Finally, she finds that he now lavishes her with exaggerated and therefore devalued praise of her feminine attributes, the better to preen himself on his own masculinity. Given Mary's role as Sovereignty maiden, these fulsome compliments carry allegorical overtones of Matthew Arnold's famously patronizing tribute to the "feminine idiosyncrasy" of the Celt. Thus, despite their courtly ring, the compliments actually work to disabuse Mary of the notion that the policeman is a "gentleman" and so grant her insight into the "condescension" animating such chivalric pretense.[84]

With the schematic serendipity we have learned to expect in this narrative, Mary's sense of rupture with the policeman and his seoininism coincides with her mother's abrupt recovery. It also directly heralds the appearance of the "young lodger," the one avowed patriot in the novel, who is, accordingly, destined to win the affections of the Sovereignty lass. The allegorical burden of this turn is pretty transparent. Once Mary, as persona of Ireland, divests of her "shoneen" adherences, the nationalist ardor necessary for her deliverance is readily discovered. The young lodger, for his part, does not merely stumble into the Sovereignty drama surrounding the Makebelieves. Rather, he gives the mytheme its most explicit articulation in the novel, bringing it from the narrative infrastructure to the textual surface, and in the process, he refigures the mytheme as well, injecting a working-class element or sensibility into this staple of middle-class Revivalism. Augustine Martin once asked of *The Charwoman's Daughter,* "Why is the note of social revolt so absent from a working class novel written on the eve of the Great Strike of 1913?"[85] The answer is that it is not so much absent as absorbed into the national question as a decisive leavening factor. Indeed, despite Stephens's close identification with Arthur Griffith's resolutely middle-class Sinn Féin movement, he seems to have constructed the young lodger with an eye to tilting the type of nationalist subjectivity toward the so-called lower orders.

In the first place, the young lodger is the one character in the novel to openly embrace the trope of Ireland as "woman, queenly and distressed and very proud," and his hypnotic invocation of the sacred names of "the Poor Old Woman, and

Caitlin the Daughter of Houlihan" (*CD,* 107) re-marks and thus educes the parallel to the Poor Old (Char)Woman and her daughter, with whom he shares a tenement.[86] In the second place, the lodger occupies the Sovereignty narrative in a manner that sustains the parallelism between gauzy romantic legend and gritty slum reality, while at the same time signaling the *distance* between these two registers as a matter of class *difference.* His performance in this regard has the effect of reminding the reader that the Makebelieves themselves are not merely "poor"—their status in the sentimental bourgeois Imaginary—but proletarians as well, which was precisely the fact Mary endeavored to obscure in telling the policeman her mother was a dressmaker rather than a maid.

In keeping with the Sovereignty thematic, the lodger's figuration of the plight of Ireland and his conception of his own redemptive agency borrow heavily upon the twinned middle-class Revivals of the time, the Irish and the Anglo-medieval, with their shared discourses of chivalric heroism: "He yearned to do deeds of valor, violent and grandiose feats," on behalf of an abducted "princess," Ireland, whose "knights . . . slept heedless of the wrongs done to their ladies and of the defacement of their shields" (*CD,* 107). But the lodger's *actual* expressions of nationalist resistance are less about the wearing of aristocratic semblance than the airing of working-class grievance. Thus, while voicing perfunctory de rigueur denunciations of "soldiers . . . and landlords," the usual object of colonial scorn, he fulminates at great length and with "eager hostility" against "policemen" and "employers of labour," who in his view represent the true banes of urban lower-class existence (*CD,* 105–6). Policemen stalk "the three capital crimes upon which a [young] man is liable to arrest . . . being drunk, or disorderly, or refusing to fight," while they themselves fight "only in squads," cravenly relying on superior numbers to physically brutalize "any resistance offered to their spleen" (*CD,* 105). As for employers of labor, many "disowned all duty to humanity . . . merely to indulge a petty exercise of power"; they simply "exploited and bought and sold their fellow men." It is these predations and the "monstrous power" they consolidate—even more than the crimes of England—that the lodger "wished to point . . . out to all people" (*CD,* 106). Significantly, however, his attacks on these localized authorities do not contravene or eclipse his investment in cultural nationalism. To the contrary, they harbor distinct resonances of displaced colonial resentment. The references to "capital crimes" and overwhelming force regarding the police, for example, sound as if they have been rerouted from their original targets in the British military regime. But the dominant middle-class nationalism the lodger has learned is here refracted through a working-class, even socialist, optic. Following James Connolly, a likely historical model, the lodger judges the rule of England and the "defense of property" to be interchangeable modes of "spoliation" and judges "true patriotism" to be "inconsistent with the selfish desire for worldly wealth gained by [such] spoliation."[87]

Not unlike Connolly, who saw socialism as a contrarian form of Irish Revivalism, the young lodger traverses the boundaries and embodies the tensions between middle- and working-class modes of rebellion. Unsurprisingly, this cleavage manifests in his masculine gender performance, wherein a certain relationship to authority is almost invariably staged. He counterbalances his express dreams of heroic gallantry and "deeds of valor" in the service of "Banba" with tales of rather less rarefied *parade virile* at his day job: the physical intimidation, muscular display, and incipient violence more closely associated with Dublin working-class life. When his own personal Banba, Mary, tellingly inquires, "Could he fight a policeman?" his cocky reply forgoes the vocabulary of chivalric devotion and discipline for the more nakedly virile lexicon of near-brawling pugnacity (*CD,* 105).

Attached once again to the novel's parallel writing styles, the allegorical and the realistic, these discrepant class styles of masculinity intersect in the climactic act of the Sovereignty narrative: the young lodger's fisticuffs with the policeman himself, the Seoinin as both class and national adversary. On the one hand, the young lodger finds himself provoked by a much larger man, a "monument" of colonial "law," to engage in "the one really great fight of his lifetime," in which he must, all bravado aside, receive a terrible beating (*CD,* 24, 118). Furthermore, the fight is for and over a sweetheart, Mary, already symbolically identified as Caitlin and Banba, the Woman/Nation. In this context, the lodger's enthusiastic participation in this bout cannot but resonate, allegorically, with the chivalric, sacrificial nationalism that infused his own political fantasies and the Sovereignty form generally. On the other hand, at the realistic level, the lodger simply enters into an old-fashioned, mano a mano brawl, an exercise not in controlled manly strength but in the furious masculine brutality all too stereotypical of Irish slum life.

There are a number of ways to read these alternatives against one another that might serve as commentary on the alternatives themselves. Is Stephens's use of the romantic nationalist allegory intended to impart a certain manly dignity to the pluck the lodger shows in confronting his massive opponent? Or is Stephens's allegorical identification of the defense of the Woman/Nation with a Dublin street fight intended to satirize the Sovereignty form itself? Or do these contrary perspectives coexist, locating the struggle in that distinctively literary space between the ironic and the nonironic? What is certain is that Stephens gives the comic form of the Sovereignty drama, marked by its culmination in a marriage of hero and Woman/Nation, a correspondingly comic tone and content. Because the ultimate Sovereignty battle—that "greatest fight"—is pitched at the level of a Dublin street brawl, the young lodger's predicament may be hopeless, as befits the scenario of blood sacrifice, but it is neither desperate nor grave. He is sure to receive a pasting, but he is equally sure to survive more or less whole. Accordingly, the lodger not only goes to defeat cheerfully, as Pearse dreamed his boy corps would do,[88] he reflects upon the defeat still more cheerfully afterward, his "deplorable appearance" notwithstanding (*CD*, 118). The lodger regards the ordeal primarily as a test of manhood, defined in terms of mettle as well as muscle, a test he has passed: "The young man did not require either condolences or revenge. He was well pleased at an opportunity to measure his hardihood against a worthy opponent. He had found that his courage exceeded his strength, as it always should" (*CD*, 120). Viewed in relation to Mary's more extended *bildung,* the clash might even be defined as a rite of passage marking his entry *into* manhood.

The "extraordinary happiness" (*CD*, 118) the lodger manages to draw from his drubbing introduces the added step that Stephens takes to resolve the Sovereignty format on an apparently comic footing. All of the major Sovereignty dramas, of course, link the higher symbolic marriage of male patriot with Woman/Nation to his imminent sacrificial death, which reverberates in turn with the prospect of collective rebirth and liberation. By contrast, Stephens's rewriting of the Sovereignty climax in the lower cas(t)e telescopes this renovative dynamic. Instead of extinction and then renewal, sacrifice and compensation, the defeat of the lodger turns immediately into the end sought rather than the means to achieve it, a spiritual tonic in itself. The notorious Irish ideology of sanctified failure, which we have traced in Gregory's "Felons of Our Land" and Pearse's blood sacrifice, here crystallizes in a pure valorizing of defeat: the good inheres not in the lost cause (Pearse), nor in the cause insofar as it is already lost (Gregory), nor even in the eternal fame of glorious sacrifice (Yeats, Gregory, Pearse), but in the very experience of loss itself, which bestows an awareness of "courage exceed[ing] strength." The lodger does not actually practice manly sublimation, *strictu sensu,* for sublimation involves deferring one's baser impulses to realize a higher good—a recognizably middle-class logic of savings and "return." Rather, the lodger engages in endless *self-contestation,* which draws upon the signature working-class virtues of endurance and resiliency in the face of hardship.

In situating the lodger between the mythic summons of middle-class nationalism and the life world of the urban slum, Stephens is able to enlist the lower- or working-class sensibility as an *immanent* challenge to the governing ideology of the Sovereignty format, what Lacan calls "the exception": a deviation from the norm that discloses its concealed truth.[89] The lodger, by cherishing his defeat not as a means to ultimate victory—the so-called triumph of failure[90]—but as success in and by itself, might be seen to practice an Irish *ascesis* even less touched by the impulses of seoininism than blood sacrifice, because it is entirely *unconcerned* with gain or profit of any sort, a theoretically purer form. Yet in a practical vein, the lodger's ethos amounts to a parody of the fantasy at the core of blood sacrifice and so of modern Sovereignty heroism: that well-intended self-destruction is redemptive, politically or otherwise; that righteous ruin, like the phoenix, is self-leveraging; that a strong-enough attachment to the wages of defeat can make it count as victory.

The lodger actualizes these self-gratifying paradoxes, to be sure, but in a purely formal, not to say empty, sense. Thus, on the strength of his masculine performance, he seems poised to consummate the Sovereignty marriage, claiming both the maiden/nation and the heroic laurels, yet he can do so properly only if the outlook underpinning this performance, the embrace of defeat as an essential good, can *itself* be defeated. The climax of the Sovereignty narrative, "the greatest fight of his lifetime," thus issues in both an explicit affirmation and an implied critique of the nationalist ethos it represents. With this gambit, Stephens sets up a closural strategy as delicate as it is clever: to round off the Sovereignty format in robustly comic terms, but to do so at the comic expense of the Sovereignty genre itself.

To this end, the closing chapter of *The Charwoman's Daughter* disentangles the two strands of the Makebelieve fairy tale, the family fortune plot and the national romance plot, as a way of prizing apart the novel's fantastic and realistic dimensions and encouraging them to be read *against* one another. Financial deliverance for the Makebelieves comes right away, in an envelope announcing a princely, unlooked-for bequest from an American relative. Arriving out of the blue and following so inorganically from the story so far, this unforeseeable deus ex machina calls heightened attention to the novel's magical subgenres, fairy tale and myth, as sites of fabulous, arbitrary, and even unwarranted wish fulfillment, cultural synonyms for the impossible-come-true.[91] The effect is to furnish a comic resolution to the family-fortunes plot but to concede in the same textual breath the stagy, manufactured quality of such a "happy ending." Without infusing the action represented, a certain ambivalence hangs over the narrative frame, calling into doubt the facile satisfactions that myth and fairy tale sometimes provide.

The ironic, self-qualifying nature of this comic denouement transfers its contaminating energies to the national romance plot. The inherited estate means that Mary's earlier rejection of Seoininism does not in the end cost her the fruits of Seoininism. With this hyperbolic wish fulfillment in place, she is all the more easy about entertaining the courtship of that symmetrical opposite of a Seoinin, the lodger, whose purified nationalism manifests precisely as an embrace of adversity for its own sake. Indeed, the bulk of the courtship in the last chapter unfolds as a single lengthy disquisition on his self-bruising life philosophy. The disquisition transpires as the lodger goes out walking with Mary "on the evening of the same day" that the notice of inheritance arrives, and this specific temporal designation should not be taken lightly. As we have seen throughout, Stephens is extraordinarily careful to wring significance from the simultaneity and contiguity of events. In this case, the coincidence invites the reader to construe the sentiments of the lodger in the fantasy light projected by the fairy-tale bequest, rather than as gospel commentary on the text itself.

No sooner does the couple's stroll begin than the young lodger becomes the focus for an encomium on hunger: "He was sad as only a well fed person could be. Now that his hunger was gone he deemed that all else was gone also" (*CD*, 125). Once his hunger returned, however, "his spirits rose. He was no longer solid, space belonged to him also. . . . Now everything was possible" (*CD*, 126). As Stephens well knew, Irish hunger could not be so steadily contemplated without raising the specter of the Great Hunger or Famine, survivors of which would still have been alive at the time he was writing. As a result, the metaphorical use of hunger as a void or lack (a "space") that breeds all manner of the "possible" crashes headlong into hunger as a material state of deprivation so basic that the possibility most valued would simply be to remedy it. The praise of adversity encounters a vicious circle in which the singular benefit of adversity seems to be providing a motive for bringing said condition to an end. And indeed, the same treatise, still attached to the lodger, lauds evil itself ("next to good the most valuable factor in life") for providing the "valorous alarms" necessary for it to be "vanquished" (*CD*, 127). That the lodger cannot enjoy his romance with Mary except as stimulated by such bodily distress not only acquires an added perversity in this light but also, given the historical resonance of Irish hunger, seems to index a nationalist attachment to the "buffer of misfortune" (*CD*, 126).

The disquisition persists in its circular, self-consuming logic. An alimentary trope connects the lodger's cherished experience of hunger with the "ripening" welts he had received from the policeman: "He felt the sting and tightness of his bruises . . . they would be his meat and drink and happiness" (*CD*, 126). Coming hard upon his strictures on satiety, the figuration of the lodger's "bruises" as nourishment, and hence the antidote to an indispensable hunger, strangely renders this wounding a negation, a bane, precisely insofar as it is a boon, a positive form of sustenance. The food metaphor thus carries a deeply ironic charge. To fill out the lodger's rite of passage to an approved, "predestined" manhood, his bruises must simultaneously counter the emptiness that his romance with Mary-Éire—the highest function of that manhood—seems to require. At this point, by mapping onto the profound contradiction at work in the Irish culture of glorified hardship, Stephens's oscillating discourse of enchantment-disenchantment concentrates itself in a single double-sided utterance that registers skepticism of that culture in and through its improbable affirmation of it.

In *Structuralist Anthropology,* Levi-Strauss famously contends that the function of cultural myths is to furnish imaginary resolutions for real social contradictions. Taking up this argument, Frederic Jameson no less famously holds that the novel serves this mythic function in modern times.[92] But in the unfolding of the "dialectic of enlightenment," the modernist novel—from Joyce's *Ulysses* to Woolf's *Between the Acts* and Orwell's *Keep the Aspidistra Flying*—has also taken cultural myths as its primary object of representation, usually with the purpose of interrogating and dismantling the imaginary resolutions they forge. For the modernist novel, that is to say, mythic narratives often act not as models for addressing social contradictions but as aspects or symptoms of those social contradictions. Poised on the historical and sociocultural threshold of modernism, *The Charwoman's Daughter* achieves its distinctive iridescence by enlisting mythic narrative to perform both roles simultaneously—that is, by aligning itself with the myth it deconstructs. As we have seen, the modern Sovereignty narrative bids to resolve the double bind of Irish manhood by translating the tactics of material-practical weakness into a sacrificial image of spiritualized potency. In the masculine *ascesis* of the relatively deprived lodger, *The Charwoman's Daughter* affirms this stratagem as a course of resistance to the colonial hegemony exemplified by the Seoinin. But in the enhancement of this spiritual *ascesis,* its detachment from any ulterior motive, the novel shows how the ethic of suffering cannot but continue to participate in, to court if you will, the material-practical futility it would rehabilitate. So in the final analysis, we find that Stephens's double take on the Sovereignty myth does something more than hedge his bets, something more too than transform ideological counterthrust into aesthetic equipoise. It opens, in a strikingly prescient manner, some of the most pressing contradictions for *post*colonial Ireland and indeed postcolonial societies across the globe: how ideological tools of decolonization and liberation can also prove instruments of self-imprisonment, how the subaltern identification with the dispossessed condition as a source of moral authority and mobilizing power can slide into a fetishism of disadvantage, and how the effective transvaluation of the colonizer's stereotypes (for example, the "tragic Celt")[93] can serve to validate nativist but nonetheless debilitating cultural habits.

Brothers in Arms

Culled from the heroic cycle of Ulster, the legend of Cuchulain furnished the Revival with a second dominant myth of Irish manhood. Here again, Augusta Gregory stood out as the indispensable agent in the transmission of national ideals of masculinity. Among the several renditions of the Red Branch tales that appeared from 1878 to 1916, her *Cuchulain at Muirthemne* excelled in the unity of its narrative form, the polish of its literary style, and its consequent popularity as a source of cultural entertainment and inspiration.[1] Her treatment, moreover, was as representative in its political agenda and ideological tendencies as it was extraordinary in the effectiveness with which it advanced them. Impelled by her characteristic obsession with restoring Irish "dignity," Lady Gregory, not unlike her colleagues in popular translation (Standish J. O'Grady, A. H. Leahy, Eleanor Hull, Betty Hutton, and Winifred Faraday), looked to validate indigenous forms of Irish civilization as a means of countering imperialist stereotypes and cultivating the nativist pride and confidence of her compatriots. This project, however, led her and her compeers into a mass of contradictions that contemporary scholars, relying on more scholarly translations, like Standish H. O'Grady, Cecile O'Rahilly, and Thomas Kinsella, are still in the process of sorting out.

Inventing Cuchulain

In *Irish Classics,* the preeminent critic of the Literary Revival, Declan Kiberd, observes that Cuchulain, like "all figures from the Irish past . . . invariably seemed on closer inspection to be a disguised version of the British Imperial present." Kiberd trains his perception specifically upon the issue of masculine normativity that occupies us here. He argues that "Cuchulain was noted for combining a propensity to Pagan violence against enemies with a Christlike sensitivity: but this was exactly the commendation much praised in the muscular Christians of Eton and Rugby." By this point, of course, we have seen that cultivated discipline rather than inborn "sensitivity" formed the muscular counterweight to naked animal aggression. Nevertheless, on Kiberd's reading, the Revivalists inherited a heroic paragon of manly virtue, already "famous for chivalry," whose peculiar blend of exemplary attributes perfectly suited the task of forging Irish national identity as a manly identity, though his profile might uncannily smack, for this very reason, of the "public school boy in drag."[2]

But scholars who focus primarily on the source materials themselves, rather than on the Revivalist movement, offer a notably different and more persuasive analysis of those materials' late-colonial adaptation. Far from locating something like a British-flavored manliness anachronistically lodged in the Red Branch cycle, the popular translators of the cycle—Standish James O'Grady, Hull, Hutton, and Gregory—undertook, for strategic reasons, to retrofit the bardic heritage to the canons of late Victorian respectability, to bowdlerize and embellish the heroic narratives so as to infuse them with the aesthetic and ethical decorum the translators would like, and would claim, to have discovered. Thus, Maria Tymoczko, in her magisterial *Translation in a Post-Colonial Context,* observes that "translated fully and accurately," the *Tain Bó Cúailnge*—the very heart of the heroic cycle—could have only proven "an embarrassment" to Irish cultural nationalism, being too "unliterary, raunchy and weird" for the dominant, which is to say English, "standards of judgment." Instead of facilitating "the political aim to shift the image of the Irish and to . . . embrace their ancient and noble culture," the *Tain* "could politically confirm the stereotypes of the Irish as wild, uncivilized and in need of conversion." To avoid this outcome while "establishing the greatness of Ireland's cultural heritage," reports Tymoczko, these translators found it necessary to engage in a pattern of partially suppressing the Red Branch cycle and, we might add, a supplementary pattern of embellishment and interpolation.[3]

According to Tymoczko, the most "important adaptation of the material," at least in structural terms, "was its assimilation to a biographical framework," which in focusing on the life of singular champions "worked to counter the depersonalization that colonized people suffer" by "stressing the individualism of Irish mythic characters," historical figures, and, by extension, the Irish people at large.[4] Indeed, it was precisely as the arch vehicle in this revisionist narrative strategy that Cuchulain came to emerge so decisively as the foremost personification of Irish revolutionary nationalism. Having said that, the individualism Cuchulain is summoned to embody for the Irish nation begins, but *only* begins, with the sort of individuality that a biographical or *bildung* framework can confer. In modern liberal societies, individualism was understood as a necessary credential for any claim upon enfranchisement or even humanity in its fullest sense, and was strongly identified with a certain gendered quality of subject—an animal vigor self-sublimated to the dignity of moral rigor—what I have been calling the "subject of freedom." Thus, to glorify his ethnic progeny, Cuchulain had to emerge not only as an individual man, against otherwise interchangeable warriors or tribesmen, but also as a manly individual, someone who channels the ferocity expected of the elite warrior into a strenuous discipline and dutifulness, born of an allegiance to an agonistic code of honor. To this end, the Revivalist translations elaborated an image of Cuchulain (subsequently monumentalized in the famous statue at the General Post Office) as a so-called hero of the tribe, a warrior celebrated for sublimating his individual valor and rapacity to the defense of the social order.

As noted Gaelicist Jeremy Lowe has shown, however, the minting of a national hero in this case involved more than framing the original texts in such a way as to set off Cuchulain as the main protagonist and to encourage an affirmative construction of his exploits; it was more too than some cursory embellishments designed to highlight virtues especially relevant to contemporary nationalism. This process was more, in sum, than the ensemble of practices that would today go under the heading of "spin." Instead, the modern coinage of Cuchulain in-volved downplaying, eliding, ignoring, or excising massive textual evidence of the powerfully destabilizing impact that the Hound's avid pursuit of a nonpareil heroic stature had upon the existing social order, its codes of honor, or even the coherence and stability of his own embodied self-identity. Indeed, on the con-sensus of today's Old Irish scholars, the "Tain" and surrounding documents were far more concerned with critiquing than with celebrating warrior culture and its violent standards of heroism. As Joan Radner puts it, "Ireland's noble warriors, however admirable, were tragically self-destructive and ineffective," a sentiment she finds Cuchulain himself confirming in his famous pronouncement, "Conscar bara bith" (Battle fury destroys the world). Daniel F. Melia seconds Radner's thesis as a kind of foundational paradox: "The more successfully [the warrior class] is able to fulfill its function, the more dangerous it is to the society which it serves." Cuchulain is not just centrally implicated in this indictment but he is also, in Lowe's words, "perfectly placed to challenge the very core of the heroic ethos."[5]

The triumphalism of the heroic cycle, then, like the Irish culture of defeat, was an "invented tradition" of Revivalism rather than a cultural inheritance. But the nature of the invention has a far greater import than the mere fact, particularly as pertains to the figure of Cuchulain. One of the principal aims of this study has been to educe that contrary to popular opinion, the revolutionary Irish nationalism with which the Revival was unevenly confederated could never simply embrace a posture of so-called colonial hypermasculinity as a bulwark against racial feminization, lest it give hostage to the typological counterthrust of racial simian or bestialization. Well, if there ever existed an authoritative Irish exemplar of such hypermasculinity, it is surely the Cuchulain of the *Book of Leinster* or the *Dun Cow*. From his scheming to find barely licit advantage to his defiance of tribal superiors, from his cruelty in combat to his easy participation in the misogyny of his culture, the Hound of Ulster personifies the Gael as "an essentially [or excessively] masculine race." Yet it was precisely this aspect of the legendary strong man that Revivalist adaptations sought to domesticate in order to sublimate.

The ultimate *parade virile* in the entire Ulster cycle is Cuchulain's patented *riastrad* or "warp-spasm," and the exorbitancy of this state of upheaval crystallizes the ideological problems Cuchulain's seemingly inestimable hypermasculinity posed for his nationalist boosters.[6] In the heat of battle, and the grip of rage, the Hound convulsively morphed into a towering, distorted, preternaturally violent figure, much as the Incredible Hulk does, only in far more graphic bodily detail. A recent scholarly translation of Cuchulain's metamorphosis after the death of the boy corps captures the horrific effect:

> Then his first distortion came upon Cú Chulainn so that he became horrible, many-shaped, strange and unrecognisable. His haunches shook about him like a tree in a current . . . every limb and every joint, every end and every member of him from head to foot. He performed a wild feat of contortion with his body inside his skin. His feet and his shins and his knees came to the back; his heels and his calves and his hams came to the front. The sinews of his calves came on the front of his shins and each huge, round knot of them was a big as a warrior's fist. The sinews of his head were stretched to the nape of his neck and every huge, immeasurable, vast, incalculable round ball of them was as big as the head of a month-old child.
>
> Then his face became a red hollow. He sucked one of his eyes into his head so that a wild crane could hardly have reached it to pluck it out from the back of his skull on to the middle of his cheek. The other eye sprang out onto his cheek. His mouth was twisted back fearsomely. He drew the cheek back from the jawbone until the inner gullet was seen. His lungs and his liver fluttered in his mouth and his throat. He struck a lion's blow with the upper pallet . . . so that every stream of fiery lakes within came into his mouth from his throat was as large as the skin of a three-year-old sheep. The loud beating of his heart . . . was heard like the baying of a bloodhound . . . or like a lion attacking bears. . . . [T]he hero's light rose from his forehead so that it was as long and thick as a hero's whetstone. As high, as thick, as strong, as powerful and as long as the mast of a great ship was the straight stream of dark blood which rose up from the very top of his head and became a dark magical mist."[7]

If size matters, not to mention gargantuan might and invincible mettle, then the transformed Cuchulain must be seen to represent the zenith of heroic masculinity in the warrior mode. But at the same time, and for the same reason, Cuchulain also falls below the spectrum of humanity altogether, becomes a pure monstrosity, and one reminiscent of the feral images of bestialized natives promulgated in imperialist popular culture. Nor does Cuchulain's lapse in properly human subjectivity derive merely from the sudden hideousness of his lineaments or the savagery of his presence (qualities Cuchulain himself regrets the following morning).[8] As Lowe notes, the terms *riastrad* and its alternate *siabrad* "are both used as impersonal passives," which indicates that the warp-spasm, though emerging from within the champion's body, occurs outside his volition or capacity for self-control.[9] At moments of warp-spasm, Lowe notes, Cuchulain is entirely prey to "bodily excitation," or what the Victorians would call the anarchy of animal spirits, which at once overwhelms and dissolves his very identity, gender and otherwise.

While Cuchulain is regularly posted along the Ulster border in order to perform the characteristically masculine duty of guarding the communal territory against foreign penetration, his signature device for mounting this defense disturbs and even destroys the integrity or boundaries of his own physical frame. This combination bespeaks the profound contradiction in hypermasculinity as a social performance: the very excessiveness whereby it comes to simulate an *ideal* of masculinity simultaneously spells a loss of the rudimentary *benchmark* of masculinity, the capacity for effective self-will. The Red Branch cycle plays this paradox out in narrative terms as a disjunction between heroic actions and their consequences. Because these actions are undertaken in such a bloodthirsty fashion, they often produce results that are not just tragic but wasteful and self-defeating—Cuchulain's slaughter of his own son being a prime example.

There is little the popular translations could do to soften the barbarous impression left by the *riastrad,* other than simply to abridge or bowdlerize the textual interludes given over to this organic emblem of hypermasculinity. L. Winifred Faraday follows exactly this path in *The Cattle-Raid of Cualange,* shrinking the cited passage to a mere fourteen lines and eliminating the graphic animal contortions and comparisons.[10] But it is Lady Gregory who takes this tactic to its tendentious extreme. First, her *Cuchulain at Muirthemne* excises the *riastrads* altogether, and what she leaves bears an import directly opposed to the original construct:

> And it is then Cuchulain's anger came on him, and the flames of his herolight began to shine about his head . . . and he lost the appearance of a man, and what was on him was the appearance of a god.

> [H]is anger came on him, so it was not his own appearance he had on him but the appearance of a god.[11]

With an apparently straight rhetorical face, Gregory here renders Cuchulain's defining experience, physical engrossment and distortion, as spiritual transcendence. Such a rarefied depiction, in turn, acts to sanctify the bloody brutish trade that Cuchulain plies and epitomizes, leaving him available for revolutionary emulation.

When it comes to Cuchulain's social expression (as opposed to his symbolic enactment) of hypermasculinity, these same editorial practices of selective elision and embellishment tend to obey, in aggregate, an organizing principle that alters the spirit of the entire heroic cycle, or at least the main hero of that cycle. More than locally airbrushing the Hound's more feral and phallic propensities, the popular translations of O'Grady, Gregory, Hall, Hutton, and others endeavor to represent his animal spirits as broadly subject to and constrained by a native species of heroic discipline. They effect, that is, an ideological translation of Cuchulain, the hypermasculine specimen, to Cuchulain, the paragon of manliness, in order to identify the Irish ethnos he personifies with the latter (and higher) standard of gender performance. These translations' primary discursive means, like those of the Sovereignty drama, involve a subterranean mapping of Irish Revivalism onto the recent vogue of Medieval Revivalism in Britain that, as noted earlier, had successfully enshrined the chivalric code as an enhanced precursor of the manly imperative.[12]

O'Grady set the tone for this pattern of culture-assimilationism in a series of very loose translations of the cycle, which were actually begun prior to the Irish Revival proper and in the midst of its medievalist counterpart.[13] As Tymoczko has observed, O'Grady transposed the Irish heroic narrative onto the generic frame of the Victorian boys' adventure tale, a preferred cultural site for conflating chivalric ideals with the public school ethos.[14] This synthesis in turn dominates O'Grady's *Coming of Cuchulain*. To take one example, O'Grady grossly sentimentalizes Cuchulain's initial rejection and ultimate acceptance by the boy corps, so that his moral sensitivity and social clubability receive equal billing with his precocious might. As a result, Cuchulain's introduction to Emain Macha, mediated by an invitation to join in team sports, resonates unmistakably with Tom Brown's introduction to Rugby, albeit in a key elevated by O'Grady's fulsomely romantic diction ("Truly he was the pure burning torch of the chivalry of the Ultonians in his time"). O'Grady seems to have envisioned the boy corps as a public school for medieval knights of the Cross, and Cuchulain's graduation in fact comes with a knighting ceremony at wide variance, ideologically and institutionally, from his "taking up of arms" in the other translations. This formal investiture of knighthood marks the young hero's inculcation not just in the skills of battle ("to hurl spears . . . to train war-horses and guide war-chariots; to lay on with the sword and defend themselves with sword and shield"), but also, and almost comically, in the high-minded menu of self-restraining virtues, the amalgamation of which went by the single name of manliness: "to speak appropriately with equals and superiors and inferiors and to exhibit the beautiful practices of hospitality according to the rank of guests[;] . . . to drink and be merry in the hall, but always without intoxication[;] . . . to respect their plighted word and be ever loyal to their captains; to reverence women, remembering always those who bore them[;] . . . to be kind to the feeble and unwarlike; and all that it became brave men to feel and think and do in war and in peace."[15] Rewriting the Red Branch as the Round Table, in an adolescent pastiche of courtly style ("plighted troth," "ever-loyal"), the catalog forecasts Cuchulain's espousal, in upcoming adventures, of ethical values that were either conspicuously eschewed by him in the original text (such as respect for rank) or were anachronistic for Red Branch society at large (for example, a medieval "reverence [for] women").

In consideration of O'Grady's role in refurbishing Cuchulain in manly form, it is telling that O'Grady was an enthusiast of Thomas Carlyle, who, as discussed in chapter 1, was both a founding apostle of the cult of manliness and a bombastic villifier of what he saw as Irish bestiality. The revivalist Cuchulain thus has his origins not just in the British Medievalist Revival but also in the gendered logic whereby it sought to give British superiority to the Irish a simultaneously natural and moral warrant.

Scholars have attributed O'Grady's portrayal of the Ultonians as a social and moral elite out of a Carlylian romance to his own Ascendancy sympathies and his distinctly aristocratic brand of irredentism.[16] But if O'Grady was the most strenuous, or least subtle, in establishing Cuchulain as the "type of chivalry," this particular brand of gendered idealization marked all the popular translations of the Revival era. Thus, as the end of the Revival's run drew near, Eleanor Hull, who had edited an earlier scholarly translation of the heroic cycle (*The Cuchullin Saga* [1898]), prefaced her own popular compendium, *Cuchulain: The Hound of Ulster* with the assurance that these tales of ancient Ireland breathe a chivalric nobility of a most authentic kind:

> As the Arthuran legend all through the middle ages set before men's minds an ideal of high purpose, purity of life, and chivalrous behavior . . . so these old Irish romances, so late rescued from oblivion, come to recall the minds of men in our own day some noble ideals. . . . For rude as are the social conditions depicted in these tales and exaggerated and barbaric as is the flavour of some of them, they nevertheless present to us a high and often romantic code of natural chivalry. There is no more pathetic story in literature than that of the fight between two old and loving friends, Cuchullain and Ferdia; there is no more touching act of chivalry to a woman than Cuchullain's offer of aid to his enemy, Queen Maeve, in the moment of her exhaustion.[17]

I've quoted this appreciation at length because it showcases the main rhetorical measures that generally appeared in the nationalist reconstruction of Cuchulainoid heroism:

1. Hull engineers a historical metalepsis wherein the Red Branch order, having been re-created in the image of Arthurian virtue, is designated the earlier and unsurpassed repository of such virtue, under the vaguely oxymoronic label, "natural chivalry." With this metaleptic gesture, Revivalist translators like Hull were able to disavow a) trimming Irish heroism to suit a foreign fashion, and so satisfy a foreign standard, and b) the metrocolonial ambivalence that motivated that practice. It was precisely this sort of metalepsis that enabled Lady Gregory to use the Morte d'Arthur, in good conscience, as the model for her *Cuchulain*.[18]

2. In elaborating this claim, Hull partitions "natural chivalry" along a distinct gender bias. As observed between men, chivalry comprises a sympathetic fraternity based on the mutual respect of equals. That is the presumed burden of the Ferdia (or Fer Diad) episode. As observed by men toward women, chivalry comprises a sympathetic willingness to provide service or protection based on the sentimentalized weakness or inferiority of the recipient. That is the presumed burden of the Maeve episode. In either case, man is always the chivalric agent, even when he is also an object of the action, while woman is always an object, even when she enjoys a compensatory form of "reverence." A political synonymy is hereby established between the medieval code of chivalry, upon which Hull and her peers draw in depicting Cuchulain, and its modern correlative, manliness, which they are actually modeling in their depiction. The subject of (medieval, aristocratic) honor could be invoked as a glorified type of the subject of (modern, middle-class) freedom, because both express and affirm the same or at least a similar patriarchal agenda.

3. Hull's apologia previews the technique of textual synecdoche whereby Revivalist translations modify the composition or proportions of the manuscript narratives in order to enable incidents of a seemingly chivalric tenor to anchor or dominate the cycle. The two episodes that Hull mentions were especially popular candidates for this sort of aggrandizement. Indeed, Tymoczko remarks that Gregory made certain that her wildly popular abridgment of the *Tain* (1904) was "heavily weighted toward the Fer Diad section," while A. H. Leahy gave the entire first volume of his *Heroic Romances of Ireland* (1905–1906) over to the Fer Diad encounter, effectively allowing it "to stand for the *Tain* as a whole." In her rendition of the *Táin* (a favorite at St. Enda's Academy), Hutton goes even further down this editorial road. She replaces all the less respectable parts of the original epic "with noble, heroic or tragic stories from other parts of the cycle," thereby fashioning the *Táin* itself into a kind of synecdoche, a condensation of the noblest moments diffused throughout the materials.[19]

For the last mode of refiguration to achieve its desired effects, which are the most concrete and widespread of all, supplementary measures of editorial intervention and alteration prove necessary. Even the most honorable encounters between well-bred warriors contained elements that chivalric decorum could not abide; even the most exalted treatment of high-born women carried misogynistic overtones far too conspicuous for the courtly paradigm to admit. And if these leading set pieces required a certain amount of sanitizing before they could be given pride of place, as touchstones of a beau ideal, so much more did other episodes, whose grosser violations of a romanticized code of manliness stood to belie the ethical integrity and disturb the aesthetic equipoise of the (revamped) whole. Surveying from the featured episodes outward, in both the "masculine" and the "feminine" registers, we can ascertain the type of emendations employed to forge the Revivalist transition from a hypermasculine to a manly Cuchulain, from a rampaging strongman to a morally disciplined warrior.

The Fer Diad episode seemed, in Hull's words, "full of the true spirit of chivalry," owing to the principal's honorable response to a tragic conflict of commitment. Foster brothers who trained together under their foster mother, Cuchulain and Fer Diad resolved to fight one another to the death out of a still greater loyalty to a tribe, a cause, and, most of all, their own sense of honor. But to preserve the chivalric nobility of the scene, the translations of Gregory, Hull (1909), Hutton, and O'Grady found it necessary to excerpt aggressively from the heroes' preparatory statements of purpose, wherein their sense of honor melded into a less rarefied *amour* propre. While each warrior deplores the other's willingness to break their intimate personal bond on the anvil of combat, the less expurgated translations of O'Rahilly and Kinsella denote that the main burden of both warriors' initial overtures is to cast aspersions on the other's prowess in arms while boasting of their own. The respective addresses read, then, like what in today's sports vernacular we call "trash talking," and they accordingly frame the ensuing clash as a hypermasculine *parade virile*. It is, at least in part, the Revivalist elision of these speeches that contours the Ferdia as a locus of the "elevation and dignity," "honor and delicacy," and "chivalrous generousity" that Hull conjures forth.[20] This trash talking, in turn, links the scene back to Cuchulain's earlier contest with his foster brother, Faerbaeth, wherein the "bond of friendship" counted for nothing compared with the vow to fight. It is no accident that the most romantic of the translations, O'Grady's and Hull's, delete the latter incident entirely, thereby protecting the tragic aura of the (bowdlerized) Ferdia.

But the conclusion of the Ferdia episode received still more consequential editorial manipulation than its prologue—once again in the interest of showcasing its putative "spirit of chivalry." As Ferdia falls by Cuchulain's notorious weapon, Gáe Bulga, he announces his doom as a reproach upon his adversary.

The popular translations either dropped the reproach altogether (Hutton) or couched it as alluding to and reaffirming the brothers' fraternal bond: "It is not right that I should die by thee, oh Hound" (Hull); "It was not right of you to kill me" (Gregory).[21] In either case, the scene passes smoothly to its chivalric climax: Cuchulain's touching eulogy for the foster brother he has slain. The scholarly translations, however, reveal another more corrosive element in the reproach, the excision of which seems vital to Cuchulain's Revivalist makeover. To some degree, in each of the fuller unsanitized renditions, Ferdia's last words can be understood to accuse Cuchulain of violating the dominant ethical mandate of his society and class, the precept of Fir Fer, fair play, literally "the truth of man."[22]

In early Irish literature, the concept of Fir Fer applies primarily to one-on-one combat and holds the participants to observe rules of conduct agreed upon or assumed, as well as less reliably demarcated principles of evenhandedness. But as Philip O'Leary has pointed out, in the Ulster cycle, Fir Fer represents a rigorous code of personal honor that is nonetheless systematically transgressed on all sides in the pursuit of *public* glory. Fir Fer thus emerges over the course of the tales as the site of a momentous ideological contradiction: it is perhaps the only internalized ethical concept in the Gaelic warrior culture, yet a treacherous infringement of its code proves an externally "acceptable means to the all-important end of fame." Adopting an ethnographical perspective, O'Leary takes the cycle's regular flouting of Fir Fer to signal that the "ethical sophistication" it marked still remained very much *in potentia,* while Lowe judges the inherently competitive nature of warrior society to have overwhelmed the creed designed to contain it. The matter looks different, however, when viewed through the more appropriate optic of literary criticism. In staging Fir Fer as an ethos at once hallowed and systematically infringed upon, the Ulster cycle continues its cited critique of battle fury—what we might today call rampant hypermasculinity—on a properly *immanent* basis. The precept of Fir Fer provides the narrative with an alternative to a material or martial success-at-all-costs philosophy, and the narrative, in turn, shows the Red Branch society sharing in that alternative standard, even as it systematically breaches it, allowing such success to stand, in O'Leary's words, "as its own validation."[23] If we take seriously the etymological meaning of Fir Fer, "the truth of man," then the approved circumvention of its dictates cannot but register as a gendered self-betrayal on the part of the warrior elite, a textually italicized failure to keep faith with their own truth as men—or, in modern terms, the truth of manliness.

Cuchulain's notorious participation in this endemic breach of honor is instanced in, though by no means limited to, the (less expurgated) Ferdia episode.[24] O'Grady's scholarly translation sees Ferdia proclaim, "I fall by that. But in truth to say, that I am sickly after thee; for it did not behoove thee that I should fall by thy hand." Ferdia's unusual complaint of sickliness makes reference to the operation of Cuchulain's signature engine of death, Gáe Bulga ("warrior fear"): "it passed . . . into him, so that every crevasse and every cavity of his body was filled with its barbs."[25] Now the uniquely destructive capacity of Gáe Bulga, to which Cuchulain alone had access, is on its face a violation of the fair-fight principle of Fir Fer, and "is repeatedly condemned by [Cuchulain's] foes" on these grounds.[26] Though these same victims, according to O'Leary, generally accept Cuchulain's use of the weapon before they die, Ferdia would seem to be the especially inconvenient exception. In the O'Rahilly translation, Fer Diad tells Cuchulain, "Yours is the guilt" for "my blood," rather than the laurels of victory, and he speaks of himself as one of the "heroes destroyed" in the "gap of betrayal," strongly suggesting a dishonorable even duplicitous practice on the part of his nemesis.[27] In Kinsella's recent translation, which specifically aims to restore material that Gregory had purged, Ferdia offers a still more explicit indictment. He tells the Hound:

> You have killed me unfairly
> Your guilt clings to me
> As my blood sticks to you.

He then charges him with "deceit."[28] Since the treacherous Gáe Bulga is not merely Cuchulain's decisive weapon but the very key to his invincibility (as his battle with Ferdia proves), Cuchulain's outsized heroic stature remains inextricably bound up with his willingness to skirt the ethical code. In this sense, Cuchulain figures centrally in the cycle's immanent critique of a social order unhinged by the violent agonism it continues to prize. Piercing the anus and irradiating throughout the body of its victim, Gáe Bulga has been said to produce "the greatest abasement of the male gendered heroic person."[29] But given the ambiguously illicit nature of Gáe Bulga, can we not deduce that this debasement is emblematic of a larger corruption, the corruption of a masculinized body politic that equivocally allows for the violation of its own heroic ideal, its own "truth of man"? Thus, in portraying the Gaelic warrior as an apotheosis of chivalry, the Revivalist translators had not only to sanitize the details of the *Tain* but also to mistake its governing point of view and hence its guiding purport. In so doing, moreover, these translators in no way mitigated the masculine violence ubiquitous in the *Tain*, but rather paradoxically validated the specifically chivalric display thereof. Here again, by giving Cuchulain's hypermasculinity an acceptably disciplined countenance, a human as opposed to animal visage, the conversion to manliness not only constrains savage display, in keeping with the stakes of a racialized counterdiscourse, but in a further twist of the dialectical screw, it selectively moralizes such display as well, in keeping with the prerogatives of revolutionary nationalism.

Cuchulain's trespass against Fir Fer extends beyond his use of Gáe Bulga.

Fighting against Nadcranntail, for instance, Cuchulain frames his breach of the announced rules of engagement as a reformulation thereof, fashioning a simulacrum of fair play that awards him a clear advantage. Cuchulain shirks Fir Fer more crudely while still in fosterage to Scḁthach, who endowed him with Gáe Bulga. During this training period, Cuchulain first encounters Aoife in battle, on "the rope of feats," and she smashes his sword to the hilt. Instead of graciously conceding defeat, Cuchulain plays upon her extraordinary concern for her chariot crew and, distracting her with words of their demise, "seized her by the two breasts . . . threw her heavily to the ground and held a naked sword over her."[30] He then extracts her promise, on pain of death, to sleep with him and bear him a son. In sum, Cuchulain responds to a legitimate straightforward challenge to his phallic mastery, symbolized by the sword, with a duplicitous, not to say brutish, reimposition of that mastery, corporealized in the act of forced sexual reproduction.

It is no surprise that the popular translations of this portion of the cycle see fit either to delete the incident altogether, as O'Grady and Hutton do, or to extenuate by revision the odiously ungallant tenor of Cuchulain's conduct. Gregory, for example, quietly drops Cuchulain's manhandling of Aoife's breasts, indicates that the warrior-queen "gave her love to Cuchulain" of her own accord, and, to cap things off, reports that Aoife gave him the Gáe Bulga herself.[31] This Revivalist whitewash is even less surprising when one considers that Cuchulain's joust with Aoife straddles the boundary between the "masculine" and the "feminine" register of chivalric expectation. If the Hound's hoodwinking of Aoife broke the protocols of fair play between equals, how much more does his move from a sexual assault on her breasts to the moral equivalent (or exaggeration) of rape break the courtly injunction to venerate and protect the weaker vessel?

As damning as the Aoife affair is in itself to the construction of Cuchulain as a Galahad *avant le Grail,* its connection to the larger subnarrative, "The Wooing of Emer," poses further challenges for the medievalizing wing of the Irish mythic Revival. As Cuchulain first parts from Emer to win her hand by heroic deed, the couple pledges mutual "chastity," providing a rare moment when the sexual mores of the cycle seem to match the respectable, button-down notions of its nationalist translators.[32] Cuchulain's ravishing of Aoife, occurring hard upon this scene, would unavoidably puncture the self-congratulatory illusion that a reverential Christianized sense of sexual morality held sway in aboriginal Gaelic society. On this count as well, the incident must be rewritten if not unwritten. Thus, Hull reorders the events, placing Cuchulain's liaison with Aoife *before* his courtship of Emer.

The narrative alacrity with which Cuchulain moves from plighted fidelity and purity to sexual rapacity indicates a lack of the self-restraint that was central to the modern take on chivalric manliness. In this regard, the cycle's peripateia, left intact, points ahead to the onset of the cattle raid itself. Cuchulain has been deployed to guard the border of Ulster against the approach of Maeve's troops. But her armies first succeed in penetrating the Ulster perimeter because Cuchulain elects to keep an adulterous assignation, despite the warning of his father, Sualtach ("Woe to him who goes thus . . . and leaves the Ulster men to be trampled underfoot by their enemies and by outlanders for the sake of a tryst with a woman").[33] Sualtach's words chime powerfully with the modern principle of manliness, which, in its political dimension, was largely predicated upon an analogy between the social injunction to secure national boundaries against infiltration and the personal duty to secure one's psychic or character boundaries against affective and libidinal agitation. Cuchulain, in refusing his father's admonition, forsakes his obligation to guard the tribal possessions out of a lack of *self*-possession, mortgaging his integrity as a warrior to a sense of sexual rivalry with women: fearing that "men's contracts will be falsified and women's words verified" if he stays, Cuchulain abandons his post for "his tryst" and allows "such a disgrace [to] come upon [him]."[34]

This incident depicts Cuchulain as defaulting not just on the chivalric code of fealty but also on the core traits of manliness, and it therefore makes the great Irish champion appear more compatible with the colonial stereotypes of his race—incontinence, impulsiveness, irresponsibility, turbulence—than with the Revivalist effort to refute them. Accordingly, while Gregory offers a refreshingly veridical picture of Maeve's initial incursion (though she does spare Cuchulain the imputation of "disgrace"), the other popular renditions show no qualms about drastically altering this key narrative crux for the purposes of ethnic uplift. Hutton expunges all evidence of the Hound's truancy and the circumstances thereof; Faraday suppresses his father's objection to and censure of the "pledged" tryst, effectively blunting the reader's awareness of the delinquency involved. In the earliest of these popular Revivalist translations, O'Grady saves Cuchulain for chivalry by inventing a motive for his defection that is diametrically opposed to the original one: instead of keeping an assignation with a mistress, he is supposedly performing an errand for his wife. Even more extreme, in the latest of these translations, Hull stoops to outright falsification. Her version records that Cuchulain, acting on a "suspicion that Maeve's host is near," proclaims, "I will stand between the men of Ireland and the province of Ulster . . . so that no harm befall the province. . . . [H]ere on the borders do I take my stand."[35] Cuchulain fulfills this grand oath, untroubled by any prospect of a tryst or other appointment. It is sometimes thought, ethnographically, that mythic heroes represent the gendered wish fulfillment of a primitive people. In this case, however, the autoethnographic wish fulfillment of a modern people retroactively contoured the gendered representation of the mythic hero.

The battle of the sexes that takes Cuchulain from his guard post reflects an

attitude of misogyny that permeates the Ulster cycle, including its central gendered battle between the forces of Maeve and the forces of Conchubar. Amply
documented in Anne Dooley's influential "The Invention of Women in the *Táin*,"
this misogyny surfaces most plainly in a series of raunchy comments reducing
women to a material-bodily stratum unworthy of man's serious attention. When
the shape changer Morrigan appears in the guise of a noble woman to ask for
or provide assistance, Cuchulain dismisses her with words unlikely to grace
the annals of chivalry: "It wasn't for a woman's backside I took on this ordeal."
During the climactic battle, Conall jibes at the prodigious feats of the great exile
Fergus with the words, "You rage very hard at your kith and kin for the sake of
a whore's [Maeve's] backside," a formula that we shall see Fergus himself repeat
at an especially decisive moment.[36]

Such ribald insults do not, however, "translate" into the more popular renditions, and leading scholars like Tymoczko have correctly deduced that these
erasures mutely testify to the nationalist desire to put a sexually modest and
therefore civilized face on indigenous Irish society. But here again, the impulse
to ethnographic cleansing serves the related ideological purpose of warranting
the Irish warriors as manly exponents of a "natural chivalry." The remarks quoted
above not only evince a strong disdain for women all too typical of homosocially
bonded military cultures but do so with an unsublimated coarseness positively
antipathetic to the chivalric sensibility that the Revivalists wished to adduce.
What is more, the frankly ungallant attitude the remarks express finds strong
reinforcement in Cuchulain's own willingness to dispatch women brutally, and
out of rage rather than necessity. Likewise edited out in all the popular renditions, Cuchulain kills the piteous Locha for her involuntary part in a hoax, kills
the beautiful Findabar on similar grounds, and, in vengeance for the boy corps
lost in battle, slaughters "a countless number besides of women and boys and
children and the common folk."[37] Unedited, these words and actions would
not only tend to vitiate of their own accord the Revivalist transposition of the
Gaelic strong man and the Arthurian knight but also radiate beyond their own
moment to compel a harsher interpretation of scenarios that the Revivalists had
come to consecrate as altars of high Irish chivalry.

The most obvious example is the episode Hull invokes as "a more touching
act of chivalry to a woman" than the medieval legends set forth: Cuchulain's
protection of Maeve.[38] Routed for the time being by the Ultonians, the "men of
Ireland" undertake a mass withdrawal, which Maeve asks Fergus to cover while
she, her menses upon her, pauses to urinate. Fergus's response to her plan, "It
is ill timed and it is not right," indicates that Maeve is attempting to use bodily
function to extort the "boon" of protection from her enemies.[39] Cuchulain's
precise motive in eventually granting her boon request never comes clear. The
popular rationale given in the unabridged translations is that he "was not a

killer of women."[40] As we have seen, however, this claim is belied on multiple occasions earlier in the *Tain*, and with less reason. Indeed, Cuchulain openly states, "It would be only right" to kill her, even as he holds his hand. Respect for Maeve, either as woman or as potentate, would not seem to be the animating factor, either, as attested by the reiteration of those earlier misogynistic formulas. Once Cuchulain vouchsafes an unhurried retreat for Maeve and her men, the queen concedes, "We have had shame and shambles here today, Fergus," and Fergus retorts, "We have followed the rump of a misguiding woman. . . . It is the usual thing for a herd led by a mare to be strayed and destroyed."[41] Although spoken to Maeve, Fergus's words address themselves to Cuchulain, as vehicles of a bonding that is not merely homosocial but phallocratic. The winner and loser of an emphatically male agon unite in the profession of their mutual superiority to the female.

The popular translations that foreground this scene (Gregory, Hull [1909], and Hutton) either eliminate or significantly moderate Fergus and Cuchulain's comments, so as to allow the opposing sides of the cattle raid—Ulster and Ireland, man and woman, Cuchulain and Maeve—a crowning moment of sentimental reconciliation through the specifically chivalric offices of the first term or "side." What is accounted the defining point of reconciliation in these redacted narratives of the Cattle Raid thus takes as its ethical hinge a leading species of Christian manliness. In this light, these narratives' suppression of any reference to Maeve's bodily function is all the more laden, and layered, with significance.

On one level, this editorial decision extends the Revivalist campaign to scour the cycle of its more Rabelasian aspect. At another, this purification effort opens space for the elaboration of a recognizable, which is to say Arthurian, paradigm of knightly solicitude and veneration of women. In Hutton, for example, Cuchulain comes upon Maeve at rest and, deeming it "were unworthy, dishonorable / So to slay her," immediately proves himself "the best for giving gifts and generous bestowing" by granting her requested "boon" unconditionally. In Hull's still more hyperbolic replacement scene, Cuchulain finds "Queen Maeve herself; fallen, forsaken and exhausted, on the ground," that is, a *classic damsel in distress*. Not only is it inserted that Cuchulain would never "hurt a woman," but the Hound himself is made to proclaim, upon hearing Maeve's request, "Never shall it be said . . . that I was heedless of a woman's appeal. Lie there in peace. I will protect the host."[42] One can even espy in this scenario—a Gaelic champion delivering a sleeping Irish queen from danger—the anachronistic suggestion of an aisling encounter, which, as we demonstrated earlier, constituted an Irish Revivalist motif particularly infused with the symbolic valences of Medieval Revivalism.

At bottom, though, and most important, the Revivalist translations' excision of Maeve's corporal discharges clears the ground for the code of chivalric idealism to operate as the primary interpretive grid on the episode. The excision eradicates the elements of a more primitive code of bodily display, aggression, and taboo that in fact governs the sexual politics of the original episode. As Anne Dooley explains, Maeve's carefully timed micturation amounts to a "sly gender performance to confound the male hero" by effectively turning her specific abjection as a woman within a patriarchal order into a highly effective if localized weapon. By combining "the embarrassment of pissing" with the charged symbolics of menstruation, Maeve activates the misogynistic taboo on the excremental female body as a site of pollution in order "to force Cu Cuchulain to observe restraint."[43] In an instance of what De Certeau calls "tactics," Maeve turns "gender differences back upon the men" from the weaker position. Given the inveterate reversibility of the sacrosanct and the proscribed, the deified and the defiled, both polarities being untouchable, even unapproachable, it is easy to grasp how Revivalist translators could effect a narrative conversion whereby the respect Cuchulain displays for the feminine taboo could be limned as reverence for a courtly lady. The means that Fergus employs for wresting control of the situation back from Maeve, the cited comment figuring her as a female animal ("mare") defined by its sexual and excremental parts ("rump"), announces a coarser, more "hyper" brand of masculinism than medieval chivalry entails, which is precisely why it had to be expunged.

Combining signifiers for "back" and "birth," the alternative name for the Irish Revival, the Irish or Celtic Renaissance, better encapsulates the Janus-faced itinerary of the movement. The enterprise of retrieving an authentic Irish past was undertaken less on nostalgic or antiquarian grounds than in the hope of leveraging the recoveries to advance the fortunes of the Irish people—socioeconomic, political, and cultural—in the present and immediate future. The doubleness of this gesture is well captured in Terry Eagleton's phrase, "the archaic avant garde."[44] Incidental to this formal doubleness is a substantive contradiction, which flowed directly from the recent history of subdominance wherein the Revival had incubated. The means and objectives summarized in the phrase "advancing the fortunes" took their definition not from the aboriginal culture to be recovered—which was more likely to be reimagined to suit this purpose—but from a colonial experience that after the Union increasingly counterbalanced, even amalgamated, resistance with assimilation. The preeminent movement of cultural nationalism in Irish history could not but refract a cultural metrocolonialism that was a condition of its very existence.

In the present case, the desire of Revivalist translators to "convert" Cuchulain from pagan hypermasculinity to Christian manliness displays something of the missionary zeal, ideological as well as religious, that energized British imperialism. What has been called Irish autoethnography comprised a certain strain of autoproselytism as well. The editorial practices cataloged here serve to mold the native Irish heroes to a gender norm inculcated in large part by the imperialist culture, and inculcated, in a further contradiction, as a manipulable index of personal and ethnic fitness for freedom. In making this editorial gesture, then, Gregory, O'Grady, Hull, and Hutton register a call for independence in the mode of cultural dependency. That is, they assert, to themselves and others, an Irish warrant of freedom, dating back to the heroic age, but they do so in a conceptual idiom they have, as metrocolonials, come to share with the colonizers. The act of creative translation that inscribed Cuchulain and his fellows as subjects of a native freedom simultaneously inscribed its authors as subjects of British ideological hegemony.

At the same time, however, on the highly charged topic of armed political resistance, this same ideological identification with the conqueror carried the potential to pass from mere colonial imitation to something like Bhabha's colonial mimicry.[45] By aesthetically refashioning native masculine violence as a crypto-Anglicized chivalric discipline, these figures help to open a margin of respectability for the option of physical force, to counter its imperialist relegation to the domain of unevolved animalism. If Irish self-respect is, on this maneuver, purchased with a tacit expression of respect for British norms of self-definition and -congratulation, the transaction does produce a certain residue of "resignification," in which the double bind of manliness is, in one aspect anyway, prized open.

Morte de Cuchulain

By consensus, Patrick Pearse emerged as the "greatest exponent of the cult of Cuchulain," and the figure most responsible for turning that hero worship into political and military action.[46] It is therefore all the more telling that Pearse was so singularly positioned, by heritage, upbringing, and training, to construct Cuchulain as a metrocolonial compromise formation, while also promoting him as a nationalist icon. Pearse was not only born of mixed blood, English and Irish; he was shaped in youth by an intersection of the mythic traditions of both lineages. His mother's sister, Margaret, famously regaled him with stories of Gaelic heroes, while his father, James, encouraged Arthurian fantasies, building him a wooden "gallant steed" named Dobbins on whom the young boy "rode . . . in quest of some Holy Grail, to the relief of some beleaguered Ascalon or Trebizond, or over the slaughtered hearts of some Roncevalle or Mugh Mhuirthemne."[47] As Pearse's childhood unfolded, he continued his interest in both Irish tales of heroism and the Crusades, attempting plays on either topic, *The Annals of Brian Boru,* for example, and *The Crusaders,* which contained verses "[his] father liked very much."[48] At every step, that is to say, Pearse's youthful exposure to ancient Gaelic legends was accompanied by an exposure to their Revivalist leaven, the medieval courtly romance.

A number of scholars have traced Pearse's manic romantic nationalism to his need to cut through the ambivalence of his Anglo-Celtic genealogy with a steely, unbending Irish-Irish allegiance. Michael Boss speaks of Pearse resolving his Oedipal conflicts with his cold, reserved father by a correspondingly strong Oedipal tie to his mother. Along similar lines, Séan Moran speculates that in order to dispel the conflicts surrounding his mixed ancestry, Pearse "overidentified with the women of his childhood." Moving from ethnic to political transference, Marie Ni Fhlathun sees Pearse identifying his father with the colonizer and allying himself with an Irish mother who also counted as Mother Ireland. Finally, Daniel O'Neill adjudges Pearse's "commitment to military action" a means for him and other doubly inscribed Easter insurgents—Clarke, Connolly, MacDonagh—to solve their "individual identity problems," collapsing their "dual nature" into a violent "singularity" of purpose.[49] By contrast, in Pearse's lifelong attachment to the figure of Cuchulain, I see the very antithesis of this strategy: an allegorized Oedipal formation, to be sure, but one that allows Pearse to fuse his paternal and Irish identifications by accommodating his father's Arthurian indices of manhood to the Irish sagas as *Irish* elements. From a psychoanalytic perspective, Pearse consolidates his *ideal ego,* all the positive determinants of his identity, on a strictly Irish basis: he absorbs the chivalric virtues of the metropole entirely within the native figure of Cuchulain. At the same time, however, Pearse internalizes his *ego ideal,* manifest in the ascesis of chivalry itself, from his father. That Pearse identifies with Cuchulain specifically as a perpetual boy hero, continually under the mentorship of strong Gaelic kings, testifies to this split mode of transference.

As a leading light in the Gaelic League and editor of its organ, *An Claidhaemh Soulis,* Pearse gained firsthand experience in the literary method whereby the metrocolonial duality, of which he was, if anything, *over*representative, was incorporated within the heroic cycle. In editing *Bruidhean Chaorthainn,* Pearse found it necessary to bowdlerize the text, owing both to "the staunch respectability of Irish scholars" generally and to his own inability to appreciate, "absorb or even understand" the "earthy and bawdy" properties of native Irish culture.[50] Beyond harmonizing Pearse's editorial tastes with those of his projected audience, this inability made Pearse himself an ideal audience for Revivalist translations of and additions to ancient Gaelic fare. Because Pearse's Victorian-Catholic sensibility recoiled from recognizing the indelicate as properly belonging to native Irish literature, he was all the more prepared, his own Gaelic fluency notwithstanding, to accept the idealized Revivalist versions of the sagas as somehow more authentic or true in the larger sense, more Irish than the (aboriginal) Irish, if you will. And just as expurgating Ulster tales proved a gateway device for translators to suffuse Cuchulain with an aura of chivalric virtue, so Pearse's willing ignorance of the sexual tone of the Gaelic life-world eased his suspension of critical judgment concerning other crucial aspects of the popular recensions.[51]

Indeed, in this area, Pearse proved to be not just a captive but also a stout apologist for the Revivalist Imaginary, as attested by his editorial "Our Heritage of Chivalry." Approving and expanding upon Sigerson's recent address "The Celtic Origin of Chivalry," Pearse insists not only that the address "established conclusively Ireland's claim to priority in the manifestation of the spirit of chivalry" but that there was "nothing essential in medieval chivalry that is not traceable to or . . . anticipated by Irish chivalry in the first century." Pearse takes his (and Sigerson's) warrant for this audacious historical counterfeit entirely from the figure of Cuchulain in his most conventional Revivalist guise. On the "masculine" side, Pearse trots out Cuchulain's fight with Ferdia, without reference to his suspected violation of Fir Fer; on the "feminine," he trots out Cuchulain's claim, "I do not slay women or children or folk," without any concession to the gross violations thereof sprinkled throughout the *Tain*.[52] Pearse's investment in this fiction, I would submit, bears less on the chivalric priority of Irish society *tout court*, Sigerson's apparent interest, than on the role of Cuchulain himself as exemplar of Irish manliness: that is, at once individual paragon and racial type, not at all unlike Thomas Hughes's "manly" Christ in relation to the human race. Cuchulain is precisely a vehicle in Pearse's writing for establishing aboriginal Irish chivalry in a Christological mode, thereby linking Pagan and Catholic Ireland, while simultaneously eliding the medieval Arthurian repository from which Pearse and his colleagues derived this particular expression of manliness. To perform this function, however, Cuchulain could not be conceived merely in "unbroken continuity" with Christ, a position famously occupied by metropolitan Grail questers like Galahad and Percival;[53] he must be somehow interchangeable with Christ, at least symbolically—an alternative Irish version of the Redeemer. Only then could "the manliness of Cuchulain" sustain spiritual precedence over these other figures and hence the racial authenticity that Pearse sought. Only then, in psychoanalytic terms, could the superegoic perspective that Pearse internalized along patrilinial lines be fully vested or absorbed into his Irish-identified ego formation.

We should not be surprised, then, to discover Pearse articulating just this sort of symbolic commutability in his lecture "Some Aspects of Irish Literature." I'll quote it at length to give the flavor of a context fully relevant to our inquiry:

> King Arthur and the Knights of the Round Table have meant more to modern men than the heroes who warred at Troy or than Charlemagne and his Paladins. But how much richer might European literature have been had the story of Cuchulain become a European possession! For the story of Cuchulain I take to be the finest epic stuff in the world. . . . The theme is as great as Milton's in

"Paradise Lost" [sic] . . . for the story of Cuchulain symbolizes the redemption of man by a sinless God. The cause of primal sin lies upon a people; . . . they are powerless to save themselves; a youth, free from the curse, akin with them through his mother but through his father divine, redeems them by his valor, and his own death comes from it. I do not mean that the Tain is a conscious allegory; but there is the story in its essence, and it is like a re-telling (or is it a foretelling?) of the story of Calvary.[54]

It is notable that Pearse conducts his comparative evaluation of these epic legacies precisely along the axis of virile heroism. Having lifted Hughes's notion of a Christ cherished primarily for his "valor," Pearse asserts the superiority of the native legend ("the finest epic stuff") to the metropolitan tradition whence sprang Hughes's conception. He does so by meticulously equating Cuchulain himself—origins, exploits, and redemptive effect—with the crucified Christ. The metalepsis central to Pearse's canonization of the Hound creeps in, almost by unconscious compulsion, at the end of the passage. Cuchulain's paganism and the historical coordinates of the Ulster cycle mean, as Pearse intimates, that Cuchulain in some sense antedates the figure in whose sacred image he supposedly follows, much as he antedates the medieval chevalier in whose image his Revivalist avatar actually follows. With that final quibble, "re-telling (or was it foretelling)," Pearse exposes ever so slightly the formal device, nativist anachronism, that had guided so much of the substantive expurgation and amendment of Cuchulain's story.

In his equation of Cuchulain with Christ, Pearse does not even stint at referring to him allegorically as "a sinless God," a move that gives all the more impetus to the much exercised will-to-censor the original.[55] Cuchulain's identity was by now constituted through the dissimulation of his recorded errancy, from his sexual peccadilloes to his brutal, indiscriminate rampages. This exigency of concealment, in turn, collaborated with Pearse's pedagogical interests (and his less welcome sexual proclivities) in directing his focus almost exclusively upon Cuchulain's comparatively innocent boy deeds. But even here selective editing proved necessary. Consider Pearse's favorite tale, Cuchulain's taking of arms, whose famous motto "dominated the front hall" of St. Enda's: "I care not though I were to live but one day and one night if only my name and deeds live after me."[56] What Pearse avoids mentioning in his many references to this incident is that Cuchulain secured the high destiny these words embrace through deceit and defiance. Yet Cuchulain's self-serving guile in obtaining a prophetic guarantee of great fame is no less central to the tale or illustrative of his character than his acceptance of certain death as the cost. Moreover, the scant regard Cuchulain pays to the authority of the king in this episode contrasts sharply with the unqualified deference the biblical Christ shows to the will of his father.

Each of these traits is in fact a symptomatic expression of the same culturally reinforced disposition, a heroic hypermasculinity at marked variance with the vision of manliness that Pearse held and taught. In a characteristic editorial in *An Claidhaemh Soulis,* Pearse wrote, "Perhaps we have yet to learn that the most manly and healthy form of independence is often found in the continuous suppression of the individual."[57] Pearse sought to train his students in this cardinal precept: "A love and a service so excessive as to annihilate all thought of self."[58] Although Pearse goes on to write, "this is the inspiration of . . . the tale of Cuchulain," the Hound actually espouses just the opposite principle of *self-aggrandizement.* Consider: Cuchulain's taking of arms and even the ensuing motto that Pearse so relished bespeak a willingness to do *anything*—to scheme, to disobey, and, yes, to die young—in order to garner the glory, the accolades, the remembrance that was for the ancient Gaels the very substance of immortality. Far from suppressing the self, Cuchulain's arrangement to die in a manner that ensures his permanent fame constitutes the approved means, in his sociosymbolic order, of dilating the self endlessly. Taking the Ulster cycle on its own terms, Cuchulain rises to preeminence among the Irish heroes in adhering to and succeeding within a value system predicated upon the pursuit of fame and the avoidance of shame at any price. Again, and again, the Red Branch fighters and their adversaries explain their motivation entirely in this vein.[59] Understood in its sociocultural context, Cuchulain's story demonstrates that martyrdom does not necessarily equal a completely selfless, disinterested, or altruistic sacrifice. There is such a thing as martyrdom to one's own reputation or legacy.

It was to avoid just such an understanding that Pearse and his cohorts subjected Cuchulain's final display of arms to a gross allegorical mystification. In what was to become the canonical reading, they treated Cuchulain's decision to strap his dying body to a giant boulder as a last-ditch gambit to defend his people and thus an analogue to Christ on Calvary, whereas the manuscripts specifically announce that Cuchulain is instead seeking to ensure that he would fall forward rather than backward to his death, thereby preserving amid defeat his *individual* dignity and "standing" as a warrior.[60] Instead of salvaging his name, a mode of self-assertion or aggrandizement fully consistent with his credo in taking arms, Cuchulain must be seen as "saving" his tribe, in conformity with the sacrificial imperative.

In grafting the later ideal onto Cuchulain from its medieval soil, Pearse contrives to indigenize the dominant metropolitan model of Christian manliness.[61] But given Cuchulain's ultimately inexpungable desire for fame, the same move contrives to give disciples of manliness, such as Pearse's students, a motivational alternative to the political capital they would reap from such chivalric sacrifice, individually and as a group, were they properly entitled subjects. As we discussed concerning the Sovereignty drama, chivalry emerged as an elite discourse, in which acts of noblesse oblige garnered a moral prestige that justified the privilege of that class of subjects able to afford those acts. Knight-errantry traversed a social landscape biased to encourage a certain form of self-abnegation by offering an organic political return on the activity. For the subaltern, who lacks the social standing to realize this sacrificial "surplus authority," whose *ascesis* would accordingly be, in a structural sense, absolute and unrelieved, the prospect of acclaim, some heightened and enduring approval, furnishes the readiest substitute form of gratification. Implicating as it does individual and community alike, this prospect of enhanced approbation or fame makes an appeal to "selfness," broadly construed, that can ease the commitment to a "selfless" endeavor. As an object of proposed identification, Cuchulain admitted Pearse's colonial audience to an interiorized simulacrum of the chivalric exchange economy: instead of reaping a camouflaged political gain from the gesture of renunciation, like their more empowered models and counterparts, they reaped a disavowed psychic remuneration. They could stand on their moral and patriotic rectitude in welcoming the summons to pure abnegation, while simultaneously nurturing the fantasy of public admiration and lasting renown. In psychoanalytic terms, Pearse's followers gain access to the enjoyment, the jouissance, of throwing everything away and the pleasure of expecting to recoup something still more.[62] If Pearse's appeal to Cuchulain was marked by a fundamental inconsistency, it must be conceded that the inconsistency formed part of the appeal.

This inconsistency attached with particular force to Cuchulain's starring role at St. Enda's, as his prominently displayed life motto has already begun to illustrate. Pearse wished for Cuchulain to become "part of the mental life of the teachers and the taught," in a very real sense the very center of the curriculum. We were "anxious," Pearse writes, "to send our boys home with the knightly image of Cuchulain in their hearts, and his knightly words ringing in their ears"—with their entire perspective, that is, "under the spell of the magic of their most beloved hero."[63] Of the many dramatic productions Pearse oversaw at St. Enda's, the Cuchulain pageant constituted, on all accounts, the centerpiece, giving a public reality to Cuchulain's transcendent stature at the school. More than a patron of the academy or the epitome of its creed, Cuchulain apostrophized the continual mindfulness of their lived purpose.[64]

Yet, as Sisson notes, the pageant Pearse composed to consolidate the Hound's institutional position, *The Boy Deeds of Cuchulain,* carefully "omits certain incidents which are unflattering to him." Philip O'Leary more specifically observes that Pearse rejects "episodes which present Cuchulain in a negative, especially an excessively violent light" and those that contain "crude sexual content"—in sum, those incidents in which Cuchulain must be seen to violate the code of chivalry that Revivalists like Pearse had enjoined upon him retroactively. As

Sisson herself uncritically remarks, "For a school which placed such a premium on chivalry and honesty it is hardly surprising that the less savoury aspects of Cuchulain's life story were expunged from Pearse's version of events." The upshot is that if Pearse strove manfully to render Cuchulain omnipresent at St. Enda's, it was, to paraphrase Althusser, omnipresence in the mode of significant absence. It was not Cuchulain but a Christianized, not to say Anglicized, surrogate with the same name who summoned Pearse's boys to a uniquely Irish species of greatness. The more prominent the Hound was to become in the life, thought, and mission of the school, the more necessary it became, from Pearse's own moral perspective, to obscure certain realities of Cuchulain's profile behind a veil of borrowed authenticity. The effectiveness of this veil, at least to the choir of believers, may be seen in the response of Che Buono, a columnist for *An Claidhaemh Soulis,* who pronounced the boys "as Irish as Cuchulain" in their display of "the chivalry of olden time."[65]

The aggrandized inconsistency accruing to Cuchulain in his pedagogical function could pass unnoticed in part because it consisted so well with the inconsistencies of Pearse's pedagogical institution itself as an avowed nursery of Irish character. What Cuchulain was to iconic Irish identity, St. Enda's was to its development. Pearse cited the genuinely "Old Irish" system of "fostering," "the wisest and most generous that the world has ever known," as the inspiration for his academy. But he proceeds to define the objective of fostering in recognizably Anglified, Victorian terms as the cultivation of character, and he delineates fostering's mission in similarly Victorian terms as "the scrupulous co-relation of moral, intellectual and physical training." Moreover, Pearse concedes that owing to the "queer turn" of civilization, fosterage "might not be easy to restore in all of its details." As a proximal substitute, he proposes an establishment that encourages student self-governance, under the rubric of "child republics," which by the "fostering of individualities," in service to a "commonwealth," should not fail to instill the "struggle, self-discipline, self-sacrifice" whereby "the soul rises to perfection."[66] The interchangeability of the warrior king and the gentleman suggested by this mode of perfection and the various measures for inducing it beg an inference that Pearse and his coadjutors would have found discomfiting in the extreme: that in seeking to replicate the fosterage system in modern terms, he rather founded a near cousin of the imperialist British public school—or, to put it another way, that the modern Macha of Emain looked more like the Rugby of Arnold.

Lest it be thought that the Anglo-Irish comparison here is too broadly drawn or the evidence of derivation too abstract, it is worth noting the striking resemblance between the particular strategies for promoting racialized manliness at St. Enda's and the strategies for doing the same thing at the classic public school. First, the "child republics" themselves, "each with their own laws and their own leaders," recall nothing so strongly as the praeposter system initiated at Rugby by Arnold and then immortalized in *Tom Brown's School Days*.[67] The praeposter system and the child republics alike reflect the primary and expressed purpose, shared by the respective institutions, "of making good citizens of the students," a common identification, that is to say, of a proper curriculum and the business of nationalist interpellation.[68] Both schemes of self-rule constitute scale models of the sort of polis the boys are expected, and are learning, to build and administer as "devoted sons of their motherland."[69] In contemplating the formation of character required for this task, Pearse placed extraordinary emphasis on the spiritual function of the school chapel, as Arnold had so famously done before him, and on the disciplinary function of athletics, which had of course become a byword in the British public school universe, ratified by no less an authority than the Clarendon Commission. Pearse's increasingly fervent subscription to the "games ethic" bore substantially the same rationale as drove that ethic's recent imperialist proponents, the belief that team sports fostered those manly traits foundational to military success: physical hardihood, strength of purpose, dependability, esprit de corps, and self-submission. This similarity explains why Pearse declared that "our boys must now be among the best hurlers and footballers," and why he even stooped to invoke the famous dictum of Wellington, the Anglo-Irish imperialist par excellence: "The battle of Waterloo was won on the playing fields of Eton." Pearse actually professed to believe that "when it comes to a question of Ireland winning battles, her main reliance must be on her hurlers." For this reason, he came to echo, with an almost eerie precision, the ascendant disciplinary ethos of the British public school in its later high-imperialist phase: "Every day I feel more certain that the *hardening* of her boys and young men is the work of the moment for Ireland."[70]

The now familiar pattern of split identification, here fully raised to the ethnocultural plane, informs Pearse's vision of St. Enda's profoundly. The "ego" of the school, the sum of its positive determinations, is aggressively Irish: the child republics claim their pedigree from the boy corps, the chapel exists for strictly Roman Catholic observances, and the sports programs participated in the cultural nationalism of the GAA movement, featuring and fetishizing Irish games to the determined exclusion of all others. But the "superego" of the school, its moral and characterological principles and the pedagogical-institutional structures they underwrite, drew liberally upon the English example that its founder so fiercely disavowed. Thomas MacDonagh, Pearse's closest associate at St. Enda's and fellow martyr of 1916, intuited the constitutive division of the school culture unerringly. Upon hearing that graduates of St. Enda's had enlisted in the British Army during World War I, the massive nationalist antirecruitment campaign notwithstanding, he exclaimed, "Begad, that's consistent anyhow," thereby acknowledging that what was anathema to the school's official credo could nevertheless fulfill the terms of its unconscious.[71] Such are the encumbrances of a metrocolonial Revival.

In trying to approximate fosterage because "such was the education of Cuchulain, the most perfect of the Gael," Pearse not unpredictably fashioned an educational agenda more perfectly suited to the Revivalist/revisionist Cuchulain out of O'Grady's Anglicized romances.[72] Drawing from the same sources, no less an aficionado of Victorian manliness than Boy Scouts founder Baden-Powell, an opponent of all anti-British nationalisms, saw in Cuchulain one of his own, a "most celebrated Boy Scout" and so kindred spirit to the public school boy. Powell's gesture of reverse cultural appropriation (or was it metrocolonial blandishment?) was met with a mixture of scorn and umbrage on the pages of *Irish Freedom,* which ridiculed this well-known imperialist's attempt to make common cause with "Irish dupes" and positively savaged his brief hagiography of Cuchulain for its errors of translation.[73] By this point, the irony of such an indictment should be all too clear.

It becomes even clearer when one considers that the objections to Baden-Powell's (re)appropriation of Cuchulain occur amid a report on developments in the Na Fianna Éireann, which had shamelessly plagiarized the Boy Scouts program in an effort to stem the inroads that organization was making among middle-class Irish youth. More to the point, Na Fianna had assiduously mapped the idols of the Gaelic sagas onto an Anglo-imperial educational and disciplinary framework, in order to give Irish boys a developmental purchase upon the metropolitan norms of manliness while allowing their influence to be disavowed. In this regard, of course, Na Fianna's founders, Bulmer Hobson and Countess Markievicz, were following the same blueprint as the curricular revival of Cuchulain at St. Enda's. But because the taboo, imperialist afflatus of Na Fianna was so concrete and proximate, the need for express denial among its supporters, Pearse in particular, grew more urgent. As a result, Na Fianna emerged not just as a companion and supplement to Cuchulianoid manliness but as an index of the compromises it entailed.

Na Fianna Éireann and the Manly Volunteer

There exists no more patent instance of politicized colonial mimesis than Na Fianna Éireann. While the troop took the great warrior brotherhood of Irish legend as its symbolic pattern, even the official Fianna handbook itself attests that its real inspiration and guidance came, uneasily, from the Boy Scouts movement, as articulated in Baden-Powell's own official and well-known handbook. As scouting came to Ireland, Countess Markievicz wondered, "Why can't we do that?" and proceeded, quite deliberately, to establish the Fianna along the same lines of "attractive indoctrination" that she discerned in Baden-Powell's movement. The topics addressed in her *Fianna Handbook* blatantly track Baden-Powell's *Scouting for Boys:* military preparedness, camp life, first aid, knot tying, sewing, and, of course, chivalry.[74] Just like the Scouts, the Fianna explicitly aimed at being a school for bourgeois manliness and employed many of the same catchphrases, including those high-minded nuggets culled from the courtly tradition. For this very reason, every effort was made to refer the boys' chivalric inheritance to the legends of the Fianna themselves. Thus, in the *Handbook* chapter "Chivalry," Roger Casement professed that Finn and his fellowship not only anticipated the Christian enactment of the knightly code but actually brought it closer to perfection. In another chapter, "Finn and the Fianna," Pearse endeavored to equate the renowned truthfulness of the Irish warrior with the more comprehensive venture of the medieval gallant. In another chapter, Markievicz herself invoked the "imperial demand" for chivalry levied by Cathleen Ni Houlihan.[75] But in each case, the arguments strain against the pressure of embarrassment, in the sense of both shame and debt. For if the object of reference was native Irish myth, the frame of reference remained British medievalism: each of these writers celebrated the Fianna for displaying masculine virtue in the romantic mode associated with, for example, the English patron Saint George, as lionized by Baden-Powell.

It is no wonder, then, that Na Fianna earned the more common name of the Irish Boy Scouts, and that its leaders continued to chafe under that label. After all, *Scouting for Boys* not only revels in the Englishness of its project, it identifies the stated goal of its subtitle, "Instruction in Good Citizenship," with the implantation of imperialist pride, purpose, and duty. Having earned his stripes at Mafeking, Baden-Powell devotes an entire chapter, "Patriotism," to instilling belief in the rightness of the British Empire and cultivating strenuous commitment to its defense—the very thing Na Fianna was created to fight within what Baden-Powell viewed as Greater Britain.[76] Still, as Pearse's address "To the Boys of Ireland" demonstrates, Na Fianna could not distance itself rhetorically from the Boy Scouts without signaling its historical dependency thereupon. Pearse begins his brief that "we are not mere Boy Scouts" by conceding that "we teach and practice the art of scouting" and that "our scheme of training" comprises the very elements the Boy Scouts helped usher to prominence: "physical culture, infantry drills, musketry, the routine of camp life, semaphore and Morse signaling, scouting in all its branches, elementary tactics and first aid." Having thus signaled, however negatively, some awareness of the filiation of Na Fianna from the Boy Scouts, Pearse proceeds to cite as manly *specifica differentiae* a series of items that do not in fact exceed but merely echo the central notes of the Boy Scout agenda: "knightly service" to the nation, the disciplined use of firearms, and the pledge "to be pure, truthful, honest, sober, kindly, clean in heart as well as body." Under an anxiety of influence at once inadmissible and inescapable,

Pearse shifts, not unlike Casement earlier, from merely disavowing a colonial debt to lodging a proprietary claim on the borrowed material. He closes his address by proclaiming the troop "chivalrous, cultured in a really Irish sense." But as the light hiccup of overemphasis ("really Irish") betrays, Pearse sensed, at least unconsciously, that precisely in their notions of chivalry, his young men were being "cultured," as young *men,* by the colonial encounter. Some such insight was certainly encrypted in Baden-Powell's invitation to Pearse to write the handbook for an Irish branch of his own Boy Scouts.[77]

In a final dialectical turn, the stifled sense of colonial belatedness, not to say inauthenticity, haunting the formation of Na Fianna factored into its *positive* function in what we might call the nationalist *bildung:* the phased trajectory toward individual manhood that was also a phased itinerary of patriotic commitment. As we have seen, Pearse's chivalric pedagogy enjoins readiness to exert physical force resistance on behalf of one's homeland, but this appeal to his students' animal spirits or masculine passion was always absorbed within and sublated by the more comprehensive moral discipline they were to espouse. While the doctrine of blood sacrifice indicated that Pearse never really diverged from this gendered ethos, its proportions, if not its components, were subtly but decisively altered in the broader discourse of Irish Volunteerism in the years preceding the Easter Rising.

If one observes the pages of the *Irish Volunteer,* the semiofficial organ of Ireland's physical-force militancy, one discovers a resolute emphasis on a like form of manly self-discipline, but here with an eye to the military advantages it brings, rather than for its own sake. Thus, in an essay "Why Volunteer: Need of Solidarity and Discipline," E. Bloxham lauds the Volunteers' discipline for "prevent[ing] outbursts of passion . . . and rioting"—the traditional function of controlling animal spirits—but only insofar as such regulation produces "concerted action and knits individual efforts into one irresistible force" of violent insurgency.[78] In a still more remarkable column, the famous national martyr Terence MacSwiney cribs directly and almost verbatim from Thomas Hughes's *Manliness of Christ* in asserting, "Moral not physical courage is the thing. Physical courage . . . is the common virtue of the physically perfect man, and its possession may blind one to the higher virtue of moral courage. . . . Place no reliance for anything on physical courage; it will lend itself readily to panic: but moral courage will make you unconquerable." As the last phrase indicates, though, moral courage has shifted from being a categorical imperative, as it is in Hughes, to a hypothetical imperative, a spiritual means to a material end, victory in arms. MacSwiney invokes moral courage as the practical assurance that its bearer "will never retreat a step," and he then summarizes its value in the following terms: "Acquire it . . . and your enemy may seize you . . . but he will never extract from you these two words . . . I surrender."[79] Whereas Pearse the educator places masculine force and manly rigor in a retentive part-whole relationship, these other Volunteer spokesmen imagined a more explosive bind-release relationship, in which self-control was the galvanizing prelude to the power of resistance.

Combining a regimen of moral instruction, an unabashedly chivalric code of honor, and an intensive practical training in military skills—from tactics to drilling to marksmanship—Na Fianna represented a perfect ideological half-way house between the allied but differently weighted agendas outlined above, a transitional point between codependent yet irreducibly dissonant ways of male being-in-the-nation. Witness the following mission statement from the newspaper *Na Fianna Éireann:*

> The making of straight and honorable men is the first object of the Fianna. The training in the arts of war without this aim is but a relapse to barbarism. We need men before we need soldiers; and when the man does not dominate the soldier that is in him he becomes a brute. The old Fianna were as chivalrous as they were strong and efficient. "By truth and strength of our arms we come safe out of every danger," said Ossian the Warrior. . . . The building up of character and the development of all that is fine and noble in the boy constitute the chief tasks of the Fianna officer. The Fianna programme is the agent through which the principles of chivalry and honor are inculcated.[80]

This passage adheres scrupulously to the classic logic of manly sublimation. The "soldier" that is in "the man" precisely figures those aggressive animal spirits that developed manliness must "dominate" if the man is not to "become a brute" and his combativeness to "relapse into barbarism." Accordingly, "the building of character and the development of all that is fine and noble in a man" take precedence over "training in arms," rather than subserving the militaristic program. At the same time, however, the primary raison d'être of manly discipline is, if not to intensify, then certainly to dignify organized revolutionary violence, which receives in turn the stature of a high moral exercise. Instead of a whole-part or means-end relation of manly rigor to masculine force, this account poses something like both, simultaneously investing a more or less seamless integration of the two. The achieved synthesis crystallizes in Ossian's exemplary boast of "truth and strength of our arms," a syllepsis in which truth stands both as a discrete substantive and a genitive modifying "arms," at once an independent moral priority and a property of the arms asserting it.

In the performance of its transitional role between the chivalric boy quest of St. Enda's and the frank militarism of the Volunteers, Na Fianna Éireann had a decisive impact in expanding the reach of this gendered nationalist *bildung* from its middle-class core to the urban working classes of Dublin. The manly ideal it propounded was a characteristically bourgeois production, but as we saw earlier with the GAA, the component parts of this *discordia concours,* taken separately, had long borne opposed class associations. In fashioning the manly ideal, the English middle class appropriated the marks of achieved sublimation for themselves—self-control, self-possession, discipline—while the matter to be sublimated, those vigorous animal spirits, were assigned to the laboring class, most invidiously in the bestial depiction of the Chartists discussed in my introduction. Exploiting this typological division within the manly complex, Na Fianna adopted a bellicose ploy for "sissifying" the original Boy Scouts in Ireland. In a cultural instance of imitation and rivalry, Na Fianna outfitted themselves as proper scouts by assaulting their nemeses—exerting "strength of arms" literally— and stealing their otherwise unaffordable gear. "The Baden-Powell Scouts never attained a vigorous life in Dublin," Padraic Colum wrote. "Parents who'd watch their sons go forth radiant in battle array saw them return later minus hats and poles and plus black eyes." On the one hand, this tactic was calculated to appeal to potential working-class recruits, because it mapped a sense of economic deprivation and resentment onto an act of nationalist aggression and revenge. On the other, the tactic actually depended on the presence of such recruits, boys whose socioeconomic backgrounds would give them more intimate knowledge of the byways and back alleys of Dublin, which were to form their escape routes. By sponsoring such politically inflected mischief, Na Fianna incurred the displeasure of certain mainstream nationalists, who regarded the practice as less than honorable—which is to say, not up to the received standards of manly deportment or chivalric grace. But as Diana Norman has pointed out, such capers also constituted informal training for urban guerrilla warfare, in which Na Fianna was to participate memorably during the Easter Rising.[81] I would add that these capers helped to prepare Dublin youth ideologically for such warfare as well. By shifting the class-associated proportions of the manly complex, they added a touch of grit, as well as "street cred," to the patriotic gallantries of Pearse's boy corps. As we have seen, however, Na Fianna simultaneously and still more vigorously fostered the manly code of self-discipline in its various aspects and so enlisted its mixed class membership under this aegis, thus reinforcing even as it reconfigured that code's hegemonic function.

With his usual epigrammatic flair, Seamus Deane has noted that at times we hear in Pearse the voice of a genuine revolutionary and at times the accents of a schoolmaster.[82] But we can now see that for advanced nationalism in the Revivalist mode these alternatives were not opposed, were not even discrete alternatives, even when the one spoke in an Irish and the other in an English "accent." Baden-Powell's *Scouting for Boys* offered a developmental schema, a course for turning boys into men in the honorific sense. By echoing this program, with an inevitable but finally inessential ethnic inflection, Markievicz, Pearse, et al. reflexively inserted it into an emergent framework of nationalist *bildung* as a bridge from a sublimated to a sanctified aggression, from the Cuchulain of Pearse's pageants to the Cuchulain monumentalized at the General Post Office. In a peculiarly metrocolonial gesture that can aptly be read in two directions, either Na Fianna Éireann performatively identified with the Boy Scouts and the bourgeois gender norms they espoused in order to contest more effectively the imperialist legal and political authority they served, or Na Fianna Éireann contested the imperialist legal and political authority underwriting the Boy Scouts only to consolidate the bourgeois gender norms fundamental to the exercise of imperialist authority.

Cuchulainoid Theater

ON BAILE'S STRAND

It was a measure of how fraught the ethos of gallant manliness proved to be for middle-class Irish nationalism that the reinvention of Cuchulain as knightly icon by his Revivalist mythographers received nothing like the same full-throated affirmation on the Abbey stage as the resurrection of the Sovereignty myth. Working in conjunction with Lady Gregory, Yeats stood as the cardinal example of this dichotomy. Just two years after he made himself party to *Cathleen Ni Houlihan,* which gave massive popular credibility to blood sacrifice on behalf of the distressed Woman/Nation, he composed *On Baile's Strand,* the first and central play in his Cuchulain cycle,[83] which just as forcefully called into question both the sacrifice itself and the idealized masculine profile it evinced.[84] The genealogy of the latter play reflects, as in a cracked mirror, Yeats's striking apostasy from the chivalric credo.[85] Yeats drew his general sense of Cuchulain from his acknowledged master of the Gaelic literary universe, Standish O'Grady, the man responsible for injecting that credo most flamboyantly into the tales of Cuchulain and his Red Branch fellows. In addition, Yeats professedly built his play on Gregory's rendition of the Hound slaying his son in *Cuchulain at Muirthemne.*[86] And yet Yeats not only departed widely from both the spirit of the former and the details of the latter, but the import of his play resides entirely in these points of departure: the portrayal of Cuchulain in middle age, a phase of life he does not attain in the legends themselves; the portrayal of Cuchulain as a bachelor, still Emer-less (and correspondingly "crazy") after all these years; and, the central conflict of the play (and one that these other inventions subserve), the dispute between the Hound and Conchubar over the taking of the "oath" and, more broadly, the proper warrior form of life.

Long viewed as purely characterological, the dramatic stakes in this clash of kings have in recent criticism acquired a combined class and ethno-national complexion. The team of Cairns and Richards helped to initiate this construc-

tive turn in somewhat problematic terms by treating Conchubar as a representative of "the solid bourgeois order" to which Cuchulain, as "the true Celt,"
must ultimately succumb.[87] Taking up this general perspective, Rob Doggett
has historicized the buried essentialist implications of Cairns's and Richard's
argument. He treats the play as self-consciously concerned to take up or on the
Arnoldian ethnic typology of the British Isles and the liberal cultural imperialism it supports. On Doggett's reading, "Cuchulain alone remains true to his
Celtic roots," which can be traced not so much in his cultural adherences as in
his temperament. Cuchulain is the "emotional Celt," the man of "wandering
passion," replete with a self-destructive "tragic nobility" manifest in the play's
conclusion. For his part, Conchubar's practical mindedness, his prudential cun-
ning, makes him, to Doggett's way of thinking, not just an Anglicized or An-
glicizing figure, but really a "Saxon" in his own right. Yeats, by thus racializing
his characteristic opposition of "emotion" and "reason," stages how the values
associated with each, dialectically engaged, factor into the following: the "process
of colonialism," understood as a drama of (Conchubar's) hegemonic manipulation; the codependency of colonialism, understood as a dynamic of mutual
disidentification; and the "psychological aftermath" of colonialism, understood
as a pathos of (Cuchulain's) subdominant ambivalence.[88]

There is much to recommend this line of analysis, not least its amenability
to the paradigm of "metrocolonialism" set forth here. Certainly, although Doggett does not raise the point, the repeated references to Cuchulain's intractable
"turbulence" deliberately recall the famous designation of "the Celt" in Arnold
as "ungovernable and turbulent," directing the audience's attention to familiar
Anglo-Irish stereotypes.[89] But the reading also bears certain pronounced limitations—and not only (though not least) the interpretive stretch required to identify
a High King of the Gaelic Heroic Age, and hence a virtual emblem of aboriginality, as a foreign, colonizing potentate. In addition, while Doggett follows the
approved (and correct) line that the Fool and the Blind Man represent, in their
squabbling, lowercase versions of Cuchulain and Conchubar, he concedes that
the comic pair also represent the left and right hemispheres of Cuchulain's own
mind, "the Fool symbolizing [his] intuition and imagination, the Blind Man his
critical and prudential intelligence."[90] If nothing else, this wrinkle in the play's
allegorical fabric qualifies Doggett's typological frame as too schematic by half.
Cuchulain simply cannot be reduced to a single ethnically essentialized faculty,
such as "emotion." Neither, I would add, can Conchubar be simply identified
with "reason," although in his case the countervailing evidence subsists not in
the symbolic framework of the play but in its diegetic backdrop.

Conchubar is always pegged as the voice of bourgeois rationality on account
of his decisive, craftily pursued political aims, which all but define the main
action: to establish for his descendants stable rule over a secure, domesticated,

one might even say "respectable" social order, and to corral Cuchulain's free-booting aesthetic, ludic, and martial energies for that order's protection. When Cuchulain is pressed to bind himself to this "settled" regime, however, he does not deride it as being typical of Conchubar, the foreseeable product of his all too circumspect, managerial nature. Quite the contrary. Cuchulain decries the new dispensation as *uncharacteristic* and *unworthy of the Conchubar he has known.* His initial objection aims precisely at bringing the High King back to his better self, a self no less at odds with the proposed social protocols than Cuchulain is. He reminds Conchubar:

> We in our young days
> Have seen the heavens like a burning cloud . . . and being more
> Than men can be now that cloud's lifted up,
> We should be the more truthful. (*B,* 18)

Cuchulain then denigrates Conchubar's children *by contrast* with their father: they "will lie soft / Where you and I lie hard." Finally, Cuchulain includes Conchubar in a chronicle of heroic glory that a calculating familialism could only diminish: "The most of men feel that [that is, the value of "one's family name"], / But you and I leave names upon the harp." Indeed, Cuchulain prophesized that their joint glory shall extend beyond the shores of Ireland: "when we die we shall be spoken of / In many countries" (*B,* 18). Certain crucial implications flow from Cuchulain's testimony. First, it becomes evident that Conchubar has partaken of the aesthetic and combative passions now identified with Cuchulain alone. Accordingly, Conchubar's personification of prudential reason cannot be judged an inherent constitutional disposition consistent with a racialized subject—Conchubar as "Saxon"—but must instead be understood as an emergent disposition consistent with a historically contingent subject, one prone to the sort of cultural mutations affecting the larger society. Conchubar's investment in the rational (self-)constraint that the "oath" enjoins is no more racial in origin or motivation than is Cuchulain's presumptively "Celtic" followers' similar investment; these followers are newly "settled" men who have likewise come to appreciate the overriding virtue of personal and public regulation. The enemy, Cuchulain himself proclaims, is "time," the "years," which "water . . . [the] blood" (*B,* 17). Instead of contrasting racial types, Cuchulain and Conchubar represent, on all the dramatic evidence, different moments in Irish culture: the old and the new, the premodern and the modern, or, translated into a political temporality, the *native* and the *national.*

With this in mind, the presentist allegory of *On Baile's Strand* does not speak to an Anglo/Irish or a metro/colonial divide so much as it signals intramural rifts within contemporary Irish nationalism over what sort of subject formation to promote, or what sort of collective *bildung* to pursue. That is, Yeats's play stages a struggle over the terms and means of *cultural* reproduction, how and in what form the so-called spiritual inheritance of the Celt would be passed down.[91] At the epicenter of this disquiet, Yeats places the issue of approved gender profile and performance, a verdict that has already been convincingly rendered by Susan Harris in her sterling essay "Blow All the Witches Out."[92] Having demonstrated how the tragic confrontation of Cuchulain and son entails a critique of the sacrificial nationalism that Yeats endorsed in *Cathleen Ni Houlihan,* Harris proceeds to connect this retraction with a critique of the gendered nationalism implicit in Conchubar's expulsion of the feminized occult, those "witches and Shape-Changers," from the patriarchal Symbolic. For Harris, then, the gender politics dominating the play primarily targets a restrictive feminine norm that mainstream nationalism shared with its colonial antagonists. As John Rees Moore observes, however, *On Baile's Strand* represents Yeats's most "masculine tragedy"—not, I would append, in the sense of asserting Irish masculinity, but rather of interrogating Irish masculinity, in large part by worrying the (re)invention of Cuchulain undertaken in Yeats's own Revivalist sources.[93]

If by the letter of its portrayal, *On Baile's Strand* offers up a Cuchulain who *never was* (middle-aged, unmarried), in its spirit, the play actually harks back to the Cuchulain who *really* was, so to speak, in the original. Instead of the stock nationalist image of the Hound as "hero of the tribe," Yeats has his strongman enact the more authentically "disruptive aspect of the warrior function" so prevalent in the *Tain.*[94] With apologies to Matthew Arnold, the "turbulence" imputed to Cuchulain has nothing to do with his being a Celt, as the contrast with an equally Irish Conchubar insists, but has to do with his being a champion in the archaic mode and hence a specimen of extreme hypermasculinity—a thrill seeker, a boaster, and an inveterate brawler. As Moore remarks, Yeats's Cuchulain "retains a certain primitive roughness" amid a modernizing allegory, and he "retains" it, I would add, from the original legends.[95] In this regard, it is noteworthy that the first bill of indictment against Cuchulain in the play is not delinquency in guarding the shore, but that Cuchulain has "killed men without [Conchubar's] bidding" (*B,* 16). Of that legendary Cuchulain, Lowe writes that his displays of virility are so extreme he not only exceeds the boundaries of masculinity, a "social category that limits and binds its members," but "*exceeds* all the [related] boundaries": boy and man, male and female, hetero- and homosexual.[96] Yeats's characterization invokes this gender exorbitancy as well, with reference to the very standard whereby Conchubar would contain it, that of manliness.

Whether as honorary "Saxon" or voice of instrumental and administrative reason, Yeats's Conchubar has been widely and plausibly seen as instituting a bourgeois code of value to which he effectively tethers the noble warrior-artist Cuchulain in his vision of a smoothly regulated collective that will serve the interests of his own children. Conchubar cuts a distinctively modern figure of rule: the chief executive officer as bourgeois paterfamilias. Yet the manner in which Conchubar "binds" Cuchulain and the framework to which he binds him bear a decidedly feudal caste. Establishing primogeniture as the rule of succession and consanguinity as the medium of dynastic obligation, Conchubar enjoins upon Cuchulain a properly medieval oath of *fealty,* in which a reciprocity of duty or responsibility ("I give my wisdom, and I take your strength" [*B,* 23]) formalizes a relation of absolute dominance.[97] Now Yeats's projected audience, both in Dublin and in London, could be expected to recognize or at least sense an allegorical allusion to a contemporary topos, chivalric manliness, where bourgeois mandates were likewise homosocially inculcated and solemnized through the use of high-medieval rhetoric and iconography.

The burden of the "wisdom" that Conchubar imparts in this fealty ritual is, in effect, to compel Cuchulain to follow the path that he himself has (that is, to discipline and sublimate the rampant "animal spirits" endemic to great warriors and to exercise such strenuous self-control in the service of the tribe—family and nation, nation as family). To this end, Conchubar reprehends Cuchulain alternately, almost interchangeably, for his truancy from his martial and marital duties, his carelessness in defending the land, and his contempt for "our queens," who could give him progeny (*B,* 19). Beyond blaming Cuchulain for securing no affectional stake in the future of Ulster, Conchubar's articulation of these two modes of delinquency in particular implicates Cuchulain in a breach of chivalry; it tags him as spoiled for knighthood—a role he would not be called upon to assume, historically, for two millennia. According to Conchubar, Cuchulain has refused the courtly respect for women that O'Grady's romantic translations made such a hallmark of Cuchulain's reputation; as a corollary, Cuchulain has also stinted on that patriotic self-abnegation that popular, anticolonial renditions of his myth had seen fit to exaggerate. In imposing a knightly mandate on Cuchulain, the High King not only gives symbolic reinforcement to bourgeois norms of being, which the current medievalist vogue had arisen to serve, he also condemns the "original" Cuchulain by the standards of his own Revivalist image. Yeats thereby suggests a more than casual accord between those (Anglified) norms and that (nationalist) image. His dramatic allegory displays a reversibility that simultaneously refers the domestication of Cuchulain to *both* "Saxon" influence, as an instance of cultural imperialism, and Irish cultural nationalism, as a matter of ethnic dignity or respectability.

Still more ingeniously, in staging the attempt to normalize the rough-hewn, hypermasculine Cuchulain, Yeats manages to turn him into a figure of gender subversion, rather than simply atavism. As our conceptual introduction delineates, a default upon the *discordia concours* of manliness, strong passions strongly checked, was understood to reflect in the male subject an affective disequilibrium that undermined his claim to sustaining a proper, self-possessed masculinity. An uncontrolled overbalance of even typically masculine attributes (aggression, willfulness, and so on) could affiliate him with the lower framing categories of manhood—the bestial, the feminine, the juvenile. In *On Baile's Strand*, Yeats overwrites the primordial excess of the legendary Cuchulain with this late Victorian code of assessment to focus gender as a primary site of the metrocolonial complicity noted above. Judged by a standard of manliness shared across Anglo-Irish lines, Cuchulain's *parade virile* in the play reads not just as exorbitant and therefore exceptional but as anomalous, even deviant, and, given his iconic heroic status for the audience, as threatening to the integrity of gender categories themselves. Cuchulain has strongly refused to strongly check his prodigiously strong passions—has refused, that is, to assume the *discordia concours* of manhood, which promises to reconcile a robust individual will, like his own, with habitual deference to legally constituted authority, such as Conchubar's. Repeatedly, the drama links Cuchulain's refusal on this score with his position at the (Celtic) fringe of Ulster society, which is also a frontier between masculinity and femininity.[98]

When Conchubar admonishes his vassal to embrace the norm of procreative, connubial love, Cuchulain counters with a harder, more feral take on Eros:

> I never have known love but as a kiss
> In the mid-battle, and a difficult truce
> . . . .
> A brief forgiveness between opposites. (*B*, 20)

His take is a vision of the romantic in which the sublimating curbs on sexual passion that demarcate its adhesive from its aggressive impetus have no sustained role. The soul mate appropriate to this vision is of course Aoife, whom Conchubar disdainfully calls "a fierce woman of the camp" (*B*, 19). From the conventional, protobourgeois vantage that Conchubar embodies, the combative intensity of this warrior-queen signals a disturbingly masculine profile, and as Harris has insightfully discerned, Aoife's evident androgyny implies a correspondingly androgynous quality in Cuchulain's powerful attraction to her.[99] Disputing Conchubar's depiction, Cuchulain strikingly denaturalizes the king's expectations of gender bipolarity, ascribing them to a complacent paternalism that cultivates subservience in women as a foil to his own increasingly lax magnificence:

> You call her a "fierce woman of the camp,"
> For, having lived among the spinning-wheels,
> You'd have no woman near that would not say,
> "Ah! how wise!" "What will you have for supper?"
> "What shall I wear that may please you, sir?" (*B*, 19)

Cuchulain here voices some awareness that the "damsel" is a creation of the chivalric system itself. Her neediness allows the knight to show his mettle while relieving him of the more formidable enterprise of dealing with a strong woman.

Cuchulain's gender dissidence in the play thus arises from and is strangely coextensive with his adherence to a primordial style of masculinity. Beyond appealing to the radical conservativism of Yeats's temperament, this paradoxical dramatic strategy enables the author:

a) to engineer a graceful transition from his youthful transvaluation of Arnoldian Celtism, in which Yeats celebrated the "feminine" imagination, to his later wish to put more masculine "salt" into his work.[100]

b) to critique the cramped sexual traditionalism of his nationalist compeers as a corruption of the aboriginal Irish warrior culture, the supposed model for contemporary, anticolonial resistance.

Cuchulain's relationship with the feminine occult bears the same pattern and reinforces the same critique. It is Cuchulain's intransigent will, an index of his excessive testosterone, that brings him into practical alignment and symbolic association with the feminine Shape-Changers. Conchubar, in fact, specifically attributes Cuchulain's habit of consorting with these daughters of "Country-Under-Wave" to a will to have "impossible things" or "nothing" at all (B, 18). To break this hypermasculine obstinacy ("the will of man"), Conchubar devises an oath ceremony that exiles the Shape-Changers, the figures of "the will of woman at its wildest," beyond the pale of the domestic polity, symbolized by "the threshold and the hearthstone" (B, 21). In so doing, the ritual encodes the imbrication of Cuchulain's old-school gender performance, identified allegorically with Celtic aboriginality, and his nascent androgyny, which challenges the normative gender bipolarity assumed and imposed by Conchubar's regime of bourgeoisified chivalry. Indeed, even as Cuchulain agrees to take the oath, he slyly renews his challenge by striking an overtly maternal posture toward his own followers: "I shall be what you please, my chicks, my nestlings" (B, 22). With this in mind, it is all the more significant that Cuchulain's destruction, although presaged in the oath ceremony, comes only later, as Skene contends, "through his turning away from the Shape-Changers . . . to whom he was formerly devoted."[101] The circumstances of this defection hold the key to its gendered import.

While Cuchulain's immediate affinity for the "Young Man" who infringes Red Branch territory has been not unreasonably deemed "an instinctive response to his own unrecognized child,"[102] the dialogue no less potently suggests that Cuchulain gravitates toward the Young Man's haughty assertiveness—"I will give no other proof than the hawk gives / That it's no sparrow!" (B, 23)—evidence of a boldness that Cuchulain no longer finds in his followers. The two men exchange words, the confrontational, not to say hostile, tenor of which steadily brings them together around a shared appreciation for traditional warrior values taken to their traditional extreme. In the end, an aggressively *male bond* supplants the *oath bond* that stamped Cuchulain as the High King's "man."

> Cuchulain: Boy, I would meet them all in arms
>   If I'd a son like you . . .
>   You and I would scatter them like water from a dish.
> Young Man: We'll stand by one another from this out.
>   Here is the ring. (*B*, 26–27)

At the same time, to dispel suspicions of sorcery, Cuchulain explains his sudden, unwonted attraction in words that mark in the Young Man's visage a trace of the androgyny that his mother displayed and that Cuchulain himself mirrored in his passion for her. Note the deft use of enjambment to underscore the point:

> Cuchulain: No witchcraft. His head is like a woman's head
>   I had a fancy for. (*B*, 26)

But given the gendered status and the gender-troubling effects of witchcraft, Cuchulain's affiliation therewith cannot be disentangled from his ambiguous sexual attachments and identifications and vice versa. Therein lies the secret of his abrupt schism with his supernatural patrons.

Critics of *On Baile's Strand* have complained about the unmotivated quality of this final peripetia, in which Cuchulain is induced to turn upon his new filial ally, killing him in combat. On an immediate experience of the play, the volte-face does seem rather arbitrary, as if Cuchulain is carried forward less by the logic of the action than the dramatic urgency of the destination. However, if one looks carefully at the formal catalyst of Cuchulain's change of heart, one finds that he has just had the concerted, if oddly assorted, elements of his gender dissidence, hypermasculinity and androgyny, reflected back to him, as the Lacanians say, in reverse order.

> First Old King: Some witch has worked upon your mind, Cuchulain.
>   The head of that young man seemed like a woman's
>   You'd had a fancy for. Then of a sudden
>   You laid your hands on the High King himself! (*B*, 27)

Everyone has been yelling that "witchcraft! witchcraft!" has maddened Cuchulain, but only when the First Old King repeats the now familiar gender cues, even using the same freighted enjambment, does Cuchulain join in the chorus: "Yes, witchcraft! witchcraft! Witches of the air" (*B*, 27). For Cuchulain to turn against the Shape-Changers on this prompting amounts in allegorical terms to a capitulation to the emergent gender norms of the Conchubar regime. Evidently panicked that his defense of a cross-gendered apparition incites him to lay violent hands upon the King, Cuchulain suddenly pivots to take possession of his errant impulses, hostile and affectional, by putting them in the service of the tribal nation and its leadership.

Cuchulain's surrender to gender normativity issues in the death of his only son at his own hand. In forging this precise and direct causal link, Yeats literalizes, biologizes if you will, the agon of cultural reproduction at work in his national allegory. With Cuchulain established as a main avatar of native Celtic ways, his unwitting extinction of his own lineage at the request of Conchubar functions as a dramatic emblem of cultural self-immolation or self-eradication, and not just any such immolation or eradication, but one undertaken in deference to newly respectable social and sexual norms. This emblematic extinction is thus the very brand of infidelity to Irish heritage that leaders of the Revival (Hyde) and Irish-Ireland (Moran) volubly lamented.[103] Only, in this case, and here we have the final turn of the allegorical screw, the gender politics of the Revival and Irish-Ireland are themselves implicated in the ethnic apostasy. *After all, the progress of Cuchulain in the play from hypermasculine original to manly reconstruction precisely tracks and invokes his progress from the ancient manuscripts to the popular, contemporary translations identified with both the Revival (O'Grady, Gregory) and Irish-Ireland (Hutton, Hull).* What was understood to salvage Cuchulain and his world for modern nationalist sensibilities, his gentrification from primitive warrior to medieval knight, figures in *On Baile's Strand* as a betrayal of his cultural roots and the stilling of their powers of regeneration (that is, of "reproducing" themselves in new "generations").

If *On Baile's Strand* mounts a critique of the sacrificial politics that Yeats himself espoused in *Cathleen,* as both Doggett and Harris have illuminated, it might further be said that the play opens a larger critique of Revivalism in its current rhetorical-methodological configuration. At either level, it is the wages of manhood, as ideological construct, that is at issue. As Tymoczko has written, "the nineteenth and twentieth century treatment of the *Tain*" delineates a "heroic paradigm" that "glorified both individualism and action on behalf of the tribe."[104] In the previous section, we witnessed the gender stakes of this paradigm: the Revival needed to fabricate a Cuchulain who would personify independence and hence the masculinized individualism inherent in the modern subject of freedom, but who would do so not for himself but for the nation at large. In its combination of political and cultural critique, *On Baile's Strand* effectively deconstructs that "heroic paradigm." It represents the sacrifice of the individual body in the cause of national liberation as continuous with or conducive to the sacrifice of the individualistic disposition or ethic to the authority of collective sociocultural norms. Yeats, we have seen, identifies such individualism with native Irish hypermasculinity, which, bearing androgyny as its complementary other, functions as a mode of gender dissent, a self-queering proposition.

Conversely, Yeats maps the upholding of social norms or conventions onto a chivalric mode of fealty that Irish nationalism and British imperialism alike adopted as a ceremonial expression of manly virtue. By thus thematizing these iconic types of male performance as profoundly conflictual in their equally profound interconnection, Yeats in effect reinscribes the double bind endemic to Ireland's metrocolonial condition, her subjacent relation to Great Britain, within the confines of its nationalist community. As a symptom of external association, this masculine aporia or double bind carries its own, admittedly contingent, promise of resolution and so can accommodate, within the space of the dramatic Imaginary, a comedy of hope and aspiration, culminating in a kind of "marriage" between the martyred Young Man and the Old Woman/ Nation. As a correlative of internal rupture, however, signifying an irreducible antagonism among the interdependent elements of the national ethos, an impasse over what Irishness is and should come to be, this masculine aporia or double bind can only take, and indeed has already taken, the form of tragedy.

THE PLAYBOY OF THE WESTERN WORLD

Throughout its history, the critical treatment of Cuchulain as a dominant analogue for Christy Mahon has rested on the secure notion that Synge's *Playboy of the Western World* comprises some form of mock-heroic parody. But everything that follows from this insight remains a matter of open debate.[105] What precisely is being mocked: Christy, the Mayo community, the Abbey audience? What in or about each of them is the target of the mockery? What ideological constellation did Synge's parody serve?[106] More recently, the questions surrounding the *import* of the Cuchulain typology have given way to doubts about its *importance.* Joseph Devlin, for example, insists that unlike Yeats, Synge was little concerned with "the resurrection of some mythical Cuchulain," while Julie Hennigan holds "there is little evidence to support the view that Synge had Cu Chulain specifically . . . in mind." Even Declan Kiberd, whose seminal *Synge and the Irish Language* gave the Cuchulain parody its saliency, came to regret the approach explicitly in *Inventing Ireland,* only to turn in *Irish Classics* and pronounce the play "an occluded parody of Gregory's [*Cuchulain at Muirthemne*]" after all, with "Christy [as] a mock-Cuchulain."[107]

My brief examination of the play cannot begin to settle the contested questions about the role of the Cuchulain antitype, though I will inevitably touch upon several of the main debates. The task I propose is far more modest: to add a single related "meta" facet to our already prismatic vision of this mythic correspondence and thus to augment its perceived import and enhance its received importance. In making the original case for his parodic reading, Kiberd invoked Synge's famous complaint to Stephen McKenna about a "fantastic, ideal, breezy, springdayish Cuchulanoid National Theatre": "The fact that the author could have mentioned a 'Cuchulainoid drama' in the famous letter to Stephen McKenna proves that the Cuchulain cycle was never far from his mind as he wrote. That his use of Cuchulainoid was pejorative should make us doubly alert to the possibilities of a mock-heroic approach in his finest play."[108] I would adjust the focus here slightly, however, to note that it is *not* Synge's use of Cuchulainoid that is pejorative, but rather the concept of a "Cuchulainoid" drama, which is to say it is not Cuchulain who is being set up for mockery nor the peasant society toiling in his allegorical shadow but rather a certain contemporary theatricalizing of Cuchulain, his "translation" into terms at once "fantastic and presentist," which is to say *revivalist.*

Having studied the "original sources [of the Ulster cycle] in the Irish language" at Trinity, Synge was in a rare position to assess the nature and effect of this revivalist tropism, of which Gregory's *Cuchulain* was of course the epitome.[109] In "An Epic of Ulster," Synge accords Gregory's effort a positive review consonant with the protocols of logrolling that characterized their Irish coterie, but a measure of disfavor presses to the surface. First, he registers a sly dig at the "difficult task" Gregory has arranging the tales. Then he admits possible criticism of "the details in her work," paying her the left-hand compliment of "tact." He concludes on an extended sour note, calling attention to the bowdlerized quality of her redaction: "A word of warning may be needed. Lady Gregory has omitted certain barbarous features, such as the descriptions of the fury of Cuchulain and, in consequence, some of her versions have a much less archaic aspect than the original texts. Students of mythology . . . for their severer studies . . . must still turn to . . . others, who translate without hesitation all that has come down to us in the MSS."[110] More than a reservation, these last words amount to a summary judgment of inauthenticity. With this in mind, the compliment Synge later paid Lady Gregory, "Your Cuchulain has become a part of my daily bread,"[111] may be understood as carrying a secondary occulted level of meaning: beneath the heartfelt praise for Gregory's experiments in rural dialect, there lurks a reference to the sustenance her work had unwittingly provided, as a touchstone of Cuchulainoid revivalism, for Synge's avidly parodic endeavors.

It is worth entertaining the proposition, then, that *The Playboy* does not mount a parody of Cuchulain or even the revivalist Cuchulain so much as the revival of Cuchulain or of revivalism per se, with Cuchulain as a focal point. And in this light, we cannot but see that the characteristic dramatic action of *The Playboy* is precisely the staging of revivals. There is the bodily revival of Old Mahon and then his second bodily revival; there is the revival of traditional Irish romance by Christy and Pegeen Mike, replete with quotations from Hyde's classic, *The Love Songs of Connacht;* there is the cultural revival of the Mayo village around their new champion; and at the center of it all, there is the revival in spirit and fortune of Christy himself from "looney" to "mighty man" and then again, at play's end, as "master of all fights."[112]

The allegorical potential of this insistent motif comes alive once we consider that the Mayo villagers may represent less an "internal" correlative of the Abbey Theatre audience than of the broader revivalist treatment of the myths and sagas of Ireland.[113] Like the Revivalist poets, folklorists, archivists, and translators, the village denizens not only mediate and help to facilitate heroic legend—here the legend of Christy Mahon—but do so in the very act of trying to recover the "original" from an obscure past. Widely credited with helping to fashion the heroic figure Christy cuts and the parricidal narrative he retails, the villagers' suggestive questionings have typically been judged the outpouring of an exuberantly poetic folk imagination, what Luke Gibbons calls the "collective fancy." But given that the group at Flaherty's pub endeavors to construct the story behind a vaguely exotic personage who is both a stranger and a native, their inquiry might still more readily be glossed as a parodic exercise in the *autoethnographic* imagination—arguably the signature faculty of the Irish Revival. Gregory Castle has persuasively treated *Playboy* as "staging ethnography," as combining an ethnographic approach to drama with a dramatic critique of ethnography.[114] I would like to add that the opening of *Playboy* stages ethnography in the sense of putting onstage a send-up of homegrown ethnography as a form of collective self-promotion.

The comic parallelism between the revivals within the play and the Revival in which the production itself seemed to participate calls in turn for a narrow but not insubstantial reassessment of Synge's dramatic approach. As the various Cuchulainoid, Oedipal, Christological, and Parnellite readings of Christy attest, Synge is widely understood to employ the kind of "mythic method" that T. S. Eliot famously credited to James Joyce, where fictive, historical, or legendary archetypes operate as glosses, frames of reference, on the present reality being dramatized.[115] But our take on the making of Christy Mahon suggests that Synge has rather developed a *mythographic* method: the mythologizing ethnography at work in the dramatized fiction operates as a satiric gloss on analogous recovery projects undertaken in the present historical reality.

The pattern of questions the pub folk put to Christy reveals an eagerness, characteristic of cultural nationalism, to emblazon (proclaim and embellish) a heroic figure, like Cuchulain. But the pattern also reveals a subliminal awareness of the dual profile, amounting almost to a *discordia concours,* that such a figure would need to possess. Thus, their queries-com-conjectures on the nature and the means of Christy's lawbreaking oscillates between probing the truly offensive or criminal on one side (larceny, mashing, bigamy) and actions authorized by legitimate grievance or political motive on the other (land war revenge, attacking soldiers, "fighting for the Boers" [*P*, 79]). Taking this rhetorical tack, they cooperate not just in building Christy up, but in allowing him to present himself, by reply, as respectable ("the son of a strong farmer" [*P*, 79]), "a decent lad" and even "a law-fearing man" (*P*, 80), as well as a "bloody-handed murderer" (*P*, 81).[116] That is to say, the villagers facilitate Christy in filling out a self-description consonant with their own standard of masculine prowess, the specifications of which closely resemble, in a rough, untutored form, the middle-class ideal of manliness. Notice that the villagers seek and appreciate an agent of robust animal spirits, in contrast with the priest-ridden Shawn Keogh, whose descendants are later described in vegetative terms ("puny weeds" [*P*, 112]). But they desire that agent to keep those animal spirits under some control, unlike "the harvest boys with their tongues red for drink" (*P*, 76), and to direct his "savagery" at appropriate objects, such as "the kharki cut throats" of the British army (*P*, 81). In sum, they wish to elicit in Christy the very thing that Synge himself found Lady Gregory attempting to refashion in Cuchulain, a belligerence purged of all "barbarous features."

The parallelism between Synge's rural townfolk and the elite urban revival should be taken to indicate not that they occupy parallel cultural universes, then, but that in certain respects, they share the same ideological space. That is to say, the natives of Synge's West possess a set of cultural realities (gender, ethnonational, and so on) of a piece with those who reify and idealize them—not because these peasants embody the genuine Irishness the Revival sought but because they likewise have access to the popular discourse on Irish identity, history, and authenticity circulating broadly during the late Home Rule period. Synge, it is worth noting, explicitly provides for such access in the play. He repeatedly indicates that Christy and his new acquaintances were practiced readers of the newspaper, which was not only, as Benedict Anderson argues, the discursive cement of the "imagined community" of nationhood but was also, in Ireland, the chief vehicle for inculcating the approved traits of national character.[117] The prevailing isolation in *Riders to the Sea* and *Shadow of the Glen* should not blind us to the conscious participation of Synge's Mayo folk in the larger drama of Irish self-definition.

Synge assigns his protagonist a crime that answers, oddly, to the villagers' bipolar conception of heroic masculinity, not by splitting the difference between the extremes of lawlessness and purposive sublimation but rather by fulfilling both, at different levels, at their very extremity. At one level, parricide is an act of the most visceral enormity. It involves not just gross violence against a fundamental blood tie but violence against a blood tie that is, within patriarchal societies, fundamental to the symbolic order itself. Partly for this reason, the Abbey theatergoers took the approval of this particular crime by their Mayo compatriots as an affront, if not an assault, upon Irishmen generally. Neverthe-

less, at a second level, parricide carries a mythic gravitas and, with it, a metaphoric fungibility that lifts it above the outrage it immediately and irrevocably
entails. The killing of the father implies a strike at the law itself, at authority
tout court, and as such, parricide asks to be read as a figure for diverse species
of transformative rebellion: antistatist, antimonarchical, antielitist, anticolonial,
anti-Church, and so forth. Some or all of these possibilities would seem to be
at work in the villagers' impulse to lionize Christy, while the impossibility of
picking and choosing among them surely helped to fuel the corresponding in-
dignation of the Abbey audience.[118] But parricide is less important in the play
for each of the politically freighted thrusts it might signify, that is, for each of
its sublimating variations than for the symbolic glamour and gravity it acquires
as a universal object of political sublimation, the master-signifier underlying
them all. This glamour and gravity cannot, however, either detach itself from
or effectively disguise the primordial social violence of parricide that forms
their enabling condition. Rather, they remain propped irremovably upon this
breach. That is certainly part, if only a part, of Synge's point in *Playboy,* and
one he encapsulates beautifully in Michael Flaherty's reaction to the prospect
of Christy's marrying Pegeen. Flaherty's initial expression of horror reflects the
gruesome physical nature of the act itself: "You'd be making him a son to me,
and he wet and crusted with his father's blood?" (*P,* 110). His ultimate expression
of acceptance sublates the bodily marker of fatality into a promise of symbolic
inheritance that is also, just to emphasize the point, an inheritance of symbolic
prowess: "It's many would be in dread to bring your like into their house for to
end them, maybe, with a sudden end; but I'm a decent man of Ireland, and I'd
leifer face the grave untimely and I seeing a score of grandsons growing up gallant little swearers . . . than go peopling my bedside with puny weeds" (*P,* 112).
Not only does the blood of the murdered father pass, in this formulation, into
the vital blood of proliferating generations to come, but the physical violence of
the parricide passes into the purely verbal aggression of the grandsons, giving
them a manly air ("gallant little swearers") in which Flaherty proleptically shares
("I'm a decent man of Ireland"). But the threat of murderous rampage ("to end
them, maybe, with a sudden end") remains the linchpin of the dialectic.[119]

The complex metonymy here between the consciousness of parricide and
the (re)production of gallantry is by no means casual. It is rather an index, a
reminder, that the mythic construction of parricide bears a structure uncannily
proximate to the *discordia concours* that defines the modern construction of
manhood. If psychoanalysis had not already indicated as much in enshrining
the story of Oedipus as the paradigm of masculine identity formation, Synge
certainly does in pairing the figure of Oedipus with that of Cuchulain as a
prototype for Christy. The timing with which those mythic links appear is particularly instructive in this regard. Declan Kiberd has convincingly demon-

strated that the character and reputation of Christy before he struck his fatal blow represented a systematic inversion of the legend of Cuchulain.[120] It is only with the collaborative transformation of Christy into an Oedipal killer that the affirmative analogues to Ireland's iconic warrior are posed. Not only do these analogies likewise emerge through the cooperative effort of the village audience, but the major ones reflect the sense of that audience—a Revivalist sense I would argue—that the *discordia concours* of a real but already sublimated or mythologized potential for violence defines the structure of (Irish) heroism:

1. Upon disclosure of his Oedipal homicide, Christy is posted to guard the public house just as Cuchulain is called to guard the borders of the Ulster community at the outset of the *Tain*. But Christy's assigned task also encompasses the Revivalist sanitation of the original. Whereas Cuchulain abandons his post to keep an adulterous assignation (see above), Christy's charge includes the protection of Pegeen's virtue as well.

2. During Christy's wooing of Pegeen, which specifically recalls Cuchulain's famous wooing of Emer, Pegeen makes much of the "rages" driving Christy to "destroy [his] da" (*P*, 94). Her words plainly allude to the "battle rages" or "war spasms" of Cuchulain.[121] But far from implicating the sort of bodily, animalistic distortions those paroxysms entail, she conflates them with the more cerebral frenzy of the poets "when their temper's roused" (*P*, 83). Just like Lady Gregory's summary of Cuchulain's *riastrad* as a "the hero light," giving him "the appearance of a god,"[122] Pegeen's description of the battle rages is self-sublimating, an elevation of feral convulsion into the creative struggle of the spirit. This is part of a broader editorial tendency among the villagers to substitute certain virtues necessary to commit the parricide— daring, bravery, and so on—for the meaning of the act.

3. The townsfolk encourage and acclaim Christy's participation in the local sports, which they see as an appropriately controlled outlet for his supposed "savagery" (*P*, 94). His triumphs not only call forth the boy exploits of Cuchulain upon first entering Emain Macha, they connect Christy with the Victorian "games ethic" of manliness that keyed the Revivalist translation of those exploits.

By the same token, the shattering of the parricidal illusion abruptly relegates Christy back to being a systematic inversion of Cuchulain's virtues, an inversion now effected by the townsfolk themselves. Where Cuchulain was the boy who took Emain Macha by storm, Christy is a child to be "pandied" for his misbehavior; where Cuchulain fought to the last, strapping himself to a rock for the purpose, Christy was "after . . . hitting a soft blow and chasing northward in a sweat of fear." In the process, Christy comes to be portrayed as an inversion of Oedipal values as well. Instead of the rebel son rising against oppressive (paternal) authority, he becomes a ridiculous, jumped-up version of such authority: "The lad thought he'd rule the roost in Mayo. Slate him now, mister" (*P*, 113). Most important, from our perspective, this inversion of Christy's status as Cuchulain-style hero correlates with an unraveling of the *discordia concours* of his supposed manliness. Having been arraigned as an "ugly liar" once his father reappears, Christy invokes his recent accomplishments, "my doings this day," as the sublimated expressions of the virile force behind his murderous blow: "I'm after hearing my voice this day saying words would raise the topknot on a poet. . . . I've won your racing, and your lepping, and . . ." (*P*, 114). His voice trails off, however, in recognition that without reference to that primal scene of agonistic violence, his associated competitive feats—what we see as his Cuchulainesque embellishments—can gather no heroic significance whatever. Hence Christy's attempt, by renewing his assault on old Mahon, to restore that primordial violence, and thus to act as the agent of his own revival.

The criticism on *Playboy* has been much occupied with why Christy's second, apparently successful parricide does not win back the approval of the townsfolk and what his rejection says about the townsfolk as an emblem of some more comprehensive Irish sensibility. These questions crystallize for all concerned around the import of Pegeen Mike's fabled proclamation: "A strange man is a marvel, with his mighty talk, but what's a squabble in your back-yard, and the blow of a loy, have taught me that there is a great gap between a gallous story and a dirty deed" (*P*, 116). One dominant reading puts most pressure on "talk" and "story" to argue that the difference in the before and after reactions of the villagers turns on the difference between fictional and real bodily mayhem.[123] Kiberd proposes that Pegeen Mike et al., like Synge's Irish contemporaries, celebrated in fiction the bloodletting they could not stomach in fact.[124] The problem with this theory is that it must suppose that the villagers did not really credit the *actual* occurrence of the first parricide, yet their acute sense of betrayal later testifies that they believed all too well.[125] The second dominant reading puts pressure on the metaphor of the "back-yard" to argue that the before and after difference answers to the relative distance of the deadly event.[126] The villagers' inclination to applaud a parricide committed far away tallies with the tendency of their contemporaries in the cultural nationalist movement to romanticize the political bloodshed of the past. While this reading is in my view the more persuasive, the willingness of a Pegeen Mike to turn about, just seconds after the "dirty deed," and bewail the loss of "the only Playboy of the Western World" (*P*, 118) suggests that we must grasp effective distance from the scene of violence in something like "aesthetic" terms rather than as a great expanse of physical space or historical time. The concept of manliness proves helpful in informing this apprehension.

Just as the return of old Mahon robs Christy's "doings this day" of the aggressive ballast necessary to give them heroic weight, so his second mortal onslaught lacks the sublimating complement of aesthetic distance necessary to give it heroic elevation. Owing to the increasingly antic and degraded familiarity of the Mahons to their Mayo audience, neither the vaguely Cuchulainesque challenge Christy poses—"I'll stretch you first" (*P,* 114)—nor the Oedipal killing he actually essays can renew the mythic stature of the original tale, the sense of a transcendental, generally appropriable significance that made it seem larger than life. Exiled from the mythic dimension, Christy can no longer integrate the component virtues of manliness that he continues to display, and because manliness is ultimately a matter of form rather than content, this failure of integration leaves him with no socially viable purchase on the estate at all. As outlined in my introduction, to enact the two sides of manliness *disjunctively*—as the metrocolonial subject was impelled to do—was to suffer being identified with either of the opposed negative "others" of masculinity: a supine, acquiescent femininity and a rampant, unrestrained animality. The self-consciousness with which Synge's Cuchulain-oid parody engages this gender construct may be gauged from his depiction of Christy at the nadir of his social fortunes—as the town prepares to lynch him after the second, desperate murder attempt. Sara Tansey has strapped a petticoat on him as a getaway disguise, and thus adorned in feminine garb he struggles against his confinement by biting Shawn Keogh "the like of a mad dog" (*P,* 117). At this climactic moment, Synge combines the androgynous and the feral to render his hero the perfect iconographic emblem of manliness undone. The crowning irony is that in thus defaulting on the Revivalist profile of a proper Cuchulain, Christy Mahon might be said to approximate the original Cuchulain—a mad yet androgynous "Hound"—more closely than ever, displaying the same boundary-busting excessiveness in roughly the same terms.[127]

Like Cuchulain, Christy can be saved only by being lost, and then revived as a sentimentalized memory. This function, of course, falls to Pegeen Mike ("I've lost him surely" [*P,* 118]), who forces him out of the community so that she might plaintively bewail his absence. That the play ends on this note is the surest sign that it constitutes not a Cuchulain "return" but a "Cuchulainoid" parody. Pegeen's final lament represents the true cry of revivalist misrecognition: *its need to lose the thing it professes to love precisely so that it can love it,* that is, can make it conform, in its reconstitution, to the prevailing standards of merit—such as manliness. Pegeen's famous last words give both Christy and the play their official "title," suggesting that only at this point of commemoration does Christy actually become the "Playboy of the Western World" promised from the start (*P,* 118). The dynamic that Christy himself identifies, "making a mighty man of me . . . by the power of a lie" (*P,* 114), proves more dialectical than even he imagines and achieves completion only with this one final negation, Pegeen's revivalist gesture. Just as Cuchulain must be translated from the ancient manuscripts into the mythopoetic world of Lady Gregory et al. in order to become a proper "hero of the tribe," so Christy must be translated into a mythopoetic space beyond Mayo in order for him to "go romancing through a romping lifetime" as the Hound's modern-day descendant (*P*, 117).[128]

Presenting, as we have seen, an intractable double bind, the problem of (metro)colonial manliness perhaps demands to be taken up and resolved in the mythical dimension—which is to say, manliness may well represent the ideal object of Revivalist elaboration. In the case of Christy, however, Synge shows that the mythologizing reflex of the Revival allows the double bind to be resolved *formally*, in the figure of the hero (Christy assumes control over his father and himself as he departs), but only at the price of reasserting the double bind *socially*, in the separation of that figure, the type of tribal manliness, from the tribe he is supposed to totemize. Thus, Christy's Mayo collaborators can "make a mighty man of [him] . . . by the power of a lie," but they can only make "a likely gaffer of [him] in the end" through the power of a ban (*P*, 117), expelling the man and thereby restoring his manliness somewhere beyond their power to benefit. As the final significant action taken by the town, it testifies to the profoundly disempowering implications of the autoethnography they allegorize: to whit, "where we are, there our most honored estates and identification-forms are not." Read in these terms, Synge's greatest play exposes the grimmest aspect of Revivalist manhood, from the treason felons to blood sacrifice to Cuchulainoid drama: the prospect of attaining the ideal always seems to depend on the disappearance, one way or another, of its champions.

5

"Mixed Middling"

James Joyce and
Metrocolonial Manliness

Reading *Ulysses* in the context of an Anglo-European prose tradition, T. S. Eliot famously proclaimed its author the pioneer of a new literary approach, the "Mythic Method," which deploys symbolic resources of past civilizations to lend a more intelligible pattern to the complexities of modern life.[1] Reading James Joyce in the context of his own native culture produces a diametrically reversed image of his achievement. What Joyce himself called the "scrupulous meanness" of his literary style registers as an ironic antidote to the strenuously mythologizing enterprise of the Irish Literary Revival: the commitment of such contemporary writers as Yeats, Gregory, Pearse, Moore, Gonne, O'Grady, Milligan, and Cousins to recover and redact ancient Gaelic legends and folklore for the purpose of reimagining and even remaking modern Ireland in their image. Nowhere, perhaps, does the comparatively demystifying cast of Joyce's work show up more clearly than with regard to the elaboration of masculine gender ideals and their psychosocial effects.

As we saw in earlier chapters, the Sovereignty myth and the Cuchulain saga figured regularly in Revivalist drama and poetry as vehicles for invoking a national spirit of manliness under and despite the pressures of colonial dispossession. Joyce not only rejected this office, like Synge and to a certain extent Stephens, but also turned his fictional enterprise to examining the impact the gender ideals circulated under this mythic aegis had on his countrymen. In *Dubliners,* male protagonists traversing much the same urban landscape as that found in *The Charwoman's Daughter* labor under an impossible yet inescapable mandate of self-restrained aggressiveness that is neither relieved nor dignified by any of the usual mythic accoutrements. In *Ulysses,* which drew Eliot's admiring notice, the varnish of Irish mythology is indeed applied, but to satirical excess. Hyperbolic parodies of Pearse, the GAA, and heroic revivalism in general serve to illuminate how the propagation of the Gaelic warrior legend as an ethno-political touchstone tended only to exacerbate the colonial plight of everyday Irish men by encouraging an internalization of imposed standards of self-conquest designed specifically to stymie and dishonor them. The sad result, as Leopold Bloom discovers to his chagrin, is a collective self-loathing manifested defensively in a phobic contempt for perceived otherness. Manliness thus emerges in Joyce's work not as some transcendent value to be espoused but as an ideologically freighted dilemma to be contended with. More specifically, by mapping the colonial bias on which this particular gender ideal plays out, Joyce subverts the hegemonic metropolitan assumption that such gender norms come by nature or represent ethical universals, while he simultaneously subverts the nationalist faith in Irish manliness as a panacea for achieving social and political autonomy.

The Ghost of Parnell: Portrait of the Artist as a Young Man

James Joyce's encounter with the problematic of manliness, like that of Gregory (chapter 2) and Yeats (epilogue), was in significant measure keyed to the figure of Charles Stewart Parnell, the betrayed master, whom Joyce likewise imaged in a gallery of typological correspondences (Christ, Moses, and so on). The difference with Joyce, however, as F. S. L. Lyons has remarked, is that he was "closer to the [Parnellite] ground and more directly involved. He had grown up inside the Parnellite tradition and he knew, far more intimately than Yeats [or Gregory] could ever know, the pettiness, the frustration, the sheer human fallibility, of nationalist politics at the grass roots." As a result, while Joyce remained "sympathetic to the Parnellite myth, it was the Parnellite actuality that provided the bass ground of his work."[2] To put it another way, Yeats was concerned to erect Parnell as a moralized Anglo-Irish ideal whose betrayal cast the Irish people out of their proper cultural Eden; Gregory was ultimately concerned to erect Parnell as a revolutionary icon whose betrayal by the Irish people, like all political calamities, carried the DNA of cultural redemption; but Joyce was specifically concerned with the social construction and erosion of the Parnell ideal as experienced from "inside the Parnell tradition," by its middle-class Catholic rank and file. He was, accordingly, not just more rooted in "Parnellite actuality" than his fellow literary observers, he was more attentive to the complex ideological dynamics at work in the myth itself. If Joyce's inherited proximity did not exactly inoculate him against the personal appeal of the martyred leader narrative—Lyons himself famously pronounced Joyce a "bad case of arrested Parnellism"—it did heighten his critical self-consciousness about the underpinnings and effects of that legend.[3]

No one displayed a greater acuity than Joyce about the importance of masculine gender norms in the circulation of Parnell's posthumous image, an insight whetted, if not generated whole, by Joyce's "growing up in the Parnellite tradition" of his family home. During the first nine years of Joyce's life, the economic wherewithal and social standing that John Joyce attained as a rate collector and Irish party operative nourished dreams of gentlemanliness, which, as *A Portrait of the Artist* tells it, he communicated to his first-born son upon enrolling him at Clongowes Wood. The complacent self-respect that Mr. Joyce enjoyed took as an ethno-national correlative an unusually fervid espousal of Home Rule,[4] replete with the kind of reverence for Parnell that I cataloged in chapter 2. Parnell's manly embodiment of the Irish will to political self-determination helped to underwrite what might be called a "new Irishness," of which John Joyce, briefly, was a sterling example: confident, assertive and structurally (socially, economically, culturally) self-possessed.

The stories that John Joyce told about Parnell, which James retailed throughout his life, belabored the Chief's manly profile: his hauteur, his reserve, his moral indomitability. In so doing, they accentuated the specifically gendered import of "growing up" Parnellite. Young James was given to appreciate Parnell as a distinctively masculine ideal that further authorized his father's imago by connecting his gentlemanly self-presentation with an affirmative vision of ethno-national identity. The legend of Parnell acquired its lifelong affective and identificatory power for Joyce from the role that it performed in his father's discourse. Over against the accumulated slights that (metro)colonial identity was heir to (such as the *Punch* caricatures, which make a salient appearance in *Stephen Hero*), Parnell stood as the symbolic guarantor of the concurrence of those gentlemanly and nationalist aspirations that John Joyce passed to his son.

It was therefore especially meaningful for young Joyce that the sudden, sharp, and irrevocable reversal in his family fortunes should have so "closely synchronized" with the fall of Parnell, which, in Richard Ellmann's phrase, henceforth marked "a dividing line between the stale present and the good old days." In addition to the steady forfeiture of rent income during this period, John Joyce lost his government post, in part because his vigorous politicking on behalf of the besieged Parnell, including a trip to Cork to rally his remaining tenants for a by-election, had attracted resentful notice in his bureau.[5] The fall of Parnell thus catalyzed, as well as dated, the long descent of the Joyces from suburban affluence to the ever-grimmer North Dublin accommodations that a big family could afford on an improvident civil servant's pension.

More important, the "dividing line" of Parnell's demise also proved an associative magnet for the psychosocial consequences of the Joyces' steep downward mobility. Prominent among them seems to have been the considerable erosion of moral authority attaching to John Joyce's position as paterfamilias. Semiretired at forty-two, yet unable to support his family in anything like the accustomed manner, lacking any political enthusiasm to rival his past devotion to Parnell or his present taste for strong drink,[6] John Joyce passed from presiding with an easy self-assurance over a flourishing brood to hastening the family's drift into disorder. Under the weight of these life conditions, which altered both his conduct and the framework of its domestic reception, his battered self-respect lapsed into embittered self-aggrandizement as he steadily lost esteem and credibility among his dependents. Even as the end of Parnellite Home Rule heralded the onset of Joycean "Home Ruin," the deposition of Parnell as Irish "Chief" heralded the dis(self-)possession of John Joyce as Irish patriarch.

This turn of events does not seem to have discredited in Joyce's eyes the manly ethos and style personified by Parnell. If anything, living through the collapse of his family situation, capped by his mother's ghastly death, spurred him to a more intensive, and defensive, personal cultivation of those gendered properties—self-containment, unflappability, aloofness—that he associated with the great man. But this same turn of events, attended by his father's increasingly transparent self-mythologization, did serve to *denaturalize* the manly ideal for Joyce, to disclose the historical contingency of its operation and of the patriarchal authority, domestic or geopolitical, that it legitimated.[7] By this route, the political nature of normative manliness became available to Joyce's conscious reflection, and, in turn, its multidimensional effects in the Irish context became available for investigation and critique in his fiction. To appreciate Joyce's overdetermined transferential identification with his father and Parnell—as respectable nationalists, self-proclaimed gentlemen, fallen heroes—is to apprehend how far his well-known preoccupation with the legal fiction of fatherhood was imbricated from the start with his inculcation in the *ideological* fiction of Victorian manhood.[8]

It is therefore not surprising that Joyce's first extended, openly autobiographical scene of father-son interaction should be mediated by the figure of Parnell. I refer, of course, to the Christmas-dinner fiasco in *A Portrait of the Artist,* which may be read as a parable of the gendered implications for both father and son of the particular contours of the Parnell affair.[9] Marking Stephen's first seasonal return from boarding school and his first holiday at the adult table, the Christmas dinner is his "coming out" as a young *man.* Indeed, Stephen feels the ritual moment on his very skin as the effect of his special outfit, which just happens to be the official uniform of manly apprenticeship, an Eton suit, which makes "him feel queer and oldish." What is more, the sight of his public school finery brings his father, Simon, to tears of generational pride at the thought "of his own father" (*AP,* 29). His sentimental reaction, confirmed by the other paterfamilias, Uncle Charles, locates Stephen's individual rite of passage within a larger class-inflected, patrilineal romance of gentlemanliness, whereby the Dedalus clan memorializes their generational ascent from "whiteboy" to Castle-Catholic.

In this regard, the ceremonial function of the dinner accords with the specific value of Parnell in the Joyce family narrative.

As Robin Gilmour has delineated, the long negotiation between a fading aristocracy and a rising middle class over the gentrifying category of the gentleman reached "an effective compromise" by the latter part of the nineteenth century. A traditional liberal education at a respectable public school now qualified one as a gentleman, even as it credentialed one for a middle-class occupation.[10] In terms of the logic of manliness anatomized in this study, such an education conferred upon a male subject the *descriptive* profile necessary for one's normative conduct, one's fulfillment of the *prescriptive* criteria of manhood, to be presumed in evidence and credited in full. Accordingly, Stephen's Eton suit marks his "public school" Clongowes Wood as a peculiarly metrocolonial enterprise, an institution that seeks to preserve and cultivate the ethno-confessional identity of the native middle class while busily assimilating that group to metropolitan economies of social authority and distinction.

But insofar as that native, ethno-confessional identity also condemns its bearer to a certain measure of inferiority, debars him, at a certain limit, from the normative stature to which he has assimilated, the dual functions of a Clongowes Wood cannot come together, or come off, without a hitch, a symptom of internal contradiction. Given its provenance, Stephen's Eton jacket cannot confer a school-certified purchase on the title of gentleman without also confessing an embattled pretense to that title. It discloses, precisely in trying to dissimulate, the profound insecurities surrounding this honored status for a professional and administrative elite mortified by their continuing subdominance. So acute is Stephen's ambivalence that he questions, "Then why was he sent to that place with them?" (*AP*, 24).

Owing to Parnell's own iconic manliness, especially for the middle-class Catholics of Dublin, the Christmas-dinner imbroglio over his demise not only coincides but symbolically coheres with Stephen's rite of passage. Surprisingly, this crucial aspect of the scene's construction has attracted little notice. That is to say, the reduplication of the great "Parnell split" within the confines of the Dedalus household has not been grasped as intimately connected with Stephen's specifically gendered debut at the holiday event. On this day, Stephen's move toward personal majority, from the nursery to the dining room, is being ritualized to affirm his gentlemanly inheritance as the basis of his gentlemanly prospects. With the debate over Parnell, however, the precarious, deeply contested nature of that gentlemanly inheritance stands revealed. Stephen finds his father figures (Simon, Mr. Casey) must struggle to assert *their own majority,* their political majority, of which the disgraced Parnell has been, in some sense, both a father (author and progenitor) and a figure (symbol and synecdoche). Thus, the unhappy political genealogy centering on Parnell not only shadows the happy personal genealogy centering on Stephen, but also threatens to abrogate the cardinal social value to be reproduced in Stephen, a status that interlinks gender, class, and national aspirations.

It is for this reason that Joyce frames the dispute over Parnell's continuing impact as a "battle of the sexes," at least in the first instance: self-assertive breadwinner (Simon) versus pious virago (Dante). In this pre-suffrage era, with the Woman's Property Act only recently legislated, Dante inhabits a subject position threatening to her male opponents by reason of its unacknowledged proximity to their own: mature, serious, articulate adulthood encumbered by the constraints of political minority. Their fight against the woman's derogation of Parnell amounts to a fight against their own feminization, which they equate to a reflexive compliance with the imperial state ("Were we to desert him at the bidding of the English people?" [*AP*, 31]).

The sexual antagonism suffusing this fracas, however, proves but the outcropping of a larger homosocial "battle of the patriarchs."[11] Dante's every retort to Simon channels the official opinion of the clergy, effectively reactivating a proxy power struggle between two groups of male eminences, the religious and the secular, the prelates and the politicians. Both drew a significant degree of their cultural influence from their respective association with the manly ideal. Even as Parnell bodied forth a new brand of *moral-force* leadership, whose volcanic yet self-contained aggression gave the Irish people back their manhood in a respectable form, the Irish clergy was practicing a more rugged, forceful species of *moral* leadership, indebted no less than Parnell's gender performance to the (Protestant) agenda of muscular Christianity. By way of confirmation, Stephen himself later finds the Jesuit "masters" to be "athletic and highspirited," prone to manly customs like washing "their bodies briskly with cold water" (*AP*, 168), and eager to add their voices to the exhortation that he be "a gentleman above all things . . . strong and manly and healthy" (*AP*, 88). Whereas the "animal spirits" that Parnell made such a conspicuous show of curbing involved political violence, the animal spirits that the Irish priesthood made a conspicuous project of repressing involved sexual desire. The glaring juxtaposition between celibacy as the sign of sacerdotal discipline and Parnell's notorious liaison with Kitty O'Shea helped to turn the cult of manliness from an adherence shared, in different ways, by priest and party, to a competitive medium in which the divorce of confessional and Parnellite nationalisms played itself out.

This development placed Catholic Irish–Irish Parnellites, such as Simon Dedalus and John Casey, in an all but impossible position, ensnaring them in yet another variation on the colonial double bind. Given the grafting and confusion of ethnic and religious identity forms in post-Reformation Ireland, Irish nationalism and even Irish national identity carried an irreducibly sectarian element. For a Dedalus or a Casey, being Irish men *at all* was wrapped up in their role as

Catholic parishioners, patriarchs, and penitents. In equating continued Parnell-
lism with "renegade" Catholicism and "black Protestant[ism]," Dante presents
Dedalus and Casey with a "cracked lookingglass" revealing the contradiction
that obtains between their unbreakable sectarian attachments and their irresistible gentlemanly aspirations—which might be translated as attachments to
a received Irish ethnicity and aspirations to a freely minted Irish nation.

Simon Dedalus, in turn, attempts to reflect the double bind of manliness back
upon the priestly caste in specific. He portrays the great prelates, like Walsh,
Logue, and Cullen, as having adopted a feminized posture of submission toward
the colonial master. Then, he suggestively imputes their quisling ways to their
immersion in animal concupiscence and comfort, which they are presumably
bent on safeguarding.

> —They are the lord's anointed, Dante said. They are an honour to their country.
> —Tub of guts, said Mr. Dedalus coarsely. He [Logue] has a handsome face, mind
> you, in repose. You should see that fellow lapping up his bacon and cabbage of
> a cold winter's day. . . .
> He twisted his features into a grimace of heavy bestiality and made a lapping
> noise with his lips. (*AP,* 32)

Given the "twisted features," the sensual "grimace," the lapping orality, Mr. Dedalus plainly endeavors to sexualize, as grossly as possible, the eating habits of
the archbishop in order to discredit priestly celibacy, that seal of the "Lord's
anointed," as proof of effective self-restraint and possession. His caricature represents priestly appetites as utterly unsublimated and thus unable to animate
the stalwart manliness necessary to mount, model, or encourage patriotic resistance, to be "an honour to their country." Further, Logue's surrender to his
baser promptings, at once beastial and feminizing, can be seen to set an allegorical tone for the feral practices of his underlings. More than merely deposing
Parnell, they tear at him "like rats in a sewer" and "lowlived dogs," a display of
rapine that Dedalus ties back to the brutish appearance of Logue at feed: "And
they look it! By Christ, they look it!" (*AP,* 33).

But Simon's performance not only adjudicates the competing scandals—the
license of Parnell, the perfidy of the cloth. In its reliance on popular anti-Irish
gender typology, it *gives* scandal as well, particularly to the boy, as everyone,
including Simon himself, agrees. That is to say, in asserting the masculinity of
his sadly "priestridden race" (a metaphor with pestilential, equine, and even
sexual connotations), Simon winds up betraying the gentlemanly standing his
genealogical reminiscences celebrated just a few hours earlier. More than catching himself in a gender double bind, he passes it on to his son. Once the dinner
breaks up, with the men openly weeping over their dead king, Stephen sits torn
between a manly identification with his now unmanned father and an identifi-

cation with the female-supported Fathers who have unmanned him. Stephen's inheritance this day is not, accordingly, the patrilineal legacy with which it began, but a traumatic attachment to the figure whose polarizing memory has started to dissolve it before Stephen's very eyes. Such an attachment could, of course, leave Stephen prey to the sort of stultifying nostalgia that Lyons attributed to Joyce under the title of "arrested Parnellism." But I would point out that for Stephen, as for Joyce, the attachment to a ghost—be it Parnell, "the beautiful May Goulding," Shakespeare, or one's own past self—is always an occasion for critiquing the self-evidence of present things. Thus, as the ghost of the compelling yet internecine construct of manhood, Parnell ultimately helped to make the call to that honored estate "hollowsounding in [Stephen's] ears" and the subject of endlessly skeptical interrogation in Joyce's prose (*AP*, 88).

Dubliners: Joyce's Counterparts

For Joyce, this subject formation I have been calling metrocolonial was exemplified not by the Irish tout court but by a peculiar species of Irishman, the Dubliner, a civic identity form that he believed to be more distinctive than comparable designations like Londoner or Parisian. By the same token, the distinctiveness of Joyce's treatment of the manhood complex in Ireland derived in large part from his focusing all but exclusively on the people of Dublin.

Under what I have coined the phenomenon of Anglo-Irish metrocolonialism, the nominally self-consistent metropolitan nation-state contrived to aggrandize itself by simultaneously absorbing and othering the proximate areas of the Celtic fringe, thereby sustaining them as doubly/divisively inscribed portions of its own now fissured identity. Instead of a properly colonial space, the Dublin of Joyce's experience instanced the metrocolonial interval or remainder, a border zone both joining and dividing an imperialist and an irredentist culture under the always contestable titles of "West Britain" and the capital of Ireland, respectively. As bearers of this split ethno-colonial inscription, the subjects of the Pale were situated to heed the contradictory summonses to both a sense of racial entitlement vis-à-vis other subject peoples of the British empire and a sense of racial subordination and grievance vis-à-vis the hegemonic peoples of the metropolitan center; both to support for Great Britain's civilizing mission abroad and to resistance to that mission at home; and, finally, to both an acceptance and a rejection of disparate values, assumptions, practices, and expressive forms alternately marked alien or native, dominant or subdominant, metropolitan or colonial.

Subject as they were to these mutually abrasive forms of identification, the metrocolonial Irish, and the Dubliners who epitomized them, were not *entirely* exiled into the occulted zone of the Other. Their imposed circumstance was at once less pathologized and more compromised, less abased and more exposed. The circumscribed sociocultural locus properly their own had become in itself *improper,* eccentric, undecidable, extraterritorial, and so appropriable in advance. As the geopolitical title the United Kingdom announces, the space of Irishness was neither fully apart from nor seamlessly a part of the conquering polis. If we might, on one hand, see such assimilation within the metropole as mitigating to a degree the subalternity of the Irish—an implicit promise of both Arnoldian and revisionist historiography—it may also be understood to have given yet another turn to the dialectical screw of colonial subjugation. The Irish were not merely dispossessed—politically, culturally, economically—but they were also in a sense *dispossessed of their dispossession,* made to suffer the grudging yet compulsory privilege of membership, junior membership to be sure, in the master nation.

During the late Victorian and Edwardian eras, when race and nationality took a leading role in subject formation, decisively inflecting other primary identity categories (gender, class, and so forth), such metrocolonial immixture could not be restricted to the geopolitical domain proper but was filtered throughout the enshrined authority structures of everyday life. The ideology of manliness was among the most salient of these structures. The dominant conception of masculinity during this period centered upon and honored the capacity to sustain sovereign, autonomous, self-contained identity formations, individual and collective, against all possible incursions or admixtures, endogenous or exogenous, on or across several ontological levels (body, ego, psyche, family, ethnos, nation). The construct of manliness perfected this ideological fantasy by transmuting the insistent male energies understood to threaten such boundary maintenance from within, the so-called animal spirits, into the prime disciplinary forces that not only would consolidate the integrity of the individual and the community but, in so doing, could help to defend them against threats or incursions from without. On this basis, the metrocolonial estate constituted *a precise negative analogue to the condition of achieved manliness.* Through the cultural dynamic of dual interpellation and correspondingly split identification that this estate entailed for its subjects, the chief external barrier to Irish self-possession and self-command, British domination, translated into an inner psychosocial impediment as well. Whereas manliness named the sublimation of internal heteronomy—the sway of animal passion—into self-coincident, self-directed agency, metrocolonial subjectivity incurred the conversion of imposed subordination into internal heteronomy, an unmastered division of cultural investments, political loyalties, and ethnic and class attachments. Under these ideological circumstances, the very attempt to perform the social script of manliness was structurally programmed not just for failure but for self-betrayal. At the same time, the title of manliness was itself a crucial part of these ideological circumstances. Because the construct had long signified the glories of the dominant (English) culture, the promise it offered Dubliners, to deliver them from the dilemma of metrocolonial hybridity and into a new collective self-ownership, only worked to reinforce their plight of psychic dependency, leaving them hostage to the moral structure of their own marginalization. Beyond licensing colonial *dispossession,* then, as an extension of the Irish failure of *self-possession,* manliness served as a conceptual lure implicating the Irish in the very predicament, individual and collective heteronomy, to which it posed as antidote.

The burden of Joyce's treatment of masculinity is to expose, explain, and help to end Irish participation in this self-defeating circle. His own account of his fellow Dubliners speaks to the task, focusing specifically on the question of self-directing agency, the aspect of manliness most scrutinized in the stories. Writing to Constantine Curran, Joyce proposed to "betray the sense of that hemiplegia or paralysis which many consider a city."[12] With his characteristic instinct for the deft pun, Joyce uses "betray" here to suggest both "disclose" and "deliver over." That is to say, he would deliver over, offload, the essential paralysis of Dublin life by disclosing or displaying it, especially to the suffering denizens themselves. Although popularly identified with loss of movement, the condition of paralysis is actually defined by a loss of local or self-control. Joyce can thus be seen as endeavoring to restore some potential for local control, autonomous agency, to his Dublin counterparts, by unveiling the social etiology of their distress. The key to this etiology rests not in simple inertia but in the historically conditioned propensity to *self-betrayal* born of the split/double inscription of metrocolonial subjectivity—an inflicted *psychomachia* that encourages an all too willing misrecognition or self-deception. The injunction to metrocolonial manliness, to a self-possession that, quite literally, is not one, not only draws upon and operates within but functions to sustain this disabling context of constitutive self-alienation. By his own testimony, the aim of Joyce's *narrative* tactics is to represent and thereby reverse the pattern wherein the Dubliners' *social* tactics perennially reversed themselves. As such, unlike certain Irish writers we have examined, he comes not to claim manliness for the people but rather to critique it in their name.

Joyce's verbal association of Dublin with doubling and "do you belong" reflects upon the importance of this curved space of split identification in any account of the Hibernian capital. Taken in this punning light, the title *Dubliners* serves as a kind of master signifier, indexing not just an urban space but a psychosocial topography, in which the question "Do you belong to *yourself?*" the baseline for achieved manliness, cannot be answered affirmatively. Reading the volume, one is struck by how far its generic, narrative, and stylistic methods justify a punning gloss on the title: Dubliners as "doublingers" as "dyoublongers" (*FW,* 13, 15). The innovative generic method of *Dubliners,* its synchronic enchainment of discrete narrative frames, diagrams the heteronomy embedded within the subject by the internal fracture of metrocolonial space. All of the characters in *Dubliners,* with their respective story lines and signature motifs, bear their import strictly and immediately in relation to elements lying beyond their own official context or horizon of pertinence, the individual story, and so each of them must literally, or literarily, operate in *the place of the Other.*

Joyce's stylistic method builds upon his generic innovation by exfoliating the relationship between the institutional and the discursive constraints upon the characters and the decentered quality of their intellection. If, as Hugh Kenner first observed, Joyce allows his indirect free style to modulate subtly into the distinctive idiolects of the protagonists,[13] he also and no less importantly ventriloquizes these idiolects, rendering them pastiches of the conflicting, overlapping threads of the larger sociolect, the dialogized and often discordant voices of Irish culture. The critical purport of this peculiar brand of double inscription is to correlate the extraterritorial character of Irish social, political, and cultural space with the extraterritorial cast of the Irish character or psyche, a mutually reinforcing condition that makes the enabling fictions of manly self-possession and self-command especially difficult to sustain.

To take one outstanding, intensively gendered example, the split identification of Little Chandler—between the feminized aesthetic "melancholy" he prizes in himself and the aggressive man of the world brio he admires in Gallagher—unfolds over the course of "A Little Cloud" as a contest of discourses for dominance of Chandler's thought patterns. The sentimental elegiac idiom distilled from his reading of Celticist literature gives way before the vigorous appeal of a pragmatic, rough-and-tumble journalese that bears Gallagher's adopted London impress: "Even when he was out at elbows and at wits' end for money he kept up a bold face"; "that was Gallagher all out, and, damn it, you couldn't but admire him for it" (*D,* 6–7). As his musings evince, in both style and substance, Chandler has been colonized by Gallagher's attitude of muscular, self-interested ambition, to which he responds with a perfect confluence of quite explicit class, gender, and subaltern resentments: "He found something mean in the pretty furniture which he had brought for his house on the hire system. Annie had chosen it herself and it reminded him of her. It too was prim and pretty. . . . Was it too late for him to try to live bravely like Gallagher? Could he go to London?" (*D,* 79). But Chandler nevertheless continues to assume the "melancholy" standards of a pseudoromantic revivalism in pronouncing Gallagher's language of the marketplace "vulgar," "gaudy," and "tawdry" (*D,* 72, 75). Even so, his underlying investment in the "Celtic note" itself proves no less commodified and careerist than the sensibility flaunted by his friend and rival, as evidenced with exquisite irony in his fantasies of future poetic éclat. By the self-feminizing strategy of inserting "his mother's name before his surname" in order to showcase his Irish-Irish roots, T. Malone Chandler ("to give him for the nonce his new misnomer")[14] hopes to attract the reviews of his dreams ("*a wistful sadness . . . The Celtic note*" [*D,* 69]), which feature just the sort of ethnically clichéd paeans that Gallagher's journalistic colleagues might concoct.

On the narrative plane, finally, Joyce carefully situates almost every protagonist at the crux of a double/divisive inscription, instanced in clashing authorities of various types: commanding figures, prevalent discourses, social institutions and customs, received ideas, and the like. This is Joyce's signature manner of supplying that basic element of conflict traditionally deemed essential to the short story form, and the result is a more or less perpetual state of crisis in masculine gender formation throughout the volume. *Dubliners* opens, tellingly, with highly Oedipalized renditions of the double/divisive interpellation of the male subject. The boy narrator of "The Sisters" and "An Encounter" is caught between opposed figures of paternal law (Cotter and Flynn, Butler and the scribbler) with opposed ethno-national associations respectively: Catholic Irish-Ireland and the secular Anglicized youth culture of cold baths and boy magazines. By "Araby" the boy finds himself solicited, on the one hand, by a putatively native but largely imported, medieval romanticism, attached to the ticket-named Mangan's sister and, on the other, by the English-accented orientalizing and commodified romanticism of the bazaar.[15] In "Two Gallants," Lenahan enacts a vulgarized species of the same ambivalence, responding both to a feminized and exposed harp, an icon of Ireland, whose romantic stylings "began to control his movements" (*D,* 52), and to the venal, predatory cynicism of Corley, the English-identified police informer, whose latest victim, likewise feminine and abjected, represents an analogous symbol of her country. In "A Little Cloud" Chandler's envious identification with the crass if energetic cosmopolitanism of his expatriot "orange" friend Gallagher confounds his phantasmatic identification with the bathetic nativism and spiritual languor of the Celtic twilight bard.[16] In the stories of public life, finally, what we might call the characters' "D(o)ublin(g) inscription" materializes in institutional presences and official ideologies. In "Grace" the Roman Catholic idea of "grace" as divine mystery is hijacked within the church itself by the Anglo-bourgeois notion of grace as social respectability. In "Ivy Day in the Committee Room," the dream of national self-respect interred with Ireland's "Uncrowned King" shrinks before the promise of imported capital affixed to the impending visit of the British monarch, Edward VI.[17]

The thematic drift of these stories is to show how the concealed structural complicity of these ideological forces and institutions, their deep if fractious collaboration in delimiting metrocolonial subjectivity, keys its paralyzing ambivalence. Being both agonistic and symbiotic, the interpellating discourses themselves do not simply converge at the level of the individual or collective subject; they are knotted together there, internally dialogized, such that the accession to one social code or mandate triggers or implies simultaneous accession to its frustrating or corrupting or negating other. It is this paradoxical curvature of the metrocolonial inscription that demands and derails the efforts of Joyce's Dubliners to "pull themselves together," to compass the sort of laminated self-containment of which manliness was the privileged social form.

The tale "Araby" crystallizes the metrocolonial male's self-contradictory struggle to accommodate himself to, and take hold of, the chivalric variant of this ruling ideal.[18] In simply purchasing a gift for the girl he fancies, the boy narrator simultaneously enacts both a *nationalist* quest and a vignette of *imperialist* (self-)othering. To the accompaniment of "come all yous" canonizing renowned Irish patriots, he plans to retrieve a love token for "Mangan's sister," a female personification of Ireland writ small. But his adventure also bears a decidedly orientalist cast, taking him to an exotic foreign resort subjugated to Western commercialism—the East as Magic Kingdom—where the crafts of subject peoples and the English accents of their purveyors lend the boy consumer a relatively metropolitan status, enlisting him as an investor, cultural and economic, in the colonial project. Taken as a whole, then, the narrative of "Araby" carefully elaborates the boy's grail quest as the function of a fissured, estranged agency that is itself an effect and a synechdoche of the ethno-national condition he inhabits.[19] On the one hand, the boy's single-minded preoccupation with his courtly venture emboldens him to wring from his reluctant guardians permission to pursue it. Since he looked to visit the fair strictly as a surrogate for a female persona of Ireland (Mangan's sister), who is romantically imprisoned in a "retreat," his success in winning the liberty to do so resonates allegorically of hopes for national self-determination. On the other hand, once he arrives at the bazaar, he actually witnesses the social meaning of his exploit undergoing an inexorable expropriation, escaping his control and even his comprehension ("Remembering with difficulty why I had come . . ." [*D*, 27]). His famous closing vision of himself, as a "creature driven and derided by vanity" (*D*, 28), answers precisely to a sense of metrocolonial heteronomy, of an alien agency belying and corroding his painstakingly sublimated *parade virile* from within. Indeed, the boy narrator apprehends and articulates the failure of his chivalric quest as a failure, specifically, of manliness: he suddenly discovers himself reduced to its disjunctive categories of otherness, to a merely animal status ("creature") by way of a stereo-typically feminine flaw or weakness ("vanity").[20]

The story "After the Race," which signals the onset of young manhood in *Dubliners,* stages the self-alienating play of gender and ethnicity in reverse order. In order to aggrandize his family's class status, an increasingly affluent Mr. Doyle abandoned his nationalist leanings and encouraged his eldest son,

Jimmy, to nurture a set of distinctively metropolitan identifications and alliances through a program of Oxbridge education and conspicuous yet strategic
consumption. At first, Jimmy operates rather effectively within the prevailing
system of social distinctions, using school contacts and a show of money to gain
inclusion into a glamorous circle of entrepreneurial young bloods and racing
enthusiasts, continental, English, and American. But his *arriviseme* requires a
certain cultural abdication. He finds his acutely felt Irishness and his vestigial
nationalism stymied by the project of assimilating to his new cohort.[21] As traveled in Seguoine's speedster, one might say, Jimmy's road to being a proper
gentleman exacts a toll on his ethically defined manhood, leaving him no less
one of the "gratefully oppressed" (*D,* 35) than those less entitled Irishmen left
cheering the great "Race" from the side of the road. In the end, even as Jimmy
relishes the postrace festivities on Farley's yacht, basks in his role as toastmaster,
and lauds the "good company" of these "jovial fellows," he sets about following
an unconscious compulsion to assert his cultural difference in an ineffectual
gesture of symbolic resistance to the metropolitan system of distinction he is
trying to "game." When the party culminates in a high-stakes game of cards, he
plays with a carelessness that simulates the wild, self-destructive Irish type dear
to certain strains of imperialist apologia and romantic nationalism alike.[22] Here
again, the final sentence of the story clinches the gender irony on which it turns.
Punctuating the "one great game for a finish" (*D,* 41), in which Jimmy Doyle
"drops" more money than he can count, a brief report, "Daylight, gentlemen" (*D,*
42), subtly yet mordantly reminds the reader that the "dawn" of Jimmy's social
prospects has proven false (it is anything but daybreak for him) in part because
he has paradoxically forfeited the cardinal mark of the "gentleman"— aggressive self-restraint and self-possession—in the effort to dispel his own sense of
assimilative cultural dependency.

In "A Little Cloud," the adult treatment of this gendered psychomachia unfolds
in a confrontation of Chandler with Ignatius Gallagher, his unacknowledged
doppelganger, towards whom he stands in antagonistic identification.[23] Witness,
for example, Chandler's much anticipated reunion with Gallagher at Corless's,
in which celebratory rounds of whiskey—traditional male bonding materials—
serve as tactical counters in a mutual, if covert, war of position. Having bought
the first installment, Gallagher immediately congratulates himself on his own
cosmopolitan lifestyle, while registering a sly dig at Chandler's masculinity:

> —Here you are Tommy. Water? Say when.
> Little Chandler allowed his whiskey to be very much diluted.
> —You don't know what's good for you, my boy, said Ignatius Gallagher. I drink
> mine neat. (*D,* 70)

Chandler responds by acceding to Gallagher's wider and wilder experience—"I drink very little as a rule, said Little Chandler modestly" (*D*, 70). But his sense of identification with Gallagher gets the better of him, and he "succeeded in catching the barman's eye" to order another round (*D*, 71). Instead of enacting the manly code of self-restraint *as* self-assertion, Chandler's gesture stages a form of self-assertion that is simultaneously a concession to Gallagher's more vulgar, Anglified canon of virility, on which Chandler himself is bound to be found wanting. Sure enough, he immediately suffers another jibe expressing Gallagher's disdainful attitude toward "pious" Chandler and "jog-along Dublin": "I say, Tommy, don't make a punch of that whiskey; liquor up . . . O, come on, another one won't do you any harm" (*D*, 71, 73).

As Chandler grows disillusioned with Gallagher's jaded cosmopolitanism, he wishes once again to "assert his manhood" (*D*, 76) and vindicate the parochial petit bourgeois morality that he associates with Irish revivalism. So he insists on purchasing yet another round "to clinch the bargain" (*D*, 75) that Gallagher would expose himself to Chandler's homier lifestyle in future. At this point, the performative contradiction at the heart of Chandler's social tactics becomes painfully legible as a self-defeating externalization of his own historically con-ditioned and deeply gendered ambivalence. By linking the defense of his do-mesticated brand of masculinity to the hard-drinking and -treating practices typical of Gallagher's man-of-the-world profile, he underwrites the standards he aims to counter by revealing his irrepressible admiration of them ("And after all, Gallagher had lived, he had seen the world. Chandler looked at his friend enviously" [*D*, 72]). Put another way, Chandler cannot hope to contest Gallagher's masculine superiority by way of social rituals designed to ratify it. But those rituals, with their associated trappings and sign values, are precisely what enthrall Chandler about his friend: "He had never been to Corless's but he knew the value of the name" (*D*, 66). For his part, Gallagher knows the turf too well to cede the advantage it gives him. He calls the drinking session to a halt with the suggestion that more compelling matters and company await him, and in the process he devalues Chandler's proposal for a last symbolic round from a gesture of stalwart homosocial *bonding* to an act of vaguely desperate, womanish *clinging*:[24]

> Ignatius Gallagher took out a large gold watch and looked at it.
> —Is it to be the last, he said. Because you know, I have an a.p.
> —O, yes, positively, said Little Chandler." (*D*, 75)

But if Chandler's emulation of his old buddy can in one sense never be enough, it is in another sense already too much. His sense of rivalry and fellowship prompts him to imbibe more than he can handle, disrupting "the sensitive equipoise of his nature" and, ultimately, the domestic harmony he is so keen to showcase (*D*, 75).

The received interpretation of this story's explosive climax argues that upon his arrival home, Chandler displaces his resentment toward Gallagher, for what he sees as unwarranted, obnoxiously flaunted success, onto his own wife and family, for what he sees as their part in stymieing his efforts at self-realization and self-aggrandizement.[25] But another layer of baffled, psychosocial desire, less apparent to the protagonist and his critics, is operating in this final scene. Just as Chandler's bitterness toward Gallagher is really less about his friend's bumptious panache than about his own inability to share in it, so his grievance with his domestic circle really derives less from any obstacle they might pose to his self-actualization and aggrandizement than from his own ethno-gendered conflict over *what type of identity he would actualize, what version of the self he would aggrandize.*

The narrative attaches this paralyzing conflict directly to Chandler's privileged site for fantasizing the discovery of his authentic selfhood, the literary. Shortly after his wife leaves him to mind their infant son, Chandler dwells upon the literary vocation in a purely material and instrumental vein: as an avenue of virile escape from the cramped bathos of his colonial existence to the intoxicating promise of the metropole: "Was it too late to live bravely like Gallagher? Could he go to London? There was still the furniture to be paid for. If he could only write a book and get it published, that might open the way for him" (*D,* 79). In encountering the genuine article, however, "a volume of Byron's poems," Chandler seizes upon the affective power and world-making potential of literature, his own unborn verse as well as the romantic lyrics before him. While he clearly projects upon the poetry he reads the Celtic "melancholy" that he fondly believes others might prize in his own, he does at this moment conceive that value as an end in itself, the expression of a certain sensibility, rather than a contingent means to worldly success: "He felt the rhythm of the verse about him in the room. How melancholy it was! Could he too write like that, express the melancholy of his soul in verse. There were so many things he wanted to describe: the sensation of a few hours before on Grattan Bridge, for example. If he could get back again into that mood . . ." (*D,* 84)

These passages featured two marked parallelisms, one interrogative ("Could he go to London?" "Could he too write like that?") and one conditional ("If he could only write a book and get it published, that might open the way for him," "If he could get back again into that mood . . ."). Taken in tandem, they elegantly encapsulate Chandler's metrocolonial agon, between a stereotypically Anglified and "masculine" ambition of a practical and material nature and a stereotypically Celtic "feminine" aesthetic sensibility. This is, if you will, the vocational expression or equivalent of the double or divisive identification that had manifested earlier in a simultaneous attraction and aversion to Gallagher himself. So while Chandler's quiet but pervasive frustration surfaces violently with the sudden eruption of his baby's cries, the local condition of that emergence is the gathering, unconscious pressure of his warring strains of masculine self-investment, at once incident to and isomorphic with his metrocolonial subject position. Understood in this light, his ultimate paroxysm of exasperation, "He couldn't do anything" (D, 79), is something of an alibi posing as an impasse. His reaction belies the deeper ambivalence surrounding his self-defining motives and priorities. Far from easing his desperation, however, Chandler's defense mechanism serves only to double it. He continues to labor in the unconscious toils of a historically contoured self-division, while simultaneously raging against the merely projected sources of his ensnarement. To paraphrase Althusser, Chandler's real ethnic-political emasculation is overdetermined, precisely in being obscured by the imaginary forms and causes of that emasculation.[26] When Chandler screams at his infant son, an archetypal innocent, the misplaced and mystified character of his masculine frustration can be seen to fuel its overwhelming intensity, which in turn drives him to forgo those crucial traits (marks/attributes) of manliness—poise, restraint, resolution, self-control—that he has been struggling to maintain since he embarked for his meeting with Gallagher. The wild swing from his accustomed "unfortunate timidity" (D, 76) to this still less fortunate burst of incontinent aggression rehearses in miniature the imperialist "stereo"-type of Irishness as a racialized negation of the manly norm. Joyce thus explores how the cultural hegemony instituted under British "domestic" or metrocolonialism can work to produce simulacra of the libelous caricatures of Irishness that were invoked to authorize that hegemony in the first place.

As normative manliness represented the telos and touchstone of maturation during this period, it is likely no coincidence that the final story of "adulthood" in Dubliners, "Counterparts," is also that collection's definitive parable of the manly double bind in Ireland. It is likewise no coincidence that the tale follows "A Little Cloud," since the two narratives and their respective protagonists are, as portraits of Irish masculinity, counterparts of one another. As we have seen, the intensely homosocial interplay in "A Little Cloud" depicts the protagonist *succumbing* to the gender ambivalence inculcated by the double/divisive interpellation native to the metrocolonial condition and forfeiting thereby any purchase upon the authorizing ideal of manliness. The even more intensely homosocial activity of "Counterparts" depicts its protagonist *refusing* any such ambivalence in his reflexive assumption and repeated assertion of his own virility and forfeiting thereby any purchase upon the authorizing ideal of manliness. "A Little Cloud" anatomizes an internal or psychic knot that short-circuits Chandler's capacity to integrate and sublimate his component masculine energies. He is left alternately prey to feminine weakness (that is, without any affectively aggressive force to control) or prey to his own animal spirits (without any affectively controlling force to exercise over them). "Counterparts" anatomizes a sociocultural knot in which the subaltern expression of aggressive force, virility in short, is indispensable to—yet works to preempt—the socially certified control of that force, that is, manliness. Taken together, the stories illustrate how, just as the ideal of manliness abided different modes of address, subsuming them within the same logic of sublimation (see chapter 1), the metrocolonial double bind abided different modes of reaction, subverting them by the same logic of exclusion.

Joyce's "Counterparts"

THE FIRST TEST OF MANLINESS

As Robert Scholes first noted, an important nominal shift occurs toward the conclusion of "Counterparts." Instead of calling Farrington by his surname, as the narrative has done earlier, it suddenly begins to designate him simply as "a man" or "the man."[27] Scholes has taught us to read this shift as an understated device for conveying the depersonalized condition to which the protagonist has come after a lengthy if unsatisfying debauch. Without discounting the value of this interpretive line, I would offer a more literal-minded yet more contextually saturated gloss on the rhetorical gambit. It ironically bestows upon Farrington the honored social status, manhood, that he has sought to assert, consciously and unconsciously, throughout the story, and it does so at the juncture when he has forfeited that status, irretrievably, through the hypermasculine manner of his assertion. Supporting this gloss and extending its implications is the Irish etymology of the name replaced: Farrington derives from the Irish word *fer,* meaning "man."[28] Thus, the lexical texture of "Counterparts" serves to introduce ethnic difference as a factor in the manliness-masculinity divide that the narrative of "Counterparts" unfolds.

Indeed, in marking this ethnically inflected divide, Joyce's language directs the reader's attention to the three classic scenarios of homosocial *parade virile* that, in warped fairy-tale fashion, constitute the main narrative thread of the tale: the confrontation with male authority, which in this case also happens to be Anglo-imperial authority; the exchange of "tall tales" combined with the ritual of treating; and the contest of strength, in this case arm wrestling an Englishman. In each of these scenarios, Farrington responds to the trauma of his colonially inflected emasculation with a self-defeating because uncontrolled aggression, which only confirms the emasculation in and through its denial.

The first scenario results from a long-standing feud between Farrington and his boss, Mr. Alleyne, which began "the day Mr. Alleyne had overheard him mimicking his north of Ireland accent to amuse Higgins and Miss Parker" (*D,* 88). That originary site of conflict comprises several elements crucial not only to the course of hostilities and the nature of the mutual antipathy but also to the ideological stakes involved. To begin with, the background informing Far-rington's action is that Mr. Alleyne, along with the other partners and execu-tives in the firm, belongs to the Anglo-Protestant settler class, who controlled much of the wealth, hence many of the economic instruments, upon which native Irish subjects, like Farrington, depended for their employment. The sting of aggrieved emasculation that Farrington would suffer under such colonial dependency found reinforcement in the hegemonic gender allegories, such as the metropolitan marriage, which reserved proper manhood exclusively to the British people and their Protestant garrison.

The *form* of Farrington's action, in turn, proceeds from the particular qual-ity of this colonial wound. To mimic the powerful is invariably a double-edged gesture. Just as any verbal negation, according to Freud, carries a moment of affirmation, however disavowed, so the debunking mimicry of the high and mighty always carries in its very structure an impulse of identification, however overridden, an assertion that the mimic can be like, and so in some fundamental sense *is* like, the mimicked. Indeed, it is only by way of such tacit identification that the ingredient of ridiculing excess that turns imitation into caricature can take on its full social meaning and effect. But precisely because mimicry identi-fies, if only in form, with the object it disparages, it must pursue an unusually tortuous path to the vantage of moral superiority that all satirical genres must by definition assume. Beyond suggesting that the elites being parodied are not all that superior, the act of insurgent mimicry implicitly designates them an imperfect version of the legitimately authoritative profile that the mimic could just as easily have impersonated—that is, such mimicry claims access to that higher moral reality of which its elite target is but an impostor. In other words, the structure of insurgent mimicry pivots from a disavowed identification with to a symbolic usurpation of the mimicked party.

It is this structural swivel that allowed mimicry to become, as Homi Bhabha observed, an ingrained method of colonial resistance.[29] Mimicry provides a means for turning the distinctive quality of the colonized condition—being forcibly inculcated in the standards and values of the conqueror—to trenchant rhetorical advantage. The regime of colonial acculturation and assimilation endeavors to inscribe the native ward as a poor reproduction, a failed mimesis, of his colonial master, thereby depriving him of culturally indigenous forms of counterattack. But the shift from enforced mimesis into strategic mimicry en-ables the subaltern to use the space of ethno-colonial difference as a screen for reflecting the master's deficiencies back to him in the shape of a being already marked out as inferior. Colonial mimicry, that is, remaps the supposed char-acterological distance between the barbarous native and the civilized colonizer as a distance between the colonizer and his own approved self-conception. Moreover, in assuming the posture of moral superiority inherent in satire, the subaltern mimic positions himself as the "better" master, worthy of supplant-ing the colonizer on his own terms.[30] For the Irish subject of "domestic" or "metro-" colonialism, the space of hierarchical difference, what Bhabha calls the "not quite, not white" phenomenon, is narrower without being less decisive, and correspondingly, the strategy of mimicry is readier without being any less subversive.[31] If, as Doherty writes, "the blotch on the colonial armor is the sedi-tious spur to the colonized," then mimicry is the response prompted.[32]

In doing a malicious impression of Mr. Alleyne's speaking voice (the mark of his settler status), Farrington presumably caricatures what he takes to be its most recognizable quality, its "piercing" timbre. Now the signifier "piercing" conveniently partakes of the two-sidedness characteristic of mimicry itself. As a synonym for "penetrating," it bears phallic overtones consistent with the mas-culinized authority that Alleyne enjoys and Farrington looks to (re)appropriate. As a vocal description, however, it indexes the upper female registers rather than the lower male registers, the soprano rather than the baritone or even the tenor, a resonance doubtless exaggerated in Farrington's comic turn. Here, the pivot from identification to ouster (from putting on the authority of another to arrogating it symbolically), upon which the genre of mimicry hinges, is a trait (mark/attribute) of gender. While borrowing the master's voice, vehicle of his authority, Farrington renders it as less than fully masculine. In his mind, clearly, the contest between these two men is more than incidentally about manhood itself.

The audience for Farrington's performance confirms as much. The presence of Miss Parker signals Farrington's pursuit of the classic patriarchal strategy of enlisting female spectatorship to countersign male power, prestige, competitive advantage, or some combination thereof. Even as patriarchal structures entail the subordination of women, they depend upon women to underwrite and ar-bitrate the phallic pretenses of men. The very first line of this story, moreover, indicates that Miss Parker is the vehicle whereby Alleyne's verbal commands reach his employees.

> The bell rang furiously, and when Miss Parker went to the tube, a furious voice called out in a piercing North of Ireland accent;
> —Send Farrington in here! (*D, 82*)

In mimicking that overbearing voice for Miss Parker's amusement, Farrington bids to commandeer the triangulated, homosocial circuitry of Alleyne's power in order to tap and reverse its current. But Miss Parker's role is still more over-determined. Given the ethnic and sectarian background signaled by her birth name, she figures as an ideal spectator in the colonial register as well. Farrington in effect solicits an Anglo-Protestant woman to bear ratifying witness to his own refusal to be emasculated or feminized by their Anglo-Protestant boss.[33] That the only other spectator, Higgins, is also the only other native Irish employee mentioned in the story italicizes the racial import of Farrington's theatrics.

The male confrontation presently represented proceeds not only from but along the same lines as this original falling out. To begin with, Mr. Alleyne elects to call for Farrington to deliver his work at the moment when the homosocial structure of his own authority is most conspicuously on display, that is, in the presence of a woman, Miss Delacours, who, unlike Miss Parker, is no mere underling but a person of independent resources, whose ethnic status gives her an orientalized desirability in their eyes. By emphasizing the pervasive odor of Miss Delacours's perfume, filtered through Farrington's quickened sensorium, the narrative gives a tangible sense of how her very presence contours the men's transaction and nudges the reader to remark how Mr. Alleyne subtly enlists her to enhance his office authority. When Farrington arrives upstairs, he discovers that "Mr. Alleyne had swivelled his chair round to face her and thrown his right foot jauntily upon his left knee" (*D*, 85). The formula "Alleyne had swivelled" as opposed to the passive "the chair was turned" is decisive in signifying intent. Alleyne has evidently disposed his body and "blocked" the action so as to channel his professional dealings with Farrington exclusively by way of his personal bond with Delacours (hence the "jauntily" crossed legs). His objective seems to be to erase the presence of Farrington in the very act of summoning it. Instead of a classic vanishing mediator "between men," Miss Delacours serves as a mediator that makes one of the opposed rivals vanish. Alleyne's attention to her even allows him to strategically ignore his employee's respectful bow, assuming the value of this obeisance all the more completely in refusing to acknowledge its execution. Mr. Alleyne's manner of dismissing Farrington, finally, amounts to a coded assertion, all the more assertive for being encoded, of the structural nature of his gendered "ascendancy": "Mr. Alleyne tapped a finger on the correspondence and then flicked it towards him as if to say: *That's all right: you can go*" (*D*, 86). Alleyne here makes a show of not making a show of force, of not exerting himself at all in exerting a gendered authority that, while remaining entirely his own, can be felt to emanate from something beyond, and less contestable than, personal endowment. His casual yet peremptory flick of his finger bespeaks a masculine agency whose unsweated composure flows from an entire battery of mutually augmenting layers of social hierarchy: occupational, class, colonial, ethnic.[34]

Lacking Alleyne's social resources, but possessed of a large, strongly knit physique, Farrington finds himself disposed to another less entitled style of masculinity, one that assumes bodily ferocity to be the master criterion of virility and virility to be the essence of manhood. After his humiliation in Alleyne's office, accordingly, Farrington longs to exhibit his enormous strength and express his masculine self-conception in acts of wholesale unbridled aggression: "He felt strong enough to clear out the whole office single-handed. His body ached to do something, to rush out and revel in violence. All the indignities of his life enraged him" (*D,* 86). But in the administered social universe of petit bourgeois, Anglo-Irish bureaucracy, the manly imperative to self-restraint serves, among other things, to harness bodily power to social power as its satellite, the meaning and value of which shift with social position. For the middle-class gentleman, the unrealized aggression implicit in his bodily strength might count as an index of vigorous good health born of self-discipline. The same unrealized aggression implicit in the power of more subaltern bodies might register as the index of a dangerous subhumanity in need of governance from above. In the former, then, a virility refined into manliness, in the latter a virility intractable to manly sublimation. Caught in this ideological vice, Farrington is compelled to stifle his aggressive impulse, to restrict any exhibition of bodily force to the realm of the wish, while being nonetheless typed as, in Mr. Alleyne's words, a "ruffian" (*D,* 87). His physical prowess proves less empowering than frustrating, a source rather than a response to indignity. The feeling that he is "strong enough to clear the room" translates, under this masculine double bind, into disability, into physical agony, into the reason his body "ached." It is this stratified regime of masculinity, with its attendant stakes and risks for the self-image of the parties involved, that gives the altercation of the heart of this tale its specific complexion.

Once Mr. Alleyne detects that the Delacours file is incomplete, he not only confronts Farrington at his own desk, in front of all the other clerks, but also brings Miss Delacours herself in tow, even though it is hardly sound business practice to expose a client to the firm's dysfunctions. All of this is to say that the objective of Alleyne's intervention is less to correct or even chastise Farrington as an employee than to shame him as a man. Not only does Farrington viscerally recognize this implication, but his reactive mental state perfectly captures, in the manner of a photographic negative, the gendered double bind he occupies. Even as he thinks to vindicate his masculinity on its own hyperaggressive terms, he registers the necessity of exercising a difficult self-control and abiding an emasculation made all the more irksome by the diminutive stature of his antagonist: "The tirade continued: it was so bitter and violent that the man could hardly restrain his fist from descending upon the head of the manikin before him" (*D,* 87). In suggesting the virtual autonomy of the "fist" from the superintending ego it would defend, the phraseology here measures the extent of Farrington's imposed alienation—how for him self-possessed manliness entails a sacrifice of the virility on which it was supposedly based, while the expression of that embodied virility could come only at the cost of manly self-possession.

Marked by a retreat into dogged nescience—"I know nothing about any other letters" (*D*, 87)—Farrington's stab at the repressive alternative is short-lived, as Mr. Alleyne, pressing his advantage, seeks to remove any shred of dignity still left his employee:

> *—You—know—nothing.* Of course you know nothing, said Mr. Alleyne. Tell me, he added, glancing first for approval to the lady beside him, do you take me for a fool? Do you think me an utter fool? (*D*, 87)

The crucial side glance at Miss Delacours signals that beyond any issue of office discipline, this confrontation represents a struggle to assert and deny manhood, the kind of phallic contest that requires a female Other as arbiter.[35] Joyce underlines the point by rendering the same glance the catalyst for Farrington's fateful rejoinder. Before speaking, he "glanced from the lady's face to the little egg-shaped head and back again" (*D*, 87), imitating Alleyne's own body language, but also absorbing the gendered import it carries. Thus cornered by the prospect of being abused in mixed company—the social equivalent of castration—Farrington again experiences a sense of separation from his body, which in this case takes him from a precarious physical repression to an oblique verbal aggression, from a barely stayed hand to an accidentally unleashed tongue.

> And almost before he was aware of it, his tongue had found a felicitous moment.
> —I don't think, sir, he said, that that's a fair question to put to me. (*D*, 87)

That Farrington manages, with this sally, to reassert for the moment his embattled virility receives strong collaboration on three fronts: his coworkers' wonder at his daring ("There was a pause in the very breathing of the clerks"), the open approval of the designated female witness ("Miss Delacours . . . began to smile broadly"), and, most important, the apoplectic, almost hysterical, reaction of Alleyne himself. First, Alleyne "flushed to the hue of a wild rose," a formulation recalling of course the feminizing icon of the wild Irish rose. Second, he "twitched with a dwarf's passion," a formulation accenting his masculine "shortcomings." Next, "he shook his fist in the man's face till it seemed to vibrate like the knob of some electric machine," an image whose futility compares unfavorably with Farrington's self-restrained "fist" moments earlier (all *D*, 87). Finally, Alleyne calls Farrington an "impertinent ruffian," a telling response to Farrington's "witticism." For does it not suggest Alleyne's felt intuition that his underling had effectively substituted the verbal for the manual jab, mockery for mayhem, impertinence *for* ruffianism, all the while preserving the blunt force of the latter?

But while the displaced aggression animating Farrington's words is crucial to the kind of virile indomitability that he, as an Irish subaltern, feels called upon to assert, the same, still legible aggression simultaneously signifies an absence or failure of manly self-control that he, as an Irish petit bourgeois, feels called upon to exercise. In his narration, Joyce not only draws the reader's attention to the sudden collapse of Farrington's efforts to "restrain" himself but also stages the action so as to *literalize* the loss of self-possession that it entails. In particular, he uses the trope of synecdoche to transfer human agency from the subject himself to his active bodily member. The "tongue" speaks in Farrington's place, but more than that, the tongue *thinks* in Farrington's place. It is the tongue that "found a felicitous moment" and the words to suit that moment. It is the tongue in Farrington's head, but beyond his conscious direction, that *exercises wit*. To turn matters around: with the "witticism" in question, Farrington has forfeited rather than displayed effective proprietorship over the prime vocal implement locating him in the Symbolic Order, whence he derives his social (including his gender) identity.

Accordingly, Farrington is "astounded no less than his neighbors" by what comes out of his mouth. However, his tongue does not operate altogether reflexively. In an especially fine-grained instance of indirect free style, Joyce's third-person narration observes that his words formed "almost before he was aware of it" (*D*, 87). They were, that is to say, sufficiently estranged from their author to seem external in origin, but sufficiently proximate to count as his own. In this respect, they represent a perfect correlative to the indirect free style itself, which is usually understood to unfold the characteristically modernist interest in psychic interiority, but only does so while marking the self-alienation of that interiority, what the Lacanians would call its ex-timacy. Shifting into the ethico-political register, Farrington's words are sufficiently inadvertent to evince a lapse of volitional self-command, but sufficiently motivated or intentionalized for him to feel, and be held, subsequently responsible for them. In this respect, Farrington's speech act represents a precise inversion of the ideological structure of manly virtue. If bourgeois manliness effectively claims to be a manner born but yet somehow earned, its subaltern defaults, like Farrington's, must likewise be accounted constitutional yet culpable, and Joyce painstakingly constructs the scene in question to reflect this paradox.

The consequences of Farrington's ultimate failure to sacrifice the appearance of virility to the demands of manliness promise to be as profound as the frustrations of doing so were acute. Because manliness, as I have endeavored to show, is a personal attribute or ethos fundamentally contingent upon authoritative social position, Farrington's momentary lapse of self-mastery is not indemnified by the more frenzied and so more disreputable bout of emotional incontinence that it provokes in his superior. To the contrary, Farrington will have to pay not only for the witty license he has taken but for Mr. Alleyne's embarrassment at losing his cool in response. Joyce highlights this boomerang effect in the key signifier of their exchange. By failing "to keep his tongue in his cheek" when answering

Mr. Alleyne's rhetorical question, "Do you think me an utter fool?" Farrington has, in his own judgment, "made a proper fool of himself" (D, 88). The double damages to be exacted of him, an abject apology now and future discharge withal, works to strip him of the very conditions, social and economic, of his self-styled virility. He is to be neither the defiant "strong man" nor the breadwinner. The operation of the gendered double bind is such that his sacrifice of manly virtue to (hyper)masculine *virtu* effects the nullification of both.

THE SECOND TEST OF MANLINESS

Centering on the homosocial pub customs of "treating" and tale telling, the circulation of lies and libation, the story's second scenario of *parade virile* forms a contradictory site of fantasy and disenchantment, wherein Farrington's confrontation with his boss is recounted, "amid . . . the clatter of glasses," to more successful effect, even as the rituals of the recounting tend toward repetition of the original failure. Thus, the thematic split between a compulsory yet impossible manliness and a compelling yet self-destroying virility may be seen to map itself onto the classic rhetorical split between the *enoncé* and the *enonciation,* what is said and the act of saying.[36] To mark this performative contradiction, the economy of the double tax or payment extends into this segment of the narrative, taking a literalized, material form, the monetary, much as Farrington's loss of self-possession took a literalized, material form, the bodily, in the first test of manhood.

Not coincidentally, the wish-fulfilling revision of the *affair d'Alleyne* begins directly after Farrington pawns his pocket watch, an emblem of the modern injunction to rationalized self-regulation, in order to secure funds for a night at the pub, a primary space for the performance of virile masculinity.[37] The infusion of cash itself allows Farrington to recover his sense of male power, which he indulges by "staring masterfully at the office girls" as they leave work. At the same time, "he preconsidered the terms in which he would narrate the incident to the boys" that evening, and his guiding principle of dramatic selection involves introducing the element missing in his earlier conduct, self-mastery, as its defining characteristic. "So, I just looked at him—cooly, you know, and I looked at her. Then I looked back at him again—taking my time, you know. *I don't think that that's a fair question to put to me, says I*" (D, 89). The one alteration of events the critics have remarked in this passage is Farrington's excision of the title "sir" from his retort ("I don't think, sir, that that's a fair . . ."), for the assumed purpose of relieving its now fabled bravado from any admixture of servility.[38] It is a narrative tactic, in other words, calculated to enhance the perceived virility of Farrington's stand. But the excision also answers to his wish that he had exercised greater control over himself and the scene than he was able to do at the time, and it is precisely to represent this baffled desire for manly self-governance as an achieved reality that Farrington introduces his more decisive fabrications, which help to frame his account.

First off, Farrington transfigures his rather dumbfounded replication of Alleyne's aggressively triangulated gaze into his own considered strategy of resistance ("I just looked at him . . ."). Second, the boastful phrase "coolly" casts that strategy as an effect of the self-possession Farrington never actually exhibited. Third, by way of elaborating his pretense to self-possession, Farrington's subsequent aside, "taking my time, you know," falsifies, even reverses, the defining temporal logic of the interchange. What had unfolded as a startlingly proleptic utterance, in which the physical speech act all but preceded the superintending will to signify, becomes in his report a studiously deferred utterance, in which the superintending will orchestrates the speech act so that it might signify beyond, or amplify upon, the words spoken. Inasmuch as these asides also suspend the punch line of the anecdote, they perform in the telling the very temporal function to which they refer, mendaciously, in the tale. They thus offer a demonstration of Farrington's capacity for judicious self-discipline, which the repeated phrase "you know" identifies with his imagined audience as well.

The specific form of braggadocio at work in Farrington's vignette testifies to his implicit awareness that the virility he asserted in his dealings with Alleyne can be valorized (given value or valor) only if subsumed within the self-disciplinary constraints associated with manliness. That is, he can assume heroic stature only if his strength and courage appear under his control. As a practical matter, however, his subdominant position impedes, if it does not preclude, him from sustaining a posture of dignified restraint in a recognizably heroic manner—except, of course, in the realm of self-glorifying fiction. And here we encounter another dimension of the masculine double bind. For Farrington to have exercised proper self-control in this instance by keeping "his tongue in his cheek" would mean offering no legible sign of recalcitrance, no evidence of backbone, no show of virility whatever.

Farrington's fantasy narrative is not the only version of events retailed in the story. Amid rounds of drinks at Davy Byrne's, "who should come in but Higgins," the native Irish coworker whom Farrington had "amused" with his impersonation of Alleyne. "Of course . . . [t]he men asked him to give his version of it, and he did so with great vivacity for the sight of five small whiskeys was very exhilarating" (*D*, 89). Now the one issue concerning Higgins's contribution prominently remarked in the criticism is the dearth of narrative evidence that he actually witnessed the face off to which he so cheerfully bears witness: inspired by the prospect of alcoholic refreshment, he may merely be recirculating the sort of hearsay that his listeners themselves could already provide.[39] That his account accords with Farrington's, the argument runs, should accordingly be greeted with suspicion. From our perspective, however, the details in Higgins's version carry that much *more* significance under those circumstances, for they must be understood as exemplary of the shared value system that produced them, rather than being simply indebted to the facts they claim to record. They are indeed legendary items, but in the strong ethnographic sense. It is therefore of less moment that the Higgins variation concurs with Farrington's as to what actually happened than that the only two items we see of Higgins's account mirror, reinforce, and thus approve the ideological priorities at work in Farrington's version: "Everyone roared laughing when he showed the way in which Mr. Alleyne shook his fist in Farrington's face. Then he imitated Farrington, saying, *And here was my nabs, as cool as you please*" (*D*, 89–90). In turning on a simple contrast between Alleyne's violent loss of composure as a source of hilarity and Farrington's unflappability as a source of admiration, Higgins locates the moral center of his report not in his friend's virile spirit of resistance but in the manly self-control with which he (claims to have) carried it off.

The kernel of the gendered fantasy that "the boys" (*D*, 56, 89) consume with their whiskey—what Freud might call the "navel" of their collective dream—resides in the signifier *cool*. *Cool* is the keyword in both available variants of the episode, the verbal ligature binding them together, and the mark of their common, mutually reinforcing attitude and perspective. In the latter respect, cool represents a gender honorific, posed in tacit opposition to the supposed tremulousness and perturbability of the feminine. This contrast in turn had long since accrued a racial dimension, as famously indicated by Matthew Arnold's identification of the Celt with the "nervous exaltation" characteristic of femininity and the Teuton with a typically masculine groundedness and reliability.[40] So among its other functions in this group fantasy, the signifier *cool* functions to vindicate the manhood of the native, gamely embodied in Farrington, over against the feminized histrionics of the Anglo-Norman intruder, Mr. Alleyne.

Finally, and perhaps most tellingly, the master signifier *cool* also constitutes, as Freudian "navels" will, the site of maximum contradiction in the dream scenario, the point at which it begins to unravel.[41] As we know, the fiction of Farrington's stout, defiant self-possession is not only made necessary but possible by a breakdown in that same self-possession, without which there would have been no show of stoutness or defiance at all and so no "incident" to speak of, no event worthy of being recounted. The production of his quotidian manliness *within* the anecdotal frame is strangely dependent upon the betrayal of this gendered touchstone outside the anecdotal frame.

The same constitutive contradiction of fictional frame and lived ground that marks the action being commemorated also characterizes, still more blatantly, the barroom act of commemoration. Higgins's motive for participating, "with great vivacity," in the restaging of Farrington's dubious triumph is but a synecdoche for the larger homosocial economy wherein all "the boys" appreciate and celebrate the cool mastery of self and situation in inverse proportion to their own display thereof. Indeed, this manly virtue seems to circulate in their lionizing narratives as a perverse stimulation to and a sentimental compensation for the gradual surrender of self-rule entailed by their signal performance of hypermasculinity: the potlatch form of endurance drinking known as treating. As I will now elaborate, this irony would have been especially clear within the historical context shared by Joyce's protagonist and his readers.

The positively datable stories in *Dubliners*—"Ivy Day in the Committee Room," "After the Race" and "The Dead"—situate the February of "Counterparts" as February 1903, just months after the much publicized formation of the St. Patrick's Anti-Treating League in Dublin, an organization alluded to in the Cyclops episode of *Ulysses*. Officially, the institution of treating came under league sanction because in pegging the perceived conviviality of each reveler to his willingness to purchase a "round" in turn, it had the effect of "prolonging drinking bouts beyond sobriety."[42] In structural terms, however, the real power and danger of treating were that it ritually soldered the practice of drinking to the enactment of hypermasculinity, by subsuming individual consumption within a circuit of reciprocal, intensely homosocial obligation and affiliation. The antitreating movement, moreover, was a subsidiary of the more established temperance movement that had, virtually since its inception, confederated with an Irish nationalism that was itself dyed in the ideology of manly sublimation, rectitude, and self-ownership. Despite the best efforts of Father Mathew, who harbored the same dream of political neutrality for the antidrink campaign that Douglas Hyde later did for the Gaelic League, early temperance processions proclaimed their nationalist allegiance in their use of allegorical personae such as Hibernia and Saint Patrick, patriotic mottoes such as "Erin go Bragh," and nativist symbols such as the harp, the wolfhound, and the shamrock.[43] As such, emblematic evocations of the '98 might suggest, the early members of the temperance movement were attracted to the nationalist campaigns of their time, specifically the Repeal and Young Ireland.[44]

The movement attracted in its turn such nationalist leaders as Daniel O'Connell and Thomas Davis. The latter explicitly linked, causally and analogically, Irish enthrallment to drink and the Irish enthrallment to Britain. In an essay for the *Nation* entitled "Irish Intoxication," he pronounced drunkenness "the saturnalia of slaves," blaming its prevalence in Ireland on long political subjugation that had robbed the people of the moral resources and life prospects conducive to self-discipline. In seeking to cultivate these resources and these prospects, "Irish temperance is," for Davis, "the first offering of an incipient freedom."[45] To amplify the point, his allies at the *Cork Examiner* endorsed temperance in a vocabulary of manliness strongly reminiscent of Davis's own essay "Memorials of Wexford" (see the introduction) in its emphasis on self-reliance: "A nation of sober men, with clear heads, with firm and erect forms, with a proud strength of moral independence about them, shall and *must* have the full completeness of their liberty."[46] Like the *Dublin Monthly Magazine,* which proclaimed "a sober people was entitled to be free," the *Cork Examiner* invokes the stock equation of manhood with fitness for freedom, substituting sobriety as the operative ingredient.[47] The *Freeman's Journal* was even more explicit: "Now that general SOBRIETY has been established . . . [w]e have proven ourselves fitted for freedom."[48]

Unlike Young Ireland itself, the triple knot of temperance, nationalism, and manliness survived the Famine years. But it was only with the new nationalism of turn-of-the-century Ireland—the period in which "Counterparts" is set—that the achievement of national independence came once again to be *predicated* upon the cultivation of a comprehensive manly *ascesis,* of which teetotalism was the all but official seal. In 1889, the capital Total Abstinence League was founded by Father James Cullen, a sympathizer with the rebels of '98, whose defeat was, to his mind, the direct result of drunkenness. He became instrumental in securing a ban upon alcoholic beverages of all functions of the Gaelic Athletic Association, which stood in the vanguard of Irish-Ireland, the first nationalist movement dominated by the Catholic middle class.[49] The GAA embrace of temperance paved the way for subsequent Irish-Ireland leaders and exponents of manliness, such as Sinn Fein's Arthur Griffith or *The Leader's* D. P. Moran, to wage patriotic war upon the entire industry of Drink or "Bung."[50] This campaign was based on the idea that Irish temperance does not merely provide the justification of Irish liberty but is the very mechanism for achieving it. Hence the unofficial motto of temperance nationalism generally, "Ireland sober, Ireland free," an expression that is at once performative (asserting sobriety *as* freedom) and metaleptic (suppressing the predicate to allow both the present and future tenses—*is, will be*—simultaneous "currency").

The logic on which temperance nationalism held drink to undermine Irish fitness for freedom owes much to an internalized, Anglo-bourgeois ideology of manliness. By all accounts, alcoholic excess induces emotional excess. Drunkenness seems to preclude or reverse the integrated dynamics of manly sublimation, whereby the robust animal spirits characteristic of masculine subjectivity were mobilized as energetic restraints upon themselves and made a material substrate of a self-regulation necessary to effective socioeconomic agency. As evidence of this pernicious effect, alcoholic consumption could be seen to produce states of psychic imbalance strongly identified with manhood's twin "Others" and the complementary stereotypes of Irishness that were based upon them: on the one side the uncontrollable aggression of the beast (the simianized Irishman), on the other the uncontrolled sentimentality of the woman (the feminized Celt), but in either case profiles adjudged unready or unworthy of full political enfranchisement.[51] In its attempt to reform Irish leisure along manly lines, temperance nationalism did not acknowledge the truth of these stereotypes, as David Lloyd has argued, but rather sought to combat the appearance of truth, without properly apprehending the discursive machinery of its production.[52] Under such circumstances, it only made sense that the movement should have come to specifically target the practice of "treating," which framed heavy drinking as a matter of ethnically inflected group membership. Treating thereby encouraged a reading of the native drinking party as a miniature version, a cameo image, of the Irish nation as bacchanal (or Donnybrook Fair) and so tended to abet the "massification" function of the imperialist stereotype, that is, its extrapolation from individual proclivities to racial verities.

"Counterparts" aims to expose the discursive underpinnings of this invidious appearance of truth that so haunted the temperance nationalists. To this end, Joyce casts *his* native drinking party as a collective extension, a "counterpart," of Farrington's earlier outburst, a sequel likewise molded by the forces of colonial dependency into a self-destructive double bind: the loss of manly self-command in the very performance of its apparent precondition, virile masculinity. In either instance, Joyce not only underscores by literalizing Farrington's loss of self-command, as noted above, but attaches this loss immediately to the "success" of his *parade virile,* as an inseparable function thereof. With Alleyne, of course, Farrington's lapsus linguae, a somaticized failure of self-control, is itself the proximate cause of his now fabled act of self-assertion—so proximate in fact that they constitute one and the same inadvertence. With "the boys," the fabling of Farrington's *tour de riposte* represents the proximate cause not only of the progressive, alcohol-fueled slackening of his faculties but also of his profligate spending, a monetized failure of self-control. This is the case, moreover, owing to *special provisions in the (homo-)social contract of treating* that Joyce quietly invokes to rivet Farrington's masculine feat and manly fiasco still more securely together.

The ordinary protocol of treating calls for each man to buy a drink for the entire company in his turn. Because on this occasion, however, the rounds of drinks unfold in concert with recitals of the day's great event, and because Farrington is the unquestioned man of the hour, he finds himself obligated to purchase every other round, instead of every fifth round, as would be his normal ante. One member of the party buys a round to toast Farrington's bold witticism and frame a retelling, and Farrington feels called upon to acknowledge the plaudit by reciprocating. His role as conquering hero thus contributes directly to a financial undoing that adumbrates the still grimmer prospect of unemployment and insolvency consequent to his blowup with Alleyne.

The depletion of the drinking party upon their removal from Davy Byrne's pub solidifies Farrington's position as the host of the treating party on this, his night. Once ensconced in the "Scotch House," he not only continues his pattern of purchasing alternate rounds, but agrees to extend his largesse to a "guest," the visiting English acrobat Weathers, who orders "a small Irish and Apollinaris," a particularly expensive combination. In keeping with the treating code and his own homosocial "notions of what was what," Farrington volunteers to buy Apollinaris all around. Notwithstanding his protests "that the hospitality was all too Irish," Weathers partakes of two more rounds of Irish whiskeys and Apollinaris without reciprocating and later, at Mulligan's pub, enjoys a glass of bitters stood him by Farrington (*D*, 90). All of this honorary treating, which flows spontaneously from Farrington's role as a minor champion of Irish (self-) mastery, diminishes not just the mental acuity but the material resources necessary for him to retain command over his night's entertainment, to remain "master" of ceremonies. Farrington comes to recognize as much, bitterly, when he suddenly finds himself without the resources to approach one of the "nice girls" (that is, quasi prostitutes [*D*, 90]) to whom Weathers introduces him in a peculiarly homosocial manner of repayment. (His gesture may be seen to repeat in a different key the competitively triangulated gender economy of Alleyne's treatment of Farrington.) Farrington's inability to approach this "girl" unmistakably recalls and belies the earlier fantasy scenario wherein he "stared masterfully at the office girls" and embellished the Alleyne incident in his mind. But in so doing, it reinforces the "real" Alleyne incident; it illustrates that owing to his subaltern position, Farrington not only must sacrifice manly control in the expression of masculine virility but that, ultimately, in making that sacrifice he ultimately squanders his claim to masculine virility as well.

That the main beneficiary of this ironic double damage is an Englishman, soon to be raised to the dignity of a national examplar, proves as galling to Farrington as it proves symbolically telling for the reader. "He watched her leave in the hope that she would look back at him, but he was disappointed. He cursed his want of money and cursed all the rounds he had stood, particularly all the whiskeys and Apollinaris which he had stood to Weathers. If there was one thing he hated it was a sponge" (*D*, 91). Like his celebrated but injudicious office retort, Farrington's honorary treating bolsters his personal and ethnic sense of virility, but only as it serves to drain him and his dispossessed tribe while swelling, like a "sponge," the advantage and privilege of their colonial ruler and adversary. Thus, with the introduction of Weathers, Joyce goes beyond literalizing the form and substance of the Irishman's double bind to personalizing its *realpolitical* stakes and effects.

THE THIRD TEST OF MANLINESS

In keeping with his role as tonight's champion, Farrington is summoned by an appeal to "uphold the national honour" in a "trial of strength," an arm-wrestling match, with the now hated Englishman (*D*, 92). Thus framed, the last of the three tests of manhood in "Counterparts" provides a crowning articulation of the personal and colonial, literal and symbolic motifs of gender formation threaded throughout the narrative.

At first glance, of course, such a test might seem to focus entirely on brute force, hence to depart from the virility/manliness *spaltung* under examination. But more careful scrutiny of the textural evidence tells another story. Notice first that the "call to arms" (and the reference to "national honour" puts this pun in play) reaches Farrington at the moment he is "so angry" over his recent sexual disappointment that "he lost count of the conversation" (*D,* 91). The phrase "lost count" here is an odd colloquialism, which seems specifically crafted to resonate with Farrington's financial carelessness this evening, all of the coins he has "lost count" of in the treating process. Together, these overt and implied significations of the phrase paint a picture of a man who has lost, or is losing, his grip—hardly a propitious state for joining an arm wrestle. And as it turns out, the issue of grip, in its different senses, factors prominently in the competition that follows.

Despite "looking serious and determined," and putting forth a mighty effort, Farrington suffers two consecutive defeats at the hand of the younger, smaller man, whom he considers "a stripling." After the first, Farrington finds fault with Weathers's grip in the literal physical sense; he has ostensibly brought illegal leverage to bear. After the second, the "curate" or bartender vocally approves Weathers's "grip" on the action, his method of controlling the struggle: "Ah! That's the knack." His comment reminds the reader that in arm wrestling, Joyce has selected, and quite deliberately selected, a "trial of strength" that is largely about technique, or rather a trial of strength harnessed and directed by technique. In this respect, and in this narrative context, the arm wrestle serves as an athletic emblem of manliness, of which no less an exponent than the novelist Thomas Hughes said that power, determination, and physical courage were necessary but decidedly lower parts, to be tempered by discipline.[53] As an acrobat, Weathers personified this exquisitely controlled power of manliness in its bodily form; as an *English* acrobat defeating an Irish champion in mock combat, he symbolically embodies the disciplinary power of manliness as a colonial ideology, its instantiation of Said's logic of "flexible positional superiority." Weathers's "knack" in the struggle is precisely to turn untrained power against itself. For Farrington's part, his response to the "curate"—"What the hell do you know about it," accompanied by a "violent expression" (*D,* 92)—exemplifies in miniature the vicious circle I have been tracing: the trauma of colonial emasculation can breed an aggressive, even violent, but paradoxically emasculating and thus self-perpetuating species of phallic display. This gendered mode of repetition compulsion has, on the obverse logic of "reversible positional *inferiority,*" fashioned only to destroy "his reputation as a strong man" (*D,* 93).

The third and final test of manhood is also the summary test of manhood; it absorbs and reconstellates the political tenor of the previous two in an elegantly chiasmatic fashion. On the one hand, the arm-wrestling episode resembles the Alleyne incident in a number of respects. In each, Farrington mistakenly relies upon his intimidating physical presence to prevail against a smaller man; each is mediated by an "exotic" woman marked out in some way for sexual conquest (the Jewess Delacours, the Londoner "nice girl"),[54] and each of course features an ethno-colonial dimension pitting Anglo against Celt, native against intruder, in a matter of "national honour." As such the victory of the diminutive Englishman amounts to a reversal of Farrington's fantasy triumph over Alleyne (test 1) that the treating ritual (test 2) seemed to substantiate. And yet the wrangle with Weathers does not reverse the aims of the night's treating, so much as continue and crystallize its inner self-defeating impetus: to "consume away," with the alcohol, the putative political gains that it celebrates. Indeed, the arm wrestle may be seen as the consummation of the treating ritual. It brings the session to an end—after Farrington's defeat, everyone pays for their own drinks ("Pony up, boys" [D, 92])—and it brings the session to its *logical* end, the utter depletion of the host. "He felt humiliated and discontented; he did not even feel drunk; and he only had twopence in his pocket. . . . He had done for himself at the office, pawned his watch, spent all his money. . . . He had lost his reputation as a strong man, having been defeated twice by a mere boy. . . . He loathed returning home" (D, 93).

Once home, Farrington locates the one person, his young son, Charlie, upon whom he can assert a rampaging form of hypermasculinity without restraint and without apparent cost to himself. To beat his son into submission, under color of parental discipline, Farrington gives "his arm free play," a phrase clearly recalling the arm-wrestling loss that he has just suffered and, by these "vicious" strokes, aims to recoup (D, 94). The repetition compulsion of traumatized masculinity thus terminates in a full-blown bout of male hysteria, which not only crushes the *spaltung* of manly "discipline" and masculine ferocity or *thumos* into a single explosive act, but also leaves in its wake the complementary stereotypes of Irish unmanliness: bestial (Farrington brutalizing a child) and feminized (Charlie offering to "say a *Hail Mary*" for his tormentor).

It is at this point, with the son, Charlie, robbed of his dignity as the father has felt himself to be, with Farrington creating a "counterpart" in thwarted manhood, that the story opens out onto the larger collection, many of whose tales ("The Sisters," "An Encounter," "After the Race," "Eveline," "The Boarding House") are precisely about pathological reproduction, the transmission of damage from parent to child. And what looks like impunity for Farrington in the story's final tableau is really the most ironic, stunning reversal of all. Farrington has passed from a local champion manqué against the quotidian forces of colonialism to a local, quotidian, but *effective* champion of colonialism itself. He now assists in inflicting the masculine double bind under which he has suffered, and the traumatized masculinity that is its fruit, upon the generation, if not generations, to come.[55]

"Neither Fish nor Flesh": Ulysses

The "Cyclops" episode of Ulysses has proved perhaps the happiest hunting ground for those scholars anxious to explore Joyce's critical anatomy of contemporary masculinity in its relation to Irish cultural and political nationalism. I would submit rather that "Cyclops" conducts a deliberate interrogation of the more dominant post-Victorian construction of manhood or manliness, its constitutive part in the delineation of ethnic differences between colonizing and colonized peoples and, most important for our discussion here, its complex effect on the exacerbation of ethnic antagonisms among the colonized themselves.[56]

It is a measure of Joyce's uncommon and imperfectly understood grasp of the commerce between gender and colonial politics that he appreciated the need to address not only the racial effects of the double bind *upon* the Irish but also how the racial attitudes it provoked *in* the Irish amounted to a second-order aporia all its own. He saw that his countrymen felt compelled to vindicate their embattled ethnic identity by stigmatizing the racial "others" in their midst and that their manner of doing so, measured against the genteel standards of manliness, would tacitly corroborate their own devalued profile as imperfectly civilized "others." This is the burden of his renowned critical anatomy of Dublin *parade virile* in the "Cyclops" episode of *Ulysses*. Moreover, by recycling the primary categories of the first double bind, feminine and bestial, in the articulation of the second, this episode draws attention to their common social origins and to the unbroken ideological violence they entail.

The brutish portrait of "Citizen" Michael Cusack, founder of the Gaelic Athletic Association, in the testosterone-soaked atmosphere of Kiernan's pub has typically been glossed either as an interrogation of the embattled will to dominance fundamental to the patriarchal construction of masculinity or, in more historically concrete terms, as an indictment of colonial hypermasculinity, the ultimately self-betraying identification of the conquered with the phallic aggression of the conqueror. Each of these lines of interpretation restricts its own scope, however, by exempting the novel's protagonist, Leopold Bloom, from the episode's gender critique; each silently translates his subjection to xenophobic racism within the narrative frame into a kind of immunity from the dueling parodic voices that articulate the frame.[57] Once this error is corrected, however, and the unforgiving sweep of the satirical perspective acknowledged, one can see that the epicenter of the chapter is not finally the Citizen qua obtrusively phallic index of a problematic (Irish) masculinism, but the underlying *logic* of his relationship to Bloom, which demarcates with astonishing precision the double bind of Irish manhood.[58]

The introduction of the principals immediately establishes the symbolic register of manliness as the framework of their growing antagonism. The Citizen, who comes to figure hypermasculinity as dehumanizing, an overflow of animal spirits, first appears in a tête-à-tête with his animal "spirit" or "familiar": "having a great confab with himself and that bloody mangy mongrel, Garyowen" (*U*, 12.118–20). The interchangeability of man and beast suggested by the formulation "confab with himself and . . ." reasserts itself in a pointedly comprehensive pattern throughout the episode. Man and dog shared a diseased outward appearance, the Citizen "puffing and blowing with the dropsy" (*U*, 12.1784–85) and the dog "growling and grousing and his eye bloodshot from the drouth . . . and the hydrophobia dropping from his jaws" (*U*, 12.709–11). They likewise share a mendicant lifestyle: " getting fed up by the ratepayers and the corporators. Entertainment for man and beast" (*U*, 12.754–55). More significantly, perhaps, they appear to share an inner life. The Citizen's irrepressible animosity toward Bloom repeatedly finds its counterpart in Garyowen's hostility: " . . . and the Citizen scowling after [Bloom] and the old dog at his feet looking up to know who to bite and when" (*U*, 12.1161–62). Finally, man and beast share a mode of expressing that inner life: "He starts . . . talking to him in Irish and the old towser growling, letting on to answer, like a duet in an opera. Such growling you never heard as they let off between them" (*U*, 12.705–7). That the Irish language is specifically marked as the medium for this unification of the higher and lower orders situates the Citizen's bestial associations as a function of his being a stereotype, both living and literary, of the "wild" Irishman.

The parodic excursions attached to Garryowen and his master serve to ratify and extend the Citizen's stereotypical role, while simultaneously lampooning the Revivalist movement for reinforcing such stock images of Gaelic savagery in the very attempt to dispel them. The "duet" triggers a hilarious parody of Gaelicist propaganda, in which the growlings of the "old Irish red setter wolfdog" are celebrated for their approximation of "the ranns of ancient Celtic bards" and "the satirical effusions of Raftery" (*U*, 12.722–23, 729–30). Not only, the passage intimates, does such promotion of "the spread of human culture among the lower animals" emulate the self-styled, British imperialist mission of soul making, but the Revivalist enthusiasm for conferring significant cultural interest or value on the most dubious if distinctively Irish execrescences of the soul enacts a refusal of aesthetic discrimination and decorum consonant with imperialist preconceptions of native barbarism. The Irish beast-as-man, Garryowen as "Owen Garry," cannot be dissociated from the (stage) Irishman as beast, the Citizen as Caliban.

It is important in this regard to recognize how and why Joyce redoubles the narrative "duet" at the level of the parodic set pieces. This entire interlude answers to an earlier pastiche of Revivalist mythography that casts the Citizen as an idealized specimen of Irish masculinity: "broadshouldered deepchested stronglimbed frankeyed redhaired freelyfreckled shaggybearded widemouthed largenosed longheaded deepvoiced barekneed brawnyhanded hairylegged ruddyfaced sinewyarmed hero. From shoulder to shoulder he measured several ells and his rocklike mountainous knees were covered, as was likewise the rest of his body wherever visible, with a strong growth of tawny prickly hair in hue and toughness similar to the mountain gorse (*Ulex Europeus*)" (*U,* 12.152–58). Like the canine poet, this primordial figure of the Citizen parodies not just a discourse but a dynamic, how the need to affirm Irish worth in the teeth of colonial ambivalence and abjection induces modes of exaggeration, both discursive and behavioral, which violate the canons of stalwart moderation informing the ideal of manhood and thereby buttress the stereotypes being contested.

Bloom, by contrast, enters onto the "Cyclops" stage as something of a paragon of self-control. Joe Hynes calls him "the prudent member" (*U,* 12.211), and the ensuing parody of Irish legend turns this epithet into an epitome of Bloom's character: "O'Bloom, the son of Rory: it is he. Impervious to fear is Rory's son: he of the prudent soul" (*U,* 12.216–17). The mock-heroic bathos of the final and defining phrase prepares the reader for the received Dublin interpretation of Bloom's signature trait as an infraction of the homosocial code that shapes immediate judgments on gender normativity and compliance. Whereas the Citizen's own narrative associations with the generic hero, Rory—"doing the raparee and the Rory of the hill" (*U,* 12.134)—betokens an attitude of spurious hypermasculine bravado, Bloom's parallel association here comes increasingly to adumbrate an effeminate or *hypo*masculine attitude of circumspection.

First, Bloom's prudence-as-wariness around the growling Garryowen raises suspicions in both the Citizen and the "nameless" narrator as to his physical courage, a baseline requirement of masculine and therefore manly self-presentation. If the assertion of masculine virility on the part of a Farrington or Cusack tends, under the weight of colonial subordination, to undercut their purchase on manliness, Bloom's display of manly temperateness tends, under obverse pressures, to cast doubts upon his masculinity. Second, Bloom's prudence-as-discretion in refusing the offer of drink—"he wouldn't and he couldn't and excuse him no offense and all to that" (*U,* 12.435–6)—violates not only local notions of sociability but also local notions of intestinal fortitude (literally), which involve the willingness to submit to homosocial rituals of self-abandon (as we saw earlier in "Counterparts"). The derision with which the Nameless One greets Bloom's demurral—"Gob, he's a prudent member and no mistake" (*U*, 12.437)—subtly modulates the key sense of the term *member,* bringing in a punning phallic connotation that qualifies Bloom's disposition as the opposite of, say, raging virility. In a decisive paradox, the very mark of elite metropolitan manhood, unaffected self-restraint, counts as a lack or deficiency in lower-class subaltern masculinity. This normative slippage, in turn, allows for what we might call a ruse of (gendered) reason: in placing an emasculating construction upon Bloom's temperate habits, the barflies not only radiate their unconscious anxiety over their own colonial emasculation but simultaneously testify to their misapprehension of and thus their incapacity for manhood proper.

Finally, there is the credited rumor of Bloom's prudence-as-calculation in his campaign to propitiate a wealthy dowager at the City Arms Hotel. Both the manner and the matter of the Nameless One's representation of Bloom's conduct speaks to its perceived effeminacy: "and Bloom trying to get on the soft side of her doing the mollycoddle playing bezique to come in for a bit of the wampum in her will and not eating meat of a Friday because the old one was always thumping her craw" (*U*, 12.505–8). From the narrator's perspective, the unmanly quality of Bloom's oblique, self-serving scheme reveals itself in the contrivances to which he resorts: participating in female-identified entertainment like "bezique" and submitting to an alien female authority in matters like dietary regulation. The effeminate gloss given Bloom's course of action is brilliantly telescoped in the phrase "doing the mollycoddle." Molly is, of course, the name of Bloom's wife, so that the phrase suggests performing as a Mrs. rather than a Mr. Bloom. But "molly" was also current slang for male homosexuality, a preference then predominantly construed on the model of sexual inversion, what Karl Ulrichs famously encapsulated as "a feminine soul enclosed in a man's body."[59] The phrase "doing the mollycoddle," accordingly, also suggests revealing one's inner feminine or homosexuality. These various associations subsequently crystallize in the Nameless One's sudden memory of yet another page from the City Arms chapter of Bloom's legend: "Lying up in the hotel Pisser was telling me once a month like a totty with her courses" (*U*, 12.1659–60). While this report and others like it in "Cyclops" chime with the many indices of Bloom's gender mobility scattered throughout the novel, their local ideological purport is just the opposite of Joyce's overall design: not to build up a character whose roundedness might exceed the sex/gender system of classification but to reduce a character to a fully and narrowly classifiable abnormality. Bloom, like the Citizen, functions in this episode less as a psychologized subject than as a discursive effect, a particular moment in the circulation and consolidation of ethno-gender stereotypes.

With this in mind, it is worth noting that the particular nexus constellating

Bloom's reputation for prudence with his gender status centered on certain stock preconceptions of the ethnic differences between Jewishness and Irishness, preconceptions that Bloom shares, in significant respects, with his anti-Semitic interlocutors. Thus, the Nameless One opposes a cliché image of the clever and devious Jew to the likewise familiar stereotype of the ingenuous and simple-minded Irishman, finding the latter to be inevitably bested by the former. "Never be up to those bloody Jerusalem . . . cuckoos," he says (*U*, 12.1571–72). But at the same time, he tacitly transposes these conventional ethnic affiliations into the register of late Victorian gender assumption, where (Jewish) sophistication and overcultivation were signifiers of racialized femininity, while the racially inflected norms of masculinity included a straightforward and uncorrupted vigor. Recounting his Kiernan's experience to Stephen in "Eumaeus," Bloom invokes a cognate if transvalued racial dichotomy. Driven "from some bump of combativeness or gland of some kind" (*U*, 16.1112), Bloom's Irish type repeats the Nameless One's ethno-ego ideal with a difference: in its bodily overdetermination, his masculinity shades into bestiality on one side ("bump of combativeness") and femininity on the other ("gland of some kind"). "Practical and proved to be so" (*U*, 16.1125), Bloom's Jewish type likewise registers the Nameless One's anti-Semitic construction with a difference: his feminized caginess and carefulness shades into the manly public virtue of economic rationality—what Bloom, in aptly metropolitan tones, calls being "imbued with the proper spirit" (*U*, 16.1124). For Bloom, finally, as for the narrator, the Jew inevitably bests or surpasses the Irish Catholic, the former bringing prosperity wherever he goes, the latter all but condemned to poverty by his sedulous adherence to Catholic "dogma" and clerical authority (*U*, 16.1129).

The Nameless One builds his typological framework on the popular ethnological classification of the Jews as bearers of feminine traits of mind and culture.[60] By this means, he moves to displace the no less prevalent ethnological thesis that the Gaelo-Irish possessed an "essentially feminine" racial cast,[61] most clearly evidenced in the culture of defeat that the narrator himself repeatedly invokes. The narrator, that is to say, treats Bloom not as an Irish Jew, a hybrid and doubly feminized identity formation, but as a Jewish negation of Irishness, feminized in its stead. In so doing, he works to counter the gender allegory of British imperialism *while and by* affirming its basic principles and presuppositions: the absolute disjunction of gender categories, the essential congruence of racial or gender identity, and the derogation of the feminine as inferior, properly subject to male command, and, in its racial dimension, humiliating. For the subaltern who internalizes these attitudes, like the narrator, the ideological aim is typically to enforce his claim to a rugged and aggressive masculinity. But this objective just as typically turns out a foil or decoy for the real exclusionary standard of entitlement, metropolitan manliness. Bloom's corresponding typological framework supplies, or at least implies, just this sort of critique. Although Bloom proclaims himself "as good an Irishman as that rude [Citizen]" (*U*, 16.1132), he no more frames his subject position in the hybrid terms of Irish Jewry than the narrator does. He too, in fact, represents Jewishness as something of a negation of Irishness, but he sees the object of that negation as the improvident passion that defines the Irish to their detriment. So whereas for the narrator the Jew constitutes the feminized other of the Irish colonial, a scapegoat of his own masculine anxiety, for Bloom the Jew forms the pragmatic, rational other of the Irish colonial, a necessary supplement to his present, unmanly condition.

Taken in combination, these racial paradigms reveal how the double bind of manhood can and perhaps must come to aggravate the interracial stresses within the colonial society and to reproduce itself along the fault lines thus en-gendered. Because proper or plenary manliness evolved under the aegis of imperialism and as a mechanism for confining the subaltern to a position of flexible inferiority, the claims of subdominant groups to such manliness could be sustained only relative to one another and through an internescine struggle of mutual abjection. In "Cyclops," the barflies on one side, noisily, and Bloom himself on the other, more quietly, exemplify this dynamic. By having Bloom answer the explicitly gendered anti-Semitism of the Citizen et al. with a "reverse" but no less racialist discourse, Joyce elaborates the problem of Irish racial antipathy as a structural effect of the colonial predicament in general and the trauma of Irish manhood in particular (a problem to which the typical response of moral censure has limited relevance).

Nowhere did this double bind of metrocolonial manhood pinch to more constraining effect than in the explicitly political arena of national resistance, and no debate topic, "Cyclops" shows, could more readily expose and sexualize Ireland's interracial division and hostility. In order to emphasize, once again, the systematic nature of the problem, Joyce stages the political disagreement between Bloom and the Citizen as a thinly mediated expression of their opposed styles of colonial "mimicry." To this end, he initially leaves the gravamen of their dispute unspecified, while foregrounding their differently gendered mode of address. What the narrator calls Bloom's politics of "moderation and botheration" seems an effect of Bloom's genteel, reasonable, and consensus-oriented cast of mind and argument—"with his *but don't you see* and *but on the other hand*" (*U*, 12.115–16, 513–14). The Citizen's politics of forcible separatism ("We want no more strangers in our house" [*U*, 12.1150–51]) seems an effect of an immediately confrontational and ferociously polarizing demeanor. In either case, the mode of address signals a fundamental link between the frustrated strain of nationalism avowed and the failed synechdoche of manhood personified.

As befits his embrace of hypermasculinity, and his correlative fall into troglyditism, the Citizen (over)embodies the cause and principles of physical-force nationalism. He is given out, first of all, to be the founder of the GAA, and his political attitudes seem to confirm its reputation as a satellite, front, and recruiting arm of the Irish Republican Brotherhood.[62] Hence Joe Hynes's otherwise inexplicable identification of the Citizen with the founder of modern Fenianism: "There's the man that made the Gaelic Sports Revival. There he is sitting there. The man that got away James Stephens" (*U*, 12.880–81). Of course, little pragmatic correlation exists in the modern age between marital and athletic prowess; to paraphrase Stephen Dedalus's mockery of Davin, a Cusack disciple, one cannot "make the next revolution with hurling sticks" (*P*, 202). The strategic connection between the movements, accordingly, must be seen to lie elsewhere (as Stephen comes to recognize in "Nestor"), specifically in the symbolic equivalence of martial and athletic endeavor as competitive mechanisms for asserting and reproducing a certain fantasy of masculinity and as dynamic signifiers of the masculinity thus asserted and reproduced: masculinity as strength, as energy, as brute mastery. For this very reason, however, the valorization of sport, like the adherence to violent political methods, opened itself to the charge of debasing the ideal of manhood to its most visceral denominator, of confusing manliness with "mere" animal spirits, a charge that the philoathleticists answered, often effectively, but could never entirely dispel.

Thus, even as British journalism had begun to press this claim with respect to simianized Irish freedom fighters, the *Dublin Review* stated much the same case with respect to athleticized British public school culture, where the higher values of religion and morality were allegedly being "strangled by the luxurious overgrowth of animal vigour."[63] Even the most famous chronicler and exponent of public school athleticism, Thomas Hughes, who extolled the moralizing and socializing discipline of team sports in particular, exclaimed against the widespread fetishism thereof. His later work *The Manliness of Christ* explicitly contrasts feats of martial daring and feats of athletic skill as "tests of animal courage" that "have come to be very much overpraised and overvalued amongst us" and true "tests of manliness," which would be more appropriately fashioned in accordance with the cerebral and spiritual attributes displayed by Jesus Christ.[64] His position finds an allusive echo in that adopted by Bloom himself, in his role as standard bearer for the spiritual and cerebral component of Irish manhood. Within a parody of the sport's society, *Slaugh na h-Eireen*, Bloom demurs at the jingoistic aggrandizement of "gaelic sports and pastimes" as being "calculated to revive the best traditions of manly strength and prowess" (*U*, 12.910–11). And shortly thereafter, he seeks to affirm the value of sport, including the English game of "lawn tennis," on a more temperate and rational basis, that is, in proportion to such pragmatic benefits as "the training and agility of the eye" and "the circulation of the blood" (*U*, 12.945–46, 952–53). It is this infringement on the hypermasculine fantasy space that elicits the first overt rebuke upon Bloom ("a mixed reception of applause and hisses" [*U,* 12.912–13]) and helps to trigger the group dynamic leading to his mock crucifixion, a "test of [his] manliness" directly conformable with "the manliness of Christ."[65]

Initially, the gripe against Bloom focuses on his apparent lack of patriotic fervor. Thus, the group answers his skeptical comments on the GAA by exhorting the Citizen to a "stentorian" rendition of "A Nation Once Again," an anthem whose apotheosis of the "ancient freemen of Greece and Rome" serves, in this context, to center an identification of Gaelic sports with Irish freedom upon their joint expression of masculine agency.[66] By these lights, Bloom's questioning of the sports revival is seen to betray the nationalist cause through a failure of personal virility. But in what proves a characteristic rhetorical gambit in "Cyclops," Joyce undercuts this easy patriotism in advance by showing hypermasculine Irish athleticism to be already caught in a web of ideological self-betrayal.

An immediately antecedent parliamentary parody conjoins the program of *Slaugh na h-Eireen* and the government mandated slaughter of suspect animals:

> Mr Cowe Conacre (Multifarnham. Nat.) . . . may I ask . . . whether . . . these animals shall be slaughtered though no medical evidence is forthcoming as to their pathological condition . . .
> . . . Mr Orelli O'Reilly (Montenotte. Nat.): Have similar orders been issued for the slaughter of human animals who dare to play Irish games in the Phoenix park? (*U,* 12.860–67)

The Irish Nationalists' question for the government not only underscores the phantasmatic linkage of athletic struggle and military discipline but, more important, hints at how the double valuation of these activities—as manly by certain lights and bestial by others—could be mapped onto the metropolitan-subaltern dichotomy to ludicrous yet deadly effect. So long as the Irish can simply be deemed "pathological" human animals, the parody stresses, casual imperialist bloodletting remains a conceivable and even respectable treatment for inherently barbarous native sport. The satiric thrust, which reflects back on the Citizen's and GAA's displaced admiration for such naked masculinized coercion, is enhanced on all counts by a sly proleptic allusion to the notorious Croke Park Massacre, where English soldiers responded to an exceptionally savage IRB outrage with the arbitrary "slaughter of human animals" out for a GAA-sponsored football match.[67] Joyce thus adumbrates a vicious metrocolonial circle in which hypermasculine identifications with the aggressor return as unmanly, in this case bestialized, self-aggression.

The same metrocolonial loop delimits the Citizen's more direct promotion of the physical force movement, with opposed yet strictly correlative typological effects. In keeping with his symbolic role, the Citizen apparently abides any stray opportunity to recite the Fenian litany of failed Irish risings: "So of course the citizen was only waiting for the wink of the word and he starts gassing out of him about the invincibles and the old guard and the men of sixtyseven and who fears to speak of ninetyeight and . . . all the fellows that were hanged, drawn, and transported for the cause," including "the Brothers Sheares and Wolfe Tone and Robert Emmet," who provide the initial reference points in his debate with Bloom (*U,* 12.479–83, 498–500). In this case, the "wink of the word" arises out of speculation on the "philoprogenitive erection" of one Joe Brady, "Invincible" assassin, on the event of his hanging (*U,* 12.45–65). As the barroom discussion unfolds, the Brady anecdote comes to emblematize not only the eroticization of political violence as a desperate assertion of colonial virility but also the eroticization of political violence *suffered,* of defeat and death at the hands of a mightier foe: indeed, it literalizes the notion of "having a hard on" for self-destruction. Fortified by the ensuing parody of Robert Emmet's hanging, which features the *homocolonial* transfer of Emmet's fiancée to a "young Oxford graduate" (*U,* 12.658–62), the Brady anecdote carries an implicit critique of the Citizen's upcoming harangue. Its burden is the profound reversibility of the colonial hypermasculine ethos into a feminized cult of (self-)sacrificial loss.

As the Citizen unpacks his rhetorical store, the deadlock at the heart of his political faith presses to the surface of the collective awareness of his barmates, where it is ultimately disavowed (acknowledged yet denied) through a transferential group dynamic that gives his debate with Bloom its distinctive trajectory. A couple of related factors enable this dawning awareness, neither of which is fully accessible nor even admissible to it. First, for many of the characters, the hybridized subject position of metrocolonialism makes for that dehiscent political sensibility we might call seminationalism, a split adherence to the institutions of empire and decolonization, operating across multiple layers of express and repressed motivation. On the terms of this highly particular psychic agon, where affective divisions cross-lines of geopolitical generality, support for local modes of cultural separatism, like playing "Irish games," does not translate into support, nor even signify robust desire for a more violent separation (in all senses) from the metropolitan marriage. To the contrary, such support often obscures and allays—in the manner of a compromise formation—the ambivalence that the prospect of outright divorce arouses. Like Irish anti-Semitism, with which it is connected, the familiar Joycean motif of Irish (self-)betrayal finally answers less to moral judgment than to structural analyses of the condition of subjectivation in what was at once the capital of Ireland, the center of the English pale, and the seat of colonial government.

It is precisely to highlight this circumstance that Joyce punctuates the proceedings with the arrival of that most politically compromised caste of Dubliners, the "Castle Catholics" (Cunningham and Power), whose seemingly benign appearance in "the castle car" occasions a medieval romance parody targeting the utterly venal privilege of their official position (*U*, 12.1588–1620). Their characteristically latitudinarian brand of politics, already articulated at this point by their colleague J. J. O'Molloy, primarily consists in the guarded "moderation" associated with Bloom and involves the affectation of a metropolitan style of gentlemanliness, what the narrator calls "doing the toff" (*U*, 12.1192). Whereas the Citizen tropes British imperial civilization as "syphilization," a foreign contagion vitiating the manly properties of the native body politic, O'Molloy seems to honor that same imperial civilization as an offspring of "the European family," a wholesome form of incorporation in which Ireland shares (*U*, 12.1197, 1202). A very different sort of identification with the colonizer underlies this viewpoint (which is shared by most of the more vocal characters of the episode), an identification not with the brute strength of his aggression but with the sublimated and legitimated fruits of that aggression.

This alternative identificatory perspective, second, is especially prone to apprehend the self-defeating impetus of the Citizen's violent separatism and to focus thereon as a way of defending itself against a full recognition of its own conflicts, complicities, and irresolution. When the Citizen grandly imagines Ireland recovering its place as a center of European trade, he is immediately reminded of the overpowering impediment posed by the British Navy, which, Lambert tellingly declares, "keep *our* foes at bay" (*U*, 12.1329; emphasis added). When the Citizen moves to belittle the British Navy by adducing the homoeroticized cruelty of its disciplinary rituals, Bloom turns the imputation back upon his own hypermasculine agenda: "But . . . isn't discipline the same everywhere? I mean wouldn't it be the same here if you put force against force?" (*U*, 12.1361) Most pointedly, when the Citizen proceeds to call for armed rebellion ("We'll put force against force" [*U*, 12.1364]), he immediately finds his message read back to him, as the Lacanians say, "in reverse order." He stakes the success of the coming revolution on the might of "our greater Ireland beyond the sea," now populated with valiant and vengeful Irish expatriates, "the sons of Granuaile and the champions of Kathleen Ni Houlihan" (*U*, 12.1364–65, 1374–75). But his interlocutors, Lambert and Nolan, are quick to indicate that Ireland's foreign dependence has always proved the flip side of its colonial corruption, figuring no less heavily in the feminized Celtic tradition of romantic expenditure without return. They reiterate the Citizen's own familiar role of Irish defeats and disappointments, for the purpose not of ennobling a thwarted past but of discouraging a self-immolative future ("We fought for the royal Stewarts that reneged us. . . . We gave our best blood to France and Spain, the wild geese. Fontenoy, eh? And Sarsfield and O'Donnell . . . but what did we ever get for it?" [*U*, 12.1379–84]). If, as Emer Nolan notes, the Citizen's list of historical grievances (*U*, 12.1239–57) derives from Joyce's "Ireland, Island of Saints and Sages," the others' dissent from his position seconds the same essay's conclusion, that it is "past time for Ireland to have done once and for all with failure."[68]

The perceived futility of the Citizen's posture, in turn, feminizes the man himself in his very troglodytism, for it exposes his hypermasculine potency as mere pose or show, the kind of self-advertising performance associated in the late Victorian Imaginary with feminine *heteronomy,* woman's inherent being-for-others. If, as Lacan has argued, the phallus can function only when veiled, it is in part because phallic display always admits of feminine construction qua display, particularly when, as in this case, the display reveals the phallus to be myth or fraud. Thus, the Nameless One sneers that the Citizen is "all wind and piss like a tanyard cat" (*U*, 12.1311–12), a formulation that neatly synthesizes the animal with the feminine. He goes on to remark how the Citizen betrayed the Land League eviction code, on account of which the Molly Maguires would like to answer his phallic pretensions, "tall talk," by putting a hole in him (*U*, 12.1312–16).

Strangely unremarked in *Ulysses* criticism, this concerted yet subterranean resistance to the Citizen's agenda neither originates nor terminates with his designated adversary, Leopold Bloom. Bloom does, however, crystallize the resistance in simultaneously symbolic and narrative terms. Consistent with his personification of the "prudent" self-controlled aspect of metropolitan manhood, Bloom stakes out the political necessity of getting beyond the endless cycle of "force against force." In keeping with the nationalist terrain of Edwardian Ireland, this priority inclines him toward an identification with, if not actual participation in, the various constituency groups of the moral force movement. At one point, Bloom sympathetically invokes "the Gaelic League and the antitreating League" and, with the phrase "drink, the curse of Ireland," the temperance movement generally (*U*, 12.683–84). In addition, he is repeatedly credited with contributing significantly to Sinn Fein's initial nonviolent strategy (*U*, 12.1574, 1625–37). As our study has shown, what these movements have in common in their respective domains—cultural, social, and political nationalism—is a commitment to enhancing Irish self-respect conceived along the lines of social respectability, a project that subscribes closely to the weltanschauung of bourgeois manliness. Thus, while the Gaelic League curriculum venerated peasant culture and folklore, its institutional organization and self-promotion aimed to advance middle-class social values and cultural prestige, so that even a sympathetic observer like George Russell could complain of its "boyscoutish propaganda," thereby affiliating the league (like the Fianna) with the institution most identified with cultivating middle-class manliness.[69] For their part, the temperance movement and the antitreating league not only held the achievement of bourgeois respectability to be essential to the decolonization of Ireland ("Ireland sober, Ireland free"), it explicitly defined such respectability in terms of self-discipline, self-control, and personal integrity, thus conflating the ethical mandates of *individual* manliness with the political goals of autonomy, unity, and self-determination that had come to delimit *racial* manhood. Sinn Fein drew out this connection with still greater force; it projected the approved manly criteria of self-reliance and self-containment directly into the public sphere and the constitutional order via its signature policy of passive resistance and parliamentary withdrawal. At the same time, insofar as this signature policy envisioned a "shadow government . . . complete with a sort of Parliament,"[70] Sinn Fein's claim to enabling national autonomy could well be judged more rather than less dependent than violent separatism on an ongoing act of identification with the colonizer. In either event, the fact that Bloom is "know[n] . . . in the castle" to have outlined precisely this policy to Arthur Griffith accentuates his own political profile in its stark and schematic opposition to the Citizen's as an image of Irish manhood (*U,* 12.1637–38).

By the time Joyce composed and revised the "Cyclops" episode, however, Sinn Fein had grown identified in the popular mind with the Easter Rising and, in consequence, had become the leading physical force party in Ireland.[71] The proleptic allusion to this turn of events in "Cyclops," reinforced by the Citizen's use of the phrase "Sinn Fein" as a war cry (*U,* 12.523), has the effect of undercutting Bloom's political credo in a manner analogous to the parodic undercutting of the Citizen's attitudes earlier. It reminds the reader that just as colonial hypermasculinity regularly issued in a feminized cult of defeat and self-immolation, exemplified by the Easter Rising, so the passive gentlemanly resistance of Sinn Fein ultimately mutated into a program of violent guerrilla insurgency in response to its own emasculation, of which a "delirium of the brave" like Easter 1916 was sharp notice.

Bloom's own moment of political advocacy in "Cyclops" epitomizes the gendered dilemma of purely moral intervention. Attempting to parry the Citizen's casual anti-Semitic thrusts, Bloom draws a parallel between the Irish and the Jews as victims of persecution, expatiating on the plight of the latter: "And I belong to a race too, says Bloom, that is hated and persecuted. Also now. This very moment. This very instant . . . Robbed . . . Plundered. Insulted. Persecuted. Taking what belongs to us by right. At this very moment, says he, putting up his fist, sold by auction in Morocco like slaves or cattle . . . I'm talking about injustice, says Bloom" (*U,* 12.1468–74). But when invited to pursue the belligerent course that his clenched fist seems to endorse ("Stand up to it then with force like men" [*U,* 12.1475]), Bloom declines on principle ("Force, hatred, history, all that. That's not life for men and women, insult and hatred" [*U,* 12.1481–82]). He further confesses by his body language to having no other effective solution: "And then he collapses all of a sudden, twisting around all the opposite, as limp as a wet rag" [*U,* 12.1478–80]). While this image of sudden detumescence and flaccidity undoubtedly proceeds from the Nameless One's already feminized construction of Bloom ("Gob, he'd adorn a sweeping brush, so he would, if only he had a nurse's apron on him" [*U,* 12.1477–78]), it nevertheless speaks to the fatal weakness of Bloom's colonial impersonation of manhood. Throughout "Cyclops," Joyce manipulates narration, dialogue, and parodic excursion in an effort to discredit without entirely discounting the invidious viewpoint of the Nameless One and to achieve thereby a measure of stylistic "binocularity." In this case, Joyce half-participates in the narrator's caustic irony by satirizing the incapacity of Bloom's political sensibility to withstand or combat just such a jaundiced perspective. Thus, Joyce carefully juxtaposes the "injustice" of Bloom's complaint with the "force" of Nolan's rejected recommendation so as to craft an allusion to Pascale's famous *pensée,* "Justice without force is impotent" (La justice sans force est impuissance),[72] which can be read as articulating metaphorically the practical futility and the personal emasculation encoded in Bloom's limp bodily attitude. These two forms of impotence ultimately converge in Bloom's facile panacea to the Irish and Jewish question: an abstract notion of "love," defined only as "the opposite of hatred" (*U,* 12.1485). Having been successively glossed along religious, political, and romantic lines, this unanchored signifier is progressively displaced and debased across one of the episode's most vicious parodies, the "Love loves to love love" interlude (*U,* 12.143–1501).

To acknowledge Joyce's supplement to the barflies' mockery of Bloom here is not to ally him in any simple way with Bloom's tormentors. Whereas they pillory Bloom for a racialized dearth of masculinity, Joyce marks the metrocolonial limitations of the mode of manliness, political and otherwise, that Bloom does in fact assume. To disregard Joyce's critique of Bloom on this score, accordingly, is to miss a crucial aspect of Joyce's subtle engagement with mimicry as a technology of imperial power. After all, self-immolation is not the only type of failure with which Ireland "must have done," according to the essay "Ireland Isle of Saints and Sages." In the same paragraph, Joyce noted that "Ireland had already had enough of equivocations" as well.[73] And for the subaltern, equivocation—as between self-possession and self-repression—is the irreducible risk of internalized "prudence" or restraint.

To appreciate this same technology, moreover, it is essential to recognize not just that the episode's "anti-Bloomite" sentiment is not entirely confined to the barroom community but also, and perhaps more important, that the barroom sentiment itself is not entirely anti-Bloomite. To the contrary, Joyce takes care to position most of the assembled characters somewhere between the gendered political polarities occupied by Bloom and the Citizen. Not, it should be noted, in a site of mediation, but rather along a curve of vacillation and (self-)betrayal that expresses, in pragmatic terms, the double/divisive interpellation of their semicolonial subjectivity and the psychomachia it en-genders. As a function of their understated opposition to the Citizen's hypermasculine extremism, many of the symposiasts league themselves with rather than against Bloom at various points in the discussion: O'Molloy in "arguing about law and history" with the Citizen (*U,* 12.1235), Lambert and Nolan in questioning the wisdom of armed revolution, and, most passionately, Nolan once again in adducing Bloom's decisive contribution to Sinn Fein. As a function, conversely, of their sense that this more "prudent" restrained political stance also fails of virtues essential to national(ist) manhood (strength, valor, fortitude, and so on), these same symposiasts find it necessary to seize opportunities for turning on Bloom and disowning his views. By the same token, the Citizen is encouraged to train his nationalist ire entirely on Bloom as a way of binding the others to him in an ongoing dissimulation of their differences. Thus, a kind of negative racial transference unfolds in which the men identify with Bloom only to project their own Irish inflected shame, anxiety, and vulnerability onto his Jewishness, bringing their structurally determined self-betrayal and their structurally determined anti-Semitism into alignment.

Such a collective dynamic, however, cannot but remain arrested in what Freud called denegation, that is, unconscious affirmation in the form of categorical denial. The scapegoat figure, in this case Bloom, cannot come to bear the constitutive frailties of the congregation except insofar as he dwells within as well as beyond its borders *in the very form of his expulsion.* He must be a participant-outcast, if you will, performing each of these conflicting offices by way of the other. Joyce fashions Bloom to fulfill this precise role in the secular context of "Cyclops" by giving him the status of social symptom as well as stereotype, and a symptom of the very men who currently stereotype him. A symptom, to paraphrase Slavoj Zizek, is something that encodes the hidden law of any system (personality, institution, community) as its most persistent disturbance. It is therefore, like the scapegoat, intensely representative of a given whole in and through its exceptionality, and Bloom occupies just such an internal ethno-gender boundary for Kiernan's patrons. He is, as Zizek would say, in them more than them.[74] Accordingly, at just the moment Bloom's racial and sexual abjection achieve their ultimate articulation, he stands forth as the image of the group in his imposed otherness, *quintessentially Irish in the social construction of his Jewishness.*

The group's final attack on Bloom begins by pushing beyond his perceived lack of patriotism to his supposed absence, as a Jew, of any proper *patrie,* and as such it clearly acts to displace the trauma of their own undecidable social inscription in the interstice of colony and metropole. Notice that the acid exchange is initiated by Nolan, periodically Bloom's most vocal supporter:

 —But do you know what a nation means? says John Wyse.
 —Yes, says Bloom.
 —What is it, says John Wyse.

—A nation? says Bloom. A nation is the same people living in the same place.
—By God, then, says Ned, laughing, if that's so I'm a nation for I'm living in the
same place for five years. So of course everyone had a laugh at Bloom and says
he . . .
—Or also living in different places.
—That covers my case, says Joe. (*U,* 12.141–42)

Joyce here arranges the dialogue so that the barflies cannot but reassert in their
implicitly anti-Semitic banter the larger parallelism the novel develops between
the Irish and Jewish condition. The very mechanism for ridiculing Bloom's
Hebraic placelessness underlines the fundamentally self-reflexive nature of the
enterprise, insistently returning the muddled question of nationhood to the
Dubliners' own place of residence, which is indeed, geopolitically speaking, a
self-different interspace, the home as foreign country.

This decentering of the domestic space of Irish life signals a form of political
castration for Irish manhood, a breakdown in corporate autonomy and self-
possession. *Dublin as gnomon equals the Dubliner as no man.* Here again, the
linkage must somehow be displaced onto Bloom as Jew; he must be made to
bear the stigma of No Man as his proper "name" or designation. Hence Nolan's
admonition to Bloom and his coreligionists, "Stand up to [persecution] then
with force, like men" (*U,* 12.1475), when not five minutes earlier he had prudently
rejected the very same course for Ireland. This particular trauma of dispossessed
Irish manhood is so pronounced in fact that its symptomatic expression shows
a compulsive tendency to repeat. No sooner do the castle hacks appear, those
personifications of metrocolonial ambivalence, than the question of Bloom's
Sinn Fein nationalism reemerges, closely shadowed by the stigma of his "Jewish" deracination.

—And after all, says John Wyse, why can't a Jew love his country like the next
fellow?
—Why not, says J. J., when he's quite sure which country it is. (*U,* 12.1628–30)

On this occasion, the analogy of the Irish to the Jewish condition finds explicit
affirmation, and in terms that speak to what the double bind of dehumanizing
violence versus feminizing restraint leaves behind as an irredentist option: "Well
they are still waiting for their redeemer, says Martin. For that matter, so are we"
(*U,* 12.1644–45). The collective psychic threat posed by this comment can be
deduced from the alacrity with which it is made the grounds for emasculating
the absent Bloom as an "every Jew" (*U,* 12.1647):

—Yes, says J. J., and every male they think . . . may be their messiah. And every Jew
is in a tall state of excitement . . . till he knows if he's a father or a mother . . .
. . . —O, by God, says Ned, you should have seen Bloom before that son of his

that died was born . . . buying a tin of Neave's food six weeks before the wife
was delivered.
—*En ventre sa mere,* says J. J.
—Do you call that a man? says the citizen.
—I wonder did he ever put it out of sight, says Joe. (*U,* 12.1646–56)

The shifting of Bloom's position from father to mother, the mockery of his uxo-
riousness and maternal solicitude, the skepticism as to his sexual experience, the
Citizen's pointed question—all of this extends the strategy previously deployed
by the Nameless One to transpose the double bind of Irish manhood onto the
received stereotype of Jewish femininity. In accordance with the transferential
logic of the scapegoat/symptom, however, the details selected for the task harbor points of Irish reference strictly pertinent to the issue at hand, including
the matriarchal strain in colonial Irish life, the renowned Mariolatry of Irish
Catholicism, the native female iconography of the Irish nation, the imposed
feminine typology of the Celtic race, and the sexual repressiveness of modern
Irish society, which conduces to expressions equating coitus with castration ("put
it out of sight"). The Nameless One's summary judgment on this interlude, that
Bloom represents "one of those mixed middlings" (*U,* 12.1658–59), also serves,
against the grain of his intent, as a summary, self-reflexive judgment on the assembled Dubliners, articulating the double inscription of their political estate
as an aporia in their gender performance.

The physical assault on Bloom that closes the episode may be seen as an
attempt on the Citizen's part to dissolve once and for all the antagonistic intimacy of the symptom/scapegoat with his host/subject—to convert, finally, the
trauma of collective self-betrayal into a more psychically manageable sense
of betrayal by the other. (Indeed, what drives the Citizen to actual battery is
Bloom's outright assertion of his proximateness to the group: "Your God was
a Jew. Christ was a Jew like me" [*U,* 12.1808–9]).[75] The nature of this transaction, however, only typifies the double bind that is the informing condition of
the symptomatic relationship. Thus, the Citizen enacts both sides of colonial
hypermasculinity: he translates his athletic strength (he was a shotputter) into
an act of patriotic violence (hurling the biscuit tin), only to bestialize himself
in the process, "puffing and blowing with the dropsy" like his dog and "shout-
ing like a stuck pig" (*U,* 12.1784–85, 1845). Bloom enacts both sides of colonial
gentlemanliness; he maintains his dignity and self-control, asserts his superior
moral and rational strength, only to wind up marked for emasculation in the
process, incurring the jeers of "all the ragamuffins and sluts of the nation": "*If
the man in the moon was a Jew, Jew, Jew . . . Eh Mister! Your fly is open Mister*"
(*U,* 12.1796, 1801–2). The others collectively enact a paralyzing, multiply fissured
affiliation and disaffiliation with both representative figures: egging the Citizen

on with laughter, "aiding and abetting" (*U*, 12.1900), trying to restrain him, mysteriously disappearing (Nolan), endeavoring to protect Bloom, attempting to silence Bloom (Cunningham), and so forth. The Nameless One epitomizes this self-division. He begins by criticizing the Citizen in words that suggest a preference for a more restrained moral-force manliness: "Arrah, sit down on the *parliamentary* side of your ass and stop making a public exhibition of yourself" (*U*, 12.172–73; emphasis added). But he ends by expressing his support for the Citizen in words that carefully endorse physical aggression: "Bloody wars, says I, I'll be in for the last gospel" (*U*, 12.1849).

When the same narrator calls Bloom a "mixed middling," unwittingly implicating the other Dubliners in that estate, he is clearly bent on likening Bloom to the pixilated Dennis Breen whom the Citizen has already declared a "half and half" (*U*, 12.1052–53). With the riotous "last gospel," Breen emerges as a kind of allegorical limit case of the trauma of Irish manhood. Like the litigious Breen, the bar dwellers prove themselves neither "fish nor flesh" (*U*, 12.1055–56) but violently torn between the two—between feminized grievance and masculinized aggression—and more than a touch hysterical from the strain.

It will be noted that no path beyond the impasse of metrocolonial manhood has been adumbrated herein. In my view, Joyce conspicuously avoids the faintest suggestion that such a path exists, and he carefully underlines this decision by emblazoning the beginning, middle, and end of the episode with twinned images of Cyclopean blinding and Oedipal castration. All of this is to say that Joyce takes the impasse quite seriously. He wishes to dispel the ready assumption that the trauma of Irish manhood can resolved strictly at the level of means, literary or political. The problem lies not in the colonial strategies of gender assumption but in the imperialist gender construct to be assumed. The normative structure of metropolitan manhood is in itself the traumatic structure of metrocolonial castration. There is accordingly no negotiation of the aporia on the terms given; the terms must be changed. Why the terms must be changed is a lesson woven into the very texture of "Cyclops," which tracks the gender double bind through its labyrinthine vicissitudes of Irish *self-othering*. Discovering how the terms might be changed can begin, and *only* begin, with a compelling and comprehensive representation of why.

"Manhood Is All"

Yeats and the Poetics of Discipline

In one of the great synopses in literary criticism, Seamus Deane describes the life of Yeats as an epic journey into cultural and political alienation: "Yeats began his career by inventing an Ireland amenable to his imagination. He ended by finding an Ireland recalcitrant to it." His gathering disillusionment prompted Yeats to reconceive his primary social attachments and with them his sense of geopolitical mission. He turned from being the self-styled bard of the rising Irish people-nation to the unofficial laureate of a declining Anglo-Irish subculture, adapting a political discourse that managed to be at once elitist and minoritarian, dissident and authoritarian, nationalist and neocolonialist. By all accounts, the clamorous protests greeting the debut of Synge's *Playboy* marked the tipping point in this conversion. Indeed, Yeats himself all but announced as much from the Abbey stage in his "Speech on the Debate" over the play and its reception.[1] Ringing a hostile variation on D. P. Moran's notorious theme, "the battle of two civilizations," Yeats drew a double Manichaean contrast between the National Theatre and the mob currently assailing it: first, an implicitly ethnic contrast between the old, gentrified vanguard of the "national movement," those "leaders," fit though few, and the now "democratised" masses who wielded "unworthy instruments of tyranny and violence," such as the rioting in question (*E,* 227); and, second, a pointedly sectarian contrast between a priest-playwright who had capitulated to "Irish disorder" in Liverpool by withdrawing his play, and the Protestant Abbey directorate, who "have not such pliant bones and did not learn in the houses that bred us a so suppliant knee" (*E,* 226–27). In one sweeping blow, Yeats both raises the English caricature of the "mere" lower-caste Irish as barbarous and addicted to violence and invokes the Protestant stereotype of Roman Catholicism as overly deferential toward and dependent upon clerical authority, identifying their devotional obsequies (kneeling, genuflection) with moral obsequiousness. He thereby follows the broad contours of the animal/ feminine canard to paint his Irish-Ireland opponents as unready for the freedom they would exercise.

It is thus not surprising, though still striking, that in the peroration of his address, Yeats enshrines not artistic license or political dissent but collective manhood as the ultimate value promoted by his faction, as "what our victory . . . means": "We are beginning once again to ask what a man is, and to be content to wait a little before we go on to that further question, What is a good Irishman? . . . Manhood is all, and the root of manhood is courage and courtesy" (*E,* 228). With the last, memorable, turn of phrase, Yeats not only signals his growing insistence upon an aristocratic style of being-in-the-world, he looks to reappropriate the chivalric discourse of manliness to the aristocratic culture whence it originally sprang. In this respect, *Yeats brings full circle the ideological progress we have been tracing in this book:* where middle-class imperialism and irredentism alike borrowed from medieval rhetoric to sanctify their shared norms of masculinity, Yeats proposes, using the *Playboy* riots as his counterexample, that modern norms of manly self-regulation could be fulfilled only with a return to medieval forms of social hierarchy, where respect for rank and for virtue reinforced one another.

Yeats's experience of the *Playboy* riots was bookended, significantly, by his mutually intensifying encounters, literary and historical, with the spirit of Bachelard Castiglione. His perspective on the event was framed by his recent reading of *The Courtier,* at Lady Gregory's urging, and then retroactively consolidated by his ensuing trip, at Lady Gregory's invitation, to the palace in Urbino where Castiglione founded his academy.[2] The peculiar utility of the courtier ethos for Yeats began with the concurrence of its defining virtue and the hallmark of Victorian manliness, that is, self-possession. Indeed, when Yeats later wrote that he had "ruffled in a manly pose," he was referring to his adoption during this period of a Castiglean mask.[3] Castiglione's treatment of self-possession, moreover, was congenially dialectical: he saw control over oneself as the precondition for placing oneself at the disposal of others, and more particularly in the service of those oligarchs who ruled the city-state. Adapting this logic, Yeats found the Castiglean standard of "courtesy and self possession" perfectly suited to authorize his own emergent cultural politics: the rehabilitation of the Anglo-Protestant aristocracy as the bearers of a standard of enlightened Irish nationalism sadly forsaken by the dominant middle-class movement of the day. The patriotic attachments of the settler gentry arose, according to Yeats, out of a certain self-mastery—a departure from rather than a pursuit of their group interest—and, as a result, they were to remain especially well equipped to fashion national unity on grounds resistant to the despotic, homogenizing solidarity of the "Mob." That is to say, Yeats's purpose in identifying this patriotic

Ascendancy tradition as a modern variant on the courtier sensibility was not merely to confer upon its leaders, a Swift or a Grattan, the reflected prestige of the Italian Renaissance, but also to recommend them as the architects of a model of collective political action that demanded sacrifice and discipline while discouraging conformity with popular shibboleths, that took a stringent devotion to the cause of Ireland as a tempered expression (rather than a suppression) of self-ownership. On Yeats's handling, the courtier ethos functions to recalibrate Thomas Hughes's motto of manliness, "self restraint is the highest form of self assertion," for the purpose of affirming the interconnection of individual and national self-determination.

But Yeats understood the dialectic implicit in *The Courtier* to extend a decisive step further. His major essay in the aftermath of the *Playboy* imbroglio, "Poetry and Tradition," observes how for Castiglione the self-possession fundamental to "good manners" seemed to entail a countervailing quality of "recklessness," control over the self achieving its purest form in the antimony of willful self-abandon, a determined nonchalance toward the ordinary concerns of security or survival, advantage or reward. "For only when we are gay over a thing," writes Yeats, "and can play with it, do we show ourselves its master."[4] *Spretazzura,* the style of being most closely identified with Castiglione, may be seen to constitute just this ethical synthesis, which Yeats proceeds to identify with none other than the subject of freedom: "In life courtesy and self-possession . . . are the sensible impression of the free mind, for both arise out of a deliberate shaping of all things" (*EI,* 253).

Yeats's well-known campaign against the middle classes and their prudentialist ideology gave him the occasion for an especially vigorous advocacy of the courtier ideal. Already, in "Poetry and Tradition," he casts "recklessness" as not merely an alternative to the guiding principle of bourgeois life, the orderly pursuit of rational self-interest, but as an index of the limitation of this instrumentalist mind-set. "They have so little belief that anything can be and end in itself," Yeats argues, "that they cannot understand you if you say, 'All the most valuable things are useless.'" Strikingly, moreover, Yeats attributes this failure of the bourgeois imagination to a failure of bourgeois mettle, a lack of manhood intrinsic to be class formation itself. According to Yeats, "beautiful things" can be created or appreciated only by those like the aristocracy, the artist, and the folk, whose rootedness in "a long tradition" grants them the courage to embrace the uselessness of aesthetic gratification, "for, being without fear, they have held to whatever pleased them." The middle class, by contrast, hold their status strictly through material acquisition and so are defined by what Barbara Ehrenreich has called a "fear of falling."[5] It is precisely their constitutive fretfulness that dooms the middle class to a debilitating inconsistency of desire and leaves them liable to an unprincipled cynicism: "Being always anxious, [they] . . . are always changing from thing to thing, for whatever they do or have must be a means to something else" (*EI*, 251). Aesthetic engagement, then, in the broad Kantian sense, would seem to grow out of a certain capacity for manliness, a capacity reserved to the noble spirit.

In the political sphere, this aesthetic manifests in impractical gestures undertaken with a resolve that lends them the look, and in some sense the reality, of principled stands. Not coincidentally, the leading specimen of such politics in this essay is John O'Leary, the very man whose public activities after his return from exile aided Yeats in mounting a bridge between advanced nationalism and committed aestheticism. O'Leary earns the poet's praise for his gender-inflected *refusal* to do whatever it takes in the name of Ireland, even when what it takes seems as tactically inevitable as it is morally innocuous. Among the things "a man must not do to save a nation," according to O'Leary, "a man was not to lie, or even give up his dignity, on any patriotic plea," and he couched that claim in a classical troupe of heroic masculinity: "I have but one religion, the old Persian: to bend the bow and tell the truth." To this policy Yeats approvingly conjoins another of his oracular strictures, "a man must not cry in public to save a nation" (*EI*, 247). Here, with superb impracticality, O'Leary not only places individual deportment *above* national redemption but also invokes the aesthetic of manliness, whence his preferred self-presentation derives, as an *end* rather than a means. He safeguards the personal indices of a fitness for freedom even at the expense of securing the (national) freedom itself.

O'Leary himself was from native stock, but Yeats is careful to trace the composed (controlled/aesthetized) "recklessness" he represents to a "thread running up to Grattan" (*EI*, 247–48) and, once again, to "the generation of Grattan . . . and that of Davis" (*EI*, 246). His aim is to give the code of courtly manliness an Anglo-Irish impress by counterposing its signature forms and virtues to the "mob" mentality of the "new" largely native middle class. This ideological agenda figures centrally in Yeats's first explicitly post-Revival verse collection, *Responsibilities,* which reads in part as a deliberate application of the principles set forth in "Poetry and Tradition."

The contest between sovereign imprudence and shrinking calculation, respectively identified with the usual ethnic subjects, forms a touchstone of *Responsibilities,* infusing such poems as "Introductory Rhymes," "September 1913," and the triptych of topical odes, "To a Friend," "To a Wealthy Man," and "To a Shade."[6] The first of these, otherwise known as "Pardon Old Fathers" (*CP,* 101), represents Yeats's military forebears as exculpated of their imperialist aggression by the daring abandon of their service. Yeats even scrambles the spatial coordinates of their exploits, through a careful manipulation of diction and syntax, in order to suggest that they helped to defend rather than to conquer Ireland:

Soldiers that gave, whatever die was cast:
A Butler or an Armstrong that withstood
Beside the brackish waters of the Boyne
James and his Irish when the Dutchmen crossed. (*CP*, 9–12)

It is almost as if the spirit animating their efforts or the strenuousness of their commitment could in itself place them on the right side of nationalist history. Still more pointedly, the poem treats Yeats's mercantile ancestors as cleansed of the heritable taint of their own "huckster's loins" (*CP*, 8) by their cultivated pursuit of "wasteful virtues" (*CP*, 18), an inversion of bourgeois merit exemplified by the "merchant skipper" (*CP*, 13) William Middleton, who risked drowning to retrieve a "ragged hat" (*CP*, 14). Given the family history he has charted, Yeats must be understood at poem's end as boasting, no less begging pardon, for the "barren passion" he bore Maud Gonne, as claiming credit (and "kin") as much as claiming responsibility for a splendid prodigality that has left him with "no child, . . . nothing but a book" (*CP*, 20–21).

For this "book" to properly uphold the cavalier ethos, however, it must not only celebrate but inscribe, textualize, the coincidence of self-control and self-expenditure. "Poetry and Tradition" had already identified this aim with the cultivation of style, which Yeats saw as the literary correlative of a manly demeanor: "In life courtesy and self possession, and in the arts style, are the sensible impressions of the free mind . . . both arise . . . from never being swept away, whatever the emotion, into confusion or dullness. . . . [A] writer . . . should never be without style which is but high breeding in words and argument" (*EI*, 253). Some years after, in the poem "The Fisherman" (*CP*, 148), Yeats epitomized this style in terms notably congruent with the *discordia concours* of "strong passions strongly checked" with which this study began: a "poem . . . as cold and passionate as the dawn" (*CP*, 39–40). But already in *Responsibilities,* Yeats had begun to forge the peculiar mode of address that would serve, throughout his later "ascendancy verse," to produce this very effect. Verbal gestures of self-abjection and self-assertion, ruefulness and defiance, are carefully interwoven so that each might act as a strong break upon the other while giving vent to a strong emotion of its own. The result is a deliberate, mannered, sometimes ceremonial style that fairly bristles with the masculinist aggression that it effectively tempers, what Yeats calls "pride established in humility." To return to our previous example, by attaching Yeats to a lineage of socially entitled recklessness, but in a deeply penitential mode, that closing flourish of "Introductory Rhymes" saved the poet from being "swept away" either by hubristic contempt for material exigency or a mawkish self-loathing, allowing him a posture of controlled dignity.

As the collection proceeds, this strategic tension is displaced outward from Yeats himself to the ethnic and class circle with which he identifies. Consider the famous lament "September 1913" (*CP*, 108–9). Here the opposition of timorous calculation to manful imprudence maps all but explicitly onto an opposition between the new Catholic middle class, who "add the halfpence to the pence / And prayer to shivering prayer" (*CP*, 3–4), and the tradition of honorable Anglo Irish revolutionism, "Edward Fitzgerald . . . And Robert Emmet and Wolf Tone, / All that delirium of the brave" (*CP*, 20–22), now past into memory with O'Leary's death. Via another muted illusion to the poet's obsession with Maud Gonne, however, the final verse of the poem gives the topos of "romantic nationalism" an unlooked-for twist. It appends Yeats to the revolutionary lineage by reason of his imprudent attachment ("maddened") to a would-be sovereignty figure (Gonne as "queen" or Cathleen Ni Houlihan) and tacitly confesses that owing to the strictly amorous nature of this attachment, he no more measures up to the canons of tragic Celtic heroism than the Paudeens he lambastes. Through this dual alignment, one self-promoting and one self-mortifying, Yeats mitigates the aggression previously leveled at the Irish Catholic middle class while still more assertively exalting his own ethno-national forebears: not just the natives but even their own people, their own bard, cannot follow properly in their footsteps. Yet this very peerlessness also points up a signal deficiency in those gallant patriots. They have proven unable to reproduce themselves in new generations, as their millennial agenda so clearly required. With O'Leary, the last of them, in the grave, Yeats is left not just to trace their nobility to their sublime impracticality but to ennoble the greatest impracticality of all, a political dead end.

If the phrase *political dead end* sounds familiar in this context, that is because I previously used it to characterize the popular nationalist ethos of blood sacrifice that Yeats helped to propagate in *Cathleen Ni Houlihan* and then renounced in *On Baile's Strand*. The figures lionized in "September 1913" all hail from the broad church of Fenianism in which this ethos took root, but the poem does not represent any simple reversion to Yeats's earlier populist support for sacrificial heroism. To the contrary, it initiates a recalibration of the political coordinates defining the principle of sanctified defeat. *As the Irish people, taken as a unified nationalist community, were to the British colonizer under classic revivalism, so the Anglo-Irish elite are now to the hegemonic segment of that community, the Catholic middle class.*[7] That is, where the Irish people-nation, in a play like *Cathleen,* was summoned to a display of chivalric manliness, to subject their bodies without complaint or concession to the entrenched military power of the British, Yeats would now have Anglo-Irish patriots, the very models of such gallantry (Tone, Emmet, Davis, et al.), exhibit yet another form of manly dignity, to abide, without complaint or concession, the suspicion, disregard, opprobrium, and worse heaped upon them by the emergent Catholic power in Ireland.

In the ensuing poems, Yeats articulates this tribal mandate quite explicitly, calling out two figures in particular who, as our study has shown, must be located among the authors of modern Irish manliness: Lady Gregory and Charles Stewart Parnell. Addressed to Lady Gregory during the Hugh Lane controversy, "To a Friend Whose Work Has Come to Nothing" counsels that the only viable response to the insults she has received from shameless vulgarians like William Martin Murphy is to affect an imperturbable self-restraint consistent with her own aristocratic breeding (*CP,* 109). Yeats masculinizes that breeding, characterizing it in term of "honour," as opposed to say grace or propriety, so that the discipline Gregory is urged to exercise under duress will resonate as strenuous even heroic ("a harder thing / Than triumph"), as opposed to merely well mannered. The iteration (in the Derridean sense) of his first injunction, "Be secret and take defeat" (*CP,* 2), in his last injunction, "Be secret and exult" (*CP,* 14), at once emphasizes the redoubled strain such effort will cost her and marks the transformative effect it will produce: outward, material failure, borne in a noble fashion and with the proper sense of commitment, constitutes and breeds in its turn spiritual triumph. Is this not the moral of the Sovereignty Drama in a different ethnic key?

Yeats's note to the poem puts a "muscular" construction on the brand of *ascesis* he commends to and reveres in his friend (*CP,* 458). Whereas the tribunes of "political Ireland," like the "brazen throat" who had slandered Gregory (*CP,* 3), mistakenly equate civic virtue with the ventilation of approved passions and opinions, the "few educated" elite, like Gregory herself, apprehend "the futility of all discipline that is not of the whole being," a phrase evocative of Charles Kingsley's previously cited insistence on "the divineness of the whole manhood" under a similar disciplinary regime. For Yeats, as for Kingsley, such comprehensive self-containment did not weaken but rather sharpened and enhanced the emotions being curbed. Indeed, the structure of "To a Friend" reflects the perpetual motion mechanism of sublimation outlined in the introduction to this book. The self-control needed to "be secret and take defeat" functions to convert the sober feelings of justified grievance into a manic jubilation, the fruits of one's fidelity to a rigorous code of honor:

> like a laughing string
> Whereon mad fingers play
> Amid a place of stone. (*CP,* 10–12)

If the stone of personal stoicism whets the antic play of passion, the exultation feeds in turn into the commandment "Be secret" and fuels the power to keep it, to perform the thing "most difficult" (*CP,* 16). By selecting music, a ready metaphor of verse, for the figural medium of this psychoethical dynamic, Yeats calls to mind how his poetic invocation duplicates the logic of his pragmatic injunction. His acceptance of defeat in Lady Gregory's name lodges claims to a dignity both personal and tribal that vindicates a counterbalancing assertion of "triumph." Yeats thus achieves the characteristic stylistic tension of his later work, between abjection and aggression, of which Lady Gregory is in this case not the object but the surrogate.

The poem "To a Shade" extends this play of surrogacy in the process of extending Yeats's contribution to the grand mythos of Parnell (*CP,* 110–11). As chapter 1 indicated, Yeats consistently enshrined Parnell as the very abstract of high-Victorian manliness, a stalwart of fierce passion rigorously controlled by a formidable will. Yeats was not slow to stitch this estimable image into the fabric of the Protestant ascendancy virtue he spins, under the impress of the courtier, in the aftermath of the Synge debate. Indeed, Yeats's cited Abbey lecture lamenting the rise of demotic leadership in Ireland receives alternative but uncannily similar expression in *Interviews and Recollections,* where Yeats specifically offers Parnell as the prime example of what has gone forfeit in the process: "When I was a young lad, Ireland obeyed a few leaders. . . . [O]rganized opinions of societies and coteries has been put in the place of these leaders. . . . [I]nstead of a Parnell, a Stevens, or a Butt, we must obey the demands of a common place and ignorant people."[8] These would be the same Catholic masses whose "formlessness" and failure of "[Protestant] self conquest," gave them over to "the unworthy instruments of violence and tyranny" (*EI,* 227).

That Yeats saw the Uncrowned King as a uniquely effective counterweight to Irish mob psychology may be gleaned from the famous episode where he stilled an unruly crowd by slowly, hypnotically incanting the name Charles . . . Stewart . . . Parnell over and over again before speaking on an entirely disparate topic.[9] In doing so, not only did Yeats mobilize Parnell as a symbolic instrument of mass affective regulation, an icon of self-possession with which the crowd might identify, but his gambit actually replicated Parnell's rhetorical gesture in announcing the newly devised strategy of boycott or "moral Coventry." As we saw in chapter 1, during that speech at Ennis Parnell deliberately stoked in order to personally quell the violence of the crowd, thus staging his own manly discipline and his exercise thereof on behalf of the Irish people. Yeats's appropriation of the name Parnell as a means of crowd (self-)control thus serves to reprise, in the historical unconscious, Parnell's own mode of public address and, with it, the gendered logic of his leadership.

Like any performative iteration, however, this one bears within itself a crucial element of difference. Because the mystique of Parnell was pegged so closely to traits of mind or temperament identified with the Anglo-Protestant background, their invocation by an increasingly vocal cotribalist like Yeats, under charged ethno-sectarian circumstances, had the aim of transmuting that legendary *personal* charisma into a select *cultural* legacy, something on which to prop the crumbling, rearguard authority of settler nationalism. It is precisely to encompass this sort of mutually reinforcing relationship of present to past that "To a Shade" features both the Ode convention of calling upon or calling down the god or commanding spirit, in this case Parnell, and the strikingly unorthodox device of bidding that god to depart (*CP*, 110).

The first of the three verse movements turns on an ironic conceit: Parnell has "revisited" Dublin a wasting specter ("thin shade"), but, as his symbolic itinerary indicates, he remains a more robust specimen of manliness than his living political progeny. He begins his undead tour by "look[ing] upon [his] monument" (*CP*, 2), a paean in stone to the sense of national self-possession he embodied. But so feckless is the Irish-Ireland that succeeded him, Yeats implies, that the monument itself has gone unpaid for, and hence been left an unacknowledged cipher of stubborn colonial dependency. Next, Parnell takes in the imposing townhouses of Dublin. Monuments in their own right to the Georgian zenith of Ascendancy culture, the mansions now loom as concrete analogues of Parnell himself, in his personification of the last great era of Anglo-Irish clout. The houses "put on" a "gaunt . . . majesty" when "the day is spent" just like the "thin shade" has now that his day is done (*CP*, 3, 6). But just as the grandeur of the Parnell legend hides from memory the squalid turbulence of his inner circle—particularly its Catholic members—concerning his scandal and fall, so these twilit edifices mask from view the squalid turbulence of the tenement life which, as Yeats well knew, had come in recent years to teem within their walls (which is why the houses are said to "put on" their "majesty" in the dusk, like an actor's paint or makeup).[10] The corruption of the party discipline that Parnell had instituted finds its contemporary avatar in a corruption of the political machine tasked with carrying out the nationalist policies of urban renewal, as dramatized in Fred Ryan's *Laying the Foundations* and, later, in Oliver St. John Gogarty's *Blight*.[11]

It should be noted that Yeats shrewdly leaves the latter analogies latent in, inferable from, the very images that cloak them. He crafts thereby a poetic manner answerable to the crepuscular cityscape depicted, a kind of "darkness visible" of the word. More important, his method evinces the restraint-in-opposition that he has found sadly lacking in contemporary Irish-Ireland, beginning with the Parnell affair itself. By passing this manliness deficit in silence, remarking it only by omission, his verse accrues a "muscular" stylistic decorum of its own. Yeats thus manages to translate the aesthetic theory of "Poetry and Tradition"—that is, style is the expressive correlative of "courtesy and self-possession" in "life"— into a poetic practice focused on just such virtues.

The second verse movement specifies the manly cachet of Parnell, passion attempered to public service, by way of a proxy, Hugh Lane, whose proposed donation of artworks to Dublin proves him to be of the same noble "kind," that is, an ethic or class type troped as an ethical or cultural exemplar. The relationship of Parnell to Lane is triangulated by the conservative mogul William Martin

Murphy (Lady Gregory's antagonist in "To a Friend"), whose demagogic part in bringing down Parnell is now compounded by his fulminations against Lane and his aesthetic largesse. Murphy's first offense, which Yeats took as typifying the Catholic bourgeoisie, had demonstrated "how base at moments of excitement are minds without culture."[12] That is to say, with only the slightest shift in vernacular, how base are strong emotions without the cultivated ability to curb, canalize, and sublimate them—how "base" is the display of unmanliness. Considered on these lines, Murphy's second offense is graver still. More than a damaging failure of "courtesy and self-possession," the capitalist's obstruction of the Lane bequest worked to forestall the future cultivation of these courtier-like attributes in the Irish public:

> what, had they only known,
> Had given their children's children loftier thought,
> Sweeter emotion, working in their veins
> Like gentle blood. (*CP*, 11–14)

But on this score, Yeats's case against Murphy contains a further dimension as well, hidden just below the surface of the poem.

In August 1913 Murphy issued a plausible, if "philistine," plea of material priority in justifying the rejection of Lane's offer: "I would rather see in the city of Dublin one block of sanitary houses at low rents replacing a reeking slum than all of the pictures of Corot and Degas ever painted."[13] His antielitist argument against Yeats and company points to constraints upon the evolution of Dublin life that were far more immediately disabling than the dearth of high art. By September, however, Murphy had commenced the infamous lockout of the tram workers' union (Irish Transport and General Workers) and extended it to the nonaligned United Builders Labor Union, in pursuit of a total war strategy against Irish labor. With these steps, he became culpable for a further dramatic deterioration of that "reeking slum" he had deplored. Yeats's uncharacteristic decision to inscribe an *exact* date, September 29, 1913, into the permanent textual apparatus of "To a Shade" serves to bring this historical framework into play. Sending the reader back to the start of the poem, the dating locates Parnell's spectral return amid a lockout that in effect reversed his signature protest strategy, the boycott; brings to mind the presently worsening plight of many living in those old slum mansions; and hints at the hypocrisy of Murphy's stated objection to the Lane gallery. But more than that, the introduction of the lockout builds upon the thematically central analogies established in verse 1. Just as Parnell is to the outside of the houses, the "gaunt . . . majesty" of each surviving as a memory of past Anglo-Protestant greatness, so Murphy is to the inside of the houses, his moral degradation corresponding with and even causing the physical and cultural degradation of their poorest inhabitants. This analogy opens in turn upon a still broader parallel that might be understood to define the agenda of the poem as a whole. Yeats again seeks to leverage the personal mystique of Parnell into a legacy of Ascendancy influence, mediated by fellow traveler Hugh Lane and capable of diffusing an air of manliness throughout the Irish people-nation. In symmetrical antithesis, Murphy is presented as trying to extend his past, animus-driven attack on the failing Parnell ("Your enemy" [*CP*, 17]) into a counterlegacy, likewise mediated by the figure of Hugh Lane, whereby the Ascendancy's leadership, cultural as well as political, would be discredited once and for all and their transmission of the "root" values of civic manliness would be aborted.

The passage from verse movement 2 to verse movement 3 testifies to the outright triumph of Murphy's campaign and the corresponding depletion of the forces of gentility. In urging Parnell "Away, away" to the grave (*CP*, 27), Yeats all but confesses the rout of the Anglo-Irish mandarins, whose sociocultural guidance now seemed as unwelcome in Éire as their canons of merit were unappreciated. Indeed, the first lines of the poem concede that Yeats, regretfully, has come not to praise Parnell but to bury him and all he represents decently. No less than Marc Anthony's ironic eulogy of Caesar, however, Yeats's valedictory carries a double valence, both surrender in the present and assertiveness for the future. Yeats warns Parnell, "The time for you to taste of that salt breath / And listen at the corners has not come" (*CP*, 24–25), implying that it is *to come*. He would, further, see Parnell "safer in the tomb" (*CP*, 27), as though sheltered for a later and perhaps triumphant return. In both turns of phrase, Yeats appears to refuse the notorious messianism surrounding Parnell—the notion that he was not really in his coffin, that he would return again—only to entertain it at a collective level, as the preservation of a tribal creed of which Parnell was the latest apotheosis and the future auditor ("To . . . listen at the corners"). Insofar as Yeats's aristocratic code demands grace in defeat, the keynote of "To a Friend," the ghost of Parnell must be laid to rest once more, if only to preserve his dignity. But insofar as that code also mandates indomitability in defeat, the spirit of Parnell must be sustained intact, as the shared dignity of his ethnos, "one of the great stocks of Europe," as Yeats had it.[14]

In thus marrying resignation with resiliency, well-bred control of personal and political passion with its proud ineradicability, "To a Shade" sets the tone for the great Big House and Ascendancy verse of Yeats's later career: "The Tower," "Ancestral Houses," "My House," "In Memory of Eva Gore-Booth and Con Markievicz," "Coole Park 1929," "The Municipal Gallery Re-visited," "The Black Tower," and, of course, "Parnell's Funeral." In that last obscure elegy (*CP*, 279–80), the shooting star marking the interment of Parnell at Glasnevin in verse 1 enters into secular association with the star of Bethlehem in verse 3, thanks to an extended communion ritual involving the symbolic ingestion of Parnell's heart.

One by one, the leaders of the new Irish Free State had the chance but declined to eat of this totemic organ emblematic of the Chief's mettle. In metaphorical terms, they squandered the opportunity to rise above the wild yet feminized "rage," the "*Hysterica passio,*" of the "crowd" they would rule:

> Had de Valera eaten Parnell's heart
> No loose-lipped demagogue had won the day,
> No civil rancour torn the land apart. (*CP,* 19–29, 33–35)

In refusing to eat Parnell's heart, they had failed to partake of the tragic, virilizing solitude that had "enriched [the] blood" of the Anglo-Irish community dating back to the "dark grove" of the Dean of Saint Patrick, Jonathan Swift (*CP,* 41–42). The name for what this communion still promises, then, what is still to be received, is none other than manhood. For if "the root of manhood is courtesy and courage," as Yeats declaimed from the Abbey stage, then the root of *cour*tesy and *cour*age, as they appear on the written page, is precisely "heart" (*coeur* FR; *cuer* OF; *cor* L). To consume Parnell's heart as the poem exhorts is not just to renew the "shade" or spirit of Parnell but to take on "the manliness of Parnell," a manliness that could only come to the whole Irish people by way of its elite (and saving) remnant.

Notes

Introduction: The Double Bind of Irish Manhood

1. This perspective is represented in Joseph Bristow, *Empire Boys* (London: Harper Collins, 1991); J. A. Mangan, *Games Ethic and Imperialism* (New York: Viking, 1985); and J. A. Mangan, "Social Darwinism and Upper Class Education in Late Victorian and Edwardian England," in *Manliness and Morality,* edited by J. A. Mangan and James Walvin (Manchester: Manchester University Press, 1987), 135–59.

2. This perspective is represented in David Newsome, *Godliness and Good Learning* (London: Murray, 1961); Jonathan Rutherford, *Forever England* (London: Lawrence and Wishart, 1997), 11–20; James Eli Adams, *Dandies and Desert Saints: Styles of Victorian Manhood* (Ithaca: Cornell University Press, 1995), 101–48; J. R. de S. Honey, *Tom Brown's Universe* (New York: Quadrangle, 1977), 1–46; and Norman Vance, *Sinews of the Spirit* (Cambridge: Cambridge University Press, 1985).

3. Claudia Nelson, "Sex and the Single Boy," *Victorian Studies* (Summer 1989): 530–31.

4. Stefan Collini, *Public Moralists* (Oxford: Oxford University Press, 1991), 191.

5. J. S. Mill quoted in Adams, *Dandies and Desert Saints,* 9.

6. Charles Kingsley, *His Letters and Memories of His Life,* edited by Frances Kingsley (London: Macmillan, 1901), 2:62; Thomas Hughes, *The Manliness of Christ* (London: Macmillan, 1879), 21; James Fitzjames Stephens quoted in Adams, *Dandies and Desert Saints,* 108; Charles Kingsley, "The Courage of the Savior," in *Village and County Sermons* (London: Parker, 1849), 184.

7. Charles Kingsley, *Letters,* edited by F. Kingsley (London: Macmillan, 1901), 1:161.

8. David Rosen, "The Volcano and the Cathedral," in *Muscular Christianity,* edited by Donald Hall (Cambridge: Cambridge University Press, 1996), 21–22.

9. Kaja Silverman, *Male Subjectivity at the Margins* (New York: Routledge, 1992), 44.

10. Jacques Lacan, *Ecrits: A Selection* (New York: Norton, 1977), 288; Slavoj Zizek, *The Sublime Object of Ideology* (New York: Verso, 1989), 70–73.

11. For the most notable elaboration of the multiplicity thesis, see Norman Vance, "The Ideal of Manliness," in *The Victorian Public School,* edited by Brian Simon and Ian Bradley (Dublin: Gill and Macmillan, 1975), 115–28.

12. See Nelson, "Sex and the Single Boy"; and Bristow, *Empire Boys.*

13. Like all self-legitimating ideological formations, manliness depended for its operation upon a *petitio principii.* Its conjunctive profile was ultimately the effect of circular assumptions. Manliness could authorize or emblematize fitness for freedom only on the condition that enfranchisement has already been attained in some socially telling fashion.

14. For "seminal fluids" in Carlyle, see Thomas Carlyle, *Past and Present* (Boston: Houghton Mifflin, 1965), 195–205. For "liveliness" in Arnold, see Newsome, *Godliness and Good Learning,* 207. For "beastliness" in Baden-Powell, see Tim Jeal, *Baden-Powell* (London: Hutchinson, 1989), 89.

15. The best-known articulation of that break is in Newsome, *Godliness and Good Learning,* 195–239.

16. Donald Hyman, *Empire and Sexuality* (Manchester: Manchester University Press, 1991), 72; Kitson Clark, *The English Inheritance* (London: SCM, 1950), 143.

17. Thomas Hughes, *Tom Brown at Oxford* (1861; reprint, London: Macmillan, 1929), 99.

18. See J. A. Mangan, *Athleticism in the Victorian and Edwardian Public Schools* (Cambridge: Cambridge University Press, 1981), 56, 22, 43; Mangan, *Games Ethic and Imperialism,* 49; Newsome, *Godliness and Good Learning,* 211.

19. J. A. Mangan, "Athleticism," in *The Victorian Public School,* edited by Simon and Bradley, 154–57.

20. Honey, *Tom Brown's Universe,* 113.

21. Ibid., 111.

22. Geoffrey Best, "Militarism and the Public School," in *The Victorian Public School,* edited by Simon and Bradley, 138.

23. Mark Girouard, *The Return to Camelot* (New Haven: Yale University Press, 1983), 169–71, 253–57. See also Jeffrey Richards, "Passing the Love of Men," in *Manliness and Morality,* edited by Mangan and Walvin, 100–101; and Allen Warren, "Popular Manliness," in ibid., 200–201.

24. Adams, *Dandies and Desert Saints,* 7.

25. Herbert Sussman speaks of Carlylean manliness as a "process . . . of marshalling tense psychic equilibrium" (*Victorian Masculinities* [Cambridge: Cambridge University Press, 1995], 28).

26. Kingsley, *Letters,* 1:161.

27. Samuel Smiles, *Self-Help* (New York: Harper, 1876), 254; Charles Kingsley, *The Life and Works of Charles Kingsley* (London: Macmillan, 1902), 5:19.

28. L. P. Curtis, *Anglo-Saxons and Celts* (Bridgeport, Conn.: University of Bridgeport Press, 1968), 70, 140.

29. See Kelly Boyd, *Manliness and the Boys' Story Paper in Britain* (New York: Palgrave, 2003), 68. This suitability was celebrated in a famous speech by J. E. C. Weldon to the Royal Colonial Institute. See Mangan, *Games Ethic and Imperialism,* 45.

30. Hughes, *The Manliness of Christ,* 23.

31. Circulated in this way, through the negative space of subdominance, the Englishman's fitness for freedom passed seamlessly into a fitness for rule.

32. George Mosse, *The Image of Man* (New York: Oxford University Press, 1996), 58.

33. Edward Said, *Orientalism* (New York: Vintage, 1979), 7.

34. Donald Hall, "The Making and Unmaking of Monsters," in *Muscular Christianity,* edited by Hall, 51–55.

35. Said, *Orientalism,* 113–201.

36. For an analysis of Ireland as a "metrocolonial" society, see my *Dracula's Crypt: Bram Stoker, Irishness, and the Question of Blood* (Champaign: University of Illinois Press, 2002).

37. See, for example, L. P. Curtis, *Anglo-Saxons and Celts;* L. P. Curtis, *Apes and Angels* (Newton Abbott: David and Charles, 1971); Liz Curtis, *Nothing but the Same Old Story* (London: IOI, 1983); Seamus Deane, "Civilians and Barbarians," in *Ireland's Field Day* (Notre Dame: University of Notre Dame Press, 1986), 33–42; Marjorie Howes, *Yeats's Nations* (Cambridge: Cambridge University Press, 1996); and Joseph Valente, "The Myth of Sovereignty: Gender in the Literature of Irish Nationalism," *ELH* 61 (1994): 189–210. In this regard, it is interesting to note that the leaders of the Chartists happened to be Irishmen, Fergus O'Connor and Joseph O'Brien.

38. Richard Ned Lebow, *White Britain and Black Ireland* (Philadelphia: Institute for the Study of Human Issues, 1976), 27.

39. Oliver MacDonagh writes, "The sexual image was in constant use in nineteenth and early twentieth century England to express the dominator's sense of the relationship between the two islands—with perhaps the Gates [Home Rule] Acts dimly perceived as a sort of counterpart to the Married Woman's Property Acts" (*States of Mind* [London: Allen and Unwin, 1983], 54–55). As the reference to the Married Woman's Property Acts indicates, the analogy also served to express a gendered sense of the geopolitical spheres of activity occupied by England and Ireland. A superpower, England moved in the geopolitical equivalent of the male public sphere as a citizen of the world. A domestic colony, literally, Ireland represented the imperialist equivalent of home ties, John Bull's ball and chain, the most troublesome yet least dispensable of his possessions.

40. Liz Curtis, *Same Old Story,* 47–48.

41. Sussman, *Victorian Masculinities,* 21–22.

42. A. P. Stanley, *Arnold's Life and Correspondence* (London: T. Fellowes, 1858), 1:200, 2:17.

43. Matthew Arnold, *The Study of Celtic Literature* (London: Smith Edder, 1902), 90.

44. L. P. Curtis, *Anglo-Saxons and Celts,* 140; Liz Curtis, *Same Old Story,* 57.

45. Quoted in L. P. Curtis, *Anglo-Saxons and Celts,* 54.

46. Hughes, *Tom Brown at Oxford,* 101–8.

47. Quoted in Liz Curtis, *Same Old Story,* 60. Personal relations between some of these figures at once drew upon and consolidated their dedication to manly self-fashioning. For example, Charles Kingsley first met Thomas Hughes at Oxford, where the latter was taking a "young Matthew Arnold out for clod dip every morning" (Girouard, *The Return to Camelot,* 136).

48. L. P. Curtis, *Apes and Angels,* 100.

49. Ibid., 37.

50. Ibid., 25, 41.

51. L. P. Curtis, *Anglo-Saxons and Celts,* 134.

52. Honey, *Tom Brown's Universe,* 33.

53. James Joyce, *A Portrait of the Artist as a Young Man* (New York: Penguin, 1968), 7–59.

54. As if to illustrate this brand of internal exclusion, the English conferred upon their most unmanly youth the Irish name hooligans, which of course remains current today.

55. Sean Ryder, "Gender and the Discourse of 'Young Ireland' Nationalism," in *Gender and Colonialism,* edited by T. Foley et al. (Galway: Galway University Press, 1995), 218.

56. C. P. Duffy, "Advice to the People in October '43," reprinted in *Voice of the Nation* (Dublin: James Duffy, 1844), 183.

57. See L. P. Curtis, *Apes and Angels,* 85–87. Tenniel's drawings of a dependent, even cowering, Erin (figures 1–2) play upon this dilemma.

58. L. P. Curtis, *Anglo-Saxons and Celts,* 102.

59. Thomas Davis, "Memorials of Wexford," in *Literary and Historical Essays* (Dublin: James Duffy, 1846), 104–7.

60. Ashis Nandy, *The Intimate Enemy* (Oxford: Oxford University Press, 1983), 7.

61. For this Fenian vocabulary, see Toby Joyce, "Ireland's Trained and Marshalled Manhood," in *Gender Perspectives in Nineteenth Century Ireland,* edited by Margaret Kelleher and James H. Murphy (Dublin: Irish Academic Press, 1998), 70–80. Joyce fails to recognize the Fenians' motivated misreading of the concept of manhood because he does not measure it against any wider usage.

62. Ibid., 73.

63. Ibid., 78.

64. L. P. Curtis, *Apes and Angels,* 17–20.

65. By this point it will be seen how my sense of the sexual ethnologies of colonial Ireland significantly complicates and volatilizes the dichotomies presented in Deane, "Civilians and Barbarians," 33–42.

66. Zizek, *Sublime Object of Ideology,* 30–33.

Chapter 1: The Manliness of Parnell

1. R. F. Foster, *Paddy and Mr. Punch* (London: Penguin, 1993), 40.

2. F. S. L. Lyons, *Charles Stewart Parnell* (New York: Oxford University Press, 1977), 616. In a similar fashion, R. F. Foster claims, "Irish history in the 1880's and 1890's is inextricably linked with the personality of one man [Parnell]," without adducing an analytic frame that might qualify the power of that "personality" (*Modern Ireland, 1600-1972* [New York: Penguin, 1988], 400).

3. See especially F. S. L. Lyons, "The Parnell Theme in Literature," in *Place, Personality, and the Irish Writer,* edited by A. Carpenter (New York: Harper and Row, 1977), 70–74.

4. T. P. O'Connor, *Memoirs of an Old Parliamentarian* (London: Ernest Benn, 1929), 2:284.

5. C. C. O'Brien, *Parnell and His Party* (London: Oxford University Press, 1957), 350–51.

6. In *The Story of Ireland,* which Roy Foster credits with popularizing a potent aristocratic variant of the "Parnell Myth," Standish O'Grady insists that Parnell "was nothing of a fanatic" and "no out and out revolutionist" (*The Story of Ireland* [London: Methuen, 1894], 207, 210).

7. In making this argument, I am specifically contesting the dichotomy of a romantic and a realistic Parnell in C. O'Brien, *Parnell and His Party,* 347–54.

8. Quoted in D. George Boyce, "'The Portrait of the King Is the King,'" in *Parnell in Perspective,* edited by D. George Boyce and Alan O'Day (New York: Routledge, 1991), 295.

9. Barry O'Brien, *The Life of Charles Stewart Parnell, 1846–1891* (London: Smith Elder, 1899), 1:249, 161.

10. John Kelly, "Parnell in Irish Literature," in *Parnell in Perspective,* edited by Boyce and O'Day, 252.

11. B. O'Brien, *Life of Parnell,* 1:41, 54–55.

12. That may well be why, as T. P. O'Connor avers, his resentment of English domination—even of English condescension—is the root of the hold he exercised over Irish hearts (*Charles Stewart Parnell: A Memory* [London: Ward, Lock, Bowden, n.d.], 95).

13. B. O'Brien, *Life of Parnell,* 2:11, 1:225.

14. Lyons, *Charles Stewart Parnell,* 423.

15. William Michael Murphy, *The Parnell Myth in Irish Politics, 1891–1956* (New York: Peter Lang, 1986), 99.

16. James Loughlin, "Constructing the Political Spectacle," in *Parnell in Perspective,* edited by Boyce and O'Day, 230, 223.

17. John Tenniel's "Irish Frankenstein" can be found in L. P. Curtis, *Apes and Angels,* 43 (see intro., n. 37).

18. Thompson's "The Irish Grievance Grinder" can be found in Roy Douglas et al., *Drawing Conclusions* (Belfast: Bladstaff, 1998), 87. For the simianization of a nationalist, see L. P. Curtis, *Apes and Angels,* 54. For Parnell's comparative immunity, see ibid., 76.

19. O'Connor, *Memoirs of an Old Parliamentarian,* 1:119; O'Connor, *Charles Stewart Parnell,* 68, 98; W. Murphy, *Parnell Myth in Irish Politics,* 42. Parnell's athleticism was evidenced most plainly in his enthusiasm for cricket and cricketers, a love famously celebrated as the very essence of independent (British) manliness in no less a scriptural authority than *Tom Brown's Schooldays:* "'What a noble game it is too!' / 'Isn't it? But it's more than a game. It's an institution,' said Tom. / 'Yes,' said Arthur, 'the birthright of British boys, young and old, as *habeas corpus* and trial by jury are of British men.' / 'The discipline and reliance on one another is so valuable, I think,' said the master . . . It merges the individual into the eleven; he doesn't play that he may win, but that his side may win'" (Thomas Hughes, *Tom Brown's Schooldays* [Oxford: Oxford University Press, 1999], 354–55).

20. Lyons, *Charles Stewart Parnell,* 105; O'Grady, *The Story of Ireland,* 202, 207; Wil-

liam O'Brien, *The Parnell of Real Life* (London: T. Fisher Unwin, 1926), 5; Lyons, *Charles Stewart Parnell,* 163.

21. W. Murphy, *Parnell Myth in Irish Politics,* 81; Lyons, *Charles Stewart Parnell,* 616; B. O'Brien, *Life of Parnell,* 2:32. Michael Davitt called the "note of self-reliance" struck by Parnell "a keynote of nationhood." See W. Murphy, *Parnell Myth in Irish Politics,* 100.

22. C. O'Brien, *Parnell and His Party,* 10.

23. W. Murphy, *Parnell Myth in Irish Politics,* 74; Loughlin, "Constructing the Political Spectacle," 231.

24. Mosse, *The Image of Man,* 101 (see intro., n. 32).

25. O'Connor, *Charles Stewart Parnell,* 213; O'Connor, *Memoirs of an Old Parliamentarian,* 2:280.

26. O'Connor, *Charles Stewart Parnell,* 68.

27. B. O'Brien, *Life of Parnell,* 2:12, 1:145.

28. Lyons, "Parnell Theme in Literature," 80; W. B. Yeats, *Autobiographies* (New York: Scribner, 1999), 191; Kelly, "Parnell in Irish Literature," 262.

29. W. Murphy, *Parnell Myth in Irish Politics,* 64; Lyons, *Charles Stewart Parnell,* 613. Sympathetic political caricatures of Parnell at his zenith helped to transpose the personal testimony of his Laocoon-like aura into a fully public or mass image. Cartoons focusing on Parnell's successes in defending himself against *The Times*'s sedition charges ("Loaded with Infamy," "Hide and Seek," "In a Fair Field in Bonnie Scotland," figure 7) show his body as not simply powerful but bursting with the suppressed volatility of its power, a coiled spring, and the same sense of manfully checked aggression marks his facial features as well.

30. W. Murphy, *Parnell Myth in Irish Politics,* 78.

31. Paul Bew, *Charles Stewart Parnell* (Dublin: Gill and Macmillan, 1978), 67; Conn, "The Irish Sphinx," *Weekly Irish Times,* September 29, 1883.

32. W. Murphy, *Parnell Myth in Irish Politics,* 77, 79.

33. B. O'Brien, *Life of Parnell,* 1:137, 295, 146.

34. O'Connor, *Memoirs of an Old Parliamentarian,* 1:114. A Fenian representative offers a similar account in B. O'Brien, *Life of Parnell,* 1:107.

35. W. O'Brien, *Parnell of Real Life,* 20. Yeats quoted in James Pethica, ed., *Lady Gregory's Diaries, 1892–1902* (New York: Oxford University Press, 1996), 169.

36. Loughlin, "Constructing the Political Spectacle," 223.

37. C. O'Brien, *Parnell and His Party,* 245.

38. For the disappointment in Parnell's oratory, both on the stump and in Parliament, see Alan O'Day, "Parnell: Orator and Speaker," in *Parnell in Perspective,* edited by Boyce and O'Day, 201–20.

39. O'Grady, *The Story of Ireland,* 210. It is perhaps worth noting that the emancipator, Daniel O'Connell, who most famously embodied the loquacious brand of leadership that Parnell eschewed, closed his career weeping futilely on the floor of Parliament for Britain to save Ireland from the Famine. His last performance was not only ridiculed as it occurred, it gave hostages to the stereotypical linkage of volubility, feminine over-emotionality, and Irishness that Parnell played off.

40. Lyons, *Charles Stewart Parnell,* 246.

41. B. O'Brien, *Life of Parnell,* 2:28.

42. O'Connor, *Charles Stewart Parnell,* 163.

43. B. O'Brien, *Life of Parnell,* 1:184.

44. O'Connor, *Charles Stewart Parnell,* 65.

45. B. O'Brien, *Life of Parnell,* 1:237.

46. O'Day, "Parnell: Orator and Speaker," in *Parnell in Perspective,* edited by Boyce and O'Day, 215.

47. The indissoluble blend of imperial presumption and nationalist purpose instinct in this gendered stratagem speaks to the peculiarly Ascendancy cast of Parnell's leadership.

48. The political cartoon "A Game Two Can Play At" captures this quality of suspensive force.

49. See B. O'Brien, *Life of Parnell,* 1:107.

50. Thus, in Joyce's classic tale of Parnellism undone, "Ivy Day in the Committee Room," the Tory Crofton and the nationalist Henchy join in respecting the deceased leader for being "the only man who could keep that bag of cats in order" (*Dubliners* [New York: Penguin, 1993], 133).

51. B. O'Brien, *Life of Parnell,* 1:312.

52. Ibid., 160.

53. Ibid., 146–47.

54. Roy Foster, *Charles Stewart Parnell: The Man and His Family* (Sussex: Harvester, 1976), 265.

55. Robert Kee, *The Laurel and the Ivy* (London: Hamish Hamilton, 1993), 329; Lyons, *Charles Stewart Parnell,* 178–80.

56. Alvin Jackson, *Ireland, 1798–1998: Politics and War* (London: Blackwell, 1989), 122.

57. Ibid.

58. Edward Norman, *A History of Modern Ireland* (Coral Gables: University of Miami Press, 1971), 210.

59. O'Connor, *Memoirs of an Old Parliamentarian,* 1:276; Lyons, *Charles Stewart Parnell,* 215–16; Foster, *Charles Stewart Parnell,* 271–72.

60. Jules Abels, *The Parnell Tragedy* (New York: Macmillan, 1966), 162.

61. B. O'Brien, *Life of Parnell,* 1:329.

62. Foster, *Charles Stewart Parnell,* 280.

63. John Howard Parnell, *Charles Stewart Parnell: A Memoir* (New York: Henry Holt, 1914), 205.

64. O'Connor, *Memoirs of an Old Parliamentarian,* 1:329–30.

65. Katherine O'Shea, *Charles Stewart Parnell* (New York: Doran, 1914), 1:245.

66. B. O'Brien, *Life of Parnell,* 1:364; Jackson, *Ireland, 1798–1998,* 124.

67. Liz Curtis, *The Cause of Ireland* (Belfast: Beyond the Pale, 1994), 112.

68. Jackson, *Ireland, 1798–1998,* 132.

69. Paul Bew, *Conflict and Conciliation in Ireland* (New York: Oxford University Press, 1987), 119.

70. Foster, *Charles Stewart Parnell,* 269.

71. Liz Curtis, *The Cause of Ireland,* 113.

72. Giorgio Agamben, *Homo Sacer: Sovereign Power and Bare Life* (Stanford: Stanford University Press, 1998), 15–29.

73. B. O'Brien, *Life of Parnell,* 1:364.

74. E. Norman, *History of Modern Ireland,* 206.

75. Joyce Marlowe, *The Uncrowned Queen of Ireland* (New York: Dutton, 1975), 259.

76. B. O'Brien, *Life of Parnell,* 2:254.

77. Emmett Larkin, *The Roman Catholic Church in Ireland and the Fall of Parnell* (Chapel Hill: University of North Carolina Press, 1979), 241.

78. Bew, *Charles Stewart Parnell,* 114.

79. F. S. L. Lyons, *The Fall of Parnell* (London: Routledge, 1960), 148, 147.

80. Marlowe, *Uncrowned Queen of Ireland,* 263.

81. "A Startling Contrast" can be found in Lawrence McBride, "Nationalist Political Illustrations and the Parnell Myth," in *Images, Icons, and the Irish Nationalist Imagination,* edited by Lawrence McBride (Dublin: Four Courts, 1999), 85. I am also indebted to Professor McBride's summary of the cartoons' details.

82. Marlowe, *Uncrowned Queen of Ireland,* 254.

83. Richard Davis, *Arthur Griffith and Non-violent Sinn Fein* (Dublin: Anvil, 1974), 7, 45.

Chapter 2: Afterlives of Parnell

1. Yeats, *Autobiographies,* 410 (see chap. 1, n. 28).

2. Roy Foster, *W. B. Yeats: A Life* (New York: Oxford University Press, 1997), 115.

3. For Fenian influence in the GAA, see W. F. Mandle, "The I.R.B. and the Beginnings of the Gaelic Athletic Association," in *Reactions to Irish Nationalism, 1865–1914,* edited by Alan O'Day (London: Hambledon, 1987).

4. Jeffrey Richards, "Irish Sport and Empire," in *An Irish Empire?* edited by K. Jeffrey (New York: Manchester University Press, 1996), 62.

5. *GAA 1907–8 Annual* quoted in W. F. Mandle, *The Gaelic Athletic Association and Irish Nationalist Politics, 1884–1924* (London: Gill and Macmillan, 1987), 155.

6. Ibid.; Charles Kickham, "On Some of Our Ancient Games and Pastimes," in *Gaelic Athletic Association for the Preservation and Cultivation of National Pastimes* (Dublin: Cahill, 1987), 27–36; Mandle, *Gaelic Athletic Association,* 155.

7. *United Ireland,* October 11, 1884, 5.

8. Celt, "Athletic Ireland II," *Sinn Fein,* January 25, 1908, 3; S. B. W., "Irish Athleticism," *Sinn Fein,* May 1, 1909, 3.

9. Celt, "Athletic Ireland I," *Sinn Fein,* January 18, 1908, 3.

10. Celt, "Muscular Sinn Fein," *Sinn Fein,* June 13, 1908, 4.

11. Amerigen, *Sinn Fein,* December 17, 1904, 4.

12. Marilyn Silverman, *An Irish Working Class* (Toronto: University of Toronto Press, 2001), 251.

13. The enduring relationship of the GAA to the Irish working class is attested by the prominent GAA officials assisting union members during the Dublin Lockout of 1913. See Padriag Yeates, *Dublin: Lockout 1913* (New York: Palgrave, 2000), 319, 482, 500.

14. Celt, "Athletic Ireland II," *Sinn Fein,* January 25, 1908, 3.

15. Marcus de Burcas, *The GAA: A History* (London: Gill and Macmillan, 1980), 62; Mandle, *Gaelic Athletic Association,* 85–86.

16. Lacan states that the phallus can only perform its function when veiled, a proposition that explains the added power given the phallic camạns by their coverings.

17. Frederic Jameson, *The Political Unconscious* (Ithaca: Cornell University Press, 1981), 73.

18. *United Irishmen,* October 3, 1903, 4.

19. R. Davis, *Griffith and Non-violent Sinn Fein,* 99, 45 (see chap. 1, n. 83).

20. Celt, "Muscular Sinn Fein," 3–4.

21. R. Davis, *Griffith and Non-violent Sinn Fein,* 35; P. S. O'Hegarty Papers, *Report of 1905 Cumann Na nGaedhal Convention,* quoted in ibid., 28; Celt, "Muscular Sinn Fein," 3–4; *The Peasant,* September 14, 1907, 5.

22. R. Davis, *Griffith and Non-violent Sinn Fein,* 103.

23. Arthur Griffith, *United Irishmen,* June 3, 1903, 2.

24. Lady Gregory, "Arabi and His Household," *The Times,* October 23, 1882, 4.

25. Mary Lou Kohfeldt, *Lady Gregory: The Woman behind the Renaissance* (New York: Atheneum, 1985), 79.

26. For Gregory's position at this time, see Greg Winston, "Redefining Coole: Lady Gregory, Class Politics, and the Land War," *Colby Quarterly* 37, no. 3 (2001): 20; Kohfeldt, *Lady Gregory,* 79–81.

27. Pethica, introduction to *Lady Gregory's Diaries, 1892–1902,* edited by Pethica, xvi (see chap. 1, n. 35). Winston contends this document shows how deeply "entrenched in status quo positions regarding land ownership" Gregory remained ("Redefining Coole," 216).

28. Lady Gregory, *Seventy Years* (New York: Macmillan, 1974), 310.

29. Kohfeldt, *Lady Gregory,* 123; Lady Gregory, *Seventy Years,* 310.

30. Pethica, introduction to *Lady Gregory's Diaries,* edited by Pethica, xvii.

31. Lady Gregory, *Our Irish Theatre* (Gerralds Cross: Colin Smythe, 1972), 141. See also Kohfeldt, *Lady Gregory,* 87.

32. Mary Lou Kohfeldt, "The Cloud of Witnesses," in *Lady Gregory: Fifty Years After,* edited by A. Saddlemeyer and C. Smythe (Gerrards Cross: Colin Smythe, 1987), 60. See also Leigh T. Partington, "Roughly Hammered Links," *South Carolina Review* 32, no. 1 (1999): 23.

33. Lady Gregory, "The Felons of Our Land," *Cornhill Magazine,* May 1900, 622–34; Lady Gregory, *Lady Gregory's Diaries, 1892–1902,* 267.

34. Lady Gregory, *Seventy Years,* 310. See Kohfeldt, "The Cloud of Witnesses," 61–62; Elizabeth Longford, "Lady Gregory and Wilfred Scawen Blunt," in *Lady Gregory: Fifty Years After,* 91–93.

35. Pethica, introduction to *Lady Gregory's Diaries,* edited by Pethica, xvii; Lucy McDiarmid, "The Demotic Lady Gregory," in *High and Low Moderns,* edited by M. DiBattista and Lucy McDiarmid (New York: Oxford University Press, 1996), 218–27.

36. Slavoj Zizek, *For They Know Not What They Do* (New York: Verso, 1991), 49–50.

37. John Kelly, "'Friendship Is the Only House I Have,'" in *Lady Gregory: Fifty Years After,* 189; Lady Gregory, *Seventy Years,* 310.

38. Quoted in Liz Curtis, *The Cause of Ireland,* 140 (see chap. 1, n. 67).

39. Lady Gregory, *Our Irish Theatre,* 20.

40. The chivalric ideal took on exaggerated force in the later nineteenth century thanks to a medievalist revival in Great Britain. In a subsequent chapter, I will discuss at length the influence of this revival on the masculine ideal promoted by the Irish Renaissance.

41. Pethica, introduction to *Lady Gregory's Diaries,* edited by Pethica, xvii.

42. Ibid.

43. Lady Gregory, *The Deliverer,* in *The Collected Plays of Lady Gregory,* Coole Edition (New York: Oxford University Press, 1970), 2:255–77; Lyons, *The Fall of Parnell,* 130 (see chap. 1, n. 79).

44. Lady Gregory, *Our Irish Theatre,* 59.

45. Lady Gregory, *Poets and Dreamers* (Dublin: Hodges Figgis, 1903), 98.

46. Lady Gregory, "The Felons of Our Land," 622–34; McDiarmid, "The Demotic Lady Gregory," 220–21.

47. Lady Gregory, *The Gaol Gate,* in *Collected Plays,* 2:10; Lady Gregory, *The Rising of the Moon,* in *Collected Plays,* 1:67.

48. McDiarmid, "The Demotic Lady Gregory," 213.

Chapter 3: The Mother of All Sovereignty

1. Nicholas Grene, *The Politics of Irish Drama* (Cambridge: Cambridge University Press, 1999), 64–65.

2. There may have been a pagan "cult of sacrifice," as Richard Kearney argues, but it was not a Sovereignty cult (*Transitions* [Manchester: Manchester University Press, 1988], 220–21). See also Susan Harris, *Gender and Modern Irish Drama* (Bloomingon: Indiana University Press, 2002), 58. Indeed, the invocation of such a pagan cult would cut against the cherished notion of a "divinely instilled [Celtic]morality, which the sacrificial ethos of the Sovereignty was seen to corroborate" (Sinead Matter, *Science, Primitivism, and the Irish Revival* [Oxford: Clarendon Press, 2004], 33).

3. For a chronicle of the Medieval Revival, see Girouard, *The Return to Camelot* (see intro., n. 23). Declan Kiberd has proposed that the chivalric affectations of the Irish Revival reflect the continental influences displayed by native Gaelic poetry, specifically the "amour courteous" tradition. As we have seen, however, the imperative to self-denial and self-conquest does not form a keynote of this tradition, while it all but defines the British resuscitation of chivalry under Victoria and its later emulation in Ireland. Kiberd's later suggestion that the element of sacrifice in Irish political ideology derives from the Irish monastery seems a far more remote causal possibility than the medieval revival transpiring contemporaneously in the colonial power across the Channel. See Kiberd, *Inventing Ireland* (Cambridge: Harvard University Press, 1994), 158, 210. In his later work, Kiberd has become much more receptive to the pervasiveness of British cultural influence on Irish nationalist discourse.

4. Elizabeth Cullingford, "Thinking of Her . . . as . . . Ireland," *Textual Practice* 4 (1990):

1–21. The Hag quoted in Muirean Ni Bhrolchain, "Women in Early Irish Myths and Sagas," in *Crane Bag Book of Irish Studies,* edited by P. Hedeman and R. Kearney (Dublin: Blackwater, 1982), 525–26.

5. Cullingford, "Thinking of Her," 2. See also Mary Hedeman, "Irish Women and Irish Law," in *Crane Bag Book of Irish Studies,* edited by P. Hedeman and R. Kearney, 548–52.

6. Robert Welch, *The Abbey Theatre, 1899–1999* (Oxford: Oxford University Press, 1999), 16; William Butler Yeats (Lady Gregory), *Cathleen Ni Houlihan,* in *Modern Irish Drama,* edited by John Harrington (New York: Norton, 1991), 3–11.

7. Cullingford, "Thinking of Her," 12.

8. Joseph Plunkett, "The Little Black Rose Shall Be Red at Last," in *The 1916 Poets,* edited by D. Ryan (Westport, Conn.: Greenwood, 1979), 201.

9. I paraphrase Jacques Lacan on the "courtly woman" (*The Seminars of Jacques Lacan, Book XX: Encore* [New York: Norton, 1998], 69).

10. Patrick Pearse, *The Singer,* in *Collected Works of Padraic H. Pearse: Plays, Stories, Poems* (Dublin: Maunsel and Roberts, 1922), 42.

11. Kathryn Conrad casts this "indelible shift of emphasis" as a shift in "agency" (*Locked in the Family Cell* [Madison: University of Wisconsin Press, 2004], 11).

12. Lionel Polkington, *Theatre and the State in Twentieth Century Ireland* (London: Routledge, 2001), 18.

13. C. L. Innes, "Virgin Territories and Motherlands," *Feminist Review* 47 (1994): 10.

14. Nicholas Grene nominates her *la belle dame* (*Politics of Irish Drama,* 68).

15. Séan Moran, *Patrick Pearse and the Politics of Redemption* (Washington, D.C.: Catholic University Press, 1994), 123–24. Pearse's homosexuality has occasioned much recent debate. See Moran, *Pearse and the Politics of Redemption,* 47–51; Harris, *Gender and Modern Irish Drama,* 144–48; and Elaine Sisson, *Pearse's Patriots* (Cork: Cork University Press, 2004), 135–52.

16. Girouard, *The Return to Camelot,* 16.

17. Susan Harris argues that sacrificial rhetoric sought to outflank the British discourse pathologizing the Irish as inherently criminal and reducing Irish violence of whatever sort to a symptom of that pathology (*Gender and Modern Irish Drama,* 125–27).

18. Kingsley, *Life and Works of Kingsley,* 5:119 (see intro., n. 27).

19. Hughes, *The Manliness of Christ,* 99 (see intro., n. 6).

20. Lionel Polkington speaks to these historical events in *Theatre and the State,* 32–34.

21. Moran, *Pearse and the Politics of Redemption,* 95. For both the repetitive and the mythic as models of history, see Richard Kearney, *Transitions,* 213ff. See also Séan Moran, "Patrick Pearse and Patriotic Soteriology," in *The Irish Terrorism Experience,* edited by Y. Alexander and Alan O'Day (Dartmouth: Aldershot, 1991), 17.

22. This legacy, in turn, was deeply complicit with an Arnoldian cultural imperialism centering on the "the Celt's tragic nobility." See Rob Doggett, *Deep Rooted Things* (Notre Dame: University of Notre Dame Press, 2003), 29.

23. Eric Hobsbawm, "Introduction: Inventing Traditions," in *The Invention of Traditions,* edited by Eric Hobsbawm and T. Ranger (Cambridge: Cambridge University

Press, 1983), 1–15. Susan Harris speaks of Cathleen tapping into a "Celtic tradition of heroic failure," but there is, strictly speaking, no such thing. There is a *Celticist* tradition of Irish failure, which the Revival tapped into, creating an invented tradition at two removes (*Gender and Modern Irish Drama,* 59). Richard Kearney identifies this tradition, wrongly in my view, with "mythic logic" ("Myth and Motherland," in *Ireland's Field Day* [Notre Dame: University of Notre Dame Press, 1986], 65).

24. Harris, *Gender and Modern Irish Drama,* 128.

25. Patrick Pearse, *Political Writings and Speeches* (Dublin: Talbot, 1962), 97–99, 194–95.

26. J. J. Lee, "In Search of Patrick Pearse," in *Revising the Rising,* edited by M. Ni-Dhonnchada and T. Dorgan (Derry: Field Day, 1991), 126.

27. Hughes, *The Manliness of Christ,* esp. 145–46.

28. Girouard exhaustively canvasses the relevant details of this cultural movement in *The Return to Camelot,* 15–29, 129–45, 163–97, 219–31.

29. Ibid., 143.

30. Ibid., 225, 261.

31. Jean Baudrillard, *Towards a Political Economy of the Sign* (St. Louis: Telos, 1981), 82.

32. Nandy, *The Intimate Enemy,* 9–10 (see intro., n. 60).

33. George Bernard Shaw noted that the rebels "had fought a fair gentlemanly fight—hence the revulsion at the subsequent executions" (quoted in Declan Kiberd, "The Elephant of Revolutionary Forgetfulness," in *Revising the Rising,* 12).

34. Ann McClintock, *Imperial Leather* (New York: Routledge, 1995), 354.

35. I first introduced this motif into the criticism of the play in "The Myth of Sovereignty: Gender in the Literature of Irish Nationalism," *ELH* 61 (1994): 198–201. Susan Harris later adapted it along the lines of separate spheres ideology in *Gender and Modern Irish Drama,* 52–54. Antoinette Quinn remarks that the upstaging of a real woman by a nationalist icon was not only thematized in Cathleen but conditioned its production "in that Lady Gregory's coauthorship was ignored" ("Staging the Irish Peasant Woman," in *Interpreting Synge,* edited by Nicholas Grene [Dublin: Lilliput, 2000], 126). See also C. C. O'Brien, *Ancestral Voices* (Chicago: University of Chicago Press, 1995), 67.

36. Cullingford, "Thinking of Her," 13.

37. Robert Hogan and James Kilroy, *Laying the Foundations, 1902–4* (Atlantic Highlands, N.J.: Dolmen, 1976), 17–18.

38. Maud Gonne, *Dawn,* in *Lost Plays of the Irish Renaissance,* edited by R. Hogan and J. Kilroy (New York: Proscenium, 1970), 73–84.

39. Patrick Pearse, "I Am Ireland," in *The Collected Works of Padraic Pearse: Plays, Stories, Poems,* 323.

40. Lennox Robinson, *Patriots,* in *Selected Plays* (Washington, D.C.: Catholic University Press, 1982), 23–62.

41. Popular melodramas such as *The Colleen Bawn* and *The Shaughran* by Dion Boucicault are cases in point.

42. Patrick Pearse, "The Mother," in *Collected Works,* 115–35.

43. Rosemary Cullen Owens, *Smashing Times* (Dublin: Fleet, 1984), 35–74, 103–12; Margaret Ward, *Unmanageable Revolutionaries* (London: Pluto, 1983), 40–102; Cliona Murphy, *The Woman's Suffrage in Irish Society in the Early Twentieth Century* (Philadelphia: Temple University Press, 1989), 1–112, 100–133.

44. David Cairns and Shaun Richards touched briefly on the potential connection between the Poor Old Woman figure and the Suffrage question in "Tropes and Traps: Aspects of 'Woman' and Nationality in Twentieth Century Irish Drama," in *Gender in Irish Writing*, edited by T. O. Johnson and D. Cairns (Buckingham: Open University Press, 1991), 131.

45. David Barry, "Female Suffrage from a Catholic Standpoint," *Irish Ecclesiastical Record* 26 (1909): 295–303. Reprinted in Maria Luddy, *Women in Ireland, 1800–1918* (Cork: Cork University Press, 1995), 280–83.

46. "Kitty and the Fight for Freedom," *Catholic Bulletin*, 1912, quoted in R. Owens, *Smashing Times,* 68–70.

47. See, for example, the notorious debate between Hannah Sheehy Skeffington and "a Sinn Feiner," who warns "the suffrage for the English Parliament granted to Irish women would not make them free . . . It would only mean another chain linking another section of Ireland to England." The debate is included in full in Luddy, *Women in Ireland,* 301–4.

48. "It was necessary for the Irish party in the interest of Home Rule to save the Liberal Ministry from the disruptive effects of Woman's Suffrage": a Redmondite deputy quoted in R. Owens, *Smashing Times,* 49. For Redmond's own anti-Suffragism, see also R. Owens, *Smashing Times,* 50; and C. Murphy, *Woman's Suffrage in Irish Society,* 172–76.

49. A "Sinn Feiner," for example, calls Skeffington "a woman scrambling for her mess of pottage" (quoted in Luddy, *Women in Ireland,* 303). For a further discussion of this attitude, see C. Murphy, *Woman's Suffrage in Irish Society,* 72–76. See also Barry, "Female Suffrage," 282.

50. See Barry, "Female Suffrage," 281; and "Kitty and the Fight for Freedom," quoted in R. Owens, *Smashing Times,* 68–70.

51. John Synge, *The Shadow of the Glen,* in *Collected Plays and Poems* (London: J. M. Dent, 1996), 1–15. Arthur Griffith quoted in R. Hogan and J. Kilroy, *Laying the Foundations,* 79.

52. Quinn, "Staging the Irish Peasant Woman," 127.

53. Rob Doggett, "*In the Shadow of the Glen:* Gender, Nationalism, and 'A Woman Only,'" *ELH* 67 (2000): 1011–34; Grene, *Politics of Irish Drama,* 73; Mary Fitzgerald-Hoyt, "Death and the Colleen," in *Assessing the Achievement of J. M. Synge,* edited by A. Gonzalez (Westport, Conn.: Greenwood, 1996), 51–56; Quinn, "Staging the Irish Peasant Woman," 117–34.

54. Ben Levitas, *The Theatre of Nation* (Oxford: Clarendon Press, 2002), 88; Grene, *Politics of Irish Drama,* 51.

55. For the stakes of the New Formalism, see Marjorie Levinson, "What Is New Formalism," *PMLA* 122, no. 2 (2007): 558–69.

56. For the derivation of shadow and source story itself, see Eilis Ni Dhibnealmquist, "Synge's Use of Popular Material in *The Shadow of the Glen*," *Journal of the Folklore of Ireland Society* 58 (1990): 141–80.

57. See, for example, Christopher Murray, *Twentieth Century Irish Drama: Mirror Up to Nation* (Manchester: Manchester University Press, 1997), 75–76.

58. Quoted in Hogan and Kilroy, *Laying the Foundations*, 78.

59. Fitzgerald-Hoyt, "Death and the Colleen," 55. Indeed, this point is a bone of contention in the criticism. Kopper, for example, argues against the infidelity thesis, while Cairns and Richards assume it into evidence. Edward A. Kopper, *A J. M. Synge Literary Companion* (Westport, Conn.: Greenwood, 1988), 32; D. Cairns and S. Richards, *Writing Ireland* (Manchester: Manchester University Press, 1988), 77.

60. Quinn, "Staging the Irish Peasant Woman," 118, 127; Lacan, *Seminar of Jacques Lacan*, 73.

61. Paul Murphy, "J. M. Synge and the Pitfalls of National Consciousness," *Theatre Research International* 28 (2003): 130.

62. See Edward Hirsch, "The Imaginary Irish Peasant," *PMLA* 106 (1991): 1116–33.

63. Cairns and Richards, *Writing Ireland*, 77.

64. P. J. Matthews, *Revival* (Notre Dame: University of Notre Dame Press, 2003), 144.

65. Coilin Owens, "The Wooing of Etain: Celtic Myth and the Shadow of the Glen," in *Assessing the Achievement of J. M. Synge*, edited by Gonzalez, 63 (see chap. 3, n. 57).

66. Nicholas Grene, "Synge's *The Shadow of the Glen*: Repetition and Allusion," in *Critical Essays on John Synge*, edited by Daniel Casey (New York: G. K. Hall, 1994), 86.

67. Murray, *Twentieth Century Irish Drama*, 75–77.

68. P. Murphy, "Synge and the Pitfalls of National Consciousness," 130.

69. If, as Ann McClintock writes, "women are typically constructed as the symbolic bearer of the nation but are denied any direct relation to national agency," chivalry is the discourse pressing that construction most effectively in Revivalist Ireland (*Imperial Leather*, 354).

70. Eugene Benson, *J. M. Synge* (New York: Grove, 1983), 77.

71. Seamus Deane, *Celtic Revivals* (London: Faber and Faber, 1984), 53; Doggett, "*In the Shadow of the Glen*: Gender, Nationalism, and 'A Woman Only,'" 1014, 1026.

72. Theodor Adorno, *Aesthetic Theory* (Minneapolis: University of Minnesota Press, 1997), 32–33.

73. Ibid., 338–39.

74. Kohfeldt, *Lady Gregory*, 182, 192–93 (see chap. 2, n. 25). See also Elizabeth Cox, *Lady Gregory* (London: Macmillan, 1961), 127.

75. James Stephens, *The Charwoman's Daughter* (Dublin: Gill and Macmillan, 1912).

76. James Stephens, "Irish Englishmen," *Sinn Fein*, June 1, 1907. Stephens wrote a closely related essay entitled "Seonin" (*Sinn Fein*, April 20, 1907). Together these essays represent the most immediate ideological background for the novel. Both appear in *Uncollected Prose of James Stephens*, edited by Patricia McFate (London: Gill and Macmillan, 1983), 17–20, 26–29.

77. James Stephens, "Irish Englishmen," in *Uncollected Prose,* edited by McFate, 26.

78. Patricia McFate, *The Writing of James Stephens* (New York: St. Martin's, 1979), 24.

79. Jochen Achilles, "The Charwoman's Daughter and the Emergence of a National Psychology," *Irish University Review* 11 (1981): 186; Augustine Martin, *James Stephens: A Critical Study* (Totowa: Rowman and Littlefield, 1977), 4.

80. Achilles, "Charwoman's Daughter," 186.

81. Ibid.

82. D. M. Anderson and D. Killingray, eds., *Policing the Empire* (Manchester: Manchester University Press, 1991), 3–4.

83. Richard Hawkins, "The Irish Model and the Empire," in *Policing the Empire,* edited by Anderson and Killingray, 28–30.

84. Such condescension is of course a function of the elite caste of chivalric discourse, its manipulation of an assumed power reserve.

85. Augustine Martin, "The Poet and the Policeman," *University Review* 3 (1962): 61. The working-class experience of nationalist ferment has finally received its due in such stellar contemporary novels as *A Star Called Henry* by Roddy Doyle and *At Swim Two Boys* by Jamie O'Neill.

86. Achilles, "Charwoman's Daughter," 190.

87. James Connolly, *Socialism and Nationalism* (Dublin: Three Candles, 1948), 24, 29.

88. Patrick Pearse cherished a dream he had of a young man condemned to die and smiling at the prospect "by way of comment" (*An Macaomb* 2 [May 1913]: 4).

89. Zizek, *For They Know Not What They Do,* 49–50 (see chap. 2, n. 36).

90. Ruth Edwards, *Patrick Pearse: The Triumph of Failure* (London: Gollancz, 1977).

91. While Mrs. Makebelieve has invoked her relative, Patrick, as a potential savior in the past, it was strictly with reference to his possible return to Ireland, still unmarried. Moreover, it was always treated as still more fanciful than Mary's marriage to a lord, a mere fantasy of a fantasy.

92. Claude Levi-Strauss, *Structural Anthropology* (New York: Basic Books, 1963), 229–30; Jameson, *The Political Unconscious,* 73 (see chap. 2, n. 17).

93. Stephens quotes Matthew Arnold's famous formulation of this stereotype, "They always went forth to battle, but they always fell," in his account of the Easter Rising. "Indeed, the history of the Irish race," he proclaims, "is in that phrase" (*The Insurrection in Dublin* [New York: Macmillan, 1916], 39–40).

Chapter 4: Brothers in Arms

1. Lady Gregory, *Cuchulain at Muirthemne* (London: John Murray, 1911).

2. Declan Kiberd, *Irish Classics* (Cambridge: Harvard University Press, 2001), 403.

3. Maria Tymoczko, *Translation in a Postcolonial Context* (Manchester: St. Jerome, 1999), 66, 68, 82.

4. Ibid., 79.

5. Jeremy Lowe, "Contagious Violence and the Spectacle of Death in Táin Bó Cúailange," in *Language and Tradition in Ireland,* edited by M. Tymoczko and C. Ireland (Amherst: University of Massachusetts Press, 2003), 84–85; Joan Radner, "'Fury Destroys the World': Historical Strategy in Ireland's Ulster Epic," *Mankind Quarterly* 23 (1982): 54, 55; Daniel Melia, "Parallel Versions of 'The Boyhood Deeds of Cuchulainn,'" *Forum for Modern Language Studies* 10 (1974): 220; Lowe, "Contagious Violence," 95.

6. Jeremy Lowe, "Kicking Over the Traces: The Instability Cuchulainn," *Studia Celtica* 34 (2000): 121–24.

7. Cecile O'Rahilly, *Táin Bó Cúalnge* (Dublin: Dublin Institute for Advanced Studies, 1967), 201–2.

8. Ibid., 203–4.

9. Lowe, "Kicking Over the Traces," 124.

10. L. Winifred Faraday, *The Cattle-Raid of Cualnge* (London: Nutt, 1904), 93–94.

11. Lady Gregory, *Cuchulain at Muirthemne,* 239, 217.

12. In her book, *Pearse's Patriots: St. Enda's and the Irish Cult of Boyhood,* Elaine Sisson notes that Pearse and other Irish Nationalists borrowed from "the medieval idea of chivalry" to fashion their ideal of native masculinity, but she sees that ideal as a fully *hypermasculine* one. Sisson argues that Irish nationalists seeking hypermasculine histories of masculinity found in the *Tain* a literary epic equivalent in content and pedigree to the Arthurian cycle and deeds of male prowess of a highly exaggerated quality. She holds that the *Tain* provided Pearse with an authentic Irish source upon which to base his school's code of honor. However, far from "equivalent in content and pedigree to the Arthurian Cycle," the *Tain* displays an "ethics" that bears little similarity to "the chivalric code of the knights," which is precisely why nationalists like Pearse needed not just to borrow from the latter but to recast the former in its image. If these nationalists were merely "seeking hypermasculine theories of masculinity," as Sisson claims, they had to look no further than that "authentic" source, the *Tain* itself. It was precisely because they sought to avoid simple hypermasculinity and its animalistic entailments that they sought the imported chivalric supplement identified with contemporary manliness. Sisson, *Pearse's Patriots,* 812–13 (see chap. 3, n. 15).

13. Standish O'Grady, *The History of Ireland: The Heroic Period (1878–80)* (London: Lemma, 1970). Maria Tymoczko notes that O'Grady suppressed the warp-spasm altogether in this volume (*Translation in a Postcolonial Context,* 22–23).

14. Tymoczko, *Translation in a Postcolonial Context,* 171. She also remarks that his Irish tales form "an analogue to medieval romance."

15. Standish O'Grady, *The Coming of Cuchulain* (London: Methuen, 1894), 44, 49. O'Grady later asserts, "Intoxication was not known in the age of heroes," apparently to refute the stereotype of the Irish as inveterate drunkards (159).

16. William Thompson, *The Imagination of an Insurrection* (New York: Oxford University Press, 1967), 21.

17. Eleanor Hull, *Cuchulain: The Hound of Ulster* (London: George Harrap, 1909), 13–14.

18. Lady Gregory, *Seventy Years,* 391 (see chap. 2, n. 28). Elaine Sisson contends that "the advantage of the *Tain*" was that it predated the Arthurian cycle, so "any similar-

ity between the chivalric code of the knights and the ethics of the Fianna was easily explained by the preexistence of the latter." In addition to misplacing the Fianna in Ulster, Sisson seems to accept the revivalist metalepsis whole and ignores the newly manufactured nature of the "similarity" (*Pearse's Patriots,* 83). Sinead Matter observes that "academic Celtologists" of this same period had established to their satisfaction that "chivalric ideals" were "not Celtic but Norman in origin" (*Primitivism, Science, and the Irish Revival,* 219 [see chap. 3, n. 2]).

19. Tymoczko, *Translation in a Postcolonial Context,* 73–74.

20. Eleanor Hull, introduction to *The Cuchulinn Saga in Irish Literature* (London: Nutt, 1898), xliii; O'Rahilly, *Táin Bó Cúalnge,* 219–22; Thomas Kinsella, *The Tain* (Oxford: Oxford University Press, 1969), 181–87; Hull, introduction to *Cuchulinn Saga,* xliii.

21. Hull, *Cuchulain: The Hound of Ulster,* 140; Lady Gregory, *Cuchulain at Muirthemne,* 240.

22. Lowe, "Contagious Violence," 89.

23. Philip O'Leary, "Fir Fer: An Internalized Ethical Concept in Early Irish Literature," *Eigse* 22 (1987): 13, 1; Lowe, "Contagious Violence," 89–90; O'Leary, "Fir Fer," 1.

24. Philip O'Leary speaks of Cuchulain's "extraordinary ability to maneuver within and manipulate the code of honor" (ibid., 2).

25. Standish Hayes O'Grady, *The Táin bó Cúailnge,* in Hull, *Cuchullin Saga,* 195.

26. O'Leary, "Fir Fer," 2.

27. O'Rahilly, *Táin Bó Cúalnge,* 229.

28. Kinsella, *The Tain,* 197.

29. Ann Dooley, "The Invention of Women in the *Táin,*" in *Ulidia,* edited by J. P. Mallory and G. Stockman (Belfast: December Publications, 1994), 127.

30. Kinsella, *The Tain,* 33. For Nadcranntail, see 123–25.

31. Lady Gregory, *Cuchulain at Muirthemne,* 38.

32. Kinsella, *The Tain,* 29.

33. O'Rahilly, *Táin Bó Cúalnge,* 150. See also Standish Hayes O'Grady in Hull, *Cuchullin Saga,* 128.

34. O'Rahilly, *Táin Bó Cúalnge,* 150, 152. Gregory translates this passage "If I break my word to a woman, it will be said from this out that a woman's word is better than a man's" (*Cuchulain at Muirthemne,* 190).

35. Lady Gregory, *Cuchulain at Muirthemne,* 190–91; Betty Hutton, *The Táin* (Dublin: Maunsel, 1907), bk. 4; Faraday, *Cattle-Raid of Cualnge,* 10; O'Grady, *History of Ireland,* 149; Hull, *Cuchulain: The Hound of Ulster,* 90.

36. Dooley, "Invention of Women," 127–29, 133; Kinsella, *The Tain,* 133, 247.

37. O'Rahilly, *Táin Bó Cúalnge,* 203. See also Kinsella, *The Tain:* "Cuchulain slew . . . an uncountable horde of dogs and horses, women and boys and children and rabble of all kinds" (156).

38. Hull, *Cuchulain: The Hound of Ulster,* 13.

39. O'Rahilly, *Táin Bó Cúalnge,* 269. See also Kinsella, *The Tain,* 250.

40. Kinsella, *The Tain,* 250. O'Rahilly has it "for he used not to strike her from behind" (*Táin Bó Cúalnge,* 270).

41. Kinsella, *The Tain,* 250, 251. See also O'Rahilly, *Táin Bó Cúalnge,* 270.

42. Hutton, *The Táin*, 433–34; Hull, *Cuchulain: The Hound of Ulster*, 168.

43. Dooley, "Invention of Women," 133.

44. Terry Eagleton, *Heathcliff and the Great Hunger* (New York: Verso, 1995), 273.

45. Homi Bhabha, *The Location of Culture* (New York: Routledge, 1994), 85–92.

46. Brian Ocuiv, "The Gaelic Cultural Movements and the New Nationalism," in *The Making of 1916*, edited by K. Nowlan (Dublin: Stationery Office, 1969), 18.

47. Patrick Pearse, "My Childhood and Youth," in *The Home Life of Patrick Pearse*, by Mary Brigid Pearse (Dublin: Nolan, 1934). Pearse said of his father, "For an Englishman, not too bad!" (Desmond Ryan, *Remembering Sion* [London: Arthur Barker, 1934], 102).

48. M. Pearse, *Home Life of Patrick Pearse*, 98.

49. Michael Boss, "Country of Light," *Irish University Review* 30, no. 2 (2000): 274, 280; Moran, *Pearse and the Politics of Redemption*, 47–48 (see chap. 3, n. 15); Maire ni Fhlathun, "The Anti-Colonial Modernism of Patrick Pearse," in *Modernism and Empire*, edited by H. J. Booth and N. Rigby (Manchester: Manchester University Press, 2000), 161, 169–70.

50. Edwards, *Triumph of Failure*, 90 (see chap. 3, n. 90).

51. To take one tangential example, he asserted that the great Irish epics were all in prose, though this was a clearly a function of the translation (Pearse, *Political Writings and Speeches*, 166 [see chap. 3, n. 25]).

52. Patrick Pearse, *An Claidhaemh Soulis* 10, no. 36 (November 14, 1908): 9.

53. Kiberd, *Inventing Ireland*, 212 (see chap. 3, n. 3).

54. Patrick Pearse, *Songs of the Irish Rebels* (Dublin: Phoenix, n.d.), 155–56.

55. Ibid., 156.

56. Sisson, *Pearse's Patriots*, 79.

57. Patrick Pearse, "Criticism and Argument," *An Claidhaemh Soulis* 9, no. 7 (July 6, 1901), 7.

58. Patrick Pearse, *Political Writings and Speeches*, 25.

59. Our earlier discussion of the trash talking between Ferdia and Cuchulain illustrates this very point.

60. See Whitley Stokes, "The Tragical Death of Cuchullin," in *Cuchullin Saga*, by Hull, 260.

61. Seamus Deane asserts the centrality of the chivalric ideal in Pearse's work, which he takes to be a nationalist mythology counterposed to the "imperial one," rather than oddly imbricated with it (*Celtic Revivals*, 64 [see chap. 3, n. 71]).

62. The same sort of split-level transaction occurs in *Cathleen Ni Houlihan*. The Old Woman tells the Gillanes that the patriot must relinquish everything without reserve for Ireland: "He must give me all" (*C*, 8). But at the same, she assures them, they will receive everlasting glory in return: "They shall be remembered forever" (*C*, 10). Since this denouement cannot, as we said, be properly staged, it remains a rhetorical rather than dramatic reality.

63. Patrick Pearse, *The Story of a Success* (Dublin: Maunsel, 1917), 17, 21.

64. Hence Desmond Ryan's sense that the boys regard Cuchulain as "an important if invisible member of the staff" (quoted in Donal McCartney, "Gaelic Origins of 1916," in *1916: The Easter Rising*, edited by O. D. Edward and F. Pyle [London: MacGibbon and Kee, 1969], 44).

65. Sisson, *Pearse's Patriots,* 95; Che Buono, *An Claidhaemh Soulis* 11, no. 17 (July 3, 1909), 11.

66. Pearse, *Story of a Success,* 32, 33, 35–36.

67. Ibid., 36.

68. Patrick Pearse, "The Schools and Citizenship," *An Claidhaemh Soulis* 13, no. 4 (January 6, 1912): 7.

69. Patrick Pearse, *Prospectus for St. Enda's,* quoted in Desmond Ryan, *The Man Called Pearse* (Dublin: Maunsel, 1919), 35.

70. Pearse, *Story of a Success,* 40–41, 65. To turn to a more humorous, but no less telling, example, Pearse "invariably accepted a boy's word as true" in the belief that his own expectations would prove fulfilling. He thereby acceded to a form of headmastership made famous by Thomas Arnold, whose Rugby students said of him, "There's no point lying to the Doctor. He'll only believe you." See Ryan, *The Man Called Pearse,* 47.

71. Ryan, *Remembering Sion,* 166.

72. Pearse, *Story of a Success,* 34. O'Grady was a frequent visitor to Cullenswood. See Sisson, *Pearse's Patriots,* 39.

73. Quoted in *Irish Freedom,* no. 8 (June 1911), 3.

74. Diana Norman, *Terrible Beauty* (Dublin: Poolbeg, 1988), 62; R. S. S. Baden-Powell, *Scouting for Boys* (London: Horace Cocks, 1908), 3; *The Fianna Handbook* (Dublin: Central Committee of the Na Fianna Éireann 1909).

75. Roger Casement, "Chivalry," in *The Fianna Handbook,* 13; Patrick Pearse, "Finn and the Fianna," in *The Fianna Handbook,* 5; quoted in D. Norman, *Terrible Beauty,* 69.

76. Baden-Powell, *Scouting for Boys,* 309–15.

77. Pearse, *Political Writings and Speeches,* 114, 115, 116; D. Norman, *Terrible Beauty,* 64.

78. E. Bloxham, "Why Volunteer: Need of Solidarity and Discipline," *Irish Volunteer,* February 7, 1914, 6. Along the same lines, see also L. M'Masder, "Discipline before All," *Irish Volunteer,* February 7, 1914, 2.

79. Terence MacSwiney, "The Trial," *Irish Volunteer,* July 31, 1915, 4–5.

80. *Na Fianna Éireann: National Boy Scouts,* February 6, 1915, 8.

81. P. Colum quoted in D. Norman, *Terrible Beauty,* 63; D. Norman, *Terrible Beauty,* 63–64, 69.

82. Deane, *Celtic Revivals,* 71.

83. Robin Skene, *The Cuchulain Plays of W. B. Yeats* (New York: Columbia University Press, 1974), 25.

84. W. B. Yeats, *On Baile's Strand,* in *Modern Irish Drama,* edited by Harrington, 12–32.

85. Susan Harris speaks of the play leaving behind "the reductive model of nationalist commitment," of which blood sacrifice was an expression ("'Blow the Witches Out': Gender Construction and the Subversion of Nationalism in Yeats' *Cathleen Ni Houlihan* and *On Baile's Strand*," *Modern Drama* 39 [1996]: 485).

86. Skene, *Cuchulain Plays of Yeats,* 13.

87. Cairns and Richards, *Writing Ireland,* 98 (see chap. 3, n. 59). As they note, their insight builds on the work of Declan Kiberd, *Men and Feminism in Modern Literature*

(London: Macmillan, 1986), 107; and Denis Donoghue, *Yeats* (London: Fontana, 1971), 102.

88. Doggett, *Deep Rooted Things,* 25–33 (see chap. 3, n. 22).

89. Matthew Arnold, *On the Study of Celtic Literature, and Other Essays* (London: Jay M. Dent, 1910), 85.

90. Doggett, *Deep Rooted Things,* 30; Skene, *Cuchulain Plays of Yeats,* 154.

91. The quoted phrase was a Revivalist cliché brilliantly deconstructed in James Connolly, *The Lost Writings* (London: Pluto, 1997), 49–53.

92. The essay is revised in Harris, *Gender and Modern Irish Drama,* 79–88 (see chap. 3, n. 2).

93. Ibid., 79–86; John Rees Moore, *Masks of Love and Death* (Ithaca: Cornell University Press, 1971), 108. He also refers to Cuchulain as a "thoroughly masculine hero" (129).

94. For this contrast, see Lowe, "Contagious Violence," 85–86.

95. Moore, *Masks of Love and Death,* 48. Yeats himself said of his creation, "He is a little hard and leaves people a little repelled" (*Letters* [London: Macmillan, 1954], 360).

96. Lowe, "Contagious Violence," 95.

97. Matter, *Primitivism, Science, and the Irish Revival,* 122. Matter points to the oath as a "ritual of fealty" that portends the plenary ritualism of Yeats's later drama.

98. See Harris, *Gender and Modern Irish Drama,* 84–85.

99. Ibid., 82–83. Declan Kiberd reminds us that the mythic Cuchulain was himself androgynous as well as hypermasculine (*Irish Classics,* 413).

100. Howes, *Yeats's Nations,* 17 (see intro., n. 37).

101. Skene, *Cuchulain Plays of Yeats,* 193.

102. Moore, *Masks of Love and Death,* 117.

103. This complaint centrally informs the best-known essays of both Douglas Hyde, "The Necessity of De-Anglicizing Ireland," and D. P. Moran, "The Battle of Two Civilizations."

104. Tymoczko, *Translation in a Postcolonial Context,* 79.

105. John Synge, *The Playboy of the Western World,* in *Modern Irish Drama,* edited by Harrington, 73–118.

106. For arguments concerning the object, meaning, and motive of Synge's mock-heroic use of Cuchulain, see M. J. Sidnell, "Synge's *Playboy* and the Champion of Ulster," *Dalhousie Review* 45, no. 1 (1965): 51–59; Diane Bessai, "Little Hound in Mayo: Synge's *Playboy* and the Comic Tradition in Irish Literature," *Dalhousie Review* 48, no. 3 (1968): 372–83; Declan Kiberd, *Synge and the Irish Language* (Totowa: Rowman and Littlefield, 1979), 109–21; Brenda Murphy, "'The Treachery of the Law': Reading Synge's Politics," *Colby Quarterly* 28, no. 1 (1992): 45–51; Edward Hirsch, "The Gallous Story and the Dirty Deed: The Two *Playboys,*" *Modern Drama* 26, no. 1 (1983): 85–102; George Cusack, "'In the Gripe of the Ditch': Nationalism, Famine, and *The Playboy of the Western World,*" *Modern Drama* 45, no. 4 (2002): 657–92; and Nelson Ritschell, *Synge and Nationalism* (Westport, Conn.: Greenwood, 2002), 41–48.

107. Joseph Devlin, "J. M. Synge's *The Playboy of the Western World* and the Culture of Western Ireland under Late Colonial Rule," *Modern Drama* 41 (1998): 378; Julie Hennigan, "'The Power of a Lie': Irish Storytelling Tradition in *The Playboy of the Western*

World," New Hibernia Review 6, no. 3 (2002): 92; Kiberd, *Inventing Ireland,* 180–81; Kiberd, *Irish Classics,* 413.

108. Kiberd, *Synge and the Irish Language,* 111, 115.

109. Ibid., 106.

110. John Synge, *Collected Works* (London: Oxford University Press, 1966), 2:370.

111. Lady Gregory, *Our Irish Theatre,* 124 (see chap. 2, n. 31).

112. According to Paul Murphy, it is precisely the claim to be "master of all fights" that "makes Christy seem more like the legendary warrior Cuchulain than the homeless tramp beaten in a pub brawl" ("Synge and the Pitfalls of National Consciousness," 136).

113. For the villagers as internal counterparts of the Abbey audience, see Levitas, *The Theatre of Nation,* 126–27 (see chap. 3, n. 54); Cusack, "'In the Gripe of the Ditch,'" 585–86; and, most important, Edward Hirsch, "The Gallous Story and the Dirty Deed," 94–95.

114. Luke Gibbons, *Transformations in Irish Culture* (Notre Dame: University of Notre Dame Press, 1996), 31; Gregory Castle, *Modernism and the Celtic Revival* (Cambridge: Cambridge University Press, 2001), 134–71.

115. Declan Kiberd specifically compares Synge to Joyce and Eliot in his use of a mythic method (*Synge and the Irish Language,* 109). More recently, Kiberd finds *Playboy* "evoking the heroic cycle to mock the reduced lives of the peasants who still told the tale." This reading is based on a classic sense of the conservative thrust of the mythic method (*Irish Classics,* 413).

116. Nicholas Grene sees in the villagers' questions an indiscriminate admiration for crime that enraged the Abbey audience, because it seemed to affirm the stereotype—backed by recent studies in the "Unionist Press"—of the Irish as innately criminal. Without disputing Grene's read on the audience reaction, I do think the notion that the interrogation lumps all types of crime together fails to take into account the force and rhythm of the interaction between the questions and Christy's answers (*Politics of Irish Drama,* 89–90 [see chap. 3, n. 1]).

117. Benedict Anderson, *Imagined Communities* (New York: Verso, 1991), 9–46.

118. Nicholas Grene has elegantly stated the ideological predicament in which typical nationalists found themselves when confronted with Christy's parricide: "Ireland as a colonised country had the sacred right . . . to destroy its tyrranic parent . . . England, but the Irish people were deeply, piously, submissive to the authoritarian, patriarchal model of the family sanctioned by their authoritarian and patriarchal church" (*Politics of Irish Drama,* 92).

119. Cusack is mistaken, I believe, in saying that "to glorify patricide is to glorify the breakdown of the patriarchal system." As Flaherty's own words intimate, the glorification of patricide has a role in the reproduction of the system qua system, by keeping the authority of the patriarchy separate and free from the power of any given patriarch ("'In the Gripe of the Ditch,'" 581).

120. Kiberd, *Synge and the Irish Language,* 115–16.

121. Ibid., 118.

122. Lady Gregory, *Cuchulain at Muirthemne,* 239.

123. For the fiction/reality conflict, see Heidi Holder, "Between Fiction and Reality: Synge's *Playboy* and Its Audience," *Journal of Modern Literature* 14, no. 4 (1988): 530, 534–35; Hennigan, "'The Power of a Lie,'" 102; Polkington, *Theatre and the State*, 56 (see chap. 3, n. 12); and B. Murphy, "'Treachery of Law,'" 49.

124. Kiberd, *Inventing Ireland*, 171.

125. This point is made in Ginger Strand, "The Enduring Problem of the Audience," in *Assessing the Achievement of J. M. Synge*, edited by Gonzalez, 12 (see chap. 3, n. 57).

126. For the argument as to distance, see ibid., 12–13. See also Polkington, *Theatre and the State*, 56. Nelson Ritschel declaims against this argument in *Synge and Irish Nationalism*, 44.

127. For Cuchulain's excessiveness, see Lowe, "Contagious Violence," 95. For Cuchulain's native androgyny, see Kiberd, *Irish Classics*, 414. Patrick Pearse's initial denunciation of the play for propagating "the monstrous gospel of animalism" indicates just how committed he was to the Revivalist purification of Cuchulain. Quoted in Welch, *Abbey Theatre*, 42 (see chap. 3, n. 6).

128. Kiberd contends that in the end the Mahons "constitute the image of a revolutionary community" while the town "lapses into revivalism" (*Inventing Ireland*, 175). I would say rather that the revivalism of the town constitutes the Mahons as the image of a revolutionary community, one based on the ideal of manliness.

Chapter 5: "Mixed Middling"

1. T. S. Eliot, "Ulysses, Order, and Myth," in *Selected Prose of T. S. Eliot* (New York: Faber and Faber), 1975.

2. Lyons, "Parnell Theme in Literature," 78–79 (see chap. 1, n. 3).

3. F. S. L. Lyons, "James Joyce's Dublin," *Twentieth Century Studies* (November 1970): 201.

4. Richard Ellmann, *James Joyce* (New York: Oxford University Press, 1982), 32.

5. Ibid., 33–34.

6. Ibid., 34.

7. Stephen Dedalus lists the final occupation of his father as "praiser of his own past" (Joyce, *A Portrait of the Artist* [see intro., n. 53]).

8. For the visceral importance of this fiction to Joyce pere and fils, see Colbert Kearny, "The Joycead," in *Coping with Joyce*, edited by M. Beja and S. Benstock (Columbus: Ohio State University Press, 1989), 55–72.

9. It is interesting that criticism of the novel has parsed the title by putting interrogative emphasis on the words *portrait, artist*, and *young*, but not *man*.

10. Robin Gilmour, *The Idea of the Gentleman in the Victorian Novel* (London: Allen and Unwin 1981), 12.

11. Katherine Mullin interprets the gender implications of the Christmas-dinner scene in terms of "true manliness," a concept of fin de siècle purity discourse that identifies the masculine ideal with sexual abstention. But just as true manliness is but a fraction of the reigning construct of manliness, so sexual behavior is but one ingredient in the Parnell dispute. See Mullin, *James Joyce, Sexuality, and Social Purity* (Cambridge: Cambridge University Press, 2003), 87–91.

12. James Joyce, *Letters,* edited by Stuart Gilbert (New York: Viking, 1965), 1:55; James Joyce, *Dubliners* (New York: Penguin, 1996).

13. Hugh Kenner, *Joyce's Voices* (Berkeley and Los Angeles: University of California Press, 1978), 15–16; James Joyce, *Ulysses,* edited by Hans Walter Gabler (New York: Viking, 1986), 16.1274–75.

14. On the importance of James Clarence Mangan to the Oriental motif in "Araby," see Heyward Erlich, "'Araby' in Context: The 'Splendid Bazaar,' Irish Orientalism, and James Clarence Mangan," *James Joyce Quarterly* 35, nos. 2–3 (1998): 309–31.

15. For a reading of the nativist-cosmopolitan dialectic in the story, see Vincent Cheng, "Nations without Borders," in *Joyce, Ireland, Britain,* edited by A. Gibson and L. Platt (Gainesville: University Press of Florida, 2006), 218–29.

16. For a fine-grained political textualization of this capitulation, see Anne Fogarty, "Parnellism and the Politics of Memory," in *Joyce, Ireland, Britain,* edited by Gibson and Platt, 113–17.

17. Ranjana Khanna suggestively proposes that "Araby becomes the colony within Ireland, as Ireland was a colony of Britain . . . the metropolitan colony . . . confronts itself in the other" ("Women's Time and the Time of the Nation," in *Joyce: Feminism/Post/Colonialism,* edited by E. C. Jones [Amsterdam: Rodopi, 1998], 100).

18. For a fuller reading of the chivalric script in the story, but without its imbrication with commercialism, see Margot Norris, *Suspicious Readings of Joyce's "Dubliners"* (Philadelphia: University of Pennsylvania Press, 2003), 51–54.

19. Susan Bazargan construes the final epiphany as hinging upon "a shameful sense of dispossession . . . a recognition of his profound [ethnic] unbelonging," triggered by the "English accents" ("Epiphany as Scene of Performance," in *A New and Complex Sensation: Essays on Joyce's Dubliners,* edited by Oona Frawly [Dublin: Lilliput, 2004], 51). I would argue that his sense of dispossession undoes a gendered ego-ideal staked upon the imperative to *self*-possession contained in the norm, the "English"-identified norm, of manliness.

20. Margot Norris notes his "slow retrieval of the advanced nationalism buried under his father's prosperity" (*Suspicious Readings,* 73).

21. As Garry Leonard observes, Jimmy is "gratified" by the "amusement" taken at "his powerless posturing as an Irishman under the influence. He plays the hero of his father's unlived story" (*Reading "Dubliners" Again* [Syracuse: Syracuse University Press, 1993], 116).

22. For a Lacanian analysis of this dynamic, see ibid., 149–69.

23. Norris's sense that Chandler "takes control" at this point badly misses, to my mind, the coded value of the jousting men's respective maneuvers (*Suspicious Readings,* 117).

24. Ibid. This loss of "control" has been where this contest has been heading from the start.

25. See, for example, Leonard, *Reading "Dubliners" Again,* 165; and Norris, *Suspicious Readings,* 118–19.

26. Louis Althusser, *For Marx* (London: Verso, 1979), 228–29.

27. Robert Scholes, "'Counterparts' and the Method of *Dubliners,*" in *Dubliners: Text,*

Criticism, and Notes, by James Joyce, edited by Robert Scholes and A. Walton Litz (New York: Viking, 1969), 384.

28. Don Gifford, *Joyce Annotated* (Berkeley and Los Angeles: University of California Press, 1982), 72.

29. Bhabha, *The Location of Culture,* 88 (see chap. 4, n. 45). For a clever reading of mimesis, colonial and otherwise, in "Counterparts," see Gerald Doherty, *Dubliners Dozen* (Madison: Associated University Press, 2004), 89–98.

30. My analysis elaborates upon Homi Bhabha's central insight on this topic. To whit, the "menace of mimicry" arises from the "ambivalence" of colonial discourse itself, which in order to cast the subaltern as an ersatz copy of the normative pattern must extend "partial recognition" to him.

31. See Bhabha, *The Location of Culture,* 86. For "metrocolonialism" and "metrocolonial" subjectivity, see Joseph Valente, "Between Resistance and Complicity: Metro-Colonial Tactics in Joyce's *Dubliners," Narrative* 6, no. 3 (1998): 325–40.

32. Doherty, *Dubliners Dozen,* 89–98.

33. The situation is thus much more complicated than Tracey Teets Schwarze imagines when she proposes that Farrington is trying to "supplant" Alleyne with Miss Parker (*Joyce and the Victorians* [Gainesville: University Press of Florida, 2002], 177).

34. Even a deceptive narrator cannot turn Alleyne's aggressive gesture into a "polite order." See Norris, *Suspicious Readings,* 133.

35. For the importance of Miss Delacours' "gaze" to the dynamics of male gender consolidation in the story, see Leonard, *Reading "Dubliners" Again,* 177. See also Earl Ingersoll, *En-Gendered Tropes in "Dubliners"* (Carbondale: Southern Illinois University Press, 1996), 100–101.

36. For the *enoncé-enunciation* distinction, see Jacques Lacan, *Ecrits* (Paris: Éditions de Seuill, 1966), 800–801.

37. David Lloyd, "'Counterparts': *Dubliners,* Masculinity, and Temperance Nationalism," in *Semicolonial Joyce,* edited by Derek Attridge and Marjorie Howes (Cambridge: Cambridge University Press, 2000), 133. Its title notwithstanding, this article is almost entirely a cultural and political critique of temperance nationalism, with little analysis devoted to "Counterparts" or *Dubliners.*

38. Leonard, *Reading "Dubliners" Again,* 178; Norris, *Suspicious Readings,* 133; Ingersoll, *En-Gendered Tropes,* 103; Gerald Doherty, "Undercover Stories," *Journal of Narrative Technique* 22, no. 1 (1992): 43.

39. Leonard, *Reading "Dubliners" Again,* 179; Norris, *Suspicious Readings,* 134.

40. Sigmund Freud, *The Interpretation of Dreams* (New York: Basic Books, 1965), 564; Matthew Arnold, "On the Celtic Element in Literature," in *Lectures and Essays in Criticism,* by Matthew Arnold, edited by R. H. Super (Ann Arbor: University of Michigan Press, 1973), 82.

41. Freud, *The Interpretation of Dreams,* 564.

42. Don Gifford, *"Ulysses" Annotated* (Berkeley and Los Angeles: University of California Press, 1986), 337.

43. Elizabeth Malcom, *Ireland Sober, Ireland Free: Drink and Temperance in Nineteenth Century Ireland* (Syracuse: Syracuse University Press, 1986), 95–97.

44. See Paul Townend, *Father Mathew, Temperance, and Irish Identity* (Dublin: Irish Academic Press, 2002), 192–234.

45. Elizabeth Malcom, "Temperance and Irish Nationalism," in *Ireland under the Union,* edited by F. S. L. Lyons and R. A. J. Hawkins (Oxford: Clarendon Press, 1980), 80.

46. Malcom, *Ireland Sober, Ireland Free,* 132.

47. Colm Kerrigan, *Father Mathew and the Irish Temperance Movement, 1838–1849* (Cork: Cork University Press, 1992), 120.

48. Townend, *Father Mathew,* 204.

49. Malcom, *Ireland Sober, Ireland Free,* 319.

50. Ibid. See, for example, *The Leader,* January 25, 1902 ("The Temperance Movement"); *The Leader,* July 26, 1902 ("The Leader"); *The Leader,* July 11, 1903 ("Drinks at Wakes").

51. Lloyd, "'Counterparts,'" 134. For a fuller discussion of these stereotypes and the relationship between them, see Joseph Valente, "'Neither Fish nor Flesh,'" in *Semicolonial Joyce,* edited by Attridge and Howes, 96–106.

52. Lloyd, "'Counterparts,'" 135.

53. Hughes, *The Manliness of Christ,* 21 (see intro., n. 6).

54. Garry Leonard sees the London "girl" as a "counterpart" of Miss Delacours (*Reading "Dubliners" Again,* 180).

55. For the generational cycle of victimization, see Tanja Verala-Vartala, *Sympathy and Joyce's "Dubliners"* (Tampere: Tampere University Press, 1998), 240.

56. James Joyce, *Ulysses* (New York: Random House, 1986). The one other treatment of the episode in terms of the of the post-Victorian construct of manliness distorts the effects of that norm by eliding its dialectical structure and reducing it to a version of aggressive masculinity. See Schwarze, *Joyce and the Victorians,* 71–92.

57. This tendency holds true for both humanistic readings, like David Hayman's well-known essay, "'Cyclops,'" and for more recent postcolonial readings, like Vincent Cheng's equally prominent exegesis in *Joyce, Race, and Empire.* Cheng's piece is especially interesting in this regard in that it repeatedly inveighs against bipolarizing constructions and "binary hierarchies" as strategies of imperialist violence while fixing Bloom and the Citizen in rigid hierarchical opposition as the bearers of political light and dark, respectively. One notable exception to this hermeneutical orthodoxy is Emer Nolan's reading of the episode, the impetus of which, very different from my own, is to rehabilitate the Citizen to some degree. Andrew Gibson's analysis of the episode's historiography also registers the importance of displacing Bloom from his place at the invulnerable moral center of "Cyclops" and concentrating instead on the modes of relationality it deploys. See Hayman, "'Cyclops,'" in *James Joyce's "Ulysses": Critical Essays,* edited by C. Hart and D. Hayman (Berkeley and Los Angeles: University of California Press, 1974), 254–76; Cheng, *Joyce, Race, and Empire* (Cambridge: Cambridge University Press, 1995), 191–218; Nolan, *Joyce and Nationalism* (New York: Routledge, 1995), 96–113; and Gibson, *Joyce's Revenge* (Oxford: Oxford University Press, 2003), 221.

58. Joyce here replays the structure of the story "Counterparts" by using the same three tests of manliness to elaborate and parody its Irish double bind: confrontation

with authority ("Stand up to it then with force like men"), treating (Bloom's failure to share his supposed winnings), and the test of strength (the Citizen hurling the biscuit tray). Enda Duffy reads Bloom and the Citizen in terms of Deane's dichotomy of civilians and barbarians critiqued above (intro., n. 65). The ideological stakes of manhood shift and volatize the grounds of his literary interpretation in much the same way they do Deane's historical interpretation (*The Subaltern Ulysses* [Minneapolis: University of Minnesota Press, 1994], 111–14).

59. Alan Sinfield, *The Wilde Century* (New York: Columbia University Press, 1994), 110.

60. For Joyce's conversance and engagement with these feminizing Semitic ethnologies, the best source is Marilyn Reizbaum, *Joyce's Judaic Other* (Stanford: Stanford University Press, 1999). See also Vicki Mahaffey, *States of Desire* (Oxford: Oxford University Press, 1998), 150–66; and Joseph Valente, *Joyce and the Problem of Justice: Negotiating Sexual and Colonial Difference* (Cambridge: Cambridge University Press, 1995), 84ff.

61. Cairns and Richards, *Writing Ireland,* 42 (see chap. 3, n. 59).

62. See above chapter 3, section 1.

63. Mangan, "Social Darwinism and Upper Class Education," 145–46 (see intro., n. 1).

64. Hughes, *The Manliness of Christ,* 24–25.

65. In her reading of "Cyclops," Marilyn Reizbaum opines, "Has that not been a vexed aspect of [Christ's] image, how to make the victim heroic, the ultimate in love and charity, manly?" But as Joyce well knew, Thomas Hughes had already undertaken that task, in print, as the spokesman for a significant contingent within the "manhood" movement and to some not inconsiderable public acclaim. The possibility of his success in making Christ "manly" arose precisely out of the decisive if fraught conceptual distance separating manliness from masculinity. That distance in turn, mapped onto the metrocolonial divide, became well nigh untraversable. See Reizbaum, "When the Saints Coming Marching in," in *"Ulysses": En-Gendered Perspectives* (Columbia: University of South Carolina Press, 1999), 182.

66. Thomas Davis, *National and Other Poems* (Dublin: Gill, 1907), 27.

67. Liz Curtis, *The Cause of Ireland,* 341–42 (see intro., n. 67).

68. James Joyce, *The Critical Writings of James Joyce,* edited by R. Ellmann and Ellsworth Mason (New York: Viking, 1959), 174.

69. Kiberd, *Inventing Ireland,* 157 (see chap. 3, n. 3).

70. Stephen Tifft, "The Parricidal Phantasm: Irish Nationalism and the Playboy Riots," in *Nationalisms and Sexualities,* edited by Andrew Parker et al. (New York: Routledge, 1992), 320.

71. E. Duffy, *The Subaltern Ulysses,* 125.

72. Quoted in Jacques Derrida, "Force of Law: The Mystical Foundations of Authority," *Cardozo Law Review* 11, nos. 5–6 (1990): 920–1045.

73. Joyce, *Critical Writings,* 174.

74. Sigmund Freud, *General Psychological Theory* (New York: Macmillan, 1963), 214–17; Zizek, *Sublime Object of Ideology,* 71–76 (see intro., n. 10).

75. For the logic of proximateness, see Jonathan Dollimore, *Sexual Dissidence* (New York: Oxford University Press, 1991), 14–17. For its operation in Joyce, see Joseph Valente, "'Thrilled by His Touch': The Aestheticizing of Homosexual Panic in *A Portrait of the Artist as a Young Man*," in *Quare Joyce,* edited by Joseph Valente (Ann Arbor: University of Michigan Press, 1999), 47–76.

Epilogue: "Manhood Is All"

1. Deane, *Celtic Revivals,* 38 (see chap. 3, n. 71); W. B. Yeats, *Explorations* (New York: Collier, 1962), 225–28.

2. Terence Brown, *The Life of W. B. Yeats* (London: Blackwell, 1999), 171; Stephen Coote, *W. B. Yeats: A Life* (London: Stoughton and Hoddler, 1997), 264.

3. W. B. Yeats, "Coole Park, 1929," in *The Collected Poems of W. B. Yeats* (New York: Scribner, 1987), 243.

4. W. B. Yeats, "Poetry and Tradition," in *Essays and Introductions* (New York: Collier, 1968), 252, 256.

5. Barbara Ehrenreich, *Fear of Falling: The Inner Life of the Middle Class* (New York: Pantheon, 1989).

6. All in Yeats, *Collected Poems of Yeats.*

7. Yeats points up this reconfiguration of the nationalist struggle in "Divorce: An Undelivered Speech," in *The Senate Speeches of W. B. Yeats* (Bloomington: Indiana University Press, 1960), 160.

8. W. B. Yeats, *Interviews and Recollections* (London: Littlefield, 1977), 54–55.

9. Lyons, "Parnell Theme in Literature," 80 (see chap. 1, n. 3).

10. Joseph V. O'Brien, *Dear Dirty Dublin: A City in Distress* (Berkeley and Los Angeles: University of California Press, 1982), 23–25.

11. Fred Ryan, *Laying the Foundations,* in *Lost Plays of the Irish Renaissance* (New York: Proscenium, 1970), 23–38; Oliver St. John Gogarty, *Blight* (Dublin: Talbot, 1917).

12. Quoted in F. S. L. Lyons, *Culture and Anarchy in Ireland, 1890–1939* (Oxford: Oxford University Press, 1979), 76.

13. Yeates, *Lockout: Dublin 1913,* 143 (see chap. 2, n. 13).

14. Yeats continued, "We are the people of Burke, we are the people of Grattan, we are the people of Swift, the people of Emmet, the people of Parnell." See "Debate on Divorce," in *Senate Speeches of Yeats,* 99.

Index

JOSEPH VALENTE, a professor of English at the University of Illinois at Urbana-Champaign, is the author of *Dracula's Crypt: Bram Stoker, Irishness, and the Question of Blood* and other works.

The University of Illinois Press is a founding member of the Association of American University Presses.

Composed in 10.5/13 Adobe Minion Pro with FF Meta display at the University of Illinois Press Manufactured by Edwards Brothers, Inc.

University of Illinois Press
1325 South Oak Street
Champaign, IL 61820-6903
www.press.uillinois.edu